Encyclopedia
of
IOWA

MEREDITH WILLSON
"The Music Man"

Encyclopedia
of
IOWA

-a volume of
ENCYCLOPEDIA OF THE UNITED STATES

SOMERSET PUBLISHERS, INC.
521 Fifth Ave., 17th Floor
New York, N.Y. 10175

Library of Congress Cataloging-in-Publication Data

Encyclopedia of Iowa.
    p.   cm. -- (Encyclopedia of the United States)
    Includes bibliographical references and index.
    ISBN 0-403-09918-8 : $89.00
    1. Iowa--Encyclopedias. I. Series.
F621.E53 1993
977.7'003--dc20   93-32272
                                             CIP

FOREWORD

Information on this State is available from many other sources. Histories and geographies abound; there are place-name books, guidebooks and biographical references; many excellent atlases provide map detail; government registers contain in-depth coverage of the political organization. It is the existence of so many varied sources of information that makes a systematic, encyclopedic reference necessary - a single source for the most useful information about the State.

A secondary purpose of this volume is to play a part in a national reference on all of the States, a systematic approach to referencing the entire nation - an Encyclopedia of the United States, with each volume following a planned outline that matches each other volume in the series - with exceptions in the format made only when necessary. This goal was partly achieved during the Great Depression years with the publication of the WPA Federal Writers' Project State and City Guidebooks, which we are proud to have republished in recent years in their original form. While containing a wealth of interesting and still useful information they are essentially *tour-guides* rather than general reference books. They were, however, very useful in the planning of this new work.

It is our hope that this Encyclopedia series will have a permanence through the issuance of revised editions at intervals to be determined by a careful watch on the availability of new material. Undoubtedly, changes in the concept will be reflected in later editions as a result of feedback from users and the observations and introspection of our editors.

We wish to acknowledge with great appreciation the cooperation of the many State and local government offices that have furnished or reviewed material. We are further grateful to the many librarians who have made their facilities so available during the years that this project has been in process.

CONTENTS

INTRODUCTION

IOWA, a north central State of the United States, is the smallest of the midwestern states. It is bounded on the north by Minnesota; on the east by the Mississippi River, which separates it from Wisconsin and Illinois; on the south by Missouri; and on the west by the Missouri and Big Sioux rivers, which separate it from Nebraska and South Dakota.

The total area of Iowa is 56,275 square miles (145,752 sq. km), of which land is 55,965 sq. mi. (144,949 sq. km) and inland water 310 sq. mi (803 sq. km). The State extends 324 miles (521 km) E-W; its maximum extension N-S is 210 miles (338 km).

Iowa ranks 25th among the states in area. Its highest elevation, at 509 miles, is located in Osceola County; its lowest elevation, 148 miles, is on the Mississippi River. Iowa entered the Union on December 28, 1846, as the 29th State. Its capitol is Des Moines.

STATE SYMBOLS

THE NAME

It is the opinion of some leading Iowa historians that the origin and meaning of the name *Iowa* are uncertain. Investigation reveals the truthfulness of the statement made by L. F. Andrews, who says that "words have been twisted, distorted and corrupted until they bear little or no orthographic relation to that which the tradition-searchers have reached in their quest."

Johnson Brigham, State Historian of Iowa, called attention to the great part speculation played in determining the origin and meaning of the name Iowa. "Is it," he asked, "(1) a tribal designation; or (2) a place name; or (3) a name descriptive of some characteristic of the region?" He presented a mass of scholarly research in which he cited annals, journals, and historical records, dating from the year 1676. He closed his introductory remarks by saying that "it is evident from these divergent views that this [the origin and the significance of the name *Iowa*] must ever remain one of the open questions confronting the student of Iowa history."

1

Historians generally agree that both the Iowa River and the State were named after a powerful tribe of Indians which, in primitive times, lived in that part of the United States now comprising the State of Iowa.

Of the various writers giving the meaning of the word *Iowa,* some have affirmed that it signifies *beautiful* or *beautiful land;* others have said that the word means *this is the place.* Augustus C. Dodge, former United States Senator from Iowa, as well as other authorities, have said that the name means *none such;* and again others stated that the term *Iowa* in the Dakota language denotes *"'something to write or paint with--a pen or pencil.'"*

Probably the chief reason that the origin and significance of the primitive Indian word for Iowa is so difficult to ascertain is the fact that its original form has been lost in the records of the French and Spanish explorers, or those of other early travelers, or of the fur traders, and in the mass of historical data which grew up later. Some of the forms of the word found in these documents are: *Ayouas, Aiouez, Ayavois, Ainovines, Aiodais, Aiouas, Aiouways,* and *Ioways.*

Brighman pointed out the fact that the early French explorers spelled the name *Ayouas;* the Spanish, *Ajoues;* and the English, *Ioways.* He also stated that the first appearance of the modern spelling of the name, *Iowa,* was found in *Morse's American Gazetteer* of 1804, "in which it was applied to the river along which Iowa Indian towns were located."

Fulton said that it should be remembered that the word is of Dakota origin and that it had great varieties of orthography, until finally the word *Ioway* was commonly used, and then the form *Iowa* "was adopted and the name applied by the whites to the territory and the State where the tribe had so long made their home."

NICKNAMES

According to some authorities, the *Hawkeye State* came to be applied as a sobriquet to Iowa from the Indian chief Hawkeye, who traveled along the border in early days. It has also been attributed to Black Hawk, who came back to Iowa to die after his release from prison, where he had served a sentence for fighting the encroachment of white settlers on Indian land.

The New International Encyclopaedia says that the sobriquet, the Hawkeye State, was attributed to Iowa in al-

Introduction

lusion apparently "to J. G. Edwards, familiarly known as 'Old Hawkeye.' Edwards was editor of the Burlington *Patriot,* afterwards the *Hawkeye and Patriot."*

The nickname, the *Land of the Rolling Prairie,* was given to Iowa because of the vast expanses of rolling prairies within the limits of the State.

The sobriquet of *Hawkeyes,* as applied to Iowans, is of the same origin as the State's nickname as the *Hawkeye State.*

THE FLAG

When the United States entered World War I, Iowa had no State flag. "It was expected that the Iowa men would fight in State regiments as they had in former wars" and this emphasized the desirability of the State flag to designate the Iowa units.

The organization most interested in this matter was the Iowa Society of the Daughters of the American Revolution, which had already prepared two designs. On May 11, 1917, Mrs. Lue B. Prentiss, chairman of the Society's flag committee, Mrs. Dixie Gebhardt, and a number of other interested persons appeared before the State Council of National Defense. They presented a flag design submitted by Mrs. Gebhardt, and asked that it be adopted as the State flag for use by the Iowa soldiers.

The Council approved the plan without much discussion. Thereupon, the Daughters of the American Revolution had a number of flags manufactured and presented one to each of the Iowa National Guard regiments, one of which-- the 168th United States Infantry--was already in France. The use of State flags, however, was soon rendered almost impossible by the policy adopted by the War Department of assigning men to military units without regard to the State from which they came.

The Iowa State flag "consists of three vertical stripes of blue, white and red, the blue stripe being nearest the staff and the white stripe being in the center, and upon the central white stripe being depicted a spreading eagle bearing in its beak blue streamers on which is inscribed, in white letters, the State motto, 'Our liberties we prize and our rights we will maintain,' and with the word 'Iowa' in red letters below such streamers..."

This flag was authorized by legislative action on March 29, 1921.

3

THE STATE MOTTO

A committee of the State Senate selected the motto of Iowa, *Our Liberties We Prize and Our Rights We Will Maintain*. It, no doubt, referred to the difficulties encountered while Iowans were establishing their statehood. It expressed the sentiment of citizens as they entered the Union in 1846, and was placed on the State seal by the first General Assembly in 1847.

THE GREAT SEAL

The Legislature of Iowa adopted the State seal on February 25, 1847. The law prescribes that the seal shall be "two inches in diameter, upon which shall be engraved the following device, surrounded by the words, 'The Great Seal of the State of Iowa'--a sheaf and field of standing wheat, with a sickle and other farming utensils, on the left side near the bottom; a lead furnace and pile of pig lead, on the right side; the citizen soldier, with a plow in his rear,

supporting the American flag and liberty cap with his right hand, and his gun with his left, in the center and near the bottom; the Mississippi River in the rear of the whole, with the streamer Iowa under way; an eagle near the upper edge, holding in his beak a scroll, with the following inscription upon it: *Our liberties we prize, and our rights we will maintain*."

THE STATE FLOWER

The wild rose was designated as the official State flower of Iowa by the State General Assembly on May 7, 1897. Some say the *Rosa pratincola,* the wild prairie rose, was the unofficial selection of the species, since there are several, and none was singled out for the designation. Others say the unofficial designation was the *Rosa virginiana* or *Rosa acicularis,* both of which also grow in the State. The Iowa Federation of Women's Clubs at Dubuque, Iowa, had previously voted to select the wild rose as the official floral emblem of the State.

THE STATE SONG

The State song of Iowa, entitled *Iowa,* was written by S. H. M. Byers in 1867. It was at that time, and has been, sung to the tune of the old German song, *O Tannenbaun.* The lyrics, however, were set to a different melody by Paul Lange, and published by Bollman and Schatzman, St. Louis, Missouri, in 1867.

Byers received the inspiration for writing this production while he was confined in Libby Prison at Richmond, Virginia, after he had been taken by the enemy in the battle of Lookout Mountain 1n 1863. His captors were accustomed to pass by his prison playing the music of *O Tannenbaun* to the song *My Maryland,* or else singing it "set to Southern and bitter words." It was at this time that Byers resolved to put that tune "to loyal words." The song *Iowa* was the crystallization of his resolve. This musical composition was authorized to be recognized as the State song of Iowa by a House concurrent resolution of the Senate on March 20, 1911. The resolution reads:

"*Whereas,* the patriotic song of Iowa by S. H. M. Byers, has, for years, been sung in all the schools of the State, and on thousands of public occasions, political and social, and wherever Iowa people come together in other States

Therefore, Be it Resolved by the House, the Senate concurring, that it be hereby declared to be recognized as the State Song."

The theme of Byers' lyrics centers about his love for and praise of Iowa: its cornfields, prairies, purple sunsets, fair women, and the patriotic sons of his beloved State.

Three other songs about Iowa are great favorites. They are: *Iowa--Beautiful Land; Iowa, Proud Iowa;* and the *Iowa Corn Song.*

The words of the first of these was written by Tacitus Hussey in 1889, and the music was composed by Horace M. Towner of Corning, Iowa. This composition is a great favorite in schools throughout the State and is popular with quartet singers.

Iowa, Proud Iowa, was written by Virginia Knight Logan. The Iowa Federation of Music Clubs adopted this composition as their State song. It was published and copyrighted by Forster Music Publisher, Incorporated, Chicago, Illinois, in 1920. A bill was introduced in the State Legislature in 1921 to use this as the State song "on all public and official occasions where the use of a State song is proper or advisable," but the bill was lost for want of action.

The *Iowa Corn Song* was written by George E. Hamilton about 1911, and sung to the tune of *Travelling.* It was popularized by the Shriner Conclave held in Des Moines, Iowa, in 1921. This production was very popular throughout the State and was sung by the people on various occasions.

THE STATE BIRD

Iowa, by concurrent resolution number twenty-two, approved by the House on March 21, and by the Senate on March 22, 1933, adopted as the official State bird the Eastern goldfinch (*Spinus tristis tristia*).

The resolution says:

"Whereas, many states have not only adopted certain named flowers as their state flowers, but have also adopted certain named birds as their state birds, and

"Whereas, the Iowa Ornithological Union, an association comprising students and lovers of birds, residing within our state at their annual meeting held in Des Moines, Iowa, in May, 1922, by resolution and vote designated the Eastern Goldfinch as their choice for a state bird, and recommended that the Eastern Goldfinch be adopted as the official state bird of Iowa, therefore,

"Be it Resolved by the House of Representatives, the Senate concurring, that the Eastern Goldfinch, Spinus tristis tristia, is hereby designated and shall hereafter be officially known as the state bird of Iowa."

The eastern goldfinch has a total length of about 4.5 inches; its tail length is 1.5 to 2 inches. It is found in the United States and southern Canada, east of the Rocky Mountains; it winters southward to the Gulf coast.

Introduction

The adult male of the species is generally pure lemon yellow or canary yellow in the summer; the forehead, crown, wings, and tail are black; and white stripes appear near the base of the wings and along the ends of the tail feathers. The adult female (and the adult male in winter) is olive brownish or grayish above; the wings and tail are blackish or dusky marked with white; the upper tail feathers are pale grayish or grayish white; and the underparts are dull grayish white tinged with yellow.

The eastern goldfinch is a flock bird, often seen in flight and singing with its friends. The birds usually sing in choral fashion, whistling high-pitched tunes that last for two or three seconds. Breeding is very late in the season (from July to September), and the male and female are constant companions as they build their nests and raise their young. Egg sets average five in number, and the coloration is plain bluish white. Seeds are the mainstay of the goldfinch's diet, supplemented in winter months by a delicacy, plant lice eggs.

THE CAPITOL BUILDING

When the first General Assembly met in Iowa City after Iowa became a State in 1846, it began to search for a new capital. In 1857, the governor declared Des Moines as the capital city.

A capital commission was formed in 1870 to construct a capitol for $1.5 million. John C. Cochrane and A.H. Piquenard were named architects by the commission, and the cornerstone of the traditional, modified Renaissance building was laid on November 23, 1871. The cornerstone had to be laid again in 1873, however, owing to the deterioration of the stone used.

The government occupied temporary quarters in Des Moines until 1884, when the new capitol was completed at a cost of $2,873,294. A fire in 1904, which occurred during repair and modernization work, resulted in additional expenditures for renovation. The total cost of the capitol building was $3,296,256.

The State capitol building represents a combination of Grecian and Roman types of architecture. It is constructed in the form of a Greek cross and has Grecian columns and Roman arched windows. A central dome, constructed of steel and stone, is covered with gold leaf (replaced in 1964-65), and surmounted by a lookout lantern that terminates in a finial. Two pairs of domes are also situated on the opposite ends of the wings.

The length of the Statehouse from north to south is 363 feet, 8 inches; the width from east to west is 246 feet, eleven inches. The "top of the finial above the dome" is 275 feet. The diameter of the dome at its base is 66 feet, 8 inches.

The area of the capitol grounds is 93.25 acres. "The foundation and basement [is] built out of Iowa stone." The walls of the main edifice are constructed out of stone obtained both from Carroll County, Iowa, and from St. Genevieve, Missouri. In the finishing work, "twenty-nine kinds of domestic and imported marble" were used. The woodwork consists mainly of "Iowa black walnut, butternut, cherry, oak, and catalpa."

OTHER FACTS ABOUT IOWA

Total area: 56,275 square miles
Land area: 55,965 square miles
Water area: 310 square miles
Average elevation: 1,100 feet
Highest point: Osceola County, 1,670 feet
Lowest point: Mississippi River, 118 feet
Highest temperature: 118 degrees Fahrenheit
Lowest temperature: -47 degrees Fahrenheit
Population in 1990: 2,776,755
Population density in 1990: 49.70 persons per square mile
Population 1980-1990: -4.7 percent change
Black population in 1990: 48,090
Hispanic population in 1990: 32,647
Native American population in 1990: 7,349
White population in 1990: 2,683,090
Capital: Des Moines
Admitted to Union: December 28, 1846
Order of Statehood: 29
Electoral votes: 8

GEOGRAPHICAL OVERVIEW

AN ANALYSIS OF THE NATURAL LANDSCAPE

By
Graham A. Tobin
Department of Geography
The University of Iowa

Situated in the middle interior of the United States, Iowa is recognized as one of the northern Great Plain States. While certainly characteristic of this geographic region in terms of physical features, notably the extensive rolling relief, the State still maintains a uniqueness which is not always apparent to the casual observer. The traits of adjacent plain states blend, often imperceptibly, into one another, and yet each maintains a distinctive lifestyle. The geopolitical boundaries of Iowa distinguish a strongly partisan people sensitive to the values of the "Hawkeye State."

The gently undulating topography of the plains and the agriculturally dominated landscape, combined with the rigorous extremes of the continental climate, have perpetuated an image of Iowa as a typically rural midwestern state with little to offer other than corn and hogs. While much of Iowa's economy, like the nation's as a whole, is intrinsically linked to agriculture and associate industries, Iowa is more than this. The subtle contrasts in landforms, the range of economic activities and the diversity of cultural backgrounds and recreational pursuits present many opportunities.

Immediately following statehood, Iowa grew rapidly, adopting much of its economic structure and characteristics during these early years. The following sections examine some of these features of Iowa, from the physical landforms and geology to the population base and economic activities.

9

PHYSICAL GEOGRAPHY

GEOLOGY:
The geology of Iowa comprises consolidated bedrock overlain by substantial deposits of unconsolidated materials; these are the products of two different physical processes. Both furnished important resources to the State, from mineral wealth, to soils, to water storage, although it is the extensive surficial deposits which provided the basic ingredients for Iowa's fertile soils.

Consolidated Bedrock: The geologic record in Iowa extends from the old Precambrian Systems to the younger Cretaceous System. This succession is not complete, however, since omissions occur in the Permian, Triassic, and Tertiary Systems, leaving unconformities where non-consecutively aged rocks are adjacent to each other. These probably represent periods of limited deposition and possibly more extensive erosion. The other systems are not always represented by a full geologic record, although much of each series is present, particularly during the Paleozoic Era.

Most of the rocks in Iowa were laid down initially as loose sediments in shallow seas and eventually compressed and hardened into sedimentary rocks. To build up these large deposits of sandstone, limestones, and dolomites which dominate the geologic record, the area undoubtedly spent a great deal of time as a marine environment. Fossil evidence further testifies to this as sea life and coral has been petrified in various strata, such as in the fine-grained limestone of the Cedar Valley Formation.

The stable nature of the interior has preserved much of this succession intact. The strata have remained relatively undisturbed, forming largely horizontal layers across the State. Large-scale tectonic activity has not been a significant process in this area, although some fracturing is evident from faulting in the distant past. As a result, the consolidated bedrock of Iowa now constitutes a gently dipping asymmetrical basin running east-west across the State. While this bedrock provides some resources, its impact on Iowa landforms is somewhat limited; the dominating influence is the surficial geology.

Unconsolidated Materials: Overlying the sedimentary bedrock formations are huge deposits of unconsolidated material, primarily the products of Pleistocene processes. During this period, the climate fluctuated to such an extent that Iowa was subject to a range of environments, from

10

tropical and sub- tropical conditions to cold arctic temperatures. While such climatic variations are not unusual over
geologic time, it was these Pleistocene conditions which sig-
nificantly changed so much of the character of the North
American continent.

The predominant influence on the physical landscape of
Iowa has been the processes of the cold environments or
"ice- ages." Four major glacial periods have been identified
during the Pleistocene; the oldest Nebraskan advance, followed by the Kansan, Illinoian, and Wisconsin advances.
Each of these was separated by substantially warmer conditions or interglacial stages (named Aftonian, Yarmouth, San-
gamon). Each glacial advance began with cooler
temperatures and a subsequent buildup of ice over the
Canadian Shield/Great Lakes region. As the ice thickness
grew, often to several thousand feet, the ice sheet spread
out under its own weight, advancing great distances and
covering the landscape. The approximate limits of each
major advance have given each stage its name.

Classical continental glaciation features, particularly
depositional landforms, were the product of these ice advances. In the source areas, the ice would remove all surficial
materials and scour the bedrock, leaving, in post-glacial
times, a barren, harsh landscape. Loose material and frag-
mented bedrock would then be transported great distances
by the flowing ice, eventually to be deposited at the margins
or beneath the decaying ice sheet. On two occasions, these
ice sheets covered most of Iowa, creating the same scouring
effect and leaving behind some glacial deposits (Nebraskan
and Kansan). During the later Illinoian and Wisconsin advances, the ice sheets were less extensive, and Iowa would
have been at the margins of the ice and subject to severe
periglacial conditions. The latter advance (Wisconsin)
covered only the northcentral portion of Iowa--now called
the Des Moines Lobe. With each major glacial advance, the
flow of ice would vary, sometimes stopping or even retreat-
ing, only to readvance later. This variable nature has com-
plicated the glacial history of the State, but because of its
good glacial record, Iowa has been the center for considerable research into continental glaciation, and particularly depositional features.

Large quantities of glacial drift in various forms have
been deposited in the State. Glacial till represents that
material which has been transported by ice sheets then
dumped en masse as the ice stagnated. This till or ground

moraine consists of mixed debris, small and large boulders intermixed with some clays, silts, and sands, and tends to be unsorted. It is usually found deposited on scoured bedrock which is frequently marked by striations from the ice and boulder movement. Most of the till now found in Iowa originated outside the State, as evidenced by the deposition of igneous and metamorphic boulders (erratics), which are not indigenous to the State. As the ice sheets receded, many areas were inundated by the meltwater carving new channels across the land surface. These rivers, especially during the summer months, would be extremely large and consequently could transport enormous quantities of sediment. Eventually, this material would be redeposited in sorted layers of sands and gravels. Such fluvio-glacial deposits are found in various parts of the State, wherever large meltwater channels occurred.

Loess Deposition. A third type of drift located in Iowa is loess deposition. These deposits consist of very fine grained materials, mainly clays and silts with some sand, which have been sorted by eolian processes. Fine sediments from dry drainage channels in winter months would be subject to ablation, the wind then transporting the material and subsequently redepositing it. The principal source area for loess in Iowa was the Missouri Valley and to a lesser extent, the Mississippi and other local tributaries.

These glacial drifts can be found in huge quantities across the State in depths up to 600 feet. The combined thickness of these deposits is such that they completely mask the original bedrock topography and form a new land surface. Streams have created new dendritic drainage patterns flowing to the southeast and southwest, which are not influenced by the underlying geologic structure. To varying degrees, the majority of the State is covered by till of different ages, depending on which particular glacial advance covered that area. In some parts, other than that most recently glaciated, loessial deposits can be found superimposed on the till. In general, this represents a relatively thin covering which does not form any distinctive landforms except in the southwest, where hills composed entirely of loess rise 150-200 feet above the land surface.

The Driftless Area. In contrast to the rest of the State, one area stands out because of its different geological history and because of its dissimilar landform features. The northeast of Iowa, for some reason which is not entirely clear, was not covered by ice during recent glacial advances, and consequently differs substantially from other parts of the state. This region has been called the "Driftless Area" which is somewhat of a misnomer since some thin isolated patches of drift, principally loess, can be found. In this area, the influence of geological structure on the surface landforms is more apparent while exposed bedrock is not uncommon as it is in the rest of Iowa.

TOPOGRAPHIC FEATURES:
     While the surficial material of Iowa was the direct result of Pleistocene activity, the present landform features are primarily the product of subsequent fluvial processes reworking these drift deposits. The influence of bedrock on surface relief is limited to the small area in the northeast, leaving most of Iowa as a young and dynamic landscape. Finally, the Des Moines Lobe is characterized by features more related to glacial activity than the product of present processes. Thus the Iowan topography ranges from a geologically controlled environment to one shaped by glacial and fluvial processes.
     The predominant feature in Iowa is a plain surface dipping gradually from the northwest of the State down to the southeast. The principal drainage networks follow this directional trend, with 69 percent of the State draining into the Mississippi River system. The rest of the State, primarily the south and west, flows into the Missouri River. This plain is further characterized by a rolling or undulating topography with subtle changes in elevation, rising to a maximum of 1,670 feet in the northwest and falling to a minimum of 480 feet in the southwest. However, an estimated 60 percent of the State lies between 800 and 1,400 feet. Geologically, these features are very young, with the oldest landforms, less than 24,000 years old, found in the Driftless Area and the youngest, alluvial deposits of less than 11,000 years, located along the Mississippi and Missouri Rivers. The physical features of the Des Moines Lobe area aged somewhere between 12,000 and 13,500 years, while the Iowa Plains features date between 14,000 and 16,000 years.
     Southern Iowa Drift Plain: This area represents "typical Iowa scenery," stretching across the whole of the southern half of the State. The relief is essentially rolling, with fairly uniform upland divides and level alluvial lowlands. Almost imperceptibly, the relief changes from east to west as the lower levels become wider and the

uplands more ridge- like. The drainage is well developed over the whole area.

Northern Iowa Plains: In the northern part of the State, located on either side of the Des Moines Lobe, are plains of subtle topographic features where the relief is less variable than in the south, with broad low lying swales and long sweeping slopes. The northwest plain consists of fairly thick loess deposits situated upon older till and gently shaped by post- glacial activity. In contrast, the plain to the northeast has experienced more extensive erosion, which has removed most of the older Kansas till and created the relatively smooth "Iowa surface." Remnants of the old till, topped with loess, are apparent as elongated ridges called "paha."

Des Moines Lobe: Such extensive erosion has not taken place on the Des Moines Lobe. This topographic region extends down through northcentral Iowa and represents the most recently glaciated part of the State. Here the topographic features are essentially a product of glacial processes illustrating classical continental glaciation landforms. Ground moraine dominates the region, banded in several places by a series of ridges representing terminal and recessional moraines. In other places, the relief takes on an irregular appearance of a "knob and kettle" terrain, where the drainage is particularly ill- defined and disorganized with a number of lakes, ponds, and marshes. Most of Iowa's natural lakes can be found in this area. Other parts of the lobe are flat, with little distinctive relief.

Driftless Area: The Driftless Area contrasts sharply with both the Des Moines Lobe and other parts of Iowa. In this area, bedrock plays a more significant role in controlling topographic features and often can be found exposed at the surface. Valleys are deeper and more incised, and generally the relief has a harsher outline. A few loess deposits can be found in the area, but do little to alter the overall relief. The geological influence can best be seen through the karst features formed on limestone and dolomite, in particular sinkholes, underground caverns and springs.

Smaller "unique" areas of relief also exist within Iowa. Alluvial floodplains can be found adjacent to many rivers, especially the Missouri, including such fluvial features as floodplains, terraces, meanders, oxbow lakes, and wetlands. A more complex fluvial feature exists in the southeast, where a series of terraces were once thought to be the result of lacustrine processes in "Lake Calvin." The evidence now indicates, however, that fluvial processes were probably responsible. In the southwest part of the State, the loess hills form a very distinctive landform and have been compared with the large loess deposits of China. Typical of this environment are sharp narrow ridges and deep ravines with relatively unstable slopes.

CLIMATE:

The climate of Iowa is classical temperate continental, with hot humid summers and cold dry winters. In winter, the average January temperature is 21 degrees F, while in summer, the July average is 76 degrees F. Across the State, this produces mean annual temperatures of 46 degrees F in the north to 52 degrees F in the south. However, like all climatic averages, these figures mask the true variations which can occur in the State. Temperatures in winter generally fall well below the average, and a record of minus 47 degrees F was recorded in 1912. In summer, temperatures regularly reach the 90 degrees F range, and frequently top 100 degrees F, with an extreme of 118 degrees F recorded in 1934. Furthermore, large temperature changes can occur over relatively short periods. During a nine day period in February, 1930, the temperature rose 106 degrees F, from -34 degrees F to 72 degrees F. For the most part, these temperatures are ideal for certain agricultural practices, the only major constraint being long hot periods, which can inflict some crop damage. The growing season for the State averages 150 days.

Precipitation totals and seasonal distribution are also conducive to agriculture. The State receives an annual average of 32 inches (ranging from 25 inches in the northwest to 35 inches in the southeast), the majority of which falls during the growing season. Snow contributes some water to this total, building up soil moisture during the spring. Extreme records for precipitation in the State extend from a high of 74.5 inches in 1851 to 12 inches in 1910. More recent extremes recorded in 1973 and 1976, respectively, were 64 inches and 13 inches. Agricultural problems, therefore, can occur during extreme years, particularly if the spring is dry.

Certain violent weather conditions also affect Iowa, inflicting damages and financial losses on both agricultural and urban areas. Severe thunderstorms are not uncommon during summer months, occurring an average 40 to 50 days a year. These can produce flash flooding and are also related to lightning and hail damage. Certain crops are particularly vulnerable to hail damage during the summer months. Tornadoes also occur throughout Iowa, averaging approximately 30 per year. These can be particularly devastating, and several communities have been the scene of extensive destruction in recent years.

NATURAL RESOURCES

The natural resources of Iowa, although not has varied as in some states, are very important to the livelihood of the State, from the population to the soils, from the mineral wealth to the water resources.

POPULATION:

The population of Iowa rose rapidly during the early years of statehood, principally as a result of European immigration. In 1840, the territory had an estimated population of 43,000, which rose to 192,000 in 1850 and to 2.232 million in 1900, an increase of more than 5,000 percent in the first 60 years. Since then, the population has increased at a much slower rate, even experiencing a small decline at the turn of the 20th century. In the 1990 census, Iowa recorded a population of 2.776 million, an increase of only 30 percent in the 20th century. This lower rate of increase is expected to continue, with a projected population figure of only 2.5 million by the year 2000. The current density for the State is 49.70 persons per square mile.

During this latter period, there have been several changes in the structure of the population, which has become older (the median age is now 30 years) bringing all the concurrent responsibilities of an aging population. One cause of this has been the net emigration from the State over the last three decades. The population has also become more urbanized. In 1900, only 25 percent of Iowans lived in communities of more than 2,500; now the figure is 43.4 percent, with the urban population reaching a majority at the 1960 census (Table 1). Urban areas, therefore, have continued to grow, and there are now seven Standard Metropolitan Statistical Areas in Iowa: Cedar Rapids, Davenport, Dubuque, Sioux City, Waterloo-Cedar Falls and Omaha- Council Bluffs (partially in Nebraska).

SOILS:

The soils of Iowa are undoubtedly the State's most valuable natural resource. The large deposits of glacial drift of all types and subsequent weathering processes have bestowed on Iowa some of the best agricultural land in the world. These soils, principally loams, are extremely fertile, occur widely over the State, and can be farmed easily on the gently undulating topography. Added to this, the "ideal" climate makes Iowa almost a perfect agricultural environment. It is not surprising, therefore, to find that 94 percent of the Iowa land surface is used for farming of one sort or another.

WATER:

The climatic conditions in Iowa have produced an adequate supply of water for most purposes and, given the low population projections, little difficulty should be encountered in meeting any increased demand in the future. At present, the demand comes from a variety of sources. By far, the largest users of water are the power utilities for energy production, although most of this water is eventually returned to the fluvial system. Agriculture is the next largest user, especially for irrigation, followed by industrial demands and finally, domestic supplies. Generally, the water supply is more than sufficient to meet all these needs and puts little constraint on future development. Some restrictions have occurred during extreme conditions, however.

For instance, in 1976, limitations were set on some irrigation because of exceptionally low rainfall. The trend for water use is rising in Iowa, although figures are well below the national average, particularly in the rural areas.

The supply of water in Iowa is undertaken partially through public water supply systems (serving 73 percent) and partially through private investment (27 percent). The rural nature of much of the population means that a substantial proportion of Iowans must rely on their own supplies, principally wells. For the public systems, water is obtained from both surface supplies (approximately 27 percent) and groundwater (73 percent). Surface water supply sources include natural lakes and streams, and to some extent, impounded reservoirs. Only four Federal dams have been constructed in Iowa, of which one will serve in part as a water supply facility in the near future.

Groundwater is utilized more extensively across the State, with wells tapping into the various aquifers. The surficial glacial deposits and alluvial materials hold important water resources for many individuals and smaller communities. Larger communities and industries requiring higher yields often sink wells into the lower bedrock aquifers. Although water is extracted from the ground across the State, yields are variable. Highest yields of water are found in the northeast and then gradually decline towards the southwest. However, estimated supplies are extremely high and should impose no real restrictions on development. Irrigation, especially in the west, could cause some problems, but licensing of wells has prevented too much mining of the water resource.

While water quantity may place no restrictions on use of the resource, water quality could impose some limitations unless action and care in management are taken in the near future. For a long time, water quality in Iowa has been very good. Physical contaminants in the form of suspended sediments in surface water, along with the chemical hardness of some groundwater, have presented some problems, but nothing of a serious nature. Recently, however, with the increased application of chemical fertilizers, herbicides, and pesticides, other contaminants have been found in the water. Surface water, in particular, and now groundwater in various parts of the State, have been polluted with nitrates, nitrites, and phosphates and, on occasion, low levels of pesticides. This pollution has not reached toxic levels as in some industrial states, but attention has been given to the problem to prevent further difficulties. Already, contaminants have had a direct impact on certain activities. For example, for a time, commercial fishing was banned in Coralville Lake near Cedar Rapids because of high levels of dieldrin found in the fish. In a few communities, high nitrate levels have made wells obsolete and forced the drilling of new, deeper ones. In general, however, water quality in Iowa can be regarded as good.

FLORA AND FAUNA:
The settlement of Iowa and the development of big business farming has all but eliminated the natural flora and fauna of the State. Once a vast open prairie, the biological environment has been transformed into a controlled agricultural landscape. A number of natural grasslands remain, but these are confined to a few small reserves. Similarly,

forests which once covered nearly 18 percent of the State are now reduced to less than 7 percent. Wetlands have been extensively drained, about 3 percent of the original area still exists, destroying unique habitats and diverse vegetation. The fauna have suffered accordingly, with species diversity and actual numbers of animals reduced over the years. Ironically, hunters have recently altered this pattern with "conservation" measures, as a result of which, more deer can be found in Iowa than before settlers entered the State. In addition, such animals as peregrine falcons, river otters, and wild turkeys have been introduced in some areas.

MINERAL WEALTH:

The original mineral attraction in Iowa was lead, and later zinc, which were mined near Dubuque. In time, these resources, while not fully exhausted, declined in importance and other mineral resources were developed. Five main mining/quarrying activities are now carried out in the State: cement, stone, sands, gravels, gypsum, and coal. In combination with a few minor resources, such as peat and clay, the non-fuel minerals had a total value in 1980 of $251.9 million, while coal added a further $12.5 million.

The carbonate rocks in Iowa provide the raw material for cement, which is mined extensively throughout the State. In 1980, this production accounted for 41 percent of the non-fuel mineral wealth. Stone, both crushed and dimensional, contributed 37 percent, and sands and gravels, 13 percent. The widespread occurrence of these resources reduces the transportation costs for such bulky material. For example, limestone is quarried in 64 counties, and sands and gravels in 81. Gypsum is found in two areas: at Fort Dodge, where it is extracted by open pit methods, and at a smaller reserve in Sperry in the southeast, where it is mined. Coal is also a valuable resource to the Iowa economy, with six mines (one underground) active in 1980. With the pressure on certain energy resources, these reserves could become more significant in future years. The official estimated number of reserves in Iowa is 7 billion tons, over 50 percent of which is proven. Most of this is located in southcentral Iowa. Unfortunately, this coal is not of the highest quality; it is primarily bituminous, which has fairly high ash and sulphur contents. With careful management, however, these problems can be overcome.

GEOGRAPHICAL
CONFIGURATION

LANDSCAPE FEATURES

Topography. A North Central State wholly within the prairie region, Iowa stretches approximately 310 miles from the Mississippi River on the east to the Missouri and Big Sioux rivers on the west; from Minnesota on the north, the prairies extend approximately 200 miles southward to the Missouri Line. The total area of 56,147 miles (of which only 561 square miles are water surface) is one-fifth larger than that of New York and just one-fifth as large as that of Texas. Across the Mississippi River are the states of Illinois and Wisconsin, and on the west are Nebraska and South Dakota. The prolongation of the southern and eastern boundaries, to include the entire channel of the Des Moines River, gives Iowa a shape somewhat similar to that of the United States.

From Keokuk at the mouth of the Des Moines River, the southernmost point in the State, where the elevation is the lowest (477 feet above sea level), the land rises in gentle swells northward and westward until the highest point is reached (1,670 feet) near Sibley in Osceola County at the northern border. The rivers, following this natural drainage, flow eastward into the Mississippi and westward into the Missouri from a broad water-parting that runs almost directly north and south. The Upper Iowa, Turkey, Maquoketa, Wapsipinicon, Cedar, Iowa, Skunk, and Des Moines rivers, which drain the eastern two-thirds of the State, flow slowly over long winding courses. The longest, the Des Moines, with its source in the far northwest, rises and lowers with the rains--in midsummer a shallow muddy stream, in spring a swift river overflowing its banks and bringing southward a burden of broken branches, driftwood, and rich earth. In the north, its valley is low and broad but, as the river moves on, high wooded hills and bluffs rise on both sides. The northern rivers in this eastern system cut through rock courses. Both the Iowa and Cedar river valleys are hill and bluff sections, sometimes marked by limestone cliffs. In the western system, the shorter courses

21

of the Big Sioux, Floyd, Little Sioux, Boyer, and Nishnabotna rivers tend to create a rapid current. The rivers here flow between steep grassy banks.

The greater part of the Iowa country is level land, a region of subtly varying contours, where yellow light spreads over the great expanses and plays through the luxurious vegetation. Fields of corn and other grains are planted in even squares and rectangles, with straight roads following the section lines and defining more squares. Groves of trees shelter the farm buildings. Large herds of stock feed in the knolly pasture lands. Sudden breaks in this level country are the low river valleys, from one to ten miles wide and covered by natural woodlands that rise to irregular lines of hills or bluffs at the valley's edge.

The most marked differences are found only in the northeast and southwest. In the northeastern section, cliffs rise abruptly from the banks of the Mississippi River, sometimes to a height of 300 to 400 feet, with tree-covered hills extending westward. Here the tributaries of the Mississippi wind through rocky ravines and wooded valleys. In the west, south of the mouth of the Big Sioux River, a line of mound-like bluffs sweeps up from the flood plain of the Missouri to heights ranging from 100 to 300 feet.

Waterways. Lakes of varying size are scattered throughout the northwestern area, extending about 50 miles from the Minnesota Line. Lake Okoboji, Spirit Lake, and the many smaller lakes in Dickinson County constitute the principal region. Storm Lake, lying to the south of this region, and Clear Lake, to the east, are other important lakes. Some of the Iowa lakes, called "wall lakes," have rock-walled beaches, where the ice has forced the glacial rocks from the lake's bottom to the shore.

CLIMACTIC CONDITIONS

Wet springs, warm summers, long growing seasons, and favorable winds, make the State admirably suited to agriculture. Temperatures range from 25 degrees below zero in winter to 100 degrees in the summer. The lowest temperature ever observed was 47 degrees below zero, on January 12, 1912, at Washta in Cherokee County. The average for winter, however, is 21.6 degrees. The highest temperature on record for summer is 118 degrees, registered in the suburbs of Keokuk, July 20, 1934. Unusual extremes sometimes occur during a single season and the temperature may vary 50 degrees in a day. A wintry morning will be followed by a warm afternoon, or two days will be like spring, and the next two, like winter. An exceptional variation occurred in 1930 in Webster City, when the temperature rose from 34 degrees below zero on February 15, to 72 degrees on February 24, a difference of 106 degrees in nine days.

Climate Extremes. Hailstorms sometimes occur during the hot summer months, but data for the thirteen years preceding 1935 show that only 1.12 percent of the crops were hail-damaged. The greatest damage was suffered in the northwest and the least in the south-central counties. Crop-destroying droughts seldom cover the entire State, although twice since 1930, crops in the western and southern part have been so damaged that much of the corn was unfit even for fodder. In 1934, the southern and western sections felt the drought most severely, but in 1936, it was more widespread, with the southern counties again the most severe sufferers. According to Charles D. Reed, a director of the Weather Division of the State Department of Agriculture, "It is not the drought but heat that causes most of the damage to crops in Iowa."

Winter. During the winters, the snowfall is frequently heavy enough to store moisture in the ground for spring planting and growing. The average annual snowfall over a 50-year period at Des Moines was 31.8 inches. The greatest snowfall in a day was in December, 1888, at which time 17 inches of snow fell. In the days before the State was more populated, blizzards roared unhindered across open country, but protecting groves of trees around many farmhouses, and the presence of towns and cities, have rendered such storms less devastating through the years.

Most of the rain, coming on the south winds, falls in the growing season when the chief crops, corn and other grains, need it most. The average of 85 rainy days a year gives an average annual rainfall of about 26 inches in the extreme northwest and about 36 inches in the southeast. Annual precipitation--averaged for 63 years--is 31.62 inches. The rainfall is an important factor in the consistent fertility of the State. The long growing season ranges from 140 days in the northwest to 170 days in the southeast, or from the last killing frost in the spring (April 20 to May 3) to the first killing frost in the fall (September 25 to October 15). Sunshine is present on an average of 215 days in the year.

NATURAL RESOURCES AND THEIR CONSERVATION

In 1933, the *Report on the Iowa Twenty-Five Year Conservation Plan* was published for the Iowa Board of Conservation and the Iowa Fish and Game Commission. Although this report was in the nature of a research study, outlining the State's recreational facilities in State parks, and its fish, game, and waterfowl refuges, it became the beginning of the State's program for the conservation of its land resources in general. Today the State Planning Board, appointed in part by the governor, supervises such fact-finding projects dealing with land use and land waste as the making of soil surveys, studies of forests and streams in their relation to land waste, and investigations of methods of preserving soil fertility.

Very little land in the State is unsuitable for agriculture. The National Resources Board (1935) reported that 25 percent of all the grade-one land in the United States is in Iowa, and that this rich soil is the State's most important natural resource. The entire north-central section is part of the Wisconsin drift area, with some of the richest soils in the world. However, this great natural fertility is in danger of being depleted, by erosion in some sections, and by intensive farming throughout the State.

The dark and heavy soil is not likely to blow away in "dust storms" in drought years, but erosion is a serious problem. Along the hillsides, the soil is being gullied constantly, but this type of erosion does not cause so much land waste as does that known as "sheet erosion." The latter, although not so apparent as gully erosion, proceeds rapidly. In extreme cases, as much as 50 tons of soil to an acre have been carried away in one rain. To regulate the flow of water, and to check the washing away of land, the State has planted trees, built artificial lakes, and dammed streams. Farmers, to guard against excessive losses, developed plans of plowing, with the furrows being laid transverse on the slopes.

From the earliest times in Iowa, farmers practiced rotation of crops, mainly wheat, oats, and barley against corn. Application of the Agricultural Adjustment Act made a more varied plan profitable. Pasture crops and such legumes as alfalfa and soybeans alternated with the regular crops, and some of the land was left idle to "rest." Much of this is in the nature of experimentation, but it is checking the loss of the soil's fertility.

Extensive field experiments made during the past ten or fifteen years show that approximately 75 percent of the soils are acid--in need of phosphate. However, they are benefited by applications of crushed limestone. Aside from this, the soils are so well supplied with organic matter, nitrogen, and potassium, that it is comparatively easy to maintain their productivity.

An abundant surface-water supply is insured by the two large boundary rivers, and the many interior streams, lakes, and marshes. Rivers and watercourses carry off the wastes of industries and communities, and drain the farmyards. Lakes and numerous marshes, valuable for recreation and as havens for wildlife, are also a means for regulating stream flow.

The potential water power of the Iowa rivers is relatively slight. Power is generated by 64 hydroelectric plants, including the one at Keokuk, among the greatest in the world, which generates power for this and surrounding states. The dam, nearly a mile long, holds back the waters of the Mississippi River, and 200,000 horse power is generated by the plant.

The urban centers of the northern part of the State depend mainly on the underground water supply. The public water supply of 500 municipalities comes from subsurface waters; few areas of equal size have so many communities thus dependent. Some of these lower water veins, tapped by larger communities, furnish as much as 4,000,000 gallons a day. However, in the southern part, where the water-bearing strata are very deep, communities often find it more practical to use the surface waters.

The underground waters flow through the sandstones that lie fairly near the surface in northeast Iowa--at depths of 1,000 to 3,000 feet. In Wisconsin and Minnesota, these strata come near enough to the surface to absorb the direct rainfall and percolation, but the movement of this absorbed water is so slow that it reaches the surface in Iowa wells many years after it has fallen as rain.

Shallow wells, developed in areas where there are glacial deposits of gravel, sand, or clay, are limited in yield. The glacial drift and the wind-deposited loess retain part of the rainfall and snowfall, carrying it underground to the lakes and streams. Tapping these top strata, drift wells (usually less than 100 feet deep) furnish the individual domestic supply as well as that of some of the smaller municipalities. Although the supply of water borne by these

25

strata is usually limited, an exception occurs in the gravel deposit adjacent to and underlying the Raccoon River, which furnishes as much as 20,000,000 gallons a day--enough for the entire city of Des Moines.

As with the land, the State is faced with a problem of water conservation. Freeflowing wells once were left uncapped when not in use; marshes were drained, to the detriment of the surrounding country; communities too close together tapped the same water- bearing strata. Industrial and community wastes have periodically polluted the streams.

Before setting up a definite program for the conservation of its valuable water supply, the State collected accurate basic data; surveying the extent of river pollution, the availability of better public water supplies, and the possibilities of flood control and reforestation are just some of the data that was utilized.

No metallic minerals are mined in Iowa, but sand, gravel, and limestone in the underlying and surface strata constitute an important resource. Almost all of the counties have clay deposits. Some types, suitable for the manufacture of common grades of clay products, are easily accessible; others, valuable in the composition of high-grade products, are more difficult to reach.

Limestones and shales necessary for making Portland cement are found, but this industry did not develop as quickly as the clay industry; this is primarily because the combination of particular kinds of rock (each conforms closely to a standard composition) was not readily available. The materials are near enough, however, for advantageous use and are utilized commercially at Davenport, Mason City, Des Moines, West Des Moines, and Gilmore City. Mason City plants have both the required limestone and shale nearby.

Limestone, from a relatively small area in east-central Iowa, is used for building purposes, while limestone suitable for road surfacing, lime, and fertilizer are found in quantity throughout the entire eastern portion. The deposits of sand and gravel in the northern half of the State are largely used for road building; by the mid-twentieth century, more than fifty plants in Iowa were using these deposits for road construction and building purposes.

An important deposit of gypsum at Fort Dodge makes possible a high State production in quantity and value. By mid-century, almost 350,000 tons were mined. The deposits at Fort Dodge, in an area of more than 30 square miles, are made available largely through stripping and sluicing operations.

Beds of coal underlie approximately 20,000 square miles in 20 counties. One broad belt extends on both sides of the Des Moines River from Webster County to the Missouri State Line. It has been estimated that, according to present needs and rate of consumption, there is enough coal to supply the State for more than 4,000 years. The bituminous coals lie comparatively close to the surface, with the deepest shaft at only 387 feet. The deposits in most places are only 18 to 30 inches thick, and are easily mined as they stretch evenly between the series of bedrock. In most of southern Iowa the beds, though seldom deep, are usually continuous enough to make commercial development profitable. By mid-century, the mines yielded 3,650,000 tons of coal. Total mining value of Iowa in 1987 was $317 million.

FAUNA

The open farming country, with its grassy nesting grounds, the rush-grown sloughs, the low brushland, the lake regions, and the wooded bluffs and hills along Iowa's streams are havens for birds of many species. Ornithologists have pointed out that this territory along the Mississippi and Missouri rivers forms a natural channel (flyway) for the passage of migratory birds. Two feathered travelers that make the longest annual journey along this route are the bobolink and the purple martin. Both make trips of approximately 5,000 miles from the northern United States to South America, crossing by way of the Canal Zone and Central America. In the autumn, wood warblers pass through by the hundreds. The birds going north to nest or south to escape the cold weather often stop in the parks and refuges in passing.

Bird Species. In the counties along the Missouri River, the species of birds differ somewhat from those to the east. Here, more characteristically western species are found: the lark-bunting, Lewis woodpecker, and red-shafted flicker are among them. Also in northern Iowa, around Clear Lake and Mud Lake, yellow-headed blackbirds are seen in large numbers, though they are seldom found elsewhere in the State.

Common Birds. Although there are hundreds of species and sub-species of birds in Iowa, the commonest are limited to relatively few species. The brown creeper, tree-sparrow, slate- colored junco, and northwestern shrike, here in the winter, migrate north in the spring to nest. The cardinal (red bird), blue jay, eastern goldfinch, crow, white-breasted nut-hatch, black-capped chickadee, English sparrow, downy woodpecker, tufted titmouse, and starling remain throughout the year. During the summer months, the eastern goldfinch, designated in 1933 as the State bird, may often be seen feeding on seeds of dandelions and thistle.

Migratory Birds. The meadow larks (eastern and western), bobolink, and red-winged blackbird, birds of the open meadows, and the bronzed grackle, fox sparrow, song sparrow, bluebird, robin, mourning dove, and rusty blackbird arrive early in the spring. Perhaps the loveliest singers among the spring birds are the white-throated sparrow and the prairie horned lark.

Migrating here in the late spring and summer are the scarlet tanager, indigo bunting, red-headed woodpecker, wood peewee, crested fly-catcher, ruby-throated humming bird, northern yellow throat and yellow warbler, dickcissel (considered the characteristic Iowa bird), rose-breasted grosbeak, Baltimore and orchard orioles, kingbird, kingfisher, cuckoos (rain crow), cowbird, brown thrasher, woodthrush, hermit thrush, olive and gray-cheeked thrushes, catbird, purple martin, migrant (loggerhead) shrike, whippoorwill, and several species of swallows. The nighthawk, in appearance similar to the whippoorwill, and one of the summer birds, is well known to city dwellers.

Birds of Prey. Among the birds of prey, the bald eagle migrates along the longer rivers and the turkey vulture nests only in the southern half of the State. There are at least ten kinds of hawks, two of which are Cooper's and the sharp- shinned, both migrants in the fall and spring, although the Cooper's hawk is sometimes a resident. The marsh sparrow hawk and the red-tailed hawk remain through the summer months, less frequently in the winter. Several species of the owl family are found in the winter, among them the screech, barred, great- horned, long-eared, and short-eared; several species remain throughout the year. The snowy owl occasionally visits from December to March.

The American bittern, often called "shite poke" or "slough pump," was one of the most conspicuous of prairie birds to early settlers, but it now has decreased in numbers. American coots (mud hens), common throughout the area, nest here, though other water birds, such as rails and gallinules, are far less plentiful. Of the shore birds, most of them migratory-- plover, woodcock, sandpiper, curlew, and snipe--the snipe (Wilson's snipe or jacksnipe) is the most common game species. The killdeer, a favorite with his melody, "kill-dee, kill- dee," lives in the marshy regions while the upland plover hunts out the higher grasslands. Mallard duck and blue-winged teal nest in the marshes of northwestern Iowa, and the Canada goose stops here during its migration. This northwestern lake region annually becomes one of the greatest concentration points for migrating wildlife in the Midwest.

Game Birds. Of game birds, the wild turkey, once common, is almost extinct, except for a small number introduced in the State parks. The quail (eastern bobwhite), although it is not numerous, is found throughout the State. Prairie chicken (pinnated grouse), here in large numbers in the early days of settlement when conditions were favorable for its development, has decreased rapidly, and few, if any, nest here. At one time there were many sharptail grouse, but now only a few winter migrants are seen; and the ruffed grouse, found in northeastern Iowa, is now limited in number.

Settlement naturally destroyed parts of the original habitats for the birds, but, realizing this, the State began to introduce birds to fit the new environment. Ringnecked pheasants, easily adaptable to the locale, now are numerous enough in the northern area to permit open seasons. The European partridge (Hungarian), imported in 1902, has also replaced some of the original supply of birds. Farmlands, meadows, and cultivated areas of Iowa now are as plentiful with bird life as the grasslands of pioneer days.

Animal Life. Game animals are rare in this region, except for white-tailed deer. Some escape from private herds. Deer can sometimes be seen around Ledges State Park near Boone, where they are confined within the park; others roam at liberty. Herds roam near the town of Avoca and in the northern part of Washington County, and all are protected by law.

Of the smaller game and fur-bearing animals, beavers (protected by closed season) are still rare, although they have returned to some areas of western Iowa along the Little Sioux River and some of its tributaries. The mink, muskrat, raccoon, skunk, and opossum are not over-plentiful, but the opossum, considered a southern animal, has increased in numbers as this animal migrates northward through the country. The civet cat and badger are not plentiful, nor is the gray fox, but the red fox, in spite of the vigor with which hunters track him down, is not in danger of extinction.

The jack rabbit is common in the northwestern area, while the smaller cottontail is found throughout the entire State. The jack rabbit can be seen bounding about the open prairie and fields, but the cottontail prefers to be in or near low brush, thickets, and willow clumps. The fox squirrel is the most common of the squirrels, with the gray squirrel next; the red squirrel is abundant only in a few places. Other rodents, such as the chipmunk and gopher, are fairly common everywhere. The groundhog (woodchuck), around which the legend of the spring's early or late arrival centers, can often be seen along the highways.

There are 25 species of reptiles here, of which only three are poisonous--the massasauga rattler, the prairie rattler, and the banded or timber rattler. The poisonous snakes are distinguished by their three-cornered heads. Other snakes are the bull-snake, fox-snake, milk-snake, king-snake, and blue racer, the food of which often consists of rats, mice, ground squirrels, and pocket gophers.

Fish. Although over 130 species of fish have been described, less than one-quarter of them are common. Streams in the northeastern region are usually cold and clear--good trout streams--where rainbow, brook (native), and brown trout are found; but the streams in southern Iowa, flowing to the east and west into the two great boundary rivers, have few fish except catfish and bullheads (a small catfish). The small-mouthed bass is one of the better game fish found in the northern lakes and some of the streams. Catfish--especially the little bullhead, crappie, bluegill (sunfish), carp, and sucker (redhorse), are the common river fish. The white sucker and buffalo are plentiful. The common pike (pickerel) is one of the best game fish of the rivers and streams, while wall-eyed pike (found in Lake Okoboji and Clear Lake) and yellow perch (found in great numbers in Spirit Lake) are also good game fish.

When the Twenty-five Year Conservation Plan was conceived in the early decades of the twentieth century, it was understood that every element of conservation would bear directly upon the restoration and preservation of wildlife. Under the plan, sanctuaries for upland game and bird refuges were set aside. Efforts were made to clear the streams and lakes, and to check pollution. Artificial lakes were built and natural lakes dredged and improved. Besides State-owned parks, some State-owned or State-leased lands were designated as game and refuge areas, mostly around the northern lakes, and were recognized by the conservation commission as wildlife refuges.

Along the Mississippi are Federal areas, which are closed to shooting. Three of these are in Allamakee County and one in Jackson County--all units of the Upper Mississippi Wildlife Refuge.

FLORA

Before the Iowa country was cultivated, the prairie grass, growing as high as the wheels of the oncoming prairie schooners, covered the entire area. To the first settler, the expanse of prairie seemed unlimited; deep within the coarse grasses, hundreds of varieties of flowers grew in profusion.

Early Flowers and Plants. In early spring, the knolls were blue with pasqueflowers. Clumps of grasslike sedge appeared. False dandelion, cream-flowered paintbrush, and mats of groundplum-vetch splashed the hilltops. Then followed the bird-foot violet, white-flowered larkspur, yellow lousewort, and lemon- and orange-colored gromwell. Along the shallow streams blossomed the marsh-marigold, small white moccasin-flower, purple heart-leaved violet, white cress, and yellow stargrass. White and yellow crowfoot floated on the ponds.

Summer brought a different color tone, with red phlox and yellow indigo side by side, silver-leaved psoraleas, prairie lilies with orange cups, porcupine grass, side-oats, New Jersey tea, spiderwort, and countless roses. Red-purple vetch, yellow parsley, golden alexander, and Canadian anemone blended their colors on the ever-changing prairie.

In midsummer, the golden coreopsis, silver-leaved leadplant, red and white prairie clovers, compassplant, stiff-bush clover, crepe-petaled primrose, and yellow toad flax, mingled with spiked mesquite grass, tick trefoil, Indian grass, Eryngium, and Indian plantain. The prairie's flowers in the fall were the goldenrod, gentian, blazing-stars of many patterns, sunflower, cornflower, and blue, white, and purple prairie asters.

Even after years of careless tillage, this grassland cover has not been entirely obliterated. Today it may be seen in a few patches--strips by railroad crossings, by country roads, and in rough lands not claimed for tillage or for pas-

ture. In State parks and occasional privately owned properties, small fragments of the natural garden are preserved.

Wildflowers and Plants. The wildflowers vary in sec-
tions--not to be clearly defined--as diverse geologic,
topographic, and climatic conditions have favored certain
plant forms, many of which have migrated into the State.
In the northwestern region, where the Kansan glacial drift
has been covered somewhat with loess soil, and southward
along the loess- covered mounds of the Missouri Valley,
plants from the western and southwestern plains of the
United States appear--the golden- aster, large-flowered
beard-tongue, narrow-leaved collomia, prairie trefoil, and
the locoweed, well known as a poisonous plant. Hidden in
the grass are prairie roses, blue, white, and purple asters,
the orange-butterfly milkweed, red and white prairie
clovers, and the deep-blue downy gentian. With the blues-
tems, common throughout the state, are the wire grass,
three mesquite grasses, buffalo grass, and other southwestern species. The wind-blown loess supports many
characteristically western plants such as the Spanish
bayonet (soaproot), Indian breadroot (*pomme de prairie*), the
red locoweed, and the pink dalea.

Honeysuckles here are represented by the western buckbrush (one of the snowberries), and primroses by the scarlet
gauras. One of the spurges known as snow-on-the-mountain, grows so profusely that often the hills are tinted by its
pale green, white-edged leaves. The silverberry is a decorative plant with woolly gray leaves and oval silver fruit. Besides the common annual sunflower, there are the
rough-leaved artichoke, and others; Maximilian's, a slender
gray-leaved perennial, flourishes across the northern part of
the State. Woolly mullen is found in the pastures. Blue-
flowered lettuce contrasts with brilliant patches of the
dotted blazing-star, and the plant known as bundle-of-
switches clings to the flat-faced loess cliffs, opening its deli-
cate pink flowers to the morning sun. In a few lakes of this
region the American lotus blooms.

In the southern third of the State, although the
majority of the plants are common to other sections, there
are some native to the Ozark and Alleghenian centers and
points as far south as Texas. Among these are the
gamagrass, a member of the corn family, and the Ruellia, related to the classic acanthus. The trumpetflower, which
kills many trees in its twining embrace, often displays its
brick-red flowers from some porch trellis. The wild potato

vine may be recognized by patches of moonflower- like bloom. Silky-leaved Virginia plantain, the rare diminutive bluet, and the long-bracted bur-marigold--all found on the Texas plains--are now naturalized Iowa flora.

In the central-northeastern section, where the boulder-strewn land is drained by the Cedar and Wapsipinicon rivers, the prairie meadows abound with pink and white shootingstars, golden ragwort, and long-plumed purple avens (prairie smoke). Throughout the state there are many honeysuckles, including the coralberry (red-berried buckbrush), the black-fruited and black haw nannyberry, and the twining trumpet-honeysuckles.

Many conspicuous plants grow on the sands of river bottoms, on dune-like banks of lakes, in sand pits, and on ancient lake beds. Some of the rarest of these sand plants are found in the bed of extinct Lake Calvin. Sand-binding calamovilfa grass (whose roots aid in forming sod by checking the blowing of loose sand), fragrant spotted horsemint, the smartweed-leaved spurge, green-flowered croton, the trailing wild bean, poisonous rattlebox, and goatsrue, all flourish in the sands. White- flowered woolly Froelichia appears like a ghost among plants of a generally greener hue; and, of the plants that successfully live on the barest sands, there are the spider-flower, blue phlox, and large-flowered beard-tongue.

Pond and Lake Flora. The distinctive flora in the ponds and lakes represent three successive stages of development- -submerged, floating, and emergent. In some of the bodies of water in northwest-central Iowa, each of these stages can be traced. Among the plants living in diffused light under water are pondweed, coontail, and bladderwort. When the duckweeds, like myriads of floating cushions, and the leaves of water-lilies begin to shade the submerged plants from the sun, the latter die and the decaying vegetation sinks to the bottom of the pond. From the accumulating soil, cattails, rushes, and sedges emerge above the water, raising their leaves to the light above the floaters and in turn shading them. As these latest emergent plants rise from the water into the light and accumulate earth about their roots, they are able to maintain themselves for a time. Then, as they too die and enrich the soil, the earth is able to support such plants as the arrowhead, the flag--making the marsh blue with its flowers--and colonies of rose-flowered water smartweed that cast a glow over the waters. The tall joe- pye-weed and fluffy-leaved lobelias, with their spikes of dazzling blue, appear along the banks of meadow streams where the slowly accumulating soil rises almost out of the water.

In the tall-grass prairie, near the sources of the Des Moines River in northern Iowa, where springs bubble forth on hilltops in the poorly-drained sections, colonies of bog flowers occasionally show themselves. One of these colonies observed in early autumn revealed a cluster of cattails, marsh-dock, and traces of marshmarigolds on the west top of a knoll, and, just below the crest of the elevation, asters with blue-fringed swamp- gentian. Here the shining cup-flowered grass of Parnassus mingled with the yellow swamp betony and the slender pink foxglove. Outside the circle was a miniature sod plain ofnut rush, deep blue lobelia of the marshes, white and rose boneset, arrow grasses, and hosts of asters inside a huge sunflower hedge. Plain asters, swamp asters, and western asters--blue, white, and purple--mingled with patches of slender-leaved goldenrod. Refugee plants of seacoast marshes, of tropical, boreal, and temperate regions, had all been able to maintain themselves in the bog.

The woodlands along the rivers and streams shelter many wildflowers--snow trillium, blood root, hepaticas (white, rose, and lavender), and white lamb's tongue. As the leafing trees shade the earth, anemones (true, false, and rue) spring forth among crowfoot, dutchmans-breeches, spring beauties, mayapple (mandrake), wild ginger, Solomonseal (true and false), and the yellow violet. On the rocky hillsides, scarlet and red trumpeted columbines cling, bushy meadow rue and cranesbill color the open spaces, and jack-in-the-pulpit, with yellow or pink moccasin flowers, grow in the deeper shade of wood or hollow.

Rare Flora. In localized areas on the Mississippi River and its tributaries where bellworts and blueberries are found, grow many rare flowers--wild lily-of-the-valley, wintergreen, dwarf Canadian primrose, the twin-flower, the panicled bluebell, wild snowball, shrubby cinquefoil, and the sweet vernal grass used in basketry.

Moss and Lichen. On the rocky cliffs along the rivers, green or black mosses and matlike lichens cover the crevices. Clubmoss and rockmosses surround the bright pink fameflowers that hold tightly to the rocks in northwestern Iowa. In the natural rock gardens of eastern Iowa, a soft green undertone is given the countryside by the many ferns--the walking fern, the purple cliffbrake, the bulblet fern, and the rusty cliffbrake. Polypody fern, beech-fern, brittlefern, maidenhair fern, and blunt-lobed woodsia often grow side by side with the blue harebell and white rockress in sandstone crevices.

While the displacement of indigenous flora was going on all over the State, other much less desirable plants were introduced that competed with the native plant life for possession of the soil. After nearly 100 years of settlement by the white man, it was estimated that immigrant flora constituted approximately 18 percent of the known Iowa flora. Records show that some of these plants were of Asiatic and European origin, introduced as impurities in garden and agricultural seeds and in straw for packing purposes. Although some plants have been introduced as ornamentals (flower-of-an-hour, butter-and-eggs, cypress spurge, snow-on-the-mountain, and Queen Anne's lace), in many cases the origin is accidental and unknown. One of these "imported" weeds is the blue vervain (verbena, sometimes called Venus's torch) that colors many farmyards and pastures with its purple and blue masses. The common white-flowered, pungent dog fennel also grows abundantly in barnyards.

Many noxious alien weeds became so widespread that the State attempted to control them through legislation. Among these are quackgrass, Canada thistle, European morning glory, Russian knapweed, Indian mustard, and many others that were unknown to the first settlers.

Timberlands. Iowa still possesses almost half of the acres of woodland (including woodlots) of its original 5,000,000 acres; of these, almost 25,000 acres are State owned. These timberlands are chiefly along the streams in the eastern and southeastern part. Very little of the original timber is still standing, and practically all is second and third growth.

Along the main valleys grow hardwood forests represented by birches, maples, hickories, oaks, elms, and basswood. This bluff woodland gives way, along stream or lake borders, to elm, bur- oak, green ash, and cottonwood, which are able to stand the severe climate of the open prairie. The green ash of open spaces assumes a hardy prairie form in the midst of the grassland where the most common tree is the willow. Occasionally, cottonwoods grow in the sandy ground remote from streams. In southeastern Iowa, the hardwood forests contain the oaks--post, swamp, swamp post, swamp white, yellow chestnut, shrubby chestnut, black jack, and shingle--and the hickories, including pecan, king nut, and pig nut. Representatives of the southern broad-leaved forest occur among these, except near the middle of the State. Yellow and paper birches grow in northeastern Iowa among the conifers such as white pine, balsam fir, and Canadian yew--probably relics of a postglacial forest.

With its trees and shrubs, Iowa presents a colorful seasonal panorama from the opening of the maple buds in February to the last witch hazel blossoms in November. Along the creeks, the greening pussy willows push forth furry catkins in the spring, and poplars and cottonwoods follow them with colorful, pendent flower clusters. Among the brushy treetops on the banks and cliffs, the feathery whiteness of the shad-bush stands out in April. Thorny brown-plum thickets whiten and, over the southern half of the State, redbud and dogwood color the river woodlands in May. Persimmon and papaw are occasionally seen along the southern border, while snowy hawthorn and rose-flowered crab apples in spring border the woodlands throughout the State. Elderberries blossom in early summer. In the autumn, sumac colors the hillsides, the wild grape displays its purple clusters, and the hazel brush is brown with drying nuts. In winter, the rare bittersweet contrasts with the drifts of snow.

One half of the small area of Iowa's original timberland was destroyed before mid-20th century, and the State developed plans for preserving the few trees it had and for reforesting the neglected areas. Besides its value for lumber, posts, and cordwood, the State realized the value of its forests in the utilization of wasteland, recreation facilities for its people, and the regulation of the flow of water in its streams. State- owned recreational parks, waterfowl and wildlife refuges (four of them Federal areas in eastern Iowa), and State-owned lakes, although not definitely set aside as forest preserves, were the nucleus of a large-scale plan for the preservation of the trees.

GEOLOGY

Geological surveys, beginning as early as the first quarter of the nineteenth century, have revealed several systems of sedimentary rock (indurated) formations that could have been deposited only in oceans as they advanced and retreated over the surface of this region hundreds of millions of years ago. The geological ages represented in these formations are: the Protozoic, the Paleozoic, and the Mesozoic.

Indurated Rocks. The indurated rocks are covered for the most part with sands, gravels, and clay laid down by glaciers coming from the north in times recent in comparison to the ages of the indurated rocks. The record of this glacial period (The Pleistocene of the Cenozoic age), which lasted probably 1,000,000 years, is clearly shown.

The indurated rock formations that form the bedrock were originally loose soft layers of sediment spread out on the bottom of prehistoric seas. As the seas gradually receded, belts of rock were left exposed at the surface. The various layers of rock--each of which formed a sea bottom for a long period of geologic time--bent down under each new layer. In general, the rock formations dip gently toward the southwest in the eastern half of the State, south in the north-central and central parts, and southeast in the northwestern section. All deposited essentially horizontally, they have been deformed to make a syncline. Numerous unconformities indicate that they were not all deposited in the same sea.

Many of the formations are visible at highway and railroad cuts throughout the State, where they will be found underlying the surface soil. Frequently they may be viewed along the banks of rivers and in various surface exposures, particularly in the northeast corner of the State.

The oldest and hardest of these rock formations is the Sioux quartzite (Pre-Cambrian), found as surface rock only in the far northwestern section. In a small area of Allamakee and Clayton counties are found the second oldest rocks--sandstone, dolomite, and siltstone formations--in the St. Croixan series of the Cambrian system.

The Ordovician rocks, constituting the third oldest in Iowa, extend in a rapidly narrowing belt along the Mississippi River from Winneshiek County on the north into Clinton County on the south. Caves and grottoes are found in the many fissured layers of Galena limestone of this system. At Decorah, in Winneshiek County, a famous ice cave presents the phenomenon of warm temperature in late autumn and winter, followed by temperatures that form layers of ice in spring and summer. The Silurian strata (next youngest to the Ordovician) with its hard Niagaran dolomite, extends from the southern half of Fayette County southeastward nearly to Davenport in Scott County, making a belt about 35 to 50 miles wide and over 100 miles long.

Limestones, shales, and dolomites of Devonian age, (next younger than Silurian) lie in an even broader strip from Worth, Mitchell, and Howard counties in northern Iowa to Muscatine and Scott counties in the southeast. West of the Devonian rocks a great belt of shales and limestones belonging to the Mississippian system (sixth oldest) reaches from Keokuk in the southeastern corner of the State to Algona in Kossuth County.

Because of its stores of coal and shales, the Des Moines series of the Pennsylvanian system (next youngest to the Mississippian) is probably the most economically important rock strata. Included in the system are the Missouri and the Virgil series in southwestern Iowa, and the Des Moines series underlying a large region in southern and central Iowa.

A rich though limited bed of red sandy shale and gypsum filled a deep valley in the neighborhood of Fort Dodge to a depth of 80 feet during Permian time, following the Pennsylvanian age. The formation of gypsum differs somewhat from the formation of most rocks, resulting as it does from the rapid evaporation of inland bodies of water. This bed is in the old valleys of the Des Moines strata (Pennsylvanian) and the Mississippian system.

Underlying the surface soil of west-central and northwestern Iowa, and cropping out in many localities of the lake region, are the youngest of the indurated rock strata of Iowa (the ninth in order numbering from the oldest to the most recent). Sandstones of the Dakota formation were formed here--comparatively recently- -during the Cretaceous period. The area covered by Cretaceous rock extends from its southern tip in Monona and Crawford counties, in a gradually widening belt, to the Missouri River on the west and the Minnesota boundary on the north, and lies next to the Pennsylvanian and Mississippian strata on the east. Indurated rocks of the Cretaceous system (the last of the systems deposited by oceans) attain a thickness of 250 feet.

Non-Indurated Rocks. Iowa owes its soils, sands, gravels, silts and clay--the non-indurated or mantle rocks--chiefly to the four great glaciers that covered all or part of the area during the Pleistocene period. It is a safe estimate that the last of these glaciers retreated only 25,000 years ago. The time involved in the advance and retreat of each glacier and in the succeeding interglacial age constitute a cycle. A striking fact is the great length of the interglacial ages in contrast to the duration of the glacial ages themselves, estimated at a minimum of 30,000 years for each.

As each glacier traveled to the region, at the estimated rate of one mile in ten years, it carried along with it the coarse and fine rock materials picked up and scraped from the ground over which it passed. When the glacier reached as far south as the region including what is now Iowa, where the climate was warmer, it began to melt, or retreat, as slowly as it had come, leaving till (boulders of all sizes and fine clay) spread out behind it. During this time, streams that flowed out from beneath the melting glaciers carried immense quantities of sands and gravels, depositing them in valleys or on top of the till. The till, sands, and gravels together are known as drift. During the interglacial periods the drift was subject to weathering by air, wind, and water, and also underwent a certain amount of leaching and oxidation.

Glacier Age Drifts. Drift of the first glacier, the Nebraskan, covered the entire region, even the area commonly called the "driftless area" in Allamakee County in northeastern Iowa. The drift of later glaciers did not cover this section and the early deposits have been almost entirely eroded away. Deep-cutting streams, valleys, and rugged bluffs characterize this section.

Perhaps 500,000 years ago (minimum estimate), the Kansas Glacier fringed the western edge of the old Nebraskan drift and covered all of the region except a small area in the northeast. About 300,000 years later, a portion of the continental Illinoisan Glacier invaded the southeastern part from what is now Scott County along the river to Fort Madison, but extended no more than 30 miles inland. The widespread gumbotil, and related materials that have undergone a chemical weathering, developed during the first three glacial periods.

Geologists have discovered that during the third glacial age, the Illinoian, the now long extinct Lake Calvin was formed, covering large areas in what is now Johnson, Cedar, Muscatine, Washington, and Louisa Counties. As the Illinoian Glacier crept westward, the Mississippi River, and the water therein, became blocked at the mouth of the Wapsipinicon River and was forced to a new channel about 25 miles west of the original. As the waters reached the vicinity of what is now Columbus Junction, the Illinoian Glacier again dammed the way on the southeast, and drift of the Kansan blocked passage on the southwest. From

Columbus Junction, the waters backed up into what is now the Iowa River Valley beyond Iowa City, and up the Cedar River Valley to West Liberty and Moscow, to form a large body of water of great depth--perhaps more than 80 feet-- over parts of the present Iowa City, and deeper in other localities. Lake Calvin probably remained for 130,000 years, or until the approach of the fourth great ice sheet, the Iowan lobe of the Wisconsin.

More than 50,000 years ago, the Iowan lobe of the fourth glacier, the Wisconsin, crept down through the central northeast from what is now Worth, Mitchell, and Howard counties on the north to Linn County on the south, and by way of a slender strip to Clinton County on the east. This Wisconsin Glacier retreated to the north for a time. Many years later, the second lobe of the last ice sheet to in- vade Iowa entered from the northern part, along a path from Osceola County on the west to Worth County on the east and continued as far south as Polk and Dallas counties. When this second lobe (called the Mankato) melted away, the streams in that region became shallow and meandered with ill- defined courses and loosely packed banks. Many lakes, shallows, and marshes are in this area. Pilot Knob State Park, in Hancock County, embraces many odd-shaped morainal deposits (mounds at the edge of the glacier when it rapidly melted) characteristic of this lake region.

The Iowan and Mankato drift areas contain some of the richest soils in the world. Following both of these glaciers the usual drift was deposited; but the chemical weathering of the drift into gumbotil and related materials did not fol- low, and a widespread black soil was formed. The alluvial soils, composed of what has been washed down from other soils plus decayed vegetable matter, may be found along the streams and river bottoms. The loess soils (deposits of wind-blown silt), covering approximately three-fourths of the State, are browner and thinner than the northern soils.

Principal Soil Areas. Iowa may be divided into five principal soil areas: the Mississippi loess area covering a strip of land in east-central Iowa; the Iowan drift area covering approximately the territory over which the Iowan lobe passed in north-central Iowa; the southern Iowa loess area extending over most of the southern part of the state; the Mankato drift area approximately identical with the land covered by the Mankato lobe of the Wisconsin Glacier; and the Missouri loess area extending along a wide belt on the western border, from Missouri on the south to Sioux City on the north.

Because of the opportunities for analyzing indurated and non-indurated rock strata, and because of the four distinct glacial ages represented in this region, Iowa has distinctive geologic importance. It was among the first states in the New World to be examined geologically. Thomas Nuttall, from England, studied the banks of the Missouri early in the nineteenth century. About 1870, an excellent cut was made in Capitol Hill at Des Moines, exposing many layers of rocks and soils and enabling geologists to verify their theories and hypotheses. At this point, the Mankato drift was found resting on soil of the Kansas drift. A bridge today over the Court Avenue Speedway on Capitol Hill connects the southern tip of the Mankato lobe on one side with the edge of the Kansan drift on the other, joining in a single arch, non-indurated soils separated in geological time by nearly a million years. Samuel Calvin, appointed State Geologist in 1892, was perhaps the first to study Iowa geology extensively and scientifically.

Fossil Remains. Paleontologists found an abundance of fossil remains embedded in the successive rock strata of almost every part of the State. Fossils of one-celled animals, water- dwelling plants, and invertebrates have been discovered in the Paleozoic rocks. Large collections of shells and early forms of marine life have been taken from the layers of Burlington limestone in the vicinity of Keokuk, Fort Madison, and Burlington. Crinoids were found in this region in such abundance that Charles Wachsmuth and Frank Springer made a collection recognized as one of the most complete in the United States, now in the Smithsonian Institution at Washington.

In the limestone quarries at Le Grand, Marshall County, finely preserved starfishes and crinoids (stone lilies) have been found. The abundance of these fossils and their state of preservation have made the limestones of the Mississippian age here of international importance. Specimens have been sent to Paris and other foreign cities. The collection made by B. H. Beane, of Le Grand, is on display in the State Historical building in Des Moines.

Besides the many crinoids discovered, coal plants have been unearthed in Marion County, and single-celled animal fossils were found near Winterset in Madison County. Fossils from shale were plentiful at Hackberry Clay Banks a few miles east of Mason City in Cerro Gordo County and near Rockford in Floyd County. Bones and teeth of ancient fishes and corals are found near Iowa City, and there are hornshaped corals near Monticello. Sponges and clam-like and snail-like fossils may be seen at Dubuque. Fossils of the trilobites and brachiopods are also embedded in the sandstone of the steep slopes at Lansing in Allamakee County.

Animal Fossils. In the sand and gravel beneath the glacial drifts, fossils of the great Ice Age have been unearthed. Bones and teeth show that hairy elephants (mammoth and mastodon), camels, musk-ox, sloths, and giant beavers once roamed over Iowa. The skull of one of these beavers found near Avoca indicated the living beaver must have been more than nine feet long. The Cox gravel pit, southeast of the Missouri River bluffs, have given up remains of prehistoric animals.

PRE-HISTORY

MOUND BUILDERS

Mound Discoveries. A long time ago, a race of what is now believed to have been copper-skinned men, slowly and painfully piled stone upon stone, and heaped basket after basket of earth, day after day for many years, leaving as monuments to their dead the thousands of mounds scattered throughout Iowa. The homes of these people were of such fragile construction that scarcely any have been preserved, but the mounds they built reveal to archaeologists something of the customs and culture of the early tribal people. Some of their mounds were fortifications, or the foundations of religious structures; the great majority were built for burial purposes.

At the base of the burial mound was a shallow grave or low platform, upon which the remains of the dead were deposited, along with offerings of personal or tribal possessions--food, tobacco, weapons, or perhaps ornaments. Sometimes this platform was enclosed by a structure of wood or stone. Earth was heaped over this crude vault, as was an outer covering of sand and gravel. More than 10,000 mounds have been found in Iowa, and archaeologists in the past century have arrived at several confident conclusions concerning the origin and lives of the mound builders.

There is little doubt that these people were ancestors of the American Indian tribes found by the first explorers. But the diversity of cultures included within the term "mound builders," and the greater diversity of Indian customs at the historic level, make it practically impossible to trace the culture of any specific tribe to a particular mound builder culture. However, on the basis of a limited number of characteristics, some archaeologists believe that the Oneota culture provided the basis for the Siouan or historic times, and the Woodland the basis for the Algonkian.

Five Cultures. The mound builders of Iowa have been divided into five groups: Woodland, Hopewellian, Oneota, Mill Creek, and Glenwood, according to the materials found. The time sequence of these cultures has not been definitely established. In northeastern Iowa, the Woodland culture is known to have preceded the Oneota. In Allamakee County, however, the remains of the Oneota have been found superimposed on those of the Woodland culture.

Woodland Culture Group. The Woodland is the most widespread mound builder culture identified by archaeologists in Iowa, and may be found in almost every county in the State. Numerous village remains were discovered in oak groves of the lake district of northwestern Iowa, and more than 60 rock shelters were located in east-central Iowa. Most of the village sites are small, generally of two acres or less. The Woodland people were master artisans in stone and flint, and left behind more than 100 known types of chipped flint implements.

They were also responsible for an individual type of pottery, the material of which was mixed with coarsely crushed granite. Woodland pottery objects were generally formed on a base in the shape of a rounded-off cone. The rims and sides were decorated with fabric impressions, and were embellished with punched, stamped, and incised designs.

Effigy mounds in the shape of birds and animals were found in Allamakee, Clayton, and Dubuque counties. The famous "Woman Mound," on the Turkey River in Clayton, was built in the shape of a gigantic female with arms akimbo. It measures 70 feet between the out-thrust elbows and is 135 feet in length. There are also linear mounds in this quarter of the State and in the middle of the Des Moines River Valley. The conical mounds are numerous in nearly all sections.

Hopewellian Culture Group. The Hopewellian culture is found along the eastern border of Iowa; upon the banks of the Mississippi River in Jackson, Scott, Muscatine, and Louisa counties; from Dubuque south to the mouth of the Iowa River. An isolated group of Hopewellian mounds is farther north, in the Turkey River Valley in Clayton County. These latter mounds average three to ten feet in height and 30 to 90 feet in diameter. The interiors are rectangular crypts of logs which served for burial congregations and sacrificial altars. The largest specimen of the Hopewellian culture in Iowa is on a bluff near Toolesboro at the junction of the Iowa and Mississippi rivers.

Oneota Culture Group. The earthworks and large village sites of the Oneota culture are widespread over Iowa. The most extensive site, called Blood Run, covers more than 100 acres in Lyon County, overlooking the Big Sioux River. Originally there were 143 mounds here, and an earthen enclosure of 15 acres. Other examples of the Oneota appear along the Little Sioux River in Clay, Dickinson, and Woodbury counties. Still others are adjacent to the Hopewellian culture at Toolesboro, and along the Upper Iowa River in Allamakee County. The mounds of the Blood Run site best show the distinctive characteristics of this culture, the majority being conical, two and three feet high and 25 to 70 feet in diameter. Numerous boulder circles are often found with the Oneota remains, and these occur invariably on high bluffs or terraces overlooking rivers or streams.

Mill Creek Culture Group. Ancient remains of the Mill Creek culture have been traced along the Little Sioux River in northwestern Iowa from Linn Grove in Buena Vista County, across the southeastern corner of O'Brien County, and southwestward through Cherokee County to its southern border. Fourteen village sites of one or two acres are left. Two of these still show a broad moat encompassing 12 to 20 earth lodge sites. Approximately 100 mounds, two to four feet high, are in the Mill Creek areas. No cemeteries have yet been discovered. A single village site of the Mill Creek group is on Broken Kettle Creek (a tributary of the Big Sioux) in Plymouth County.

The pottery of this culture is dark and, like the Woodland, has crushed granite in its composition. Most of the specimens are globular, decorated with cross-hatched rims, rounded indentations, diagonal and horizontal incised lines, and molded heads of birds and animals.

Glenwood Culture Group. Glenwood is the name of a culture of pre-historic peoples who lived in semi-subterranean lodges scattered along the Missouri flood plain in southwestern Iowa from about the center of Monona County to the Missouri State Line. The lodges here were large--from 20 to 60 feet in diameter. Today they appear as circular depressions from one to four feet deep, standing singly or in groups of two or three. A somewhat attenuated line of seven lodge sites, two miles west of Glenwood, is an unusual concentration. The pottery found here is quite different from that of the other Iowa cultures, and the other artifacts are also more or less differentiated. The bodies of many vessels, and sometimes the outer rims, show impressions of a coarse fabric or matting which had been partially smoothed. Tool remains indicate that the people used numerous knives made of chipped stone, roughly diamond-shaped.

Location of Earthworks. Invariably the mounds and earthworks of the mound builders are found along the bluffs and terraces of rivers and smaller streams, or on lake shores, almost never on the wider, more open prairie areas. Village and campsites are frequently discovered in connection with burial mounds. A series of 30 or more along the Little Sioux River constitutes what was once probably one of the more thickly settled areas in the State, and, in eastern Iowa, caves and rock shelters in the cliffs bordering the tributaries of the Mississippi indicate another such center.

Burial Customs. Cemetery burial apparently was almost as common as mound interment. In some cases, collected bones were removed from trees or scaffolds and buried in mass "ossuaries." Sometimes the bones of a single skeleton were tied and interred in a "bundle" burial. Many cemeteries containing such burials have been found in the Upper Iowa River Valley in northeast Iowa, and numbers of great ossuaries have been discovered in the cave region of east-central Iowa. Cremated remains were eventually unearthed and burials in stone-covered graves were not infrequent. Some bodies were found to have been interred lying on the back, others in a squatting position, or on the side with knees drawn up to the chin.

Early Industries. It is evident that agricultural activity was not uncommon among the mound builder peoples, and garden crops were raised in large quantities. Another important industry was the quarrying and working of stone. This is not surprising since there was an inexhaustible supply of glacial boulders and deposits of flint and hematite. Several of the stone quarries used by these men of antiquity were exactly located, and stone mauls and axes were found scattered over the hills from Burlington to Fort Madison, as well as in other places.

One of the most unusual and impressive structures built by Neolithic man in Iowa is the large stone dam across the Iowa River at Amana, but the nearest approach to actual masonry among the mound builders was found in the numerous rows of stones sometimes forming irregular enclosures within many of the mounds.

Artifacts. The most widespread art was that of flint chipping. Ceremonial blades, daggers, and knives were skillfully chipped from flint rock. Catlinite was used for pipes and ornaments; copper was hammered into useful and decorative articles; and wood, worked by fire and cutting, was fashioned into bows, arrows, spears, and other necessary articles. Artifacts uncovered in Iowa have included fetishes, ceremonial weapons, and sacred articles probably belonging to the priests and medicine men. Pottery-making was apparently a late development.

There are a large number of private and public archaeological museums and collections in the State. Outstanding are those of the State Historical Society of Iowa, collected for the most part by Charles R. Keyes, Mount Vernon, and Ellison Orr, Waukon; the Historical, Memorial, and Art Department; the Frank E. Ellis Museum at Maquoketa; the Hermann Museum; and the Davenport Museum.

Historic Indian Tribes. Although no mounds were constructed by the historic Indians, their burials were as elaborate and often as complex as those of the mound builders; it is evident that they had as great an awe of the supernatural and as intense a belief in an afterlife as did their primitive forefathers. The Effigy Mounds National Monument, near Dubuque, is among numerous historic sites throughout the State today.

The Iowa (Ioway), from whom the State takes its name, are Siouan and came here from the Great Lakes region, adopting to some extent the Algonkian culture. The Iowa roamed in all quarters of the Iowa county, but settled mainly in the central part along the Des Moines River Valley. French explorers, hearing the Sioux speak of these people, added their own terminals, forming the words "Ay-u-vois" (I-u-wa) and "Ay-u-ou-ez" (I-u-oo-ay), thus influencing the two different spellings of the word--Iowa and Ioway. The meaning of the word in the Sioux dialect is "dusty-faces," or "dust-in-the-faces"; but other interpretations, such as "drowsy one," "here is the place," or "beautiful land," have been accepted.

The Omaha, Oto, and Missouri tribes lived in the western and southwestern part of the region, where they were in continual fear of warring bands of Sioux. Along with the Iowa Indians, the Oto and Missouri belonged to the Chiwere group of the Siouan stock, while the Omaha were allied to another division, the Thegiha.

The Sac (Sauk) and Fox, originally two distinct tribes of Algonkian stock, joined in defense against common enemies, and were forced by this warfare westward through the southern part of the Iowa country. The hostile Sioux, of the Dakota branch, hunted and fought and trailed their skin tipis all over the northern third of the area. The Winnebago, also Siouan, transferred here by the Government, built their villages in what is now northeastern Iowa. The Pottawattamie (Algonkian) were given homes in the far southwestern corner; the Mascoutin settled on the Mississippi River, giving their name to the present county and city of Muscatine. Generally, the tribes of Algonkian stock came down upon the area from regions east and north, the tribes of the Siouan stock entering from the north and west.

The Iowa region was a battle and hunting ground for all these tribes. Before white men settled in the country, various tribes warred with one another to possess the rich hunting ground, one driving out another, then each in turn either drifting on or being driven out. The history of Indians in Iowa centers around the Sac and Fox, and their leaders--Chiefs Black Hawk, Keokuk, and Wapello--and the ultimate purchase of their lands by the whites.

The Sac, although they were described as the most savage people Father Allouez had met (1667), were an agricultural group. In the fall, they left their bark or reed houses to go into the woods to hunt game, but usually returned to their houses in the spring when planting time came. The women raised crops of pumpkins, corn, beans, potatoes, and melons. About 1780, after the Fox tribe had been almost annihilated by the French in Wisconsin, they joined the Sac. Described as a warlike, quarrelsome, but courageous group, their culture, like that of the Sac, was of the eastern wooded area.

Trade and Treaties. Events of the spring of 1804 led to confusion and bitterness among the Sac and Fox, and laid the foundations for conflict between Black Hawk and the white settlers. An Indian killed a white man, and out of the confusion came a treaty (1804) which Black Hawk considered unjust, since the makers did not properly represent the Indians and had arranged the treaty while the Indians were drunk.

It had been the practice of the British traders to let the Indians buy their supplies on credit, paying for them in the spring after the hunting season was over. This time the American trader refused to do so. His action, coupled with Indian resentments aroused by trickeries often used to acquire claims to Indian lands, brought about an alliance between Black Hawk and his followers with the British during the War of 1812. A battle fought at Credit Island forced the Americans to retreat. When the war ended, Black Hawk signed a treaty (1816) ratifying the treaty of 1804. Of this he wrote in his autobiography, "Here, for the first time, I touched the goose quill to the treaty not knowing, however, that by that act, I consented to give away my village."

In making these treaties, frequently negotiated with the aid of whiskey, the whites persuaded the Indians to sign documents they did not understand; this led to confusion that was not lessened by the failure of the whites to carry out their own treaty obligations. Because of a provision in the treaty of 1804 providing that "as long as the lands which are now ceded to the United States remain their property, the Indians belonging to the said tribes shall enjoy the privilege of living and hunting upon them," Black Hawk felt that he and his people had a right to live in the Illinois village of Saukenuk, at the mouth of Rock River, until the land was sold. The Government, ignoring this clause, in 1831 sanctioned the action of squatters who invaded the Indian villages. The squatters tore down the lodges, plowed up the cornfields, and beat those who protested--even Black Hawk himself.

Angered by the actions of the whites, who had not even permitted the Indian women to harvest the corn they had planted, Black Hawk, in the spring of 1832, tried to incite his tribesmen in Illinois to battle against the whites. Chief Keokuk was more conservative. Whether motivated by the realization of the hopelessness of struggle, or by the thought of gain he might secure for himself, he bowed to the will of the white man. He and Wapello persuaded many of the Sac and Fox to follow them across the river into Iowa. Black Hawk crossed to the west side also, but his stay there was short.

Final Battles. Early in April, Black Hawk, with about 1,000 braves, women, and children, recrossed the Mississippi River and set out for the north country of Illinois to visit the Winnebago, among whom he hoped to find allies. Failing in this, he sent scouts to the whites to admit his defeat, and to say that he was ready at last to go across the Mississippi River. His emissaries were captured, and one of them was murdered. Convinced that his band would ultimately be destroyed, and enraged at the treachery and injustice of the whites, Black Hawk and a few of his braves made a surprise attack and routed a strong army of white men. Then the Indian chief, with his people, moved slowly northward in a great arc, up the Rock River, across the site of what is now Madison, Wisconsin, and down to the mouth of the Bad Axe River. Black Hawk had hoped to cross before being overtaken, but the reorganized pursuers caught up with the little band just as they reached the river. Black Hawk raised the white flag of surrender. But the enemy paid no heed, firing on the Indian women and children as they struggled to cross. Most of those who reached the opposite bank were killed by the Sioux Indians who had been summoned for that purpose by the whites.

Black Hawk gave himself up to a band of Winnebago, who turned him over to his conquerors. He was kept prisoner for a time and then released through the intervention of Chief Keokuk. The chief's last home was on the Des Moines River in the northeast corner of Davis County. Here Black Hawk died in 1838.

Later Tribes and Half-Breeds. It is estimated that 8,000 Indians were in the Iowa country during the first decade of the nineteenth century. Traders, trappers, and soldiers had intermarried with them and the half-breed children began to make claims for a share in the Indian land. In 1824, as a provision for these half-breeds, the Sac and Fox Indians made their first cession of land in the Iowa region. A small triangle between the Mississippi and Des Moines rivers in the southeastern corner was turned over to the half-breeds and became known as the Half-Breed Tract.

In 1825, at a conference of Indians at Prairie du Chien, Wisconsin, a neutral line was established to divide the territories of the warring Sioux from that of the Sac and Fox. In 1830, the Sac and Fox ceded a strip 10 miles wide south of this line, and the Sioux made an equal cession north of this line. Later the Winnebago were transferred to this neutral strip. In 1832, the Sac and Fox, after the Black Hawk War, were compelled to move farther westward. The Black Hawk Purchase, effected by the United States Government in 1832, pushed the Indians beyond a line 50 miles west of the Mississippi River. A strip of 400 square miles around Chief Keokuk's village was reserved for the chief, but in 1836, this also was ceded to the whites.

Friends of the Indians. Antoine Le Claire, great-grandson of a Potawatomi chief, and interpreter for the Indians, was one of their best friends during the days the Indians were being driven from the Iowa country. Joseph M. Street, appointed Indian agent in 1827, was another friend. He was stationed first at Prairie du Chien in Wisconsin, and then at Fort Armstrong in Illinois prior to 1838, when he was transferred to an agency (which later became a town called Agency) in the Iowa country. Street manifested a kindly interest in the Indians and their problems that was unusual for those times. Understanding that, as the game supply became scarce, it would be increasingly hard for them to gain a livelihood by hunting, he advised the Government to teach them farming. It was said of Street that he was "an Indian agent whom the spoils of office could not buy."

Tribal Lands Ceded. Within 20 years after the Black Hawk Purchase, all the country that had been occupied by Indians was ceded to the whites. In 1837, a million and a quarter acres of land had been given up by the Sac and Fox, and in 1842, these Indians signed a treaty at Agency promising to be out of the State by 1845. The Potawatomi Indians, who had been living in southwestern Iowa, were moved out in 1846, and the Winnebago, in northeastern Iowa, moved to Minnesota in 1848. The warlike Sioux alone remained in Iowa up to 1851, when they, too, were forced to give up their lands.

Wapello, a friend of the white settlers, died in 1842 at Rock Creek, in Keokuk County. He was buried at Agency, where a monument was erected to his memory. Keokuk lived until 1848, dying on a Kansas reservation. In 1883, his remains were moved to the city of Keokuk.

The Spirit Lake massacre of 1857, in which 42 whites were killed, was perpetrated by a renegade Sioux Indian and his band who wanted to avenge the killing of a relative by a white trader. The massacre was the last outbreak of Indian warfare in Iowa.

After 1845, small groups of Sac and Fox kept moving back into Iowa from Kansas to rejoin the remnants of their tribes. In time, there were 80 of these Indians in the State, and in 1856, the State passed a law permitting them to remain. The governor was instructed to urge the Federal Government to pay the Indians their share of annuities. The government refused to do this, however, until the Sac and Fox had been joined by more influential tribes from Kansas who had saved money from annuities for the purchase of land.

In July 1857, with Governor James W. Grimes acting as trustee, the Indians secured their first 80 acres in Tama County. Later this group, which had grown to 265, received $5,500 from the Federal Government. They used $2,000 of it to buy 80 more acres. Since then, their holdings have increased, and the Sac and Fox Indian lands in Tama County harbor a large group of Indians in Iowa. The cultural background of Sac and Fox Indians have fitted them in many respects for the life they live today on their own farms in Iowa.

HISTORY

EARLY EXPLORATION

French and Spanish Discoveries. Late in June 1673, Pere Jacques Marquette noted in his journal: "To the right is a chain of very high mountains, and to the left are beautiful lands ..." He and six companions, including the French- Canadian trapper, Louis Joliet, and five voyageurs, looked from their canoes in the quiet waters of the upper Mississippi upon the steep bluffs just south of the present city of McGregor. After being chosen by the governor of New France to explore the great river about which they had heard so much from the Indians, Marquette and Joliet set out from St. Ignace (Michigan) on the long route across Lake Michigan, through Green Bay, and up the Fox River to the portage where they embarked on the Wisconsin River. They entered the Mississippi in late spring when the wilderness was, in truth, a beautiful land.

The party landed on June 25 on the west bank of the river, probably at some point near the mouth of the Iowa. It must have been with great joy that they marked the signs of human footprints on the prairie trail. "We silently followed the narrow path," wrote Marquette, "and, after walking about two leagues, we discovered a village on the bank of a river ... then we heartily commended ourselves to God ... and approached so near that we could hear the savages talking ... and I therefore spoke to them first, and asked them who they were. They replied that they were Illinois; and, as a token of peace, they offered us their pipes to smoke." The chief thanked the white men for making the earth bright with their visit. The explorers rested for two days in the Indian village.

In 1680, from Fort Crevecoeur at the mouth of the Illinois River, Robert de La Salle sent Michel Accault (Aco) to explore the upper Mississippi. Accault's expedition, which included the Belgian missionary, Louis Hennepin, and Antoine Aguel, passed along the shore of what was later to be known as Iowa. La Salle, proceeding southward, reached the mouth of the Mississippi in 1682, and claimed the whole of the great fan-shaped valley for France, naming the country Louisiana in honor of King Louis XIV.

By the terms of the secret Treaty of Fontainebleau in 1762, France transferred control of all the country west of the Mississippi to Spain, but the actual transfer was not completed until 1769. The upper Mississippi region remained a wilderness where Sac and Fox Indians hunted and warred at will; it was visited at infrequent intervals by white fur traders, missionaries, and army detachments. It is believed that Jean Marie Cardinal, who came to Prairie du Chien some time previous to 1763 to establish a trading post, visited the Iowa country from time to time. He may have known of, and possibly even worked in, some of the lead mines there; although credit for the discovery of lead in what is now Iowa is commonly given to the wife of Peosta, a Fox warrior.

Trade Conflicts. Toward the close of the eighteenth century, American, Spanish, French, and English interests in trade on the Mississippi began to conflict seriously. Napoleon Bonaparte, then First Consul of France, demanded from Spain the return of Louisiana. By a treaty made in 1800, and a second signed in 1801, the Louisiana country was retroceded to France, but remained under Spanish administration. Napoleon, realizing that the territory was a political burden, sold it to the United States in 1803, scarcely a month after French control had been formally established.

The northern part of the Louisiana Purchase was organized as the Louisiana District and was attached for a short time to the Territory of Indiana. By a treaty at St. Louis (ratified by Black Hawk in 1816) with the Fox and Sac Indians, much of the land that they controlled in eastern Iowa on the east side of the Mississippi River was ceded to the United States on November 3, 1804. Earlier in the same year, Captains Meriwether Lewis and William Clark had started out on their two-and-one-half-year trip through the Northwest, traveling up the Missouri River along the Iowa shore. A member of the expedition, Sergeant Charles Floyd, died on August 20, 1804, and was "buried on a high bluff overlooking the (Missouri) River." This was the first recorded burial of a white man on Iowa soil.

On March 5, 1805, the United States Government created the Territory of Louisiana from the Louisiana District, and a few months later sent a second Government expedition to explore the region of which Iowa country was a part. The expedition, headed by Lieutenant Zebulon M. Pike, went up the Mississippi River, stopped at a village of

Sac and Fox Indians, and visited Julien Dubuque's settlement (1788). A site on the heights near the present city of McGregor was designated as a possible location for a fort. However, the first fortification in Iowa was not built until 1808, on the site of the present Fort Madison.

During the War of 1812, one battle with the Indians under Black Hawk was fought at Credit Island, near what is now Davenport, and another around Fort Madison. In 1813, after several Indian attacks, the guards set fire to the fort and abandoned it.

First Settlements. Meanwhile, trappers and traders had entered the wilderness, and a few adventurous individuals even had attempted settlements in the Iowa country. During the period of Spanish rule, Julien Dubuque, the first white man to establish a home in Iowa, arrived at the west bank of the Mississippi. A French voyageur and adventurer, Dubuque was attracted by the commercial possibilities of the lead mines near the site of the city which now bears his name. In 1788, he received permission, in a document signed by the Fox chiefs, to work the mines and to occupy a certain tract of land. Spanish title was given to his grant in 1796. The claim, which Dubuque deferentially named *Les Mines d'Espagne,* extended for twenty-one miles along the Mississippi from the Little Maquoketa to the Tetes des Morts River. Dubuque, as miner, farmer, and trader, was held in high regard by the Indians. At his death in 1810, the members of his party disbanded and the Indians resumed control of the mines.

Another settlement was made in 1799 by Louis Honore Tesson, in what is now Lee County. Riding upon a mule, Tesson brought from St. Charles, Missouri, a hundred seedling apple trees to plant in Iowa's first orchard. A rail fence enclosed his orchard, potato patch, and cornfield. A year later, the Frenchman, Basil Giard, obtained from the Spanish Governor a grant of 5,680 acres in the present Clayton County, title of which was confirmed in 1803 by a patent issued by the United States Government.

Trading Posts. The Des Moines and Mississippi rivers and the regions nearby, rich in fur-bearing animals, were profitable territory for trappers and hunters. The first trading posts were erected on the east side of the Mississippi, and here the Indians exchanged skins and pelts for firearms, blankets, ornaments, and whiskey. The American Fur Company in St. Louis was influential in founding a number of posts in Iowa that later developed into towns:

among these were Council Bluffs, Sioux City, Eddyville, Muscatine, and Keokuk. Later the Des Moines River region became the center for the Iowa fur trade, which, in 1809, was valued at $60,000.

One of the best known fur traders was George Davenport, who came west with the United States soldiers as early as 1816. He traded with the Indians at Rock Island, south of the present city of Davenport until 1845, winning their confidence and friendship. Maurice Blondeau, another well known pioneer in the industry, opened a trading post on the Des Moines River under the auspices of John Jacob Astor.

Early White Settlements. Many of the trappers and some of the soldiers intermarried with the Indians, and in 1824, a small area in the extreme southeastern corner of the Iowa country was turned over to the children of these men. White settlement really began in what was called the Half-Breed Tract. In 1820, Dr. Samuel C. Muir, a former Army surgeon who had married an Indian girl, built his home within the limits of the present city of Keokuk. Moses Stillwell also came to this district, and his daughter, Margaret, was the first white child born in Iowa (November 22, 1829). Isaac Galland organized the first school, which opened on October 4, 1830, in a crude log structure near the town that now bears his name.

Noted men who crossed the Iowa country during the first decades of the nineteenth century were George Catlin, painter and student of Indian life; G.C. Beltrami, Italian traveler; and John J. Audubon, the great naturalist. Captain Stephen W. Kearny and a body of United States dragoons crossed the region in 1820 in an attempt to establish a route from Camp Missouri (Omaha, Nebraska) to Camp Coldwater (Fort Snelling, Minnesota). According to Kearny, who kept a record of his observations along the way, this was the first exploration made of the route by white men.

TERRITORY OF IOWA

Although the Iowa country was included in the Territory of Missouri in 1812, after Missouri was admitted to the Union in 1821, this part was left unorganized. Hunters, traders, and trappers moved across the area at will. Some cabins were built and trading centers established, but settlement could not legally begin until matters were adjusted with the Indians. However, settlement began along the Mississippi River long before the legal entry dates. White settlers rushed into take the lead mines near the present city of Dubuque in 1830, after warring Sioux almost annihilated a band of Sac and Fox who had been in possession. United States troops under Lieutenant Jefferson Davis immediately drove the usurpers out. But settlers continued to advance. Finally, a treaty with the Sac and Fox Indians was signed in 1832 at Rock Island, Illinois, under the terms of which the Indians ceded a part of eastern Iowa to the whites. This territory, called the Black Hawk Purchase, became part of the public domain on June 1, 1833. Federal laws prohibited settlement in such regions, but as the Government was lax in enforcement, settlers began to move into the Iowa country in large numbers. They were permitted to establish homes, and many laid out claims and built log cabins.

A group of miners took the first step toward establishing law and order. They met in Dubuque on June 17, 1830, for the purpose of drafting a compact by which they might govern themselves. Settlers upon the public lands, too, found it necessary to establish rules and regulations for taking and holding claims. Claim associations were organized to limit the number of acres in any one claim and to fix the value of improvements required to make a claim valid. By this time the nuclei of future towns were beginning to take form. Dubuque was founded in 1833, and in 1836, Antoine Le Claire and others laid out the city of Davenport. John King established the first newspaper, the *Du Buque Visitor,* which appeared on May 11, 1836.

Order is Established. Meanwhile, a legal problem arose that drew the attention of the Federal Government to the need for established control in the new country. A group of men in Dubuque, organized as a vigilante "court," tried and sentenced to death Patrick O'Connor, a lead miner, for murdering his partner. O'Connor challenged the court: "Ye have no laws in the country and cannot try me." The case was appealed to the governor of Missouri and to President Andrew Jackson, but both refused to grant a pardon because, they said, they lacked proper authority. O'Connor was hanged in June of 1834, a month after the murder.

To remedy this embarrassing situation, the Iowa country was promptly made part of the Territory of Michigan (1834) and the first two counties were formed--Des Moine and Du Buque. A fort, the first of three to be named Des Moine, was established about the same time near the present site of Montrose (abandoned in 1837). Since the land had not been surveyed, claims officially could not be made; but the country was now under the jurisdiction of lawfully established courts. In June 1832, not more than fifty persons lived within the Iowa country; during the next eight years, more than 43,000 settled there, most of them coming from the eastern and southern states. Slavery was barred from the territory by the terms of the Ordinance of 1787 and the Missouri Compromise. The census of 1840 enumerated only 188 African-Americans.

Farming. In the years 1836 and 1837, the roads following the watersheds and Indian trails were lined with wagons from the eastern states, usually in groups of two to five. The farmer came with his yoke of oxen, his cows, and his pigs. Along the way, wild birds and game were plentiful. Captain Benjamin Clark, operating the first interstate ferry across the Mississippi at Buffalo--the transriver crossing from Illinois into Iowa--was kept busy night and day. Each family was numbered, and crossed in its turn; wagons were driven onto a flatboat, and every able-bodied man assisted in the rowing.

With the exception of farmers, it is said that there were more millers and millwrights in those early years than all other tradesmen combined. It was common for travelers to be hailed with the question, "Is the mill a-runnin'?" Quite often the response was, "Crick too high," "Crick too low," or "Froze up." A variation of three feet in the water might clog the mill wheel or leave it dry; and since it was usually a long trip to the mill, it meant much to the farmer to know before he set out whether the mill was operating or not.

The prairie sod was tough to break, and six or seven yoke of oxen were required to plow it. Except for a few necessities such as salt and tobacco, the pioneer was self-sufficient. He hunted and fished for food, raised his own sheep and sheared them. His wife carded and spun the wool. She also raised food for the household in her garden, and gathered berries, greens, and roots in the woods and on the prairie.

In 1836, the Iowa area was included in the newly-formed Territory of Wisconsin. However, by this time, the idea of the formation of a separate Territory was growing in favor, and the name Iowa began to be associated definitely with the region. Lieutenant Albert M. Lea, writing in 1836 of his travels with a party of United States dragoons through the Iowa country in 1835, referred to it as the Iowa District. Previously the name Iowa had been used for one

of the local rivers, but Lea's little book effectively chris-
tened the territory.

In an issue of the *Patriot,* an early newspaper first
published in Illinois and later at Fort Madison, editor
James G. Edwards, wrote about the creation of a new territory west of the Mississippi: "If a division of the territory
is effected, we propose that the Iowans take the cognomen
of Hawk-eyes. Our etymology can then be more definitely
traced than can that of the Wolverines, Suckers, and
Gophers, etc., and we shall rescue from oblivion a memento,
at least, of the name of the old chief."

Madison was selected as the site of the capital of the
Territory of Wisconsin, but men from the Iowa counties
prevailed upon the lawmaking body to meet for the second
session in Burlington. In 1838 a bill was introduced in Congress to subdivide the Territory. Senator John C. Calhoun
of South Carolina, fearing the creation of another abolition
State, opposed the bill, while George Wallace Jones,
delegate from the Territory of Wisconsin, lobbied in favor of
the division. Finally, on June 12, 1838, the Territory of
Wisconsin was divided to create the Territory of Iowa.
Laws passed by the Territorial Legislature had to be approved by Congress. The President of the United States appointed the principal officers, including the Governor and
the three judges of the highest court.

Territorial Government. On August 15, 1838, Robert
Lucas was welcomed as the first Governor. The first Territorial Legislature met on November 12 in a Methodist
church building in the temporary capital at Burlington.
Governor Lucas believed in his executive right "to veto what
he did not like," and tried to retain personal control of all
expenditures. The Legislature, considering this attitude opposed to the idea of democracy, requested President Martin
Van Buren for the "immediate and unconditional release" of
Governor Lucas because of his "unfitness and stubbornness."
The request was refused.

Government surveys were made of the new Territory;
land offices were opened; a fixed price of $1.25 an acre was
set. Meeting at Burlington from 1838 to 1841, the Legislature provided for the building of roads, protection of
settlers' claims against speculators, and the establishment
of schools. After some debate, a committee appointed by the
Legislature selected a site in Johnson County for the permanent capital, which was to be called Iowa City. The
cornerstone of the Capitol was laid on July 4, 1840, but the

first Legislature to meet there in 1842 had to find other quarters. The Capitol, constructed of stone quarried in the vicinity, was first occupied in the fall of 1842.

The establishment of a capital city at this point in Iowa's history shows the speed at which the State had changed from a wilderness to a settled area. In less than 10 years, the frontier line moved inland 80 or 90 miles from the west bank of the Mississippi River. Fort Des Moines, the second fort of that name, was erected at the fork of the Raccoon and Des Moines Rivers, on the western line of settlement. (This fort was abandoned in 1846, when the Indians under its control were moved to Kansas.) Other forts following the frontier as it moved westward were Camp Kearny (1838-1840), near the present site of Council Bluffs; Fort Atkinson (1840), on the site of the Iowa town of that name; Fort Croghan (1842), at what is now Council Bluffs; and Fort Sanford (1842), on the Des Moines River near Ottumwa.

A notable decision was handed down by Chief Justice Charles Mason of the Territorial judiciary in the case of Ralph, a black. Ralph had worked in the lead mines of Dubuque for five years trying to accumulate the price of his freedom plus the interest agreed upon with his master in Missouri. The master, tired of waiting, attempted to force Ralph to return to Missouri and to slavery. Ralph's friends took the case to court. The Supreme Court of the Territory, which sat on Ralph's case in 1839, decided that since Ralph was not a fugitive slave, his master could not force him to return to Missouri. (The Kansas-Nebraska Act of 1854 and the Dred Scott Decision of the United States Supreme Court of 1857 both nullified this Iowa decision.)

A dispute over the Missouri boundary line occasioned the Honey War in 1839. An early Government survey (in 1816) had fixed the Sullivan Line, or the northern boundary of Missouri, with reference to "the rapids of the River Des Moines." The Iowans claimed that this clause described the rapids of that name in the Mississippi River, just above the mouth of the Des Moines. But in 1837, by order of the Missouri State Legislature, a line was run westward from the rapids in the Des Moines River, just above the present site of Keosauqua, thus reducing by some 2,000 square miles the area that was to become Iowa Territory.

Although tempers were boiling on both sides when Missouri undertook to extend its jurisdiction officially by collecting taxes in the disputed area, the destruction of bee trees in 1839 was the overt act that nearly brought about a civil war. Both Governor Lucas of Iowa and Governor L.W. Boggs of Missouri authorized the calling out of volunteer militia in December 1839. The Iowa militia from Burlington, Bloomington, Davenport, and Dubuque assembled at Farmington. The forces were still being mustered on both sides when the Honey War came to an abrupt close with an agreement to leave the decision to the United States Government. (The Supreme Court decided the case in Iowa's favor in 1851.)

STATEHOOD

As early as 1839, Governor Lucas had proposed that steps be taken toward statehood, but the voters were not ready. Under the Territorial regime, the United States Government paid the salaries of the majority of the officials; with statehood, responsibility for these salaries would greatly increase taxation, a burden which the people did not wish to assume. Despite the rich farmland, the pioneer was not wealthy; with hard work and few farm implements, he was able to produce abundant crops, but it was not easy to market them.

First Constitutional Convention. Not until 1844 did the people vote in favor of a constitutional convention. The convention, meeting at Iowa City that year, drew up a constitution, the crux of which was settlement of the boundaries of the proposed State. When Congress had established the Territory of Iowa (1838), it had included all the area north of the State of Missouri, west of the Mississippi River, and east of the Missouri. The constitution fixed the boundaries of the new State as they are today, except for the northern line, but Congress rejected these limits. Had Iowa accepted the suggestions of Congress, the western boundary would have been only 40 miles west of the city of Des Moines, and the northern boundary would have been 30 miles beyond the present Minnesota line. These changes were twice rejected by a vote of the people, who preferred to remain under Territorial government rather than give up the Missouri River as the western boundary. The present boundaries were agreed upon at a second constitutional convention meeting in May 1846, and later were approved by Congress. The second constitution was approved by the voters of the Territory on August 3, 1846, and Iowa was admitted into the Union that year, the bill being signed on December 28 by President James K. Polk.

Iowa is Admitted into Union. The debate preceding the admission of Iowa was of more than local interest, since the extension of slavery had become a vital national question. Florida had been earnestly seeking admission as a slave state ever since 1838; so, when Iowa applied for admission, it was paired with Florida to maintain a balance of power between the North and the South.

The first Iowa legislatures were evenly divided between Whigs and Democrats. In 1848, the Democrats elected the first United States Senators, Augustus Caesar Dodge and George Wallace Jones.

Many of the provisions of the second constitution were the same as those in the one rejected; the one important change was the prohibition of banks of issue. The frontier needed money, and much of the paper currency then in circulation was of doubtful value or entirely worthless. The one legally chartered bank in the Territory, the Miners' Bank at Dubuque, earlier incorporated by an act of the legislature of the original Territory of Wisconsin, was in disrepute.

Times were hard on the frontier. Corn and oats sold for 10 cents a bushel, and wheat for 20 cents. The framers of the constitution of 1846 attributed much of this financial trouble to the "wild cat" bank notes, and decided to authorize no such banks. Ansel Briggs, later the State's first governor, expressed popular sentiment when he said, "No banks but earth, and they well tilled."

Farmers had already discovered that here the corn grew "taller than any other place in the world," and many early inland towns grew up around mills started for the purpose of grinding the grist. Keokuk was the "gate city," and one of the liveliest points on the Mississippi above St. Louis in this hey-day of the river town. Burlington, Davenport, and Muscatine grew rapidly. (William F. Cody, later known as "Buffalo Bill," was born in 1846 at Le Claire, one of the smaller river towns.) Council Bluffs, on the Missouri River, was an outfitting point for those on their way to California in 1849. Here, and at other such places, sometimes as many as a thousand teams were gathered together at one time, preparing for the westward trek. Returning prospectors brought a flow of gold into the State.

Beginning in the 1840s, many Europeans who had emigrated to escape poverty, famine, religious persecution, or political oppression in their native country were attracted by the undeveloped lands of the rich prairie. Particularly, many Irish, Scots, Swedes, Germans, and Hollanders came into Iowa. Racial groups sometimes settled in communities; some, like the French Fourierites carried away by visions of Utopia, planned socialized colonies.

War with Mexico. In May 1846, the United States declared war against Mexico. An outstanding soldier from the Territory of Iowa, Lieutenant Benjamin S. Roberts of Fort Madison, led the advance into the capital of Mexico and pulled down the Mexican flag. Later he was made a lieutenant colonel, and the Iowa Legislature voted him a sword. Many Iowa counties and cities became organized during this period, their names taken from military leaders and battlefields. Among battalions that served with distinction was one formed by the Mormons, who had come to Iowa early in the spring of 1846.

Immigration. Owing to the influx of immigrants, the population of Iowa had increased to 192,214 by 1850. The pioneers joined together to establish schools and churches, and to participate in farming and business activities. Annual fairs, where farmers and merchants exhibited their commodities, were great diversions. Hunting parties, sleigh rides, quilting and husking bees, church picnics, school parties, and celebrations of all kinds expressed the cooperative spirit and hospitality of the early pioneer.

Three of the State's important schools had their beginnings in the decade of intense development that ended around 1850. Iowa's Wesleyan College at Mount Pleasant traces a continuous history from 1844, when the school was incorporated under the name of Mount Pleasant Collegiate Institute. Iowa College at Davenport, opened to students in 1848, was founded by the "Iowa Band," a group of twelve graduates of Andover Theological Seminary who came to the West as missionaries in 1843, and three pioneer settlers. The college was moved in 1859 to Grinnell, where it has continued as Grinnell College. Both town and college were name in honor of Josiah Bushnell Grinnell, one of the founders of the town and trustee of the college for thirty years. The State University at Iowa City, established in 1847 by an act of the first General Assembly, did not begin instruction until 1855. Anticipating the transfer of the capital to a more central location, the First General Assembly turned over the old Capitol Building and grounds to the new seat of learning.

Fort Clarke, later Fort Dodge, the most northerly fort in Iowa, was built early in the 1850s; its abandonment in

1853 meant the passing of the military frontier. Later, when Sioux Indians massacred white settlers around Spirit Lake in 1857, volunteer border brigades were organized. And after the Sioux outbreak of 1862 in Minnesota, temporary stockades were erected. One of these, Fort Defiance, was built on the site of Estherville, and occupied by soldiers for a short time.

During the 1850s, the population more than tripled, with the westward movement this time directed to northern Iowa. A caravan of 50 ox teams carrying immigrants arrived in Mitchell County in 1852. In the late 1850s, the first Czechs settled in Johnson and Linn counties, and French Icarians established a communistic colony in Adams County. The Danes made a permanent settlement in Benton County in 1854. A German religious communistic colony, the Amana Society, built homes on the Iowa River in Iowa County, establishing the village of Amana in 1855. By 1861, five more villages had been laid out within a short radius of Amana, and the town of Homestead had been purchased.

In 1856, about 1,300 Mormons arrived in Iowa City by railroad and camped near Coralville (just outside of the city) while arrangements for their trip to Utah were being completed. The second planned journey was called the Handcart Expedition, for the new converts were obliged to load their supplies on carts and pull them to the new city.

Upper Iowa University at Fayette began instruction of students in 1857, although it did not receive its charter until 1862. People interested in the farming possibilities of the State began to plan a school that would teach farming scientifically, with the result that in 1858, the Iowa State College of Agriculture and Mechanic Arts was established by law at Ames. The school was ready for students in 1868.

The constitution of 1846 had scarcely been ratified when the people of Iowa began to take steps toward revision of the fundamental law. As long as the Democrats controlled the General Assembly, however, the Whigs refused to allow revision, even though the prohibition of banks and corporations brought serious problems. Many Iowa Democrats grew dissatisfied with their party. Because of the strong Quaker element and the New England ancestry of many of the people, both Whigs and Democrats joined the new Republican Party--organized in Iowa in 1856--which was becoming an anti-slavery party. This new party elected James W. Grimes as governor, and immediately set about to make changes in the Iowa government. One of the results of the political upheaval was a new constitution for the State; it was ratified on August 3, 1857, and provided for the removal of the seat of government from Iowa City to Des Moines, and authorized the incorporation of banks, including a State bank. The first Capitol Building in Des Moines was ready for occupancy in 1857.

Railroads. The development of railroads began with the passing of the frontier to the inland settlements. Ground was broken for the Mississippi and Missouri Railroad at Davenport on September 1, 1853, and the first locomotive in Iowa was ferried across the Mississippi to Davenport in 1854. The Mississippi and Missouri Railroad (later the Chicago, Rock Island, and Pacific) had completed its road to Iowa City by January 1856.

From 1850 to 1870, railroad construction reached its height. Communities and individuals donated land and money, and townships, towns, and counties levied taxes and issued bonds for their benefit. An early State assembly had asked Congress to grant land to the railroad companies, and paid lobbyists worked successfully to that end. Every alternate section for six sections on each side of the proposed railroad (a total of more than 4,000,000 acres) was granted. The railroad companies dictated what Iowa's future should be. Towns were platted where they chose to plat them, and money from the sale of lots was used for building more roads. Freight rates were set as the railroads desired, and, consequently, the farmer suffered. The Constitution of 1857 limited the assistance that any community or organization might furnish the railroads.

Iowa played an important part in the agitation for the emancipation of slaves. Many Quakers lived in the State, and the Underground Railroad frequently carried an escaping slave through the Quaker towns to freedom. John Brown, an abolitionist with headquarters established at Tabor and Springdale, made Iowa the middle ground for three years for his band of followers.

Civil War Years. When the call for troops was issued by Abraham Lincoln in 1861, Governor Samuel J. Kirkwood asked that one regiment be formed in Iowa; ten times that many men offered themselves for enlistment. The State, in all, furnished President Lincoln with 48 regiments of infantry, nine regiments of cavalry, and four batteries of artillery. Nearly 80,000 men were enlisted. Among the battles and campaigns in which Iowa troops figured prominently were those of Wilson's Creek, under General Nathaniel

Lyon; Fort Donelson, Shiloh, Vicksburg, and Chattanooga, under General Ulysses S. Grant; and Atlanta, under General William Tecumseh Sherman. While in a prison camp in Carolina, Adjutant S. H. M. Byers, an Iowan, composed the marching song, *Sherman Marched Down to the Sea.* Among Iowans with the rank of major general were Samuel R. Curtis, Grenville M. Dodge, Frederick Steele, and Francis J. Herron. Annie Turner Wittenmyer of Keokuk was prominent for her work in installing diet kitchens in the military hospitals.

During the bitter debate over Reconstruction, which culminated in the impeachment of President Andrew Johnson, Senator James W. Grimes of Iowa, stricken with paralysis, was assisted to his feet in the Senate Chamber to vote "not guilty." In 1868, the State Constitution of Iowa, which previously had granted suffrage only to white male citizens over 21, was amended to give African-Americans the franchise and the right to hold office.

After the Civil War, a period of inflated prices was followed by a panic causing hard times and unemployment. The dissatisfaction of farmers with existing conditions gave rise to many suggestions for change. The Patrons of Husbandry was organized in 1868 at Newton, and for a number of years, had more than 500 granges.

The North Western Railroad reached Council Bluffs in 1867, and the Chicago, Rock Island and Pacific Railway completed a trans-state railroad from Davenport to Council Bluffs in 1869. Later the Rock Island joined with the Union Pacific, forming part of a continuous line from New York to San Francisco. At the same time, the Burlington Lines were laid across the State, and by 1870, the Illinois Central reached Sioux City, giving Iowa four east and west trunk lines, with a total mileage of 3,000. Des Moines, Cedar Rapids, Fort Dodge, and Waterloo grew into active railroad centers. Funds were appropriated for a new Capitol Building at Des Moines to replace the old one, which had become inadequate, and the cornerstone was laid on November 22, 1871, and dedicated in 1884.

By 1870, the State's population had risen to 1,194,020. The mining of coal, development of factories, centralized marketing of farm products, and widespread advertising had their beginnings in these years. Iowa already ranked high in the production of corn and hogs. The so-called "herd law," an act passed in 1870, represented another step forward in agricultural development. Before this, most of the country had been unfenced. Often the farmer's fields were damaged or entirely destroyed by a herd of carelessly tended cattle. By the act of 1870, owners were held responsible for all damage done by their stock.

The depression of 1873 aroused general discontent with the economic structure. The struggle for railroad extension merged into a conflict for control of the companies, the farmers charging the existing management with discrimination and extortion. In the fall of 1873, the Anti-Monopoly Party, with a program for State control of railroads, elected 50 of the 100 representatives chosen. (At that time, the Grange had 1,800 subordinate granges and a membership of nearly 160,000.) The abundant crops and consequent low prices of 1874 so intensified the unrest that, in the Fifteenth and Sixteenth General Assemblies, the Anti-Monopoly Party, backed again by the Grange, enacted the so-called Granger Laws. Railroads were classified according to earnings, with a detailed schedule of rates for passengers and freight; classes were also established for the various shipments. In 1877, under pressure from the railroad companies, the Granger Laws were repealed. A commission was appointed to act as mediator between people and railroads, but was given little authority. Peter A. Dey, member of the commission from 1878 to 1895, was an outstanding figure in the development of the State's transportation system.

Although railroad traffic was gradually supplanting river traffic, a canal was completed in 1877 to take care of the lightering service around the rapids of the Mississippi River north of Keokuk. Here much of the freight had been carried over tracks.

The last settlement of any size made in Iowa by any racial group occurred in the late 1870s, with emigration from England promoted by press agents. These English people established large farms in northwestern Iowa, particularly around Le Mars (1876) in Plymouth County.

Prohibition. In 1880, the population of 1,624,615 represented a growth of almost half a million in one decade. The Iowa Normal School, now the State Teachers College, had been opened in 1876. Drake University was founded in Des Moines in 1881.

The 1880s were a stormy period in politics. Besides the railroad question, which was still before the people, prohibition was becoming an important issue. The movement had grown gradually from the time the first temperance society was organized in 1838 at Fort Madison. Robert Lucas, the first Governor, had advocated temperance. A State-wide prohibitory law, adopted by popular vote in 1855, was amended in 1857 to provide a license system; and a form of county local option followed in 1870. All this culminated in a constitutional prohibitory amendment adopted in 1883. However, on July 4, 1884, the State became dry by statutory prohibition.

In spite of the fact that the Grange had instituted a successful purchasing plan for the benefit of farmers, obtained railroad regulation, and managed factories for making its own machinery, the organization began to decline after 1885. Inner strife was responsible. When the question of railroad regulation came up during the administration of William Larrabee (1886- 1890), and the governor called upon railroad companies to revise their freight rates, he found them as defiant and arrogant as ever. Proponents of railroad control coined the slogan: "freight rate is the skeleton that lurks in every farmer's corn crib." During this period, Judge N. M. Hubbard, representing the Chicago and North Western Railway, became almost a legendary figure in Iowa politics, the power behind the scenes of all political conventions. In Governor Larrabee's administration, the commission that had been established in 1877 was given authority (1888) to formulate the schedule for railroad rates based on distance traveled.

The Federal census of 1890 did not report a population growth for the decade comparable with that of the preceding ones, but its numbering of 1,912,297 showed an increase over 1880.

Industry. In the decade between 1880 and 1890, industry was beginning to take a definite place in the State and, with the advance of industrialization, the farmer became increasingly interested in politics. There were many followers of the Greenback Party; and though the State had been Republican since 1856, it had registered its discontent by electing Democratic Governor Horace Boies in 1889 and reelecting him in 1891. In 1892, General James Baird Weaver of Iowa was the People's Party candidate for President of the United States. In the gubernatorial campaign in 1893, Governor Boies was defeated by the Republican, Frank D. Jackson, whose program called for retention of the prohibition law but permitted the sale of liquor in municipalities which met the required conditions. This led to the adoption of the Mulct Law of 1894.

In 1893, a depression year, an army of unemployed, whose march brought into the open the political sentiments of Iowans, started moving across the country. Charles Kelly's army, arriving in Omaha in April 1894 on a Union Pacific train it had seized, was hustled across the Missouri River into Iowa. Worried by the presence of this formidable army, State officials persuaded Governor Jackson to call out the National Guard to stop an invasion of Iowa and to protect railroad property. Three hundred soldiers assembled at Council Bluffs. Kelly, an experienced soldier in the Salvation Army, ordered his men to their knees. Singing gospel hymns and waving flags, Kelly's marching army was cheered across the State of Iowa--the railroad companies refused transportation--and Jackson's army was jeered until the governor withdrew the troops. General Weaver and the People's Party Political Club welcomed the men in Des Moines.

In the free-silver campaign of 1896, William Jennings Bryan came to Des Moines, and crowds of his supporters milled about the building of the old State *Register* (which adhered to the gold standard) shouting, "Down with the *Register.*" Later, when William McKinley came to Des Moines as a Presidential candidate upholding the gold standard, the cries changed to "Gold! Gold! Gold!" The sentiment in Iowa was strong for annexation of the Philippine Islands, and McKinley is said to have based his campaign in this State on that sentiment.

In the war with Spain in 1898, Iowa furnished four regiments of infantry, two batteries of artillery, a signal unit, and one company of African-American soldiers.

IOWA IN THE TWENTIETH CENTURY

Prosperity. The period from 1900 (when the population had grown to 2,231,853) to World War I in 1914 was one of increased general prosperity in Iowa. Six great crops--corn, wheat, barley, hay, oats, potatoes--brought top prices in the markets. Bank statements indicated the wealth of many citizens. Good roads and the introduction of the automobile added strength to the back-to-the-farm movement which offset, in part, the migration of Iowans to California and the Northwest.

In the first decade of the twentieth century, the idea of the Farm Bureau Federation began to grow. District agents were appointed by the Government in 1900 to teach farmers by actual demonstration how to farm with profit and success. The first farm bureau was organized in Black Hawk County at Cedar Falls in September 1912, and a State federation was organized in 1918 at Marshalltown. About the same time, a group of farmers organized a branch of the Farmers' Union in Monona County (1915), which received a State charter in 1917. The purpose of the union was to discourage the credit and mortgage system, to develop cooperative buying and selling among farmers, and to secure cost of production plus a reasonable profit, at the same time eliminating speculation in farm products.

The word "male" is still in the section of the State Constitution relating to suffrage, but was nullified by the Nineteenth Amendment to the Constitution of the United States. A proposed amendment to the Constitution granting women the right to vote was defeated in 1916, but the Federal suffrage amendment was ratified by the Iowa General Assembly in 1919, and went into effect in 1920. This, however, did not give women the right to seats in the General Assembly, and a special amendment (1926) to the State constitution was required to admit women to the Legislature.

In 1915 Iowa, without benefit of women's suffrage, but probably largely through the influence of women, returned to Statewide prohibition; in 1919, the Eighteenth Amendment to the Federal Constitution was ratified. By amendment to the State law in 1933, sale of malt beverages with not more than 3.2 percent alcoholic content was permitted; and, in the same year, a popularly elected convention ratified the repeal of the Eighteenth Amendment to the Federal Constitution. Provision was made in 1934 for State-owned liquor stores under a State Liquor Control Commission.

World War I and After. During World War I, Iowa contributed 113,000 men to the Army, Navy, and Marine Corps. The third fort in Iowa to be named Fort Des Moines (established just outside that city in 1901) was used for a time as a training camp for African-American reserve officers. Camp Dodge, a cantonment of nearly 2,000 buildings, was also erected near Des Moines. The Third Iowa National Guard Regiment, part of the Rainbow Division (42nd), reached France in December of 1917, and served until the Armistice. One of the first three Americans to die in the war was Private Merle Hay of Glidden. In all, there were more than 2,000 casualties among Iowa soldiers and sailors.

During the war period and the years immediately following, land in Iowa sold at boom prices. As early as 1920, however, farms were mortgaged heavily, and the land itself was being worked by an increasingly large percentage of tenants rather than by independent farmers. From 1920 on, farm debts increased as farm assets declined. By the time the Depression was acknowledged formally in 1929, a rapidly increasing number of farmers were losing their land through mortgage foreclosures. In the national election of 1932, conditions had grown so bad that Iowa, although Republican since 1856 (except for a short interlude), swung over to the Democrats.

Farmers' Movement. The Farm Holiday Association, a militant group of farmers drawing its main strength from the Farmers' Union, was created in 1931. Loosely organized and without any set program, its main purpose was to prevent farm foreclosures and to fight against prevailing low prices. At the first meeting in May of 1932, the members decided to inaugurate a Farm Holiday; they would buy nothing and sell nothing. To save the farms of impoverished owners, the association members used persuasion, and at times intimidation, against "outsiders" present at the foreclosure sales as prospective bidders. The "penny sale" became well known in this period. Mortgaged personal property was bought up at the auctions for several dollars, sometimes for less than a dollar, and turned back free of burden, to the farmers who had just lost it. By 1933, the association was organizing picket lines and strikes, while clashes with local officials were common.

Out of this and similar movements elsewhere came a focusing of State and national attention to the needs of the farmers. State moratorium acts were passed, but two years of drought (1934 and 1936) produced the most serious crop shortage on record in the southern and western counties, and left the farmer still in a precarious position. Farm mortgages continued to be foreclosed, until more than half of the farmland was operated by tenant farmers. Land that had once been homesteaded or tilled by farmers who owned their own land, was turned over to absentee owners. Although the problem of farm tenancy remained, Federal subsidies and loans gave the farmers as a group a breathing spell, and saved them from immediate economic ruin. In 1936, when farms were again being operated without loss, farmers began to recognize the importance of solving their problems through the actions of their own groups. The

Farm Holiday Association was no longer a factor, having been largely absorbed by the Farmers' Union. A number of farmers' cooperatives on a State- wide scale developed, particularly in northwest Iowa. The movement gained strength as the farmer found it more and more difficult to survive on the old independent basis as an owner of land.

Before the end of the first half of the twentieth century was ended, Iowa had joined other states in support of World War II with manufactures and military personnel. The State celebrated its 100-year anniversary in 1946, and in 1948, it led all states in the production of corn, oats, poultry, eggs, and hogs and finished cattle for market.

In the 1950s, Iowa hosted a visit by Nikita Khrushchev to the Roswell Garst farm at Coon Rapids. Tornadoes and floods hit the State in 1965, and President Johnson declared it a disaster area. Capital punishment was abolished in 1965. Also in 1965, Iowa's unemployment rate was the lowest ever in the State's history.

In the 1970s, Drake University campus was bombed, causing $200,000 in damages to its science building. And in 1979, Eschel M. Rhoodie, a former official in South Africa's Information Ministry, reported that his country was involved in interference with the U.S. electoral process to keep Senator Richard C. Clark, liberal Democrat, from election to the Senate. (Clark was a major critic of the country's racial policies and supported economic sanctions against it.)

In 1986, prohibition once again became an issue, when the State's 52-year monopoly on liquor sales ended; 212 State-owned liquor stores were sold.

EDUCATION, POLITICS, AND CULTURE

Education. Education has been important to many Iowans from its earliest days of settlement. In 1856, Governor Grimes asked Horace Mann, the distinguished educator from Massachusetts, to head up a commission that would study Iowa's educational needs. The Mann report called for a central Board of Education "with full power to legislate and make all needful rules and regulation in relation to Common Schools." This was embodied in the State Constitution of 1857 and the general school law in 1858. Several strings were attached, however. The actions of the board could at any time be "altered, amended, or repealed by the General Assembly." Few legislators had Grimes' vision of education. In his inaugural address, he expressed

72

his view by stating, "The safety and perpetuity of our republican institutions depend upon the diffusion of intelligence among the masses of the people ... the prevention of the evils of poverty and crime is much less expensive than the relief of one or the punishment of the other."

In a rural state like Iowa, however, population was spread thinly over a large area, and limited educational resources were also spread thin. The one-room rural schoolhouse was common, and poor as it was, it often provided the only means of education for Iowa's youth. Many teachers had only an eight-grade education themselves, and average attendance for country school pupils was little more than two months per year. The answer lay in a unified township school district.

Standards Set. In the final decade of the nineteenth century, many of the State's schools were still teaching little more than the basics. But finally, some standards were set. Buffalo Township in central Winnebago County established the first consolidated township school in Buffalo Center in 1897. Children were transported to the new central school in town by horse-drawn hacks. The General Assembly authorized $500 in State aid annually for the transportation of student to each district that would consolidate, and the movement began to accelerate.

Albert Deyoe, State Superintendent of Public Instruction, and his assistant, James Woodruff, traveled the State persuading local independent schools to consolidate. In 1902, the General Assembly finally made school attendance compulsory between the ages of seven and 16. By 1921, Iowa had 439 consolidated districts.

Tax Burden Lifted. Depression and World War II caused the consolidation movement to come to an almost complete halt for the next 25 years. But in 1945, the Legislature appropriated $2 million for transportation costs, and passed the Agriculture Land Tax Credit Act, which had the effect of shifting some of the tax burden for education from the farmers' local property taxes to the State's general tax fund.

In 1955, the old 1897 law on consolidation was replaced by the Community School District Act, and by 1966, all county schools in the State were closed. Farm children now had the same educational opportunities as town children, and bright yellow school buses became common on Iowa's country roads.

Higher Education. The history of higher education in Iowa is not dissimilar to the development of primary and secondary education. Demands of the economy and the priorities given to the tax dollar were set against the need to provide adequate educational facilities and resources in an increasingly more complex and technological agrarian and industrial society. As with primary education, the first colleges in the State were private schools, most of them little more than academies; they were founded and supported by various church denominations. Clark, Coe, Cornell, Grinell, Loras, and Iowa Wesleyan were among the first institutions of higher education. Each had a fixed classical curriculum, and more attention was given to rigid social regulations than to free academic inquiry. Many additional colleges were founded in small towns during the post- Civil War period; most of them had a visionary purpose little support, but they carried the major burden of providing higher education for the State.

One of the first acts of the General Assembly after Iowa became a State was to charter a "State University of Iowa." It was not until March 1855 that the university, having been granted two townships of land by Congress, opened its first classes with two faculty members. Even before the first classes were underway, there were continuing controversies about location. There were proposals in the legislature to establish five branches of the nonexistent university, but all attempts were resisted by Governor Grimes. The Constitution of 1857 apparently settled the question for all time by permanently fixing the location in Iowa City. But as late as the 1960s, serious consideration was still being given to building another State University in the western part of the State.

For the first several decades of the university's existence, it was little more than a university in name only; its educational standards were not very demanding. However, in 1887, the regents selected George Shaeffer of Cornell University to be its president, and soon the university began to fulfill the hopes of its founders. The university began to win academic distinction throughout the Midwest, and its Medical School and Law School were particularly strong among State universities in the region.

Iowa State Agricultural College was the second higher education institution to become established in Iowa. Founded in Ames in 1858, it did not begin to function until the Morrill Land Grant College Act provided funds to build a campus, hire a faculty, and attract able administrators. With a grant of over 200,000 acres of land, Iowa State College had less growing pains than its predecessor.

The third State college to be founded in the State was Iowa State Teachers College, which eventually achieved university status as the University of Northern Iowa. Founded in 1876, it initially took over the abandoned buildings of a Civil War Orphans Home in Cedar Falls.

Funding. Funding for Iowa public universities has been difficult from the beginning. In a study made by the Carnegie Institute in 1975, Iowa ranked 26th among states in percentage of appropriations allotted to higher education from the State's general revenue. In the 1960s, State appropriations for higher education were greatly increased, but much of the allotment went into creation of a much needed sixteen-area, post- secondary educational system to provide vocational and technical training, adult education, and community services, as well as two year programs of pre-professional liberal arts education. Previously existing secondary vocational schools and municipal junior colleges were moved into this system as well. And area colleges began to provide sub-branches to provide the State with educational opportunities previously offered only in some larger towns.

Iowa has from the first been a true pioneering State in making available what the Ordinance of 1787 called "the means of education" to all persons, regardless of sex or race. The University of Iowa in 1857 was the first State university in the country to open its doors to women. Iowa College (now Grinnell College) was one of the first coeducational colleges in the country, and among the first women admitted in 1860 was a young black woman.

These important precedents in the history of Iowa education have had immeasurable impact both on individuals and upon the culture of the State and the nation. Botanist George Washington Carver, a former slave from Missouri, completed his college education at Iowa State College. Alexander Clarke, who organized and pushed for an amendment to the Iowa Constitution to extend suffrage to blacks in 1868, began his law studies at the University of Iowa at the age of 57; he was the first black to argue cases before the Iowa Supreme Court. And Iowa resident Arabella Babb Mansfield, a graduate of Iowa Wesleyan in 1869 was the first woman in the United States to be admitted to the bar. Women were admitted to the first class of the University of Iowa Medical College.

The general level of education in Iowa is still high. The State has the nation's lowest rate of adult illiteracy, and State students consistently rank near the top in standardized testing, including college entrance exams. Rural depopulation and rising curricular demands have led to more rounds of school consolidation, reducing the number of districts to 425 in 1990.

Rather than build several additional State-supported schools, Iowa recently opted to subsidize its private institutions by giving tuition grants valid at any accredited college in the State to qualified Iowa residents. The State's private colleges have prospered in recent decades.

Political Branches. Under the Constitution of 1857, three branches of government were created: the executive, the legislative, and the judicial. Legislative power was vested in the General Assembly, composed of a Senate and a House of Representatives, which meet regularly once in two years at the seat of government, on the second Monday of January of each odd- numbered year. The Executive Department, with its supreme power vested in the Governor, was charged with the enforcement of all laws enacted by the General Assembly. The Supreme Court was the "cap sheaf of the judiciary." Beneath it were the district courts and inferior courts, provided by the General Assembly.

The governor, whose term of office is four years, conducts all official business, makes recommendations to the General Assembly, and has the power of veto over legislation. He is authorized to appoint the members of most of the many boards and commissions, and to grant reprieves or pardons for all offenses except treason and impeachment. In cases of necessity, he may convene the General Assembly by proclamation before the regular time of meeting. The governor is commander-in-chief of the military forces of the State.

Other elected executive officers include the Lieutenant Governor, Secretary of State, Auditor of State, Treasurer of State, Attorney General, and Secretary of Agriculture.

General Assemblies are designated by number; the Senate has 50 members, elected for four-year terms, and the House has 100 members, elected for two-year terms. The Lieutenant Governor is the presiding officer of the Senate, but the Speaker of the House is elected by the representatives. The Assembly passes all laws, creates all commissions, and can pass legislation over the governor's veto by a two-thirds vote.

The Supreme Court has "appellate jurisdiction over all judgments and decisions of all courts of record, except as otherwise provided by law." Each district has from two to six judges, the number being determined by statute. Below these courts are the municipal, superior, police, and mayors courts (in municipalities without special courts).

Important in the history of the Iowa Supreme Court are the names of George C. Wright (1855-1870), John F. Dillon (1864- 1870), Horace E. Deemer (1894-1917), and C. C. Cole. Judge Dillon won recognition when he upheld the right of the State to regulate railroads.

Taxation. One of the most important governmental powers is that of taxation. The system includes property, sales, income, and corporation taxes. In addition to these, inheritance, license, gasoline, motor vehicle, cigarette, beer, and chain store taxes provide a considerable portion of the total tax revenue. Special privilege licenses, such as those for hunting and fishing, add to the maintenance of their respective departments.

Government Units. The county, divided into several townships, is the State's unit of local government. Each of the counties has its own administrative set-up, including a board of supervisors, which decides most of the policies of county administration. Other officials who aid in carrying on the county government include the auditor, clerk of the court, treasurer, recorder, sheriff, coroner, attorney, and, in some counties, engineer.

The county superintendent of schools is elected at a convention of the presidents of school boards throughout the county. The civil township--so important in the New England District from which came so many of Iowa's first residents--is not important here. Assessors are the only important township offices; in many cases, trustees or justices of the peace are not even elected.

Each city and town provides itself with one of three types of government: commission, manager, or mayor-council form. Unless the city votes for either of the other two, the mayor- council type is provided. There are four special-charter cities: Muscatine, Camanche, Wapello, and Davenport--whose government dates back to pioneer days, when the form of government was granted either by the Territorial Legislature or the General Assembly of the State.

The constitution of 1857 prohibits the granting of special charters, but these four are still held legal.

Any citizens of the United State, 21 years old or more, who has lived in Iowa six months and in the county 60 days, is entitled to vote. A foreigner must complete the process of naturalization before he may vote at any election.

Notable Iowans. Many native Iowans, from early pioneer days to the present, have been outstanding in the National Government. Notable are Henry A. Wallace, Secretary of Agriculture; Harry L. Hopkins, Works Progress Administrator; and Herbert Hoover, Secretary of Commerce from 1921 to 1929 and President of the United States from 1929 to 1933. George Windle Read, a former major general with the United States Army, and an officer of distinction, was born in Indianola, Iowa. Another notable Iowan was Henry Wallace, who served as United States Secretary of Agriculture under President Franklin D. Roosevelt.

Other prominent people identified with the State include Bess Streeter Aldrich (1881-1954), author of pioneer life novels; James Wilson Grimes, Iowa's Governor from 1854 to 1858, and founder of the Republican Party; George Wallace Jones, Iowa's first U.S. Senator and one of those who helped create Iowa Territory; MacKinlay Kantor, a writer whose novel, *Spirit Lake,* was set against the background of the 1857 Spirit Lake Massacre; Carl Van Vechten, whose novel, *The Tattooed Countess,* recounted his Iowa childhood; Henry Cantwell Wallace, publisher, whose *Wallace's Farmer,* an Iowa-based publication, became one of the leading farm journals in the U.S.; and Grant Wood, whose painting, *American Gothic,* portrayed an Iowa preacher-farmer and his daughter.

Culture. Culture in the State includes museums, art festivals, and various art programs. Des Moines and Iowa City both have important art museums, and all the major State universities and some larger cities host concerts and plays throughout the year. Several cities support symphony orchestras. Summer artistic experiences include the Bix-Beiderbecke Jazz Festival in Davenport, the Iowa Arts Fest in Iowa City, the Nordic fest in Decorah, and the Grant Wood Festival in Stone City. Iowa's flagship State university, the University of Iowa, is renowned for its Writer's Workshop.

Libraries and Museums. The State's major libraries are located at the universities and colleges, and a large amount of material of Iowa's history can be found in the State Historical Society of Iowa in Iowa City and the State Department of History and Archives in Des Moines. The latter also maintains the Iowa State Museum, which includes history, art, and science collections.

Other museums in the State include the Museum of Natural History at the University of Iowa, the Thomas W. Sinclair Memorial Art Gallery at Coe College in Cedar Rapids, and the Iowa Wesleyan College Museum at Mount Pleasant.

Historical Sites. Iowa also has several important historical sites. The Effigy Mounds National Monument, located on a bluff overlooking the Mississippi at the north of Dubuque, contains outstanding examples of prehistoric Indian Mounds in the shapes of birds and other creatures.

The Herbert Hoover National Historic Site, which includes the presidential library and museum, is located at West Branch. The library houses papers, books, and memorabilia of the 31st president of the United States. Also in the park are Hoover's restored birthplace cottage and a duplicate of his father's blacksmith shop. The graves of the president and his wife are on a knoll overlooking the park.

The Old Capitol in Iowa City, which was once the territorial capital, is one of a number of historical buildings restored and maintained by an active preservationist movement throughout the State.

State Areas. There are approximately 100 State-owned areas; most of them include recreational parks with camping, picnicking, hiking, fishing, and boating facilities. In addition, there are about 100 wildlife refuges and more than 250 public hunting and fishing areas. The State's largest park, Lacey-Keosauqua State Park, occupies a wood tract in a bend of the Des Moines River at Keosauqua; it is a recreation area as well as a wildlife preserve.

Population. The State's population declined substantially by the 1980s, and the 1990 census for Iowa was 2,776,755. Although the State has more than 900 incorporated municipalities, only about 30 of the cities have more than 10,000 population. The capital, Des Moines, is the largest city by far. Other large population cities include Cedar Rapids, Davenport, and Sioux City.

Industry. As Iowa moves into the 21st century, it has changed from a strictly agricultural State to one with a diverse economic base. However, in 1988, income from agriculture still netted the State $9.1 billion. In 1989, Iowa had over 100,000 farms that produced such crops as corn and soybeans as well as dairy and livestock. The latter commodity continues to rank Iowa as the top hog-producer in the United States. Manufactures include electrical products, high-tech machinery, meat-packing, and tractors and other farm equipment. In addition, publishing and gambling also fill the State coffers.

CHRONOLOGY

1541— Hernando de Soto discovers the Mississippi River.

1671— Sieur Saint-Lusson takes possession of whole unexplored northwest for France.

1673— Louis Joliet and Father Jacques Marquette are the first white men to set foot on Iowa soil.

1679— Daniel de Greysolon Sieur du Lhut (Du Luth) takes possession of Upper Mississippi region for France.

1680— Michel Accault, with Antoine Auguel and Father Louis Hennepin, travels along the Iowa shore of the Mississippi.

1682— Robert Cavalier, Sieur de la Salle, takes possession of the entire Mississippi Valley for France and names it Louisiana.

1689— Nicholas Perrot takes possession of the Upper Mississippi region for France.

1735— French soldiers under Des Noyelles fight battle with Sac and Fox Indians near the present Des Moines.

1762— By a secret treaty, France cedes to Spain part of Louisiana west of the Mississippi; it is later known as the Louisiana Purchase.

1766— Trader, Jonathan Carver, arrives in Iowa country.

1781— Wife of Peosta, a Fox warrior, reports the discovery of lead deposits in the Iowa country.

1787— July 13. Congress of the Confederation adopts Northwest Ordinance.

1788— Julien Dubuque, fur trader, obtains sanction from Indians to work lead mines; he settles near site of city now bearing his name.

1796— Julien Dubuque receives grant of land, including lead mines, from the Spanish Governor of Louisiana.

1799— Louis Honore Tesson receives from Spanish Governor grant of some 6,000 acres in the present Lee County; he plants first apple orchard in Iowa.

1800— Spain agrees to retrocede Louisiana to France.
--Basil Giard is given a grant by Spanish Governor of 5,760 (or 5,680) acres in the present Clayton County.

1801— Spain retrocedes Louisiana to France.

1803— United States purchases Louisiana, including the present Iowa, from France for $15,000,000 with cancellation of certain debts.

1804— At St. Louis, Captain Amos Stoddard, on behalf of the United States, receives Upper Louisiana from France.
--Captain Meriwether Lewis and William Clark ascend the Missouri River along what is now western Iowa.
--Sergeant Charles Floyd, member of Lewis and Clark expedition, dies near present Sioux City; he is the first white man known to be buried in Iowa.
--District of Louisiana is established and placed under jurisdiction of the Governor and Judges of Indiana Territory.
--United States makes treaty at St. Louis with five representatives of Sac and Fox tribes for the cession of lands in Illinois.

Chronology

1805—
Territory of Louisiana, including Iowa country, is established.
--Lieutenant Zebulon M. Pike poles his keelboats up the Mississippi and passes Iowa shore.
--An estimated 8,000 Indians are living in Iowa; they include Sauk, Fox, Winnebago, Iowa, Sioux, Omaha, Oto, and Missouri.

1808—
--Fort Madison, first in Iowa country, is built as a government trading post for the Indian trade.

1809—
Annual fur trade in the Iowa country is valued at $60,000.

1810—
Julien Dubuque dies and his settlement disbands.

1812—
Territory of Missouri is established, including Iowa area.

1813—
Fort Madison is abandoned and burned in the War of 1812, after several Indian attacks led by Sauk and Fox leader, Black Hawk.

1814—
American troops under Zachary Taylor are defeated at Credit Island in the Mississippi.

1816—
Fort Armstrong is established on Rock Island.
--Treaty is signed by Indians, including Black Hawk, ratifying Treaty of 1804.

1819—
--The steamboat, *Western Engineer,* reaches Fort Lisa on the Missouri River opposite Iowa Country.

1820—
Missouri Compromise makes Iowa region free territory.
--Colonel Stephen W. Kearny writes account of expedition across Iowa country.
--Dr. Samuel C. Muir builds home within limits of present Keokuk.
--*Western Engineer* arrives at foot of Des Moines Rapids in the Mississippi.

1821— Missouri's admission as a State leave Iowa country without civil government for 13 years.

1824— Half-Breed Tract is established in present Lee County.

--Trader Hart sets up trading post near site of present Council Bluffs.

1825— Neutral line is established between Sioux, Sac, and Fox Indians.

1829— November 22. Margaret Stillwell is born at present-day Keokuk; she is the first white child born in Iowa.

1830— First school in Iowa is established by Dr. Isaac Galland and taught by Berryman Jennings.

--Neutral Ground is established between Sioux, Sac, and Fox Indians.

--Miners' Compact, drawn up by miners at Dubuque, is the first instrument of government formulated in Iowa country.

1832— Black Hawk War terminates in cession of strip of Indian lands west of Mississippi River known as Black Hawk Purchase.

--Winnebago Indians are given part of Neutral Ground.

1833— Indian title to Black Hawk Purchase is transferred to United States Government; settlers are permitted to remain.

--Dubuque, Burlington, Fort Madison, Peru, and Bellevue are founded.

--Ottawa, Pottawattamie, and Chippewa Indians are given lands in what is now southwestern Iowa.

1834—   --Patrick O'Connor commits murder at Dubuque; the first trial and execution in Iowa (both extralegal) take place.

--Iowa country is made part of the Territory of Michigan.

--Half-breeds are given simple title to Half-Breed Tract by act of Congress.

--Fort Des Moines (No.1) is established on the west bank of Mississippi River at head of Des Moines Rapids, by Lieutenant Colonel Stephen Watts Kearny and three companies of dragoons.

--First church building in Iowa, a log cabin, is constructed at Dubuque by Methodists.

--Michigan Territorial Legislature establishes Du Buque and Demoine counties.

1835—   First court under act of Michigan Territorial Legislature is held in log house at Burlington.

--Colonel Stephen W. Kearny and three companies of the first United States Dragoons march up Des Moines Valley to present site of Boone, then move northeastward to the Mississippi.

--Roman Catholics erect church at Dubuque.

1836—   First post offices in Iowa are established at Gibson's Ferry (later Augusta) and at Iowa (later Montpelier).

--Territory of Winconsin is established, including Iowa country.

--*Du Buque Visitor,* Iowa's first newspaper, is started at Dubuque by John King.

--Congress authorizes laying out of towns of Fort Madison, Burlington, Belleview, Du Buque, and Peru.

--Albert M. Lea publishes guide book, *Notes on the Wisconsin Territory,* publicizing the name

Iowa for that part of the Territory west of the Mississippi.

--Sac and Fox Indians cede Keokuk's Reserve to the United States.

--First election of members of Territorial Council and House of Representatives is held in Dubuque County.

--First session of Wisconsin Territory Legislature is held at Dubuque.

--First bank in Iowa, the Miner's Bank, is established at Dubuque.

--Population of Iowa country is 10,564.

1837—

Second newspaper in Iowa, the *Western Adventurer,* is published at Montrose.

--Oldest post office (under same name) in Iowa is established at Wapello.

--Sac and Fox Indians cede to the United States 1,250,000 acres of land, known as the second Black Hawk Purchase.

--Convention of delegates meets at Burlington to consider separation of Iowa District from Territory of Wisconsin.

--Second session of Wisconsin Territorial Legislature meets at Burlington.

--Fire destroys first Capitol at Burlington.

1838—

Bellevue and Peru are authorized to incorporate.

--Burlington and Fort Madison are granted special charters by legislature of the Territory of Wisconsin, the first incorporated municipalities in Iowa.

--James G. Edwards suggests nickname of "Hawkeyes" for residents of Iowa.

--July 4. Territory of Iowa is established, including approximately all land between Missouri and Mississippi rivers north of State of Missouri.

--Robert Lucas is appointed first Governor of the Territory.

--September 10. First election is held.

--November 12. First Legislative Assembly convenes at Burlington.

--Land offices are established at Dubuque and Burlington, and first sales of public lands are made.

--First temperance society in Iowa is organized at Fort Madison.

--Camp Kearny is established near site of present Council Bluffs.

--October 3. Black Hawk dies at his home near the Des Moines River in Davis County.

--Iowa Territorial Legislature enacts law providing for incorporation of agricultural societies.

--Population of Territory of Iowa is 22,859.

1839— Iowa Territorial Legislature enacts first law, setting up system of common schools.

--Territorial seal is authorized by act of Territorial Legislature.

--Iowa City is made capital of Territory of Iowa; Congress gives the territory a section of land for capital site.

--Dispute, popularly known as the "Honey War," begins between State of Missouri and Territory of Iowa over boundary.

--Penitentiary is established by law at Fort Madison.

Territorial Legislature authorizes laying out of road from Dubuque through Iowa City to Missouri boundary; Lyman Dillon plows furrow marking this road from Dubuque to Iowa City.

--Johnson County Claim Association adopts constitution.

--Supreme Court of Territory of Iowa decides, in the case of Ralph, that slavery is not recognized under Iowa law.

1840—
July 4. Cornerstone of Territorial capitol building is laid at Iowa City.

--Fort Atkinson is founded.

--Proposal for statehood is defeated in referendum vote.

--Population (U.S. census) is 43,112.

1841—
Office of Superintendent of Public Instruction is created by law.

--John Chambers is appointed Governor of Iowa Territory.

--Legislative Assembly convenes for the first time in Butler's Capitol at Iowa City.

1842—
Referendum on statehood is held; proposition is defeated.

--Office of Superintendent of Public Instruction is discontinued.

--Sac and Fox Indians cede all remaining lands in Iowa, and agree to evacuate the State within three years.

Legislative Assembly meets in Capitol Building (now Old Capitol) for first time.

1843—
Land office is moved from Dubuque to Marion.

--May 1. Sac and Fox Indians vacate lands east of line passing north and south through the Red Rocks in Marion County.

--Fort Des Moines (No. 2) is established at mouth of Raccoon River.

--"Iowa Band" (Congregational and Presbyterian ministers) begins work in Iowa.

1844— Mount Pleasant Collegiate Institute (now Iowa Wesleyan College) is incorporated.
--First constitutional convention is held at Iowa City.
--Population is 75,152.

1845— Congress passes act for admission of Iowa (and Florida), and gives Iowa the 16th section in each township for school purposes.
--Constitution of 1844 is twice rejected by popular vote.
--Colonel George Davenport is murdered on Rock Island.
--Sac and Fox Indians withdraw from Iowa.
--James Clarke is appointed Governor of Iowa Territory.
--Augustus Caesar Dodge sponsors bill in Congress defining boundaries of Iowa.

1846— Second constitutional convention meets at Iowa City.
--Constitution of 1846 is adopted by popular vote.
--Mormons migrate across southern Iowa.
--Pottawattamie Indians relinquish lands in western Iowa.
--Land office is located in Iowa City.
--October 26. First election is held for State officers.
--November 30. First General Assembly of the State of Iowa convenes at Iowa City.
--December 3. Ansel Briggs is inaugurated as first State Governor.
--December 28. President signs act of Congress admitting Iowa to Union as 29th State.

1847— State University of Iowa is established at Iowa City; classes will begin in 1855.

--Hollanders settle at Pella.

--State seal is authorized by act of General Assembly.

--Population (State census) is 116,454.

1848— First telegraph line is laid in Iowa between Bloomington (now Muscatine) and Burlington.

--First United States Senators from Iowa are chosen by General Assembly.

--Removal begins of Winnebago Indians.

--Iowa (now Grinnell) College opens at Davenport.

1849— Exodus to California begins, with Council Bluffs as an outfitting point.

--Trappist Abbey is established near Dubuque.

1850— Population is 192,214.

--Hungarians make a settlement at New Buda.

--Underground Railroad begins operations in Iowa.

--Fort Clarke (Fort Dodge) is established.

1851— Sioux Indians cede lands in northern Iowa; it is the last Indian cession in State.

--First Iowa daily newspaper is established at Dubuque (moved to Burlington in 1854.)

1853— Company is incorporated to build Rock Island Railroad bridge.

--Iowa State Agricultural Society is organized at Fairfield.

--Fort Clarke is abandoned.

--State asylum for the blind is established at Iowa City (moved to Vinton in 1862).

Chronology

1854— Railroad is completed as far as Rock Island (Illinois).

--Private school for the deaf is opened at Iowa City.

--First State Fair is held at Fairfield; it will be moved to Des Moines in 1885.

1855— State university is opened at Iowa City.

--State school for the deaf and dumb is instituted at Iowa City; it will be moved to Council Bluffs in 1868.

--John Brown passes through Iowa.

--First prohibition law is enacted.

--Amana Colony, a German religious commune, moves into Iowa.

--First railroad in Iowa, the Mississippi and Missouri Line, is completed from Davenport to Muscatine.

1856— April 14. At Davenport, train crosses first bridge completed across Mississippi River.

--Mississippi and Missouri Railroad (later Chicago, Rock Island) is completed from Davenport to Iowa City.

--Land grants are made to railroads in Iowa.

--Mormon hand cart expeditions travel on foot from Iowa City to Salt Lake.

--Steamboat *Effie Afton* destroys railroad bridge at Rock Island.

1857—
Third constitutional convention convenes at Iowa City.

--State Historical Society of Iowa is organized.

--August 3. State constitution is adopted by popular vote.

--Banking corporations, previously prohibited, are authorized.

--Legislature creates State bank; it will be closed in 1865.

--Spirit Lake Massacre; Sioux Indians kill 30 settlers.

--Capital is moved from Iowa City to Des Moines.

--Abraham Lincoln takes part in the Rock Island Bridge Case.

--Comprehensive system of free common schools is established by law.

--Small band of Sac and Fox Indians return; they are permitted to buy 80 acres of land in Tama County.

--Prohibition law is amended to provide license system.

--Followers of John Brown spend winter of 1857-58 near Springdale.

1858—
Educational system is outlined by General Assembly.

--Law is enacted, providing for State college of agriculture at Ames.

1860—
Population is 674,913.

--Barbed wire is invented by Iowan.

Icarians start communistic settlement near Corning.

Chronology

1861—   First patients are received at hospital for the insane at Mount Pleasant.
--Civil War; Iowa furnishes nearly 80,000 men during war.
--April 15. First regiment of volunteers is called out by Governor Kirkwood.

1862—   Homestead Act is adopted by Congress.
--Blockhouses are erected in northwestern Iowa for protection against the Sioux.
--Iowa is first state to accept terms of Morrill Land- Grant College Act; federal funds are made available to endow colleges, and the State's grant is awarded to Iowa Agricultural College (later Iowa State University).

1863—   First national bank under the general banking act of the United States is opened at Davenport.

1864—   Soldiers' Orphans' Home is founded at Farmington; it will be transferred to Davenport in 1865.
--Little Brown Church (near Nashua) is dedicated.

1865—   Soldiers' Orphans' Home is established at Cedar Falls; it will be discontinued in 1876.

1866—   State begins extensive railroad building; first railroad reaches Des Moines.
--Soldiers' Orphans' Home is established at Glenwood; it is discontinued in 1875.

1867—   First railroad (later Chicago and North Western) is completed across the State to Missouri River.

1868—   First Grange Society in Iowa is organized at Newton.

--Iowa reform school for boys is established at Salem; it is moved to Eldora in 1873.

--First five amendments to the Iowa State Constitution are ratified; black men are granted right to vote and hold office.

--Gypsum block for Cardiff Giant is purchased at Fort Dodge.

1869—   *Western Stock Journal* is published at Sigourney.

--Trans-state railway is completed from Davenport to Council Bluffs.

1870—   Population is 1,194,020.

--Iowa attains second place among corn-producing states.

--Local option (liquor law) is adopted.

1871—   Cornerstone is laid for new State Capitol Building at Des Moines.

1872—   First creamery is built at Spring Branch, near Manchester.

1873—   Men's reformatory at Anamosa is established.

--Oatmeal mill is established at Cedar Rapids.

--Union Pacific bridge across Missouri River at Council Bluffs is completed.

1874—   Granger Law is passed, regulating railroad rates.

--August 10. Herbert Clark Hoover, first president born west of the Mississippi River, is born at West Branch.

1875—   President Ulysses S. Grant delivers speech at Des Moines.

1876—   State institution for feeble-minded children is established at Glenwood.

--Knights of Labor is organized in Iowa.

--State Normal School, later State Teachers College, is opened at Cedar Falls.

1877—
First telephone lines are built.
--William H. Voss and Henry F. Brammer start manufacture of washing machines.
--Canal (7.5 miles) is opened on the Missouri River above Keokuk.
--English begin settlements in vicinity of Le Mars.

1878—
Granger Law is repealed.
--Meat packing plant opens at Ottumwa.

1879—
Girls' industrial school is established at Mitchellville.

1880—
Population is 1,624,615.
--Wheat belt begins to pass westward; Iowa turns to production of corn.
--Amendment is ratified, admitting blacks to General Assembly.
--James B. Weaver is Greenback Party candidate for president.

1881—
Drake University is opened at Des Moines.
--Kate Shelley, age 15, crosses bridge over flooded Des Moines River on hands and knees to save a train.

1882—
Amendment is made to State Constitution, prohibiting sale and manufacture of intoxicating liquors.

1883—
State Supreme Court declares prohibitory amendment not legally adopted.

1884—
Present State Capitol is occupied for first time.
--Date of general election is changed by constitutional amendment.
--Statutory prohibition is adopted.

1887—
Soldiers' home is opened at Marshalltown.
--First Corn Palace is built at Sioux City.

1888—
Iowa Bureau of Labor Statistics is established.

1890— Population is 1,912,297.

--Iowa leads states in production of corn.

--Ottumwa Coal Palace opens, with President Benjamin H. Harrison giving address.

1891— Blue Grass Palace is built at Creston.

--Baseball World Series is held at Sioux City.

--Manufacture of pearl buttons is begun at Muscatine.

1892— James B. Weaver is Populist candidate for President.

1893— Cyclone hits at Pomeroy.

--Iowa Federation of Women's Clubs is organized.

--Mulct Law is adopted, to permit sales of liquor.

--Iowa branch of American Federation of Labor is established.

1894— Severe drought hits.

--Business faces general depression.

--Charles T. Kelly and army of unemployed men march through Iowa.

1896— Beginning of consolidated schools in Iowa.

--Site is purchased for Historical, Memorial, and Art Building.

--Battleship *Iowa* is launched.

1897— First child labor laws are passed.

1898— Spanish-American War; infantry is sent to Cuba and the Philippine Islands.

--Board of Control of State Institutions is established.

--Icarian Community is disbanded.

1899— First automobiles in Iowa are displayed at fair in Linn County.

Chronology

1900—   Population is 2,231,853.
             --State Department of Agriculture is established.
             --Washing machine factory is established at Newton.
             --Good roads movement is begun.

1901—   --Fort Des Moines (No. 3) is established near Des Moines.
             --Cardiff Giant exhibit at Buffalo results in world-wide publicity for Iowa gypsum beds.

1904—   Constitutional amendment is adopted, changing date and year of State elections.

1908—   State sanitarium for treatment of tuberculosis is established at Oakdale.
             --Board of Parole is established.

1909—   State Board of Education is established.

1910—   Population is 2,210,050.
             --Iowa is the only state to have lost population in first decade of the 20th century; lure of cheaper lands farther west and the mechanization of agriculture are believed to be responsible.

1911—   Free high school education is extended to all qualified pupils.

1912—   Beginning of Farm Bureau in Iowa.
             --State Board of Arbitration is appointed to settle disputes, prevent strikes.

1913—   Keokuk Dam is completed.
             --State Highway Commission is established.

1914—   Iowa Art Guild is organized.
             --Farmers' Union is organized in State.
             --William C. Robinson makes non-stop airplane flight to Chicago.
             --World War I begins.

1915—   Mulct Law is repealed; State-wide prohibition is readopted.

--Provision is made for State care of indigent children needing medical or surgical treatment.

1916—   Iowa Federation of Music Clubs is organized at Davenport.

1917—   Camp Dodge is built near Des Moines.

--Third Iowa National Guard Regiment, the 168th United States Infantry, becomes part of Rainbow Division (42nd) and reaches France in December.

--Provision is made for State parks.

--Child Welfare Research Station is set up at Iowa City; it is the first in the United States.

1918—   World War I ends; Iowa has furnished 113,000 in war effort.

--Primary road law is passed; Iowa begins to come "out of the mud."

--Women's reformatory is built at Rockwell City.

1919—   State Board of Conservation is created.

--Free medical and surgical treatment of indigent adults is provided at State university hospital.

--Iowa General Assembly ratifies Eighteenth and Nineteenth Amendments to Federal Constitution.

--State University radio station (WSUI), first west of the Mississippi, begins to broadcast.

--168th Infantry returns to Des Moines.

--State juvenile home is established at Toledo.

1920—   Population is 2,404,021.

--Farm prosperity begins to decline.

1921—   WOC is established at Davenport; it is the first commercial radio station in Iowa.

1923—   Battleship *Iowa* is sunk in target practice.

1924—   First regular transcontinental air mail service begins across Iowa.

Chronology

1925— State Highway Commission is given charge of primary roads; paving is begun.

1926— Constitutional Amendment is adopted, admitting women to the General Assembly.

1927— Iowa Artists Club is organized.
Clarence D. Chamberlin of Iowa make one of the earliest trans-Atlantic flights.

1928— Little Art Gallery opens at Cedar Rapids.

1929— Herbert Hoover, first Iowa-born president of the United States, is inaugurated.

1930— Population is 2,470,939.

1931— Cattle tuberculin-test "war" starts at Tipton.
--Grant Wood, Iowa artist, paints *American Gothic.*

1932— First Reconstruction Finance loan is given by Federal Government to finance relief operations.
--Art Colony at Stone City is founded.

1933— Farm Holiday Association meets in Des Moines to demand legislative action from Forty-fifth General Assembly, with farm moratorium legislation resulting.
--Iowa convention ratifies repeal of Eighteenth Amendment to Federal Constitution.
--State enacts liquor law.

1934— Drought hits Iowa.
--State begins to grant old age pensions to indigent persons past age 65.
--State stores for sale of intoxicating liquors are opened.

1936— Iowa's first law for administration of Social Security Act is approved.
--University of Iowa's Writing Workshop is created.

1937— New Board of Social Welfare is created.

1940— Population is 2,538,000.

--Governor G. A. Wilson is nominated for reelection by Republicans.

1941— State Secretary E. G. Miller announces he will bar Communist party from 1942 ballot.

1942— Senator Herring is defeated.

1943— Governor Hickenlooper calls special legislative session to provide for armed forces voting.

1944— Legislation is passed, permitting service men and women to vote in 1944 election.

1945— Broadcasts are permitted from warship during bombardment of Japan.

1946— Iowa marks 100th anniversary of Statehood.

--Iowa Battleship sails from Japan for U.S.

1947— Resolution urges House of Representatives retirement on Nov. 1., when members average age reaches 55.

1948— G. M. Gillette wins Senate election from Senator Wilson, based on incomplete returns.

--Iowa leads all states in production of corn, hogs, oats, poultry, eggs, and finished cattle for market.

1949— Senator Hickenlooper denies political motives in AEC probe.

1950— Population is 2,621,000.

--Hickenlooper vote is more than all candidates' totals combined.

1951— Bill requiring public employees loyalty oaths is defeated.

1952— Governor Beardsley is renominated.

1953— Republicans count on President Eisenhower's popularity to help defeat Senator Gillette.

Chronology

1954— Governor Beardsley dies; Elthon acts as governor.

1955— Governor Hoegh is inaugurated.
--Iowa will drop title "The Corn State" from license plates.

1956— Hickenlooper is re-elected; Loveless defeats Hoegh.
--Democrats win first congressional seat since 1940.

1957— Iowa and Nebraska legislators propose Missouri River be boundary between states.
--Aluminum Company of America's Davenport Works becomes world's largest integrated aluminum plate and sheet mill.

1958— Governor Loveless is reelected.

1959— Soviet leader Nikita Khrushchev tours Iowa, visits the model Roswell Garst farm at Coon Rapids.

1960— Population is 2,758,000.
--Erbe defeats McManus for Governor; Miller defeats Loveless.

1961— State Supreme Court upholds W. E. Hawks $228,000 bequest to State to aid music.

1962— High iodine levels reported; the levels had reached the permissible maximums.
--Governor Norman A. Erbe, 43, is renominated in Republican primary.
--Senator Bourke B. Hickenlooper wins GOP nomination for another term.

1963— Reapportionment plan is rejected by Iowa voters.

1964— Bourke B. Hickenlooper and Jack Miller are elected Senators of Iowa.
President Lyndon Johnson visits Des Moines, where he is greeted by a crowd estimated by

the police as the largest crowd (177,000 people) in Iowa history.

1965— Iowa is hit by tornadoes and floods; President Johnson declares it disaster area.

--President Johnson signs bill to establish Herbert Hoover National Historic Site at the Hoover birthplace in West Branch.

--Capital punishment is abolished.

--Illinois tops Iowa in corn production for first time.

1966— Jack Miller (R) is elected Senator, with 82.6 percent of total vote; Prof. E.B. Smith wins Democratic nomination.

--Iowa's unemployment rate of 1.6 percent is lowest in State's history.

1967— Feb. 5. Twenty-fifth Amendment becomes part of U.S. Constitution.

--Thomas Urban wins mayoral election.

1968— Hughes is elected Senator; Ray is elected Governor.

1969— President Nixon declares Iowa disaster area.

--Court rules that Des Moines violated First Amendment rights of three children who were suspended for wearing black armbands in protest against Vietnamese War.

1970— Population is 2,824,000.

--Two Iowa women, Mrs. Cornell Deeny of Eagle Grove and Mary Sandmann of New Vienna, are first lay women in the U.S. permitted to distribute Holy Eucharist; they are among 49 extraordinary ministers named by Archbishop James J. Byrrie.

--Bomb explodes at Drake University campus, causing $200,000 damage to the science building.

--Sex discrimination is banned in housing, employment, and public accommodations.

--Iowa-born Norman Borlaug wins Nobel Peace Prize for development of an improved variety of wheat.

1971— President Nixon visits Des Moines and remarks on bomb explosion: "The important thing is that these great buildings not be closed to the public."

--GOP Senator Bourke B. Hickenlooper dies of a heart attack.

1972— At Democratic convention, McGovern wins Democratic presidential vote 35 percent over Chisholm, Sanford, Jackson, and Wallace.

--Former State Treasurer Paul Franzenburg wins Democratic gubernatorial primary.

--Governor Robert Ray is reelected; Senator Jack Miller is elected to third term.

1973— U.S. Senator Hughes, Democrat, says he will retire at end of his term so that he may better serve God.

--Republican D. M. Stanley announces his candidacy for nomination of U.S. Senate seat.

1974— President Ford makes campaign appearance in Iowa on behalf of U.S. Representative Wiley Mayne, farm belt Republican who reportedly is trailing Democrat challenger Berkley Bidell, protege of Democrat U.S. Senator Harold E. Hughes.

1975— Governor Robert D. Ray, after winning reelection, calls for enactment of several economic measures; he notes that number of jobless

Iowans is increasing, and previous year was one of hardship for many farmers.

1976— After being scorned by Gov. Robert Ray and residents of many small towns for dropping tours, Iowa Transportation Department will print one million new State maps, listing some 185 of State's 267 unicorp towns.

--At meeting held at Drake University, coalition of Iowa publishers and broadcasters announces plans for formation of Iowa Freedom of Information Council; council is being organized to alert public to growing trend toward secrecy in Iowa's government and public affairs.

--Criminal code is rewritten, for the first time in 125 years.

1977— Democratic Senator Dick Clark stresses walking along Iowa highways as campaign tactic for '78 reelection bid; his likely Republican opponents include Governor Robert Ray, Mary Smith, and Thomas Stoner.

1978— Governor Robert Ray is reelected.

--Republican Roger Jepsen defeats Democrat Senator Richard C. Clark.

1979— Eschel M. Rhoodie, former official in South Africa's Information Ministry, who has been in hiding in Europe, reportedly says his country interfered with electoral process in U.S. in 1978, with aim of defeating Senator Dick Clark, liberal Democrat; (Clark was defeated by Roger Jepsen, conservative Republican; Rhoodie alleges that South Africa secretly was a major financial backer of Jepsen (Clark had been major critic of South Africa's racial policies and had supported economic sanctions against their country); Jepsen calls allegation 'ridiculous and totally false.'

1980— Population is 2,914,000.

--U.S. Representative Charles E. Grassley, with boost from easy victory of Republican Presidential candidate, Ronald Reagan, wins upset over U.S. Senator John C. Culver.

--Iowa Beef Processors Inc. names Perry V. Haines executive vice president.

1981— Renovation of Governor's mansion begins; mansion was built in Des Moines in 1869.

--Occidental Petroleum Corporation and Iowa Beef Processors sign agreement for $800 million merger. FTC and Justice Dept. reportedly will not oppose proposed merger.

--Iowa Beef names David C. Layhee president of company.

1982— President Reagan appears before Iowa Legislature in Des Moines to defend proposed Federal budget and 'new federalism.'

--Unemployment rate is 8.3 in October, highest in State since Great Depression; it is still lower than national average.

--Robert Ray announces he will not seek reelection.

1983— Des Moines Register poll finds Jepsen running even with Harkin.

--Iowa Electric Light & Power names Lee Liu its president.

1984— Republican Tom Harkin wins Senator race over Roger Jepsen.

1985— Actor Fred Grandy, known for role on Love Boat television series, will seek Republican nomination for Congress in Iowa's Sixth District seat of Democrat Berkley Bedell.

--Executive order imposes one-year moratorium on foreclosure of farmland.

1986— Fred Grandy, former actor and Republican candidate for House in Iowa's Sixth District, has relented and will allow release of videotapes of controversial remarks he made on Johnny Carson's Tonight show in 1982 and 1984.

--Iowa University announces policy forbidding faculty members to have romantic relationships with students, as part of effort to rule out sexual harassment.

--Fifty-two year State monopoly on liquor sales is ended; 212 State-owned liquor stores are sold.

1987— Businesses in Iowa, whose caucuses are first major contests in races for Presidential nominations, expect to reap $25 million sales bonanza as result of campaigns.

1988— Iowa (considered the place where leading drama of Presidential election is played out), is described as one of most American of American states, a State filled with small, tightly knit communities where people cling to ideals and traditions of their European ancestors.

--Governor Michael S. Dukakis takes 55 percent of Presidential vote in Iowa.

1989— Supreme Court decision authorizing State limits on abortion energizes abortion-rights supporters and creates powerful new variable in Iowa; the State is often considered a political laboratory.

1990— Population is 2,776,000.

--Abortion rights supporters win crucial victory in Iowa's Democratic gubernatorial primary when State House Speaker Don Avenson, supporter of abortion rights, defeats Attorney General Tom Miller, abortion opponent.

1991— *Des Moines Register* receives Pulitzer Prize for series by Jane Schorer about experiences of a rape victim.

Chronology

1991— Gang Lu, Chinese physics graduate student at University of Iowa, shoots and kills five people and critically injures another, then shoots himself to death on Iowa City campus; Lu is said to have been distraught over failure to be nominated for the school's academic award, the Spriesterbach Dissertation Prize.

1992— Iowa Democrat, Thomas Richard Harkin, wins Senate seat in November election; he will take office January 5, 1993.

--December. General Motors Corp. names nine plant closings by the end of 1995 in sweeping restructuring program; assembly plant in Sioux City is among those listed.

1993— April. Plane crashes about 15 miles southwest of Dubuque; eight persons are killed, including George S. Mickelson, Republican Governor of South Dakota.

--May. Michigan couple, Jan and Roberta De-Boer, are ordered to return their two-year-old adopted daughter to her biological parents, Cara and Daniel Schmidt, after Michigan Court of Appeals defers to Iowa court ruling that natural parents are rightful ones; case is said to highlight need for revision of adoption laws in U.S.

--June. Heavy rains in Midwest, continuing since April, affect Mississippi River and its tributaries; flood levels have been reached in some areas.

--July 4. Major rain damage is reported in Midwestern states; President Clinton visits flood-ravaged Davenport, which borders on Mississippi River.

--July 11. Des Moines is without safe drinking water after levee on Raccoon River breaks, disabling area's principal water-treatment plant; about 250,000 residents are affected.

--July 12. U.S. Agriculture Department lowers

forecast of 1993 corn harvest and soybean production; nearly five million acres of Midwest have been washed out or gone unplanted due to muddy conditions from heavy rains.

--July 14. Clinton announces emergency-assistance program of nearly $2.5 billion; flood damage is regarded as among worst in U.S. history; Iowa is among eight states declared disaster areas.

--July 15. Clinton announces he may seek increase in emergency assistance to flood ravaged areas.

--October. Scientists report in medical journal, *Cell*, that Dr. Michael J. Walsh and others at University of Iowa College of Medicine have discovered gene therapy to effectively correct underlying molecular defect believed to cause cystic fibrosis; currently developed therapy is neither cure nor treatment for disease, but successful alteration of nose-lining cells suggests that gene therapy could eventually restore normal functioning to lungs of cystic fibrosis patients as well.

--December. Republican Robert Grandy, after eight years as Iowa member of House of Representatives, announces he will not seek reelection; Grandy says he intends to seek other office.

1994— Controversy erupts after Clinton administration directive requires states to pay for abortions for low-income women in pregnancies resulting from rape or incest; Iowa is among three states refusing to pay for abortions in cases other than to save a woman's life; Iowa's Medicaid Director, Donald W. Herman, says that "as a matter of principle," he will join other directors who resist state implementation of the federal directive "when the language of the statute is permissive."

GOVERNORS

LUCAS, ROBERT (1781-1853), first territorial governor of Iowa (1838-41), was born at Shepherdstown, Jefferson County, Virginia on April 1, 1781. Paternally he was a descendant of William Penn; his mother was of Scotch ancestry. His father freed all his adult slaves, making humane provision for them, and moved to Chillicothe, Ohio, becoming one of the first settlers of that state.

Lucas was educated under a private tutor, and received special training in mathematics. Becoming a skillful surveyor, he secured profitable employment before reaching adulthood. In 1804, he was appointed surveyor of Scioto County. Two years later, he was commissioned justice of the peace for Union Township in the same county.

As a member of the Ohio militia, he advanced through various grades to the rank of major-general. While accompanying General Hull on the invasion of Canada, he became so popular with the other officers that many urged him to wrest command from the unpopular general. By strategy, he avoided capture with the rest of the army at Detroit and escaped to Cleveland, Ohio, after which he was commissioned a captain in the regular army, and rose to the rank of colonel before retiring to civilian life.

In 1816 he was elected a member of the Ohio Legislature, and served for nineteen consecutive years in the House and the Senate. He acted as Presidential-Elector in 1820 and 1828, and was chairman of the Democratic National Convention which renominated President Jackson at Baltimore in 1832. During the latter year, he was elected governor of Ohio. He was reelected in 1834. By his efforts, the serious difficulties between Ohio and Michigan were peaceably settled. Upon the expiration of his second term, he declined a renomination.

When the Territory of Iowa was organized by Congress on June 12, 1838, President Van Buren appointed Lucas its first Governor. Arriving at Burlington, Iowa on August 16th, he assumed the administrative office, combined with duties he incurred as Superintendent of Indian Affairs. Although he was subsequently involved in many serious political conflicts, he maintained a strong position without sacrificing his self-respect through his entire term.

Iowa is indebted to Lucas for much of its prosperity. The common school system was zealously advocated by him, and his administration arranged for its support by appropriations of public lands. He was against gambling and alcohol, and his influence in the latter secured prohibition of liquor traffic in the State.

Lucas married Elizabeth Brown in 1810; she died in 1812, and the couple had one daughter. In 1816, he married a second time, to a Miss Sumner. Lucas died in Iowa City, Iowa on February 7, 1853.

CHAMBERS, JOHN (1780-1852), second territorial governor of Iowa (1841-45), was born in Bromley Bridge, New Jersey on October 6, 1780, the son of Phoebe Mullican and Roland Chambers. In 1794, when he was thirteen years old, his father moved the family to the state of Kentucky, which was then sparsely settled.

Owing to conflicts between the settlers and the Indians, every cabin was a little fort. Chambers grew to manhood in this atmosphere, and at an early age became familiar with weapons of defense; every man and boy learned to use a rifle, not only to hunt game in the forests, but to hunt and fight the Indians as well.

Chambers studied for a time at Transylvania Seminary in Lexington, Kentucky, but it is probable that he received his early training primarily from his parents, and was otherwise self-taught.

After reading law, Chambers eventually entered into the profession. He rapidly became a success, which was demonstrated when he was chosen Prosecuting Attorney of his district. During this period, the State was overrun by lawless characters who were terrorizing its citizens, but by teaming up with other prosecuting officers, Chambers soon established a vigorous system of enforcing criminal laws, which made safe the lives and property of residents.

Chambers was enlisted in the service of his country; he participated in the Indian War of 1811 and the War of 1812 with Great Britain. At the Battle of the Thames, he served on the staff of General William Henry Harrison, who then commanded the American forces.

As Chambers advanced in years, he became politically active; he was part of the galaxy of Whig statesmen and orators which, headed by Henry Clay and John J. Crittenden, long controlled the politics and swayed the destinies of Kentucky. While not the equal of those leaders as an orator, he was a strong and forcible speaker. In 1812, 1815, 1830, and 1832, he served in the Kentucky House of

Representatives. In 1827, he was elected to Congress, and served one term. In 1835, he was again sent to Congress, where he served for four years and became the respected colleague of Thomas Corwin, former governor Vance of Ohio, and others.

Chambers was a great admirer of Henry Clay and a devoted friend of General Harrison. When, in 1839, the latter was nominated for the presidency, Chambers took an active part in his support and was one of those who escorted the President-elect from his home to the capitol of the nation to witness his inauguration.

Although Harrison's period of administration was short, he did not forget his friends; one of his earliest appointments was that of Chambers as Governor of Iowa and Superintendent of Indian affairs in that territory. Chambers took the oath of office before Judge McLean of the United States Supreme Court; that oath is now on file in the historial collection of Iowa.

Chambers was past the age of sixty when he became governor, and was frail of health, his constitution having been impaired by his many previous hardships and experiences. He was faithful in the discharge of his duties, however, and watched with dedicated care over the interests of the Territory.

Chambers remained in office throughout the administration of President Tyler, but did not desert his principles for the sake of office, as did many Whigs. He was an intense Whig and a bitter partisan, and although he made political enemies, the hostility was partisan, not personal. He was described as a courteous, affable Kentucky gentleman of the old school, and was famous for his hospitality.

After James K. Polk became president in 1845, Chambers left gubernatorial office and returned to his home. In 1849, he was appointed by the Taylor Administration as a commissioner to negotiate a treaty with the Sioux Indians, in which he was successful.

Governor Chambers was married to Margaret Taylor, and later to Hannah Lee Taylor; his children came from his second union. He died in Paris, Kentucky on September 21, 1852.

CLARK, JAMES (1811-1850), third territorial governor of Iowa (1845-46), was born in Greensborough, Westmoreland County, Pennsylvania in 1811, the son of John Clark, who was chief clerk of the county. At a young age, he was apprenticed to the printing trade at Harrisburg, Pennsylvania.

After mastering the art of printing and learning how to publish a paper, Clark traveled west in 1835, and was made territorial printer of the first legislature of Wisconsin, which met at Belmont, Wisconsin in the fall of 1836. He established the *Gazette* in the town of Burlington, Iowa in 1837.

Clark was appointed Secretary of the Territory of Iowa by President Van Buren, and was later named Governor by President Polk in 1845. He was the last territorial governor of Iowa; when the State was admitted into the Union on December 28, 1846, Ansel Briggs became the first governor elected by the people, and Clark stepped down from office.

Clarke edited the oldest and leading Democratic paper of the State, and thus exerted a commanding influence. In 1850, the town of Burlington was visited by the fearful epidemic of cholera brought by the boats up the Mississippi River from New Orleans. Clark's wife and child were two of the victims, and he was so completely devastated by grief that he died two weeks after their death, at the age of thirty-nine. At the time of his death, he was just coming into the full maturity of his powers. Clark was married in 1840, to Christiana Dodge, daughter of the late General Henry Dodge; the couple had four children. He died in 1850.

BRIGGS, ANSEL (1806-1881), first State governor of Iowa (1846-50), was born in Vermont on February 3, 1806, the son of Benjamin Ingley and Electa Briggs. He received his early education in the schools of his native town, and afterwards spent three years at the Norwich Connecticut Academy.

In 1830, Briggs moved with his parents to Cambridge, Ohio, where he engaged in commercial pursuits. He was twice elected sheriff of Guernsey County, and competed with John Ferguson for the office of county auditor, but was defeated.

In 1836, Briggs moved to Iowa, settling first at Davenport, where he contracted with the post office department for establishing mail routes and conveying the U.S. mails between Davenport and Dubuque and Iowa City; later he moved to Andrew, and became deputy treasurer of Jackson

County. In 1842, he represented the county in the Territorial House of Representatives.

At the State convention held in Iowa City on September 24, 1846, he was nominated for Governor on the Democratic ticket; he was the first to be elected by the people. The beginning of his term of office marked an epoch in the State's history.

Under his administration, the State government was organized, the boundary line between Iowa and Missouri was established, and the free and normal school system was put into operation. So ardent was he in support of the school system that he advanced about $2,000 of his own money for its establishment; the money was afterwards repaid to him by the State. He served as chief executive of Iowa until December of 1850.

In 1854, Briggs established himself as one of the founders of Florence, and became a member of its land company. This town, situated six miles above Council Bluffs, on the Nebraska side of the Missouri, was a successful rival of Omaha. He also had large property interests in Council Bluffs, Columbus, and Bellevue, the latter being another rival of Omaha. Here Briggs was one of the founders of Nebraska Lodge No. 1, Free and Accepted Masons, which was moved from Bellevue to Omaha in 1888.

From 1860 until 1865, Briggs and his son, John Shannon, engaged in overland freighting to Colorado and Montana. From 1876 to 1879, he resided at Council Bluffs, and for the remainder of his life lived at Omaha.

Briggs aimed to be true to his convictions of truth and right. He was a wise counselor, a man of strong will, but not tyrannical; he was plain and unostentatious, and of great kindness and benevolence. A writer at the time of his death said: "In honorable old age he lived to see the full realization of the desire he had expressed in his retiring message to the general assembly in 1830, that this, his adopted state, might ever be distinguished for virtue, intelligence and prosperity."

Briggs was married twice: to Nancy M. Dunlap, with whom he had eight children, and to Frances Carpenter. He died in Omaha, Nebraska on May 5, 1881.

HEMPSTEAD, STEPHEN (1812-1883), second governor of Iowa (1850-54), was born in New London, Connecticut on October 1, 1812, the son of Celinda Hutchinson and Joseph Hempstead. He moved with his parents to St. Louis, Missouri in 1828, and the family eventually settled on a farm near Bellefontaine. Soon after, he began working as a clerk in Galena, Illinois.

During the Black Hawk War in 1832, Hemstead served as an officer of an artillery company organized to protect the town from the Sac and Fox Indians, who, under their leader, Black Hawk, were threatening the area near Rock River. After the defeat of this renowned chieftain, Hempstead studied for two years at Illinois College, later reading law with his uncle, Judge Charles S. Hempstead, a prominent lawyer of Galena.

In 1836, Hempstead was admitted to practice in all courts of Wisconsin (in which territory the Iowa district belonged), and settled in Dubuque, Iowa, where he made his permanent home. Upon the organization of the territorial government of Iowa in July 1838, Hempstead was elected to represent Dubuque and adjoining counties in the legislative council, which assembled at Burlington in November of that year. He was considered a born leader, and always held a foremost position in that body. At the next session, he was elected president of the council, and in 1845, was reelected at the session held in Iowa City, at the time it was the capital of the territory.

In 1848, Hempstead was appointed with Judge Mason of Burlington, and Judge Woodward of Muscatine, to the codifying commission which compiled "The Code of Iowa" of 1851. He was elected Governor of Iowa in 1850, a position which he honorably filled for four years (the term as per the constitution of 1846, under which Iowa became a state). His oratory was forcible and eloquent, and his administration of affairs highly commendable.

After leaving gubernatorial office, in 1855 he was elected a county judge of Dubuque County, and held the office for a period of fourteen years. Upon the abolishment of the office in 1869, he was at once elected auditor of Dubuque County, serving by reelection until 1873; when his health became impaired, he retired from public life. He was induced about a year before his death, however, to accept the office of justice of the peace. His decisions were considered equitable and just.

Hempstead was married to Lavinia Moore; the couple had three sons and three daughters. He died on February 16, 1883.

GRIMES, JAMES WILSON (1816-1872), third governor of Iowa (1854-58), was born in Deering, Hillsboro County, New Hampshire on October 20, 1816, the son of Elizabeth Wilson and John Grimes. His ancestors were Scotch-Irish emigrants from the north of Ireland who settled at Londonderry, New Hampshire in 1719; his father was a farmer.

Grimes received his education at Hampton Academy and Dartmouth College. He then studied law under James Walker at Peterboro, New Hampshire. In May 1836, he began a practice at Burlington, Iowa, which was then a part of the Black Hawk purchase in Wisconsin Territory. He was highly successful as a lawyer, and from 1841 to 1853 practiced in partnerhship with Henry W. Starr.

His first public service was as secretary of the Indian Commission at Rock Island, on September 27, 1836, where the Sac and Fox relinquished to the United States their lands along the Missouri River. During 1837-38, he was assistant- librarian in the Wisconsin library. After the formation of Iowa Territory, he represented Des Moines County in its Legislature in 1838 and 1843, serving in the General Assembly of the State in 1852.

In August 1854, he was elected by both Whig and Free-Soil Democratic parties as Governor of Iowa. Though reared among Whig principles, his whole career was marked by freedom from party bias. During his administration, he opposed the Missouri Compromise and did much to foster Free- Soil sentiment throughout Iowa.

In 1856, the capital of the State was changed from Iowa City to Des Moines. Grimes served as commissioner for the founding of the Insane Hospital at Mt. Pleasant, giving careful attention to the trust. In July, 1856, he convened a special session of the General Assembly to act on land grants received from Congress for the construction of railroads. In August of the same year, he addressed a remonstrance to President Pierce against the treatment of Iowa settlers in Kansas.

Grimes relinquished the position of governor in January 1858, and in the same year was elected to the U.S. Senate for a term of six years. He was reelected and served from March 4, 1859 until December 6, 1869, when he resigned on account of ill-health.

Grimes was one of the founders of the Republican Party, which he represented in the Senate. Though seldom making a rehearsed speech, he was a ready and vigorous debater. He was a prominent worker on committees for pensions, naval affairs, the District of Columbia, and other issues. On July 4, 1861, he obtained an order from the Secretary of War setting free the escaped slaves confined in a Washington jail, thus inaugurating the first official act of emancipation.

Grimes also urged the building of iron-clads, and on March 13, 1862, he spoke on the achievements of the western naval flotilla, becoming a recognized authority in all matters pertaining to the Navy. Among the works due largely to his advocacy were the return of the Naval Academy from Newport to Annapolis, establishment of a national armory at Rock Island, and construction of a navy yard at League Island. Politically he was known for his independence of character. Although he was a Republican, he opposed a high protective tariff and President Lincoln's enlargement of the regular army.

During the impeachment trial of President Johnson, Grimes considered himself in the light of a judge rather than a representative, and although his physical condition required severe fortitude to do so, he entered the Senate and cast his vote for acquittal. He later said: "Neither the honors nor the wealth of the world could have induced me to act otherwise than I did; and I have never for a moment regretted that I voted as I did. I shall always thank God that He gave me courage to stand firm in the midst of the clamor, and by my vote, not only save the Republican Party, but prevent such a precedent being established as would in the end have converted ours into a sort of South American republic, in which there would be a revolution whenever there happened to be an adverse majority in Congress to the President for the time being." Though then greatly censured by his party, the *New York Times* said years afterward: "No braver or more faithful man ever sat in the Senate than Mr. Grimes, who, almost alone, saved his party from an incalculable blunder..."

Grimes founded a free library in Burlington, a professorship in Iowa College (Grinnell), and scholarships both at that college and at Dartmouth. The degree of LL.D. was conferred upon him by both Dartmouth and Iowa colleges in 1865.

Grimes was married to Elizabeth Sarah Nealley. After living in Europe for two years, with temporary intervals of improved health, he died suddenly in Burlington, Iowa on February 7, 1872.

LOWE, RALPH PHILLIPS (1805-1883), fourth governor of Iowa (1858-60), was born in Warren County, Ohio on November 27, 1805, the son of Martha Per-Lee and Jacob Derrick Lowe. He received his early education in the schools of his hometown, and entered Miami University in 1825. He went to Asheville, Alabama before graduating, where he taught school and studied law, then formed a law partnership with his brother, Peter P. Lowe, in Dayton, Ohio.

In 1840, Lowe moved to Bloomington (now Muscatine), Iowa, where he practiced his profession and engaged in farming. He was a member of the First Constitutional Convention, and was also a District Attorney and District Judge. In 1858, he was elected Governor of Iowa, and served until 1860.

After leaving gubernatorial office, in 1860 Lowe was elected a judge of the supreme court by popular vote; before this, the election to this office had been made by the Legislature. Lowe was conspicuous in his connection with the so-called "Five Per Cent Claim." He held that the lands offered soldiers to enlist, in addition to a certain amount of pay per month, was "pay," and not "bounty"; that the lands were offered as cash as offered, and that they were earned; and, as between the United States and the State of Iowa, no other agreement was known than that the State should not tax lands for five years after being located, and the United States should pay the State five per cent of the sales. Accordingly, the State did not tax lands located under military warrants. If the claim were allowed, the United States would pay the State of Iowa over $800,000; Lowe left the supreme bench in 1868 to prosecute the claim.

Lowe then served as U.S. District Attorney for a few years, and for ten years lived in Washington, laboring to induce Congress to pay the claim. He had the support of William M. Evarts of New York; Allen G. Thurman of Ohio; the late Senator McDonald, of Indiana; and Judge Shellabarger of Washington, D.C. The court decided adversely (Miller and Field dissenting), and, knowing that Lowe was fatally ill, withheld the announcement of the decision until after his death, that he might be spared the disappointment.

Lowe was married to Phoebe Carleton. He died in Washington, D.C. on December 22, 1883.

KIRKWOOD, SAMUEL JORDAN (1813-1894), fifth and ninth governor of Iowa (1860-64; 1876-77), and Secretary of the Interior under President Garfield, was born in Harford

County, Maryland on December 20, 1813. He received an academic education in Washington D.C.

At the age of fourteen, Kirkwood was employed as a druggist's clerk at the capital, and remained in that business for seven years. In 1835, he moved to Richland County, Ohio, where he studied law and was admitted to the bar in 1843. For four years, he was prosecuting attorney for the county, and in 1850 was a member of the judicial committee of the constitutional convention, which contributed largely to the State constitution adopted in 1851. In 1855 he moved to Iowa, where he engaged in farming and milling, near Iowa City.

In 1856, Kirkwood was elected to the State Senate, and served through the last session held in Iowa City, and the first held in Des Moines. In 1859, he was chosen Governor of Iowa over the Democratic candidate by a majority of 2,964. His administration proved so satisfactory during the critical period at the onset of the Civil War that he was reelected again in 1861. It was said of him that he saved the State $500,000 to $800,000 appropriated for defense bonds. He was a strong Union man, and as governor sent about fifty regiments to the war, nearly all of them for three years; the result was that Iowa was one of the few states in which there was no draft.

After the end of his term, President Lincoln offered Kirkwood the post of U.S. Minister to Denmark, but he declined. In 1866 he was elected a member of the U.S. Senate, to fill out the unexpired term of James Harlan; while holding this seat, he served on the committee on public lands. In 1867, at the expiration of his Senate term, he returned to Iowa City where he continued to pursue his private business.

In July 1875, Kirkwood was nominated for governor for a third term by the Republicans and won the election. In February, 1877, he was again elected to the U.S. Senate, where he served until 1881.

During his career in the Senate, he was distinguished for his clear and thoughtful consideration of all subjects brought before him, particularly those pertaining to the domestic affairs of the nation. It was probably his special knowledge in this particular area, and his wise treatment of the Indian question, that induced President Garfield to appoint him Secretary of the Interior on March 5, 1881. He continued in that post after President Garfield's death until

April 6, 1882, when he was succeeded by Henry M. Teller of Colorado, who had been appointed by President Arthur.

Kirkwood ran for the United States House of Representatives in 1886, but was defeated by the Democratic candidate, Walter I. Hayes. Kirkwood died in Iowa City on September 1, 1894.

STONE, WILLIAM MILO (1827-1893), sixth governor of Iowa (1864-68), was born in Jefferson County, New York on October 14, 1827, son of Lovina North and Truman Stone. His early educational advantages were limited to common schools.

At age sixteen, he became a driver for two seasons on the Ohio Canal. From age seventeen until about twenty-three, he was employed as a chairmaker while also studying and reading law. He was admitted to the bar in 1851, and began practice in partnership with his first preceptor, Judge James Mathews, at Coshocton.

In 1854, Stone moved to Knoxville, Iowa, followed by Mathews, and the partnership continued until Stone's election to the bench. In 1855, he became the editor of the Knoxville *Journal*. In February 1856, he was a member of the convention which organized the Republican Party of the State. He was chosen judge of the 11th Judicial District in April 1857, and when the new constitution went into effect the following year, was elected Judge of the 6th District. He was a delegate to the Chicago Convention in 1880, and was an earnest supporter of Abraham Lincoln for the Presidential nomination.

At the start of the Civil War, Stone enlisted as a private and assisted in organizing Company B of the 3rd Iowa Infantry, becoming captain of the company,. Upon the organization of the regiment, he became its first major. In May 1861, he was wounded in the battle of Blue Mills, Missouri. Later, while he was in command of the regiment, he was taken prisoner in Shiloh. In 1862, he was appointed by Governor Kirkwood as a colonel of the 22d Iowa, and with his command, participated in the battles of Fort Gibson, Champion Hills, Black River, and the charge on the works at Vicksburg, May 22, 1883. At Fort Gibson he commanded the brigade, and at Vicksburg, he was wounded in the left arm.

In June 1863, Stone was nominated for Governor by the Republicans of Iowa; that August, he resigned his commission in the army. In 1864, he was brevetted a brigadier-general.

Stone assumed the gubernatorial chair in January, 1864, holding the office for two terms. As one of the war governors, he was called to Washington several times for conferences with President Lincoln. He was in Washington at the time of Lincoln's assassination, and was a witness to the murder at Ford's Theatre. He was with the President constantly until his death, and was one of the pall bearers who accompanied Lincoln's remains to Springfield, Illinois for burial.

Stone retired from the executive chair in January 1868, and resumed the practice of law at Knoxville, Iowa, having for a partner his brother-in-law, Judge O. B. Ayers. In 1877, he was elected to the lower house of the Iowa Legislature, serving for one term.

In 1880, he became interested in mining operations in Arizona, and for several years also practiced law sporadically. In 1883, having formed a partnership with Judge T. J. Anderson, they moved to Pueblo, Colorado, but in 1885, Stone returned to Iowa and settled in Des Moines as a member of the firm of Stone, Ayers & Gamble.

He was elector for the State at large on the Harrison ticket in 1888, and was appointed Assistant Commissioner of the General Land Office by President Harrison, becoming commissioner upon the resignation of Judge Thomas Carter. At the close of his official term in 1893, Stone moved to Oklahoma City, Oklahoma Territory. While engaging in the practice of law there, he also devoted some time to agriculture.

Stone was married in 1856 to Caroline Mathews, daughter of his former partner, James; the couple had one son. He died on July 18, 1893.

MERRILL, SAMUEL (1822-1899), seventh governor of Iowa (1868-72), was born in Turner, Oxford County, Maine on August 7, 1822, the son of Abigail Hill Buxton and Abel Merrill. He was brought up on his father's farm, and received only a brief academic education.

He began to teach in the common schools at the age of seventeen, and taught successfully for eight years, subsequently becoming superintendent of schools. He moved to Tamworth, New Hampshire in 1847 and engaged in merchandising. He was a member of the New Hampshire Legislature during the exciting years of the repeal of the

Missouri Compromise, and participated in the celebrated election of John P. Hale and James Bell to the United States Senate.

Merrill moved to Iowa in 1856, continuing as merchant and banker until the outbreak of the Civil War. He was later a member of the Iowa Legislature. He was commissioned as colonel of the 21st Iowa Infantry, and served in the western department with General Grant, participating in the Battle of Missouri. While commanding the forces in the battle at Hartsville, Missouri, he was severely wounded. He was forced to resign before the end of the war because he was unable to endure the hardships of the service. When he was granted a pension for his wounds, he donated the entire proceeds to a hospital in Des Moines, Iowa, for sick and disabled soldiers.

At the end of the war, he engaged in merchandising and banking until 1868, when he was elected Governor of Iowa. In his first inaugural address, he combated the theory that U.S. bonds should be paid in depreciated paper issue, declaring the theory to be in every way vicious and dishonest. In 1868, an amendment to the State constitution was adopted by a public vote, with the word "white" being dropped from the qualification of electors.

While he was governor, Merrill held the plough to break the ground for the State capitol. As chairman of the building commission, he combated speculation and jobbers, and secured the construction of the building by honest day labor. Merrill watched over the charitable institutions of the State, introducing many reforms. Before receiving applications for pardons, he required public notice to be given, and a written opinion of the judge, district attorney, and jury before whom the case was tried. Before granting pardon in capital offenses, he had a private interview with the prisoner. He organized a Sunday-school in the chapel of the prison, and secured the services of the justice of the supreme court to superintend the same, which proved to be a success.

Retiring at the end of his second term in 1872, he returned to his occupation as a banker. In 1889, he moved to California, where he spent the last years of his life. Merrill was married three times: to Catherine Thomes, who died in June 1845; to Elizabeth D. Hill, who died in March 1888; and to Mary S. Greenwood. Merrill died in Los Angeles on August 31, 1899.

CARPENTER, CYRUS CLAY (1829-1898), eighth governor of Iowa (1872-76), was born in Harford, Susquehanna County, Pennsylvania on November 24, 1829, the son of Amanda Thayer and Ashhel Carpenter. Through his mother, he was descended from General Sylvanus Thayer, "Father of West Point Military Academy," and founder of the Thayer School of Civil Engineering at Dartmouth College.

Carpenter was left an orphan before he was twelve. In 1852, he started for the West, teaching for a time in Licking County, Ohio, and arriving in Des Moines, Iowa in 1854. He taught the first school opened in Fort Dodge, and devoted much time to land surveying for the general government. He also opened a land agency on his own account, locating land-warrants, paying taxes for non- residents, and buying, selling, and surveying lands. He was chosen to the Iowa House of Representatives for the session of 1858.

At the start of the Civil War, Carpenter enlisted as a private, but was at once commissioned as captain and commissary of subsistence, continuing in this office until the close of the war; he was advanced to the rank of lieutenant-colonel, and achieved the rank of colonel by brevet. He served mostly on the staffs of Generals Rosecrans, Thomas, Dodge, and Logan.

In 1866, Carpenter was elected register of the State Land Office in Iowa, and was reelected two years later. At the Republican State Convention, in 1871, he was nominated for Governor on the first ballot. He was elected by a large majority, and was reelected in 1873. His administrations were distinguished by his support of the State university and the agricultural college.

In his first inaugural address, he advanced the proposition that the rates for freight and passenger fares on railroads should be subject to State control; this came more conspicuously to the front in the "Granger Law," which was affirmed by the Supreme Court of the United States in a suit carried up from Iowa. The Legislature placed $10,000 at the disposal of Carpenter for the prosecution of this suit; however, he employed competent counsel and accomplished the work with an expenditure of only $2,000.

Carpenter appointed the first visiting committee to the hospital for the insane, and although this measure was bitterly fought in the Legislature, it afterward became very popular. After completing his second term, he was appointed second comptroller of the United States Treasury department, and remained for fifteen months, resigning when appointed by Governor Gear to the first Board of Railroad Commissioners. Being elected to Congress soon after, he resigned his office, and two years later, he was reelected.

Carpenter's congressional career was very successful, meeting the highest expectations of his constituency. He originated the policy of establishing experimental stations in connection with the agricultural colleges, but his bill did not pass until the next session, when the proposition was reintroduced by his successor. He also secured passage of the bill dividing the State into two districts for the Federal courts. He was again chosen to the lower House of the Iowa State Legislature in 1883. After returning from the army, he devoted many years to cultivating his farm on the Des Moines River near Fort Dodge.

Carpenter was married in 1864 to Susan C. Burkholder, who survived him when he died at Fort Dodge on May 29, 1898.

NEWBOLD, JOSHUA G. (1830-?), tenth governor of Iowa (1877-78), was born in Fayette County, Pennsylvania on May 12, 1830. After receiving a common school education, he moved to Iowa in 1854, settling in Hillsboro, Henry County, where he entered upon a mercantile career.

In 1875, Newbold was elected Lieutenant-Governor of the State of Iowa, and by virtue of this office, succeeded to the governorship upon the resignation of Governor Samuel J. Kirkwood in 1877. Upon the expiration of his term of office in 1878, he moved to Mt. Pleasant, Iowa, and served as mayor of that city in 1901.

GEAR, JOHN HENRY (1825-1900), eleventh governor of Iowa (1878-82), was born in Ithaca, New York on April 7, 1825. In 1836, his family moved to Galena, Illinois, and in 1838, to Fort Snelling, which was then located in Iowa Territory. He received a common school education; in 1843, he was engaged in merchandising in Burlington, Iowa.

Gear was one of the first citizens of Iowa to join the ranks of the Republican Party, and was elected mayor of Burlington in 1863. He was a member of the Iowa Legislature for six years, and was Speaker of the Lower House for four years. In 1878 he became Governor of Iowa, and served in that office until 1882. He was a member of Congress from 1887 to 1891, and again from 1893 to 1895.

During 1892-93, Gear was assistant secretary of the United States Treasury, and in 1894, he was elected to the United States Senate as a Republican, serving from March 4, 1895 until his death in Washington, D.C., on July 14, 1900.

SHERMAN, BUREN ROBINSON (1836-1904), twelfth governor of Iowa (1882-86), was born in Phelps, Ontario County, New York on May 28, 1836, the son of Eveline Robinson and Phineas L. Sherman; his father was an axe maker by occupation. His early education was received in the public schools in his native town, and at the Elmira (N.Y.) Academy.

Sherman was admitted to the bar in 1859, and began a practice in Vinton, Iowa with Judge J. C. Traer. The following year, he was admitted to the Supreme Court of Iowa. In 1875, he became a member of the U.S. Circuit Court, and in 1879, sat on the Supreme Court of the United States. In the interim, he enlisted in the Federal Army at the outbreak of the Civil War; he served as a second lieutenant, was promoted to captain, and on April 6, 1862, at the Battle of Shiloh, was severely wounded, a situation which eventually forced him to resign from the service.

Sherman was the judge of Benton County during 1865-67, and served as clerk of the district court from January 1869 to December 1874. In October of the latter year, he was elected auditor of the State of Iowa, and was reelected twice, serving until 1881.

Sherman was elected Governor of Iowa in October, 1881, and was inaugurated on January 12, 1882. He was reelected to that post, serving until January 1886, when he retired from politics.

The degree of LL.D. was conferred upon him in 1883 by the University of Iowa. Sherman was married to Lena Kendall. He died on November 4, 1904.

LARRABEE, WILLIAM (1832-1912), thirteenth governor of Iowa (1886-90), was born in Ledyard, Connecticut on January 20, 1832, the son of Hannah Gallup Lester and Adam Larrabee. His father was a graduate of West Point Military Academy, a captain of artillery in the War of 1812, and was severely wounded in the battle of La Cole Mills, Canada.

Larrabee was educated in common schools. In 1853, he moved to Iowa. During the first winter there, he taught school in Hardin, Alamakee County, and for three years afterwards, he ran a farm near there. He then became engaged in milling and manufacturing. In 1872 he engaged in banking, although still continuing his manufacturing interests. His well known integrity and financial standing helped him to succeed in building extensive business connections. He was one of the founders of the Republican Party in Iowa, and was always an active and consistent supporter of its principles.

In 1867, Larrabee was elected to the State Senate and served continuously for eighteen years, being five times renominated by acclamation, and as regularly reelected. At the commencement of his second term, he was appointed chairman of the Committee on Ways and Means, thus becoming prominent in the management of State monies and other important trusts. He took an active part in the passage of laws regarding railroads, and rapidly became a marked figure among the lawmakers.

In 1885, before the expiration of his last term, he was nominated for Governor and was elected for two successive terms, declining a renomination in 1890. He was appointed chairman of the State Board of Control and continued to serve in that capacity for two years, resigning the office in February 1900. He spent about six months visiting Palestine and various countries in Europe. He authored *The Railroad Question* (1893), which was recognized as an authority on the subject. He was also the inventor of a grain separator, for which he had obtained a patent.

Larrabee was married to Ann M. Appelman, and the couple had six children. He died on November 16, 1912.

BOIES, HORACE (1827-1923), fourteenth governor of Iowa (1890-94), was born near Aurora, Erie County, New York on December 7, 1827. He was brought up on his father's farm, attending school during the winter seasons. As soon as his own earnings enabled him to pay the necessary fees, he began the study of law and was admitted to the bar in 1849, in Erie County, New York.

Boies began a practice in Buffalo, where he continued to reside until 1867. Early on, he identified himself with the Republican Party, which elected him in 1857 to the Lower House of the New York Assembly. In 1864 he was a candidate for District Attorney for Erie County, but was defeated by two votes, after which he retired from politics for some time.

In 1867, Boies moved to Iowa, settling in Waterloo, Black Hawk County. He was soon recognized as one of the ablest lawyers in the State. When not actively engaged in his professional duties, he devoted himself to the cultivation of a farm in Grundy County.

Boies opposed the Prohibition movement in the ranks of the Republican Party from the start, finding in this a reason for reentering the political arena. With regret, he severed his connection with that party and supported Presidential candidate Grover Cleveland in 1884, his convictions on the tariff issue being as pronounced as on the temperance question.

Having fully identified himself with the Democratic Party, in 1889 Boies received the Democratic nomination for Governor of Iowa. The campaign that followed centered on the State Prohibition law. He attacked the existing statute in every section of the State, and was elected by a plurality of 7,000 votes. He was the first Democrat to be elected to the governorship in thirty-five years.

During Boies's administration, he won the confidence of the people, and his energy and sincerity secured him the respect of even his political opponents. He was reelected in 1891, but was defeated for a third term in the election of 1893. During his life, he also contributed extensively to agricultural literature. He died on April 4, 1923.

JACKSON, FRANK DARR (1854-1938), fifteenth governor of Iowa (1894-96), was born in Arcade, Wyoming County, New York on January 26, 1854. Both his father and mother entered the service of the Union during the Civil War, the former holding the rank of first lieutenant of the 78th regiment, New York volunteers, and the latter being at the front for fourteen months as a hospital nurse. At the end of the war, his family moved to Jesup, Buchanan County, Iowa.

In 1870, Jackson entered the Iowa Agricultural College in Ames. Three years later, he took up the study of law at the State University in Iowa City, where he graduated in 1874. He was admitted to the bar in 1875, and at once began the practice of law in Independence, Iowa. In 1880 he moved to Greene, Iowa, where he was highly successful as a lawyer and politician.

Jackson became secretary of the Senate of the 19th General Assembly, and was reelected to that office in 1884. He was soon recognized as the leader of the young Republican element of the State, and in 1884, was elected

Secretary of State by a large majority, being reelected in 1886 and 1888. At the close of his third term, he, with others, formed the Royal Union Life Insurance Co. (of which he was made president) with headquarters in Des Moines.

In 1893, he was nominated for Governor and carried the State by a 33,000 plurality. He was inaugurated on January 11, 1894. In all emergencies, Governor Jackson acted with a firmness and energy which showed his sympathies with the laboring people of the State; still, however, he would exhaust every resource if necessary to maintain law and order.

In December 1894, he declined a nomination for reelection; he retired from public life at the end of his administration to devote all his energies to his insurance company.

Governor Jackson was married to Anne F. Brock, and the couple had four sons. He died on November 16, 1938.

DRAKE, FRANCIS MARION (1830-1903), sixteenth governor of Iowa (1896-98), was born in Rushville, Illinois on December 30, 1830, son of Harriet Jane O'Neal and John Adams Drake. His parents moved to Davis County, Iowa in 1846, and founded the village of Drakeville, where Francis attended school until he was sixteen years old. Becoming a clerk in his father's general merchandise store, he assisted in carrying on the business until 1852.

At the age of twenty-two, Drake led a train across the Plains to California, fighting and defeating on the way a party of 300 Pawnee Indians, although his own force numbered but twenty men. Encouraged by the success of this venture, he again crossed the Plains in 1854, reaching Sacramento, California, with ninety-seven cows, five oxen, and five horses, having lost on the way only three cows, a result which made the trip one of the most notable ever undertaken.

Returning by sea, he was devastated when the steamer *Yankee Blade* went down with a loss of several hundred lives. Drake then entered into partnership with his father and brother in a general mercantile business, the connection continuing until 1858, when he withdrew to engage in business for himself at Unionville, Iowa.

At the outbreak of the Civil War, Drake raised a company among his townsmen, and on the governor's order, joined the independent regiment of Iowa volunteers commanded by Colonel Edwards. He was commissioned as major and commanded the Federal troops which defended the city of St. Joseph, Missouri, against the Confederate, General Price. In 1862, he became lieutenant-colonel of the 36th Iowa Infantry, with which he served for several years. At the battle of Elkin's Ford, Arkansas, in April 1864, he defeated General Marmaduke and his forces, gaining from his brigade commander the commendation: "Too much praise cannot be given Colonel Drake for his distinguished gallantry and determined courage in this contest." A few weeks later, having been assigned to the command of the 3rd Brigade of Solomon's Division, Drake set out with a large train to gather supplies for the forces of General Steele; the expedition was attacked by Confederate cavalry, and he was wounded and taken prisoner; he was released because the nature of his injury was such that recovery was thought to be impossible. Howevever, he was away from his command only six months, returning to camp and active duty while still on crutches. He was brevetted brigadier-general and served until the end of the war.

When Drake returned to Centervile, Iowa, he began the practice of law in partnership with Judge Amos Harris. Later he gave up law to engage in the development of railroads, supplying capital for five companies in his own State, among them the Albia and Centerville, of which he was president, and the Indiana, Illinois and Iowa. He was also president of the Centerville National Bank and the First National Bank of Albia.

In 1895, Drake was elected Governor of his State, and served one term. Drake University at Des Moines, Iowa, an institution under the patronage of the Disciples of Christ, was so named from his large gifts to it; Iowa College at Grinnell and the Wesleyan College at Mt. Pleasant, Iowa also enjoyed his beneficence.

Drake was married to Mary Jane Lord of Bloomfield, Iowa, and the couple had two sons and four daughters. He died on November 20, 1903.

SHAW, LESLIE MORTIER (1848-1932), seventeenth governor of Iowa (1898-1902), was born in Morristown, Vermont on November 2, 1848, the son of Louisa Spaulding and Boardman Osias Shaw. His great-grandfather, Ebenezer Shaw, was one of the earliest settlers of Morristown. In early childhood, his father moved the family to a farm in Stowe, Vermont where he spent his childhood.

He received his early education in the common schools of his county and the People's Academy of Morrisville, Vermont. Moving to Iowa in 1869, he graduated from Cornell College at Mt. Vernon in 1874. He was dependent upon his own efforts in obtaining an education, but with characteristic persistence, by teaching school, selling nursery stock, and working in the harvest fields, he earned enough money to complete his college and professional courses, and graduated from the Iowa College of Law in 1876. In the same year, he settled in Denison, Iowa, and from the start, took high rank in his profession.

Shaw was the largest contributor towards establishment of an academy and normal school at Denison, and he held the position of president of the board of trustees from its organization. He was also a trustee of Cornell College, and for several years was president of the school board of Denison, Iowa. He was also president of the Bank of Denison at Denison, and the Bank of Manilla at Manilla, Iowa.

Although always prominent in local campaigns, speaking in defense of the principles of the Republican Party, Shaw was not active in politics until 1896. At the beginning of the memorable free silver controversy that year, he was requested by adherents of the gold standard to reply to an address made in his town by William Jennings Bryan. From that date to the end of the campaign (which resulted in the election of President McKinley), he was in constant demand, and proved one of the most efficient speakers in that notable canvass. His speeches brought his name before the State.

In 1897, when Governor Drake declined renomination because of ill-health, Shaw was nominated by the Republican Party for Governor. He had a solid platform, fighting distinctively for the gold standard without equivocation, and was elected by a plurality of 29,975. He was selected by the Sound Money Commission to preside at the Indianapolis Convention of 1898, where his address attracted national attention. He served as the State's chief executive until 1902.

Shaw was married to Alice Crawshaw. He died on March 28, 1932.

CUMMINS, ALBERT BAIRD (1850-1926), eighteenth governor of Iowa (1902-08), and United States Senator, was born on February 15, 1850 near Carmichaels, Pennsylvania to and Sarah Baird Flenniken and Thomas Layton Cummins. He attended Waynesburg College in Pennsylvania, graduating in 1869.

After moving to Iowa, Cummins got a clerical position with the Clayton County recorder's office in the town of Elkader. He also worked a short time for the Milwaukee & St. Paul Railway as an express messenger.

Cummins got into engineering by accident, when he was asked by a friend to take the position of assistant surveyor for Indiana's Allen County. Cummins did such an impressive job while working on the construction of the Cincinnati, Richmond & Ft. Wayne Railroad that he was promoted to the position of assistant to the chief engineer. His next and final engineering job was for the Northern Central Michigan Railroad.

Deciding to pursue a law career, he got his education working and studying at the Chicago law firm of McClelland & Hodges. After passing the Illinois bar in 1875, he went into law practice at the firm of McClelland & Cummins. Three years later, he moved back to Iowa and became a partner with his brother, James, in their own law office. After James retired from practicing law, Albert became a partner at the law firm of Wright, Cummins & Wright, a prominent firm known throughout Iowa. In later years, he was a partner in the firms of Cummins & Wright, and Cummins, Hewitt & Wright.

Interested in politics for a number of years, Cummins was a supporter of the Republican Party, attending, and serving in various posts at a number of State and national conventions. From 1888 to 1890, he served as a member of the Iowa General Assembly. He twice ran unsuccessfully for the United States Senate, in 1894 and in 1900.

In 1901, Cummins ran for the Iowa governorship, and was elected into office. The Republican Party was broken up into two factions during that time, and while the progressives aligned themselves with him, he often had to struggle with the conservatives. However, he was a popular governor, and was reelected in 1903 and 1905.

Cummins resigned from the governorship and became a member of the U.S. Senate in November 1908, to fill the unfinished term of the incumbent, William B. Allison. He was reelected for three subsequent terms, but was defeated in the 1926 primary. While chairing the Senate Committee on Interstate Commerce, he helped draft the Esch-Cummins Act, initially called the Transportation Act of 1920, which was to take control of the nation's railroads out of the hands of the Federal Government. Although Congress did not agree with the main issue, the measure offered financial help in the refurbishing of the nation's railroad system.

One source described Cummins thusly: "Although his career was a stormy one, he himself was even-tempered, conscientious, deliberate in judgment, and, while tenacious in his views, always courteous and tolerant."

Cummins was married to Ida Lucetta Gallery, and the couple had one daughter. He died on July 30, 1926, in Des Moines, Iowa.

GARST, WARREN (1850-1924), nineteenth governor of Iowa (1908-09), was born on December 4, 1850, in Dayton, Ohio, the son of Maria Louisa Morrison and Michael Garst. After attending public schools, Garst got a position as a brakeman for the Chicago & Northwestern Railroad Co. in Boone, Iowa. He later moved to Coon Rapids, where he became involved in the family mercantile business with his father and brother.

Garst became interested in banking when he became one of the founders of the Bank of Coon Rapids. Politics became his next inclination, and he was elected to the Iowa State Senate on the Republican ticket in 1893, as well as for two subsequent terms. From 1894 to 1906, the State was going through a major growth period. As chairman of the Appropriations Committee, Garst was instrumental in many changes in State policy while revisions were sought in such areas as railroads, taxation, public utilities, education, and highways.

In 1906, Garst was nominated for, and won, the post of Lieutenant-Governor. When his superior, Governor Cummins, left office to take a vacant seat in the United States Senate, Garst took over the governorship in November of 1908.

After his tenure, Garst retired from public office for a time, pursuing business interests. He reentered the political arena after Governor Clarke named him the State's first industrial commissioner, a post in which he was overseer of the new Workmen's Compensation Law; after the law was firmly established, he retired for good.

Garst was married twice: to Lizzie P. Johnson (who died in 1881), and Clara Clark. He had three children. He died on October 5, 1924 in Des Moines.

CARROLL, BERYL FRANKLIN (1860-1939), twentieth governor of Iowa (1909-13), was born on March 15, 1860 in Salt Creek Township, Davis County, Iowa, the son of Christena Wright and Willis Carroll. He first attended the Southern Iowa Normal and Scientific Institute at Bloomfield, then enrolled at the North Missouri State Normal School, where he received a B.S. degree in 1884.

Carroll worked as a teacher for five years, and served as principal of a school in Missouri during 1886-87. During 1988-89, he was superintendent of schools in Rich Hill, Missouri.

Deciding to join his brother in a business venture, Carroll returned home to Iowa. After two years, he bought the Davis County *Republican*, a newspaper for which he also served as publisher and editor. It was around this time that he became involved in politics. A member of the Republican Party, in 1892, he served as a presidential- elector. Carroll next ran for, and won, a seat in the State Senate, serving in that post for two years (1896-98). In the latter year, he resigned to serve as postmaster of Bloomfield, Iowa.

From 1903 to 1909, he served as State auditor, then secured the governorship, making him the first native of Iowa to be elected to the position. He was reelected for a second term in 1910. During his tenure, Carroll initiated various new programs and departments, including the Office of Commerce Counsel, which was established to represent the citizens of Iowa in business matters. Other departments included a new State fire marshal division, a State Board of Education, which helped consolidate the State's numerous educational facilities under one source, and a new highway improvement and construction division.

After leaving the governor's office, Carroll returned to his business interests, creating and serving as president of the Carroll Investment Co. and the Provident Life Insurance Co. Carroll was married to Jennie Dodson, and the couple had two sons. He died on December 16, 1939 in Louisville, Kentucky.

CLARKE, GEORGE WASHINGTON (1852-1936), twenty-first governor of Iowa (1913-17), was born on October 24, 1852, in Shelby County, Indiana, the son of John and Eliza Jane (Akers) Clarke. He grew up on a farm near Drakesville, Iowa after his family moved there when he was four.

Clarke attended Oskaloosa College, receiving an A.B. degree in 1877. He continued his education at the State University of Iowa, garnering an LL.B. degree in 1878. He began practicing law in the town of Adel, and served as justice of the peace there for four years. In 1882, Clarke teamed up with John Bushrod White to create the company of White & Clarke, which became a prominent law firm.

Clarke entered the political arena in 1899 when he was elected to the lower House of the State General Assembly on the Republican ticket; he was reelected for three subsequent terms. In 1908, he was elected Lieutenant-Governor of the State, and in 1912, he secured the governorship, winning a second term in 1914. During his two terms, he helped push through legislation including stopping unfair discrimination regarding trade; curtailing false advertising; expansion of the State capitol grounds (for which he had virtually no support); upgrading of schools; building of highways; and workmen's compensation.

After leaving office in 1917, Clarke spent a year at Drake University as Dean of the College of Law. Beginning in 1918, he once again practiced law as a private citizen, and was involved in public affairs only once again, in 1926, when he headed the campaign team for the reelection of Albert B. Cummins to the United States Senate.

According to one source, Clarke "...possessed outstanding ability as a public speaker and was universally esteemed for his high character and his honesty in politics, as well as in all other activities of life." He was married to Arletta Greene and the couple had four children. He died on November 28, 1936, in Adel Iowa.

HARDING, WILLIAM LLOYD (1877-1934), twenty-second governor of Iowa (1917-21), was born on October 3, 1877 in Sibley, Iowa, the son of Emma Moyer and Orlando Boardman Harding. He attended Morningside College in Sioux City, Iowa, then secured a law degree from the University of South Dakota in 1905. After graduating, he headed a successful law office in Sioux City.

Harding became involved in politics with an election to the Iowa State Legislature in 1906 on the Republican ticket, a post to which he was twice reelected. Creating an impressive record there, he was elected Lieutenant-Governor in 1912, and again in 1914. He secured the governorship in 1916, serving two terms.

Due to the fact that he was Governor during World War I, he was forced to deal with many additional issues concerning the war effort. He also supported education for children, both in the cities and rural areas; established State parks, and sought to create a foreign trade corporation that would oversee the buying and exporting of American agricultural products to other countries.

After stepping down from the governorship, Harding returned to the practice of law as a private citizen in the Des Moines firm of Oliver, Harding & Oliver. He also spent a great deal of his time lecturing. Harding was married to Carrie May Lamoreaux, and the couple had one daughter. He died on December 17, 1934, in Des Moines, Iowa.

KENDALL, NATHAN EDWARD (1868-1936), twenty-third governor of Iowa (1921-25), was born on March 17, 1868 in Greenville, Iowa, the son of Lucinda Stephens and Elijah L. Kendall.

After studying law at a private law firm, Kendall passed the Iowa bar in 1889, and was soon practicing in Albia, Iowa. Between 1890 and 1892, he was the city attorney for Albia, and from 1893 to 1897, he served as prosecuting attorney of Monroe County.

Kendall entered politics in 1898 when, on the Republican ticket, he was elected to the State legislature; he served for ten years. In 1908, he ran for and won a seat in the United States Congress from Iowa's Sixth District, serving two terms.

Kendall secured the governorship in 1920, also serving two terms in that post. During his tenure, he implemented a major reorganization of State government, expanded the park system and the State highway program, made physical education mandatory in the State's public schools, created a State soldiers' bonus law, made sure that abused, forgotten, or troubled children were taken care of under the State system, and offered vocational rehabilitation skills for disabled citizens.

One source described Kendall thusly: "He was a man of clear vision, moral courage, integrity and broad sympathies, was quick of wit and was celebrated for his gift of repartee." Kendall was married twice: to Belle Wooden (who died in 1926), and Mabel Mildred (Fry) Bonnell. He died on November 4, 1936 in Des Moines.

HAMMILL, JOHN (1875-1936), twenty-fourth governor of Iowa (1925-31), was born on October 14, 1875, in Linden, Wisconsin, the son of Mary Brewer and George Hammill. He attended Iowa State University, receiving an LL.B. degree in 1897, and soon after began practicing law in Britt, Iowa.

Hammill entered the political arena when he ran for attorney of Hancock County on the Republican ticket, serving two terms, from 1902 to 1906. Between 1908 and 1912, he served in the Iowa State Senate. From 1920 to 1924, he was Lieutenant-Governor of the State. In 1824, he secured the governorship and served for three terms.

One of Hammills's first decisions as Governor was to convince the State Legislature to pass a measure in favor of the creation of the State Banking Board, whose responsibility it was to establish banking laws. Another measure he was able to secure was making the State Highway Commission responsibile for the State's primary roads. Other decisions made during his tenure included the creation of the Child Welfare Department, whose responsibility it was to oversee State institutions that took care of children; the inclusion of junior colleges under the public school system umbrella; and the admittance, by a constitutional amendment, of women to the State's General Assembly.

After retiring from the governorship in 1931, Hammill returned to private law practice. He also had a large farm, where he engaged in a thriving livestock business. Although no longer in politics, Hammill served on the Better Iowa Schools Commission and the National Committee of Prisons and Prison Labor. One source, describing him, said: "a sincere, straightforward and unassuming man, he was one of the most popular governors in the history of Iowa and was much loved by the people of his community."

Hammill was married to Fannie Richards. He died on April 6, 1936 in Minneapolis, Minnesota.

TURNER, DANIEL W. (1877-1969), twenty-fifth governor of Iowa (1931-33), was born in Corning, Iowa on March 17, 1877, the son of Almera Boher and Austin Turner. He attended Corning Academy in 1898, and was a member of the Iowa Volunteer Infantry during 1898-99. In the latter year, Turner turned to farming to make a living.

Turner's first foray into politics was when he was elected to the State senate in 1904, serving in that body until 1909. Several years later, in 1930, he secured the governorship of Iowa on the Republican ticket. While in office, he faced many issues having to do with the Great Depression, and he sought to reduce taxation for the State. He was chief executive during the conflict dubbed the "Cow War," and was forced to ask the National Guard to protect veterinarians from angry farmers when the vets tried to test cows for tuberculosis, which had become an epidemic.

In a show of support for his State's citizens, Turner tried to persuade President Herbert Hoover to stop forclosures on farms; however, his efforts did not garner him a second term as governor--he lost to Democrat Clyde Herring by over 50,000 votes. Turner ran against Herring once again in 1934, but lost a second time as well.

Turner returned to public life in 1941 when he served on the War Production Board during World War II, a post he held until 1945. He was married to Alice Sample and the couple had three children. He died on April 15, 1969.

HERRING, CLYDE LAVERNE (1879-1945), twenty-sixth governor of Iowa (1933-37), and United States Senator (1937- 43), was born on May 3, 1879 in Jackson, Michigan, the son of Stella Mae Addison and James Gwynn Herring. After receiving his education in public schools, Herring secured a job in Detroit as a jewelry store clerk. He then moved to Colorado, where he worked as a rancher; it was there that he received the appointment of postmaster from President Theodore Roosevelt.

Herring returned to Iowa in 1906, he settled in Massena and ran a farm. His next business venture was in the automobile industry, where in Atlantic, Iowa, he sold cars for Henry Ford, whom he had met earlier in Detroit. He did the same work for the Ford Automobile Co. in Des Moines. In 1912, he established the Herring Motor Co., which manufactured and sold not only cars, but car supplies, tractors, and even Curtis airplanes. By 1926 he had founded and was overseer of the Herring Wissler Company, which distributed wholesale automobile parts.

Herring's interest in politics was sparked by his post as U.S. fuel administrator for Polk County during World War I. After the war, he was unsuccessful in a bid for governor of Iowa and the U.S. Senate, both on the Democratic ticket. In 1932, he again ran for the governorship, and this time was successful. He was the second Democrat in Iowa to win that office. His first decision as governor, in the midst of the Great Depression, was a ban on any foreclosures on farms and homes; soon after, he helped push through the Farm and Home Mortgage Moratorium Law. Initially there was some resistance to the measure, but eventuallly the U.S. Circuit Court of Appeals upheld the decision, and the law ended up being used as an example for other states to follow.

Another somewhat courageous decision of Herring's was closing Iowa banks for a time in order to protect both the stockholders and the depositors. He went one step further by creating legislation in which the banks would be reorganized and rehabilitated. The law, known as "Senate File 111" was impressive enough to be used as a model by the U.S. Government; President Franklin D. Roosevelt proclaimed a holiday for national banks, which according to one source, "brought about nationwide conservation and rehabilitation of the entire banking system." Other decisions by Herring included the establishment of a financial control system, under which the State government could only spend the exact amount of whatever revenues were available at any given time; a State monopoly liquor system; and the issuance of old-age assistance legislation.

Herring served in the United States Senate from 1937 to 1943. His subsequent appointment was as Senior Deputy Administrator for the Office of Price Administration, a post he served in for less than a year, after which he left public life and returned to his business interests.

Herring was married to Emma Pearl Spinney, and the couple had three sons. He died in Washington, D.C. on September 15, 1945.

KRASCHEL, NELSON GEORGE (1889-1957), twenty-seventh governor of Iowa (1937-39), was born on October 27, 1889 in Macon, Illinois, the son of Nancy Jane Poe and Fred K. Kraschel. After attending public schools, Kraschel found that he enjoyed auctioneering, and made his living at that for several years, often calling auctions throughout the United States and Canada. According to one source, he was able to sell over $50,000,000 worth of agricultural property.

Between 1933 and 1937, Kraschel was Lieutenant Governor of Iowa, serving under Governor Clyde L. Herring. In most instances, the number two spot is known to be somewhat of a figurehead position; however, Kraschel was often involved in State matters, sometimes acting as Herring's emissary on visits to Washington, D.C.

In 1936, running on the Democratic ticket, Kraschel secured the governorship; he served from 1937 to 1939. One of the biggest issues he had to face while Governor concerned a strike at a Maytag plant in Newton, Iowa, instigated by the Congress of Industrial Organizations, during which the strikers occupied the plant. The governor immediately established a three-man board to attempt some kind of mediation; in the meantime, he called out the militia to secure calm and reopen the plant. The National Labor Relations Board then got involved in the situation, and in a further show of force, Kraschel requested an injunction to prevent angry strikers from striking on the plant premises. Eventually a compromise was reached by both sides, and the strike was ended.

During his tenure, Kraschel helped establish the Board of Social Welfare. He ran for a second term in 1938, but was defeated by George Wilson. After leaving office, he returned to his business interests until 1942, when he made another attempt at the governorship, this time being defeated by Bourke Hickenlooper.

In 1943, Kraschel was asked to serve as general agent for the Farm Credit Administration in Omaha, Nebraska, a post he held until it was phased out in 1949. Kraschel was married to Agnes Johnson, and the couple had three sons. He died on March 15, 1957 in Harlan, Iowa.

WILSON, GEORGE ALLISON (1884-1953), twenty-eighth governor of Iowa (1939-1943), and United States Senator, was born on April 1, 1884 in Menlo, Iowa, the son of James Henderson and Martha Green (Varley) Wilson. From 1900 to 1903, he was a student at Grinnell College. He subsequently studied at the University of Iowa, where he received an LL.B. degree in 1907. After being admitted to the Iowa bar, He went into private law practice.

Wilson was first exposed to politics when, in 1898, at the age of fourteen, he spent time in the Iowa State Senate as a page. Eventually aligning himself with the Republican Party, he served in several different political posts, including assistant secretary of the State Senate from 1906 to 1909, and secretary in 1911. After serving some time as assistant Polk County attorney, he was elected to the attorney's position in 1914. In 1917 he was appointed to the post of district court judge, resigning in 1921 to once again take up private law practice, this time as a partner in his own firm, Wilson & Shaw.

Wilson returned to politics in 1926, serving in the Iowa State Senate until 1935. Three years later, he was elected to the governorship, and with an interim reelection, served until 1943. During his tenure as Governor, one of the first decisions he made was to eliminate the three-man State Board of Control, due to that department's neglect of the State's fifteen penal institutions, a situation which had caused inhumane conditions for the inmates. New departments he created included the Tax Commission, the Department of Public Safety, and the State Industrial and Defense Commission. In addition, he also reorganized the Board of Social Welfare, and helped pass the Teacher-Tenure Law.

His next political post was as a U.S. Senator, a seat he held until 1949, during which time he served as a member of the small business, armed forces, and agriculture committees. When his last term was finished, Wilson teamed up with his son, George, to create the law firm of Wilson & Wilson.

Wilson was married to Mildred E. Zehner and the couple had four children. He died on September 8, 1953.

HICKENLOOPER, BOURKE BLAKEMORE (1896-1971), twenty- ninth governor of Iowa (1943-45), and United States Senator, was born on July 21, 1896 in Blockton, Iowa. He attended Iowa State College, earning a B.S. degree in 1920, and continued his education at the University of Iowa, where he received a law degree in 1922, passing the Iowa bar soon after. His first law position was for the firm of Johnson, Donnelly, and Lynch. In 1935, he teamed up with another attorney and established the law firm of Hickenlooper and Mitvalsky, a company name which one reporter wryly noted, made for a "tricky shingle."

1935 was also the year that Hickenlooper entered the political arena, when he was elected to the Iowa House of Representatives on the Republican ticket. During 1939-43, he served as Lieutenant-Governor, and in the latter year, was elected to the governorship, where he served one term.

During his tenure, the Hickenlooper's impressive legislation was helping to increase the State's income by $9,000,000, which gave the budget a surplus of $54,000,000. After leaving the governorship, Hickenlooper served in the United States Senate from 1945 to 1969, during which time he was appointed to two powerful committees: the Senate's

Special Committee on Atomic Energy, and the Joint Congressional Committee on Atomic Energy.

Hickenlooper was married to Verna Eilene Bensch; the couple had two children. He died on September 4, 1971.

BLUE, ROBERT DONALD (1898-?), thirtieth governor of Iowa (1945-49), was born on September 24, 1898 in Eagle Grove, Iowa. He attended Des Moines's Capital City Commerical College for a year, then studied forestry at Iowa State College, during which time he also served in the student army training corps.

After deciding to pursue a law career, Blue attended Drake University, taking his LL.B. degree in 1922. He went into private practice and teamed up with his brother to establish Hobbet, Blue, and Blue. From 1924 to 1931, he served as attorney for Wright County. In 1932, he was named city attorney for Eagle Grove, and starting in 1934, he served for four terms in the Iowa House of Representatives, which ended in 1942.

In 1943, Blue was elected Lieutenant Governor of Iowa, and in 1944, he secured the governorship. When he ran for reelection in 1946, the campaign was somewhat peculiar in that it was, according to one source, "marked by indifference on both sides." To prove the point, Blue was quoted as saying: "There is no public interest in the campaign, so why should I stir it up?" Even with apathy surrounding the entire affair, he won a second term by over 95,000 votes.

During his tenure, Blue pushed for a County Assessor Law, which the State Legislature passed in 1947; created to standardize property assessments, it was described as "one of the most forward-looking pieces of legislation adopted in years." He also lobbied for more aid to cities and towns throughout the State. In addition, according to *Current Biography*, he "secured two hundred new factories in Iowa through the Iowa Development Commission; extended the hospital program to local communities; started a new program for the care and rehabilitation of mental patients; (and) inaugurated a retirement program for public employees."

After being defeated for a third term in the 1948 primary, Blue retired from public life and returned to his law practice and farming interests. Blue was married to Cathleen Beale; the couple had two children.

BEARDSLEY, WILLIAM S. (1901-1954) was Governor of Iowa from 1948 to 1954.

Born in Beacon, Iowa on May 17, 1901, he attended the Bowen Institute of Pharmacy, graduating in 1921. The following year he began what would be a sixteen year career in the retail drug business. In 1938, he retired from that line of work and began farming on a parcel of land that he had purchased.

During his years as a pharmacist, he ran for the Iowa State Senate on the Republican ticket, and after winning his campaign, served from 1933 to 1941. Six years later, he began serving in the Iowa House of Representatives (1947-49). In 1948, he ran for Governor of Iowa and won, beating the incumbent governor, Robert Blue in the primary, and his Democratic opponent, Carroll O. Switzer, in the general election. Beardsley went on to win two more terms for the gubernatorial office.

While governor, Beardsley worked hard to balance the state budget. He used funds he had appropriated in order to upgrade schools and roads, and also added more officers to the highway patrol, made gambling illegal, and gave the workmen's compensation a much-needed raise.

Beardsley intended to retire from office after his third term, but he was killed in a car accident, and died on November 21, 1954. He was buried in New Virginia, Iowa, and was survived by his wife, Charlotte Manning, and their four children.

ELTHON, LES (1898-1967), served as Governor of Iowa for only a month following the death of Governor William Beardsley.

Born in Fertile, Iowa on June 9, 1898, he attended Augsburg Seminary, then went on to Iowa State Teacher's College and Hamilton's University of Business. He worked at three careers after his schooling; as a high school teacher (and later principal), farmer, and overseer of a quarry.

In 1932, Elthon, a Republican, won a seat in the Iowa State Senate where he served until 1953, becoming Lieutenant Governor that same year. After the death of his superior, Governor William Beardsley, Elthon served as governor for a little over a month, then returned to his former position as lieutenant governor after the election of a new governor. After leaving office in 1957, he returned to his hometown of Fertile, where he was elected Mayor. He served in that postion until 1963 when he was reelected as a Senator for the state of Iowa. Due to failing health, he resigned in 1965.

Elthon died on April 16, 1967, and was survived by his wife Synneva Hjemebud and their six children.

HOEGH, LEO A. (1908-?), was Governor of Iowa from 1954 to 1957.

Born in Audubon City, Iowa on March 30, 1908, he attended the University of Iowa, receiving a Bachelor of Arts degree in 1929, and a law degree in 1932. In 1937 he began serving in the Iowa House of Representatives, a position he held until 1942. During 1941, he was the City Attorney for Charton, and during 1953-55, he served as Attorney General of Iowa.

In 1954, he was the victor in the governor's race against Democratic candidate, Clyde E. Herring, taking office in January of 1955. His accomplishments during his term included escalation of the highway construction program, modernizing the school system, which included the increase of state funds to education, and the upgrading of Iowa's agricultural research facilities. He was able to implement these improvements after raising the sales tax on such things as alcohol, cigarettes and gasoline, as well as increasing corporate income tax.

However, his decision to raise these taxes contributed to his defeat in the subsequent election, which he lost to Herschel Loveless. His post- governor jobs included serving as a civil defense administrator (1957-58); director of the Office of Civil and Defense Mobilization; and director and general counsel of the Soypro International.

Elthon is married to Mary Louise Foster and the couple have two daughters.

LOVELESS, HERSCHEL C. (1911-?) was Governor of Iowa from 1957 to 1961.

Born in Hedrick, Iowa on May 5, 1911, he was an employee of the Chicago, Milwaukee, Saint Paul, and Pacific Railroad from 1927 to 1939. In the latter year he got a job working at the John Morrell Company, then in 1944, returned to his railroad position where he remained for the next three years.

From 1947 to 1949, he worked for the city of Ottumwa as superintendent of streets, then became that city's mayor in 1949. In 1953 he left that office and became owner and manager of the Municipal Equipment Company until 1956.

His first bid for governor failed after he lost to the incumbent, William Beardsley, and he also failed in his bid for a Congressional seat in 1954. However, he ran against Republican Governor Leo Hoegh in the 1956 race and won due to voter anger at Hoegh's tax increases.

Loveless served two terms as governor, implementing such decisions as a small monthly stipend for teachers, a workmen's compensation and unemployment compensation increase, and the creation of a mental health fund. He also refused to extend the sales tax left by his predecessor. Loveless served as governor until January of 1961.

Later that year, he began serving on the Renegotiation Board, staying in that position until 1969 when he took the post of vice president of the Chromalloy American Corporation.

Loveless is married to Amelia R. Howard and the couple have two children.

ERBE, NORMAN A. (1919-?), was Governor of Iowa from 1961 to 1963.

Born in Boone, Iowa on October 25, 1919, he went into the United States Army at the beginning of World War II, and was an infantry company commander during 1941-42. He then transferred to the United States Air Force, serving as a pilot between 1943 and 1945. After the war, he attended the University of Iowa, earning a Bachelor of Arts degree in 1946, and a law degree the following year, after which, he went into a private law practice.

His career in politics began in 1952 when he became the County Attorney General for the Iowa Highway Commission. He held that post until 1955, and was elected as Attorney General for the state in 1956, serving until 1961. He ran for Governor of Iowa on the Republican ticket in 1960 and won, taking office the following year. While in office, he increased funding to educational programs and formed a commission to study the problem of alcoholism. He also got involved in the study of prisoners, going as far as having the State Board of Control create a diagnostic clinic in order to get an idea of the viability of rehabilitation. Under his term, the Iowan people became participants in the Kerr-Mills medical program, and were able to utilize the federal low rental housing program as well.

Erbe ran for a second term, but was defeated by Harold Hughes. After leaving office, Erbe began working as an assistant to the president of Diamond Laboratories. He later became the executive director of the National Paraplegia Foundation, and also worked as regional representative of the Secretary of the United States Department of Transportation.

He is married to Jacqueline Doran and the couple have three children.

HUGHES, HAROLD (1922-?), was Governor of Iowa from 1963 to 1969.

Born in Ida Grove, Iowa on February 10, 1922, he studied at the State University of Iowa during 1941-42. In the latter year he entered the United States Army, serving until 1945. The following year, he began working in the field of transportation and commerce, at one point, creating his own rate and tariff service, the Iowa Better Trucking Bureau, which was eventually responsible for equitable truck rates in at least thirty counties. Due to his impressive work in that area, he was elected to the Iowa Commission of Commerce in 1958, a position he ran for because of what he felt was a lack of responsibility by those already in the commission. Toward the end of his term in that post he noted: "I believe we have restored dignity to the commission and people again have a feeling of confidence and fair play."

While with the commission, Hughes made a bid for the governor's office in 1960, on the Democratic ticket, not making it past the primary. However, in his second try, two years later, he was successful, due to his no-nonsense approach in campaigning, which, according to *Current Biography*, "was free of the glad-handing, back-slapping, and baby-kissing that sometimes mark political campaigns."

Elected in November of 1962, some of his decisions as Governor included the revoking of the death penalty, the formation of a State Civil Rights Commission, the creation of a radio-television system for education, and an upgrading of the laws concerning unemployment compensation and workmen's compensation.

As Governor, Hughes made his first address to the Iowa Legislature in January of 1963, saying: "It is sometimes said that the knack of skillful government is to hang back, do as little as possible, and make no mistakes. I hope there is another way--for between you and me, this prospect does not invite my soul. Frankly, I expect to experiment and make some mistakes-- whether it be in installing new programs in departments or hiring a band. But I can assure you that this new administration will not stop moving-

-towards the goals to which we have pledged ourselves with the people of Iowa...The time has come to set aside old prejudices, face our problems squarely, and work together to fulfill our state's immeasurable potential."

Hughes moved on from the governor's office to the United States Senate, serving from 1969 to 1975. He is married to Eva Mae Mercer and the couple have three children.

FULTON, ROBERT D. (1929-?) was Governor of Iowa for a very short time during 1969.

Born in Waterloo, Iowa on May 13, 1929, he studied at Iowa State Teachers College from 1947 to 1949. He went on to State University of Iowa, earning a Bachelor of Arts degree in 1952 and a law degree in 1958, after which he went into private law practice. His education was interrupted for two years, between 1953 and 1955 while he served in the United States Air Force.

Three years after his discharge, he was elected to the Iowa House of Representatives, serving in that post until 1961. He went on to the State Senate the following year, serving until 1965. In 1964, he had also been elected Lieutenant Governor, under Democratic Governor, Harold Hughes, serving in that capacity for five years.

After Governor Hughes resigned to serve in the Senate, Fulton served as governor for fifteen days in January of 1969 until the newly-elected governor, Robert Ray took office. Having made the decision to quit as lieutenant governor even before the election, Fulton returned to private practice after the transition was made. He later ran against Ray in the 1970 contest, but was defeated.

Fulton is married to Rachel Marie Breanlt and the couple have four children.

RAY, ROBERT D. (1928-?) was Governor of Iowa from 1969 to 1983.

Born on September 26, 1928 in Des Moines, Iowa, he attended Drake University, earning a B.A. degree in 1952. He went on to Drake University Law School, receiving his J.D. degree in 1954. Not long after, he passed the bar exam and was given a partnership at the law firm of Lawyer, Lawyer, Ray & Crouch, which later became Lawyer, Lawyer, Ray & Dunn.

In 1956, Ray, a Republican, decided to enter politics, running unsuccessfully for county attorney and state representative. In 1968, he made a bid for the governor's office. His campaign was interrupted when he was involved in a twin-engine plane crash, which caused a six-week stay in the hospital due to his serious injuries. His campaign was kept alive by his staff and friends, and when he was able to get around, he resumed his activities. Although his opponent was supported by incumbent governor, Harold E. Hughes, Ray easily won the election by over 90,000 votes.

A liberal, and supporter of several reforms, Ray was a popular governor and was elected to four consecutive terms. During his administration, a law was passed that prohibited any sort of discriminatory practices concerning housing, employment, or gender. Other measures he supported include: the lowering of the voting age from twenty-one to nineteen; a new "no- fault" divorce law; and the creation of both a Department of Transportation and a Department of Environmental Quality; and a veto to a bill that would have permitted wiretapping. Also, sympathizing with the Native American community, he ordered the state historical museum to eliminate its display of the remains of five Indian graves.

Ray retired from office in 1982 and later went into the insurance business. He served in the United States Army from 1946 to 1948. He is married to Billie Lee Hornberger and the couple have three children.

BRANSTAD, TERRY E. (1946-) became Governor of Iowa in 1983.

Born on November 17, 1946 in Leland, Iowa, he attended the University of Iowa, earning a B.A. degree in 1969. He went on to Drake University Law School, receiving his J.D. degree in 1974.

Branstad became involved in politics in 1968 when he served as a delegate to various Republican conventions. His first political office was in the Iowa House of Representatives in 1972, and he was reelected to his seat two more times. He became lieutenant governor in 1978, serving under incumbent governor, Robert Ray during the latter's last term in office. After Ray resigned in 1982, Branstad was elected as governor.

During his first term, Branstad was faced with a crippling farm crisis, during which he made budget cuts of over 90 million dollars, feeling it was important that the state government join the farmers and "pare back and adjust to

146

the economic realities of today." Other programs he supported had to do with a bigger fund for highways, the increase of teachers' salaries, and the upgrading of academic and research programs at colleges throughout the state.

Branstad served as chairman of the Midwestern Governor's Association, the Committee on Agriculture of the National Governors' Association, as well as the Task Force of the NGA's Committee on International Trade.

He is married to Christine Ann Johnson and the couple have three children.

DIRECTORY OF STATE SERVICES

ADJUTANT GENERAL, OFFICE OF
7700 NW Beaver dR.
Camp Dodge
Johnston, IA 50131

ADMINISTRATION, DEPARTMENT OF
Hoover State Office Bldg.
1300 E. Walnut St.
Des Moines, IA 50319

AERONAUTICS, OFFICE OF
Des Moines International Airport
Fleur Dr.
Des Moines, IA 50321

AGING, DEPARTMENT OF
Jewett Bldg., Room 236
914 Grnad Ave.
Des Moines, IA 50319

AGRICULTURE, DEPARTMENT OF
Wallace State Office Bldg.
E 9th & Grand aVe.
Des Moines, IA 50319

AIR POLLUTION CONTROL, DIVISION OF
Wallace State Office Bldg.
E 9th Grand Ave.
Des Moines, IA 50319

ALCOHOLISM, DEPARTMENT OF
Lucas State Office Bldg., 4th Fl.
E. 12th & Walnut Sts.
Des Moines, IA 50319

ARCHIVES AND RECORDS, DEPARTMENT OF
Historical Bldg.
600 E. Locust
Des Moines, IA 50319

ARTS AND HUMANITIES, DEPARTMENT OF
Capitol Complex
Des Moines, IA 50319

ATHLETICS BOARD
1000 E. Grand Ave.
Des Moines, IA 52242

ATTORNEY GENERAL, OFFICE OF
Hoover State Office Bldg.
1300 E. Walnut St.
Des Moines, IA 50319

AUDIT, DEPARTMENT OF
State Capitol Bldg.
10th St. & Grand Ave.
Des Moines, IA 50319

BANKING
East Grand Office Park
200 E. Grand Ave.
Des Moines, IA 50309

BUDGET, DEPARTMENT OF
State Capitol Bldg.
10th St. & Grand Ave.
Des Moines, IA 50319

CHILD WELFARE SERVICES
Hoover State Office Bldg., 5th Fl.
1300 E. Walnut St.
Des Moines, IA 50319

CIVIL DEFENSE, DEPARTMENT OF
Hoover State Office Bldg., Room A-29
1300 E. Walnut St.
Des Moines, IA 50319

CLERK OF THE HOUSE
State Capitol Bldg.
1015 E. Grand Ave.
Des Moines, IA 50319

COMMERCE, DEPARTMENT OF
1918 SE Hulsizer Ave.
Ankeny, IA 50021

COMMUNITY AFFAIRS, DEPARTMENT OF
200 E. Grand Ave.
Des Moines, IA 50309

COMPTROLLER, OFFICE OF
State Capitol Bldg.
10th St. & Grand Ave.
Des Moines, IA 50319

CONFLICT OF INTEREST BOARD
Colony Bldg.
507 10th St., 7th Fl.
Des Moines, IA 50309

CONSUMER AFFAIRS, OFFICE OF
Hoover State Office Bldg.
1300 E. Walnut St.
Des Moines, IA 50319

CORRECTIONS, DEPARTMENT OF
Capitol Annex
523 E. 12th St.
Des Moines, IA 50309

COURT ADMINISTRATION, OFFICE OF
State Capitol Bldg.
10th St. & Grand Ave.
Des Moines, IA 50319

DATA PROCESSING
Hoover State Office Bldg., Level B
1300 E. Walnut St.
Des Moines, IA 50319

DEVELOPMENTAL DISABILITIES DIVISION
Hoover State Office Bldg., 5th Fl.
1300 E. Walnut St.
Des Moines, IA 50319

DRUG ABUSE, DEPARTMENT OF
Lucas State Office Bldg., 4th Fl.
E. 12th & Walnut Sts.
Des Moines, IA 50319

ECONOMIC DEVELOPMENT, DEPARTMENT OF
200 E. Grand Ave.
Des Moines, IA 50309

EDUCATION (HIGHER)
Lucas State Office Bldg.
E. 12th & Walnut Sts.
Des Moines, IA 50319

EDUCATION (PRIMARY, SECONDARY, AND VOCATIONAL)
Grimes State Office Bldg.
Des Moines, IA 50319

ELECTIONS DIVISION
State Capitol Bldg.
10th St. & Grand Ave.
Des Moines, IA 50319

EMPLOYMENT SECURITY, DEPARTMENT OF
1000 E. Grand Ave.
Des Moines, IA 50319

ENERGY AND NATURAL RESOURCES, DEPARTMENT OF
Wallace State Office Bldg.
E. 9th & Grand Ave.
Des Moines, IA 50319

ENVIRONMENTAL AFFAIRS
Wallace State Office Bldg.
E. 9th & Grand Ave.
Des Moines, IA 50319

FINANCE, DEPARTMENT OF
State Capitol Bldg.
10th St. & Grand Ave.
Des Moines, IA 50319

FISH AND GAME DIVISION
Wallace State Office Bldg.
E. 9th St. & Grand Ave.
Des Moines, IA 50319

FOOD AND DRUGS DIVISION
Lucas State Office Bldg., 3rd Fl.
E. 12th & Walnut Sts.
Des Moines, IA 50319

FORESTRY DIVISION
Wallace State Office Bldg.
E. 9th & Grand Ave.
Des Moines, IA 50319

GENERAL SERVICES, DEPARTMENT OF
Hoover State Office Bldg.
1300 E. Walnut St.
Des Moines, IA 50319

GEOLOGY DIVISION
Wallace State Office Bldg.
E. 9th & Grand Ave.
Des Moines, IA 50319

HANDICAPPED, COUNCIL ON
Lucas State Office Bldg., 1st Fl.
E. 12th & Walnut Sts.
Des Moines, IA 50319

HAZARDOUS MATERIALS, DIVISION OF
Wallace State Office Bldg.
E. 9th & Grand Ave.
Des Moines, IA 50319

HEALTH, DEPARTMENT OF
Lucas State Office Bldg.
E. 12th & Walnut Sts.
Des Moines, IA 50319

HIGHWAY SAFETY, OFFICE OF
Wallace State Office Bldg., 3rd Fl.
E. 9th & Grand Ave.
Des Moines, IA 50319

HIGHWAYS DIVISION
800 Lincoln Way
Ames, IA 50010

HISTORIC PRESERVATION AGENCY
Historical Bldg.
600 E. Locust St.
Des Moines, IA 50319

HOUSING, DEPARTMENT OF
200 E. Grand St., Suite 222
Des Moines, IA 50309

HUMAN RIGHTS, DEPARTMENT OF
c/o Grimes State Office Bldg., 2nd Fl.
211 E. Maple St.
Des Moines, IA 50319

INSURANCE, BUREAU OF
Lucas State Office Bldg.
E. 12th & Walnut Sts.
Des Moines, IA 50319

JUVENILE DELINQUENCY
Hoover State Office Bldg., 5th Fl.
1300 E. Walnut St.
Des Moines, IA 50319

LABOR, DEPARTMENT OF
1000 E. Grand Ave.
Des Moines, IA 50319

LEGISLATIVE RESEARCH, DEPARTMENT OF
State Cpitol Bldg., 3rd Fl.
Des Moines, IA 50319

LIBRARY SERVICES, OFFICE OF
E. 12th & Grand Ave.
Des Moines, IA 50319

LICENSING (CORPORATE)
Hoover State Office Bldg.
1300 E. Walnut St.
Des Moines, IA 50319

LICENSING (OCCUPATIONAL AND PROFESSIONAL)
1918 SE Hulsizer Ave.
Ankeny, IA 50021

LIQUOR CONTROL COMMISSION
1918 SE Hulsizer Ave.
Ankeny, IA 50021

LOTTERY DIVISION
2015 Grand Ave.
Des Moines, IA 50312

MASS TRANSIT DIVISION
Des Moines International Airport
Fleur Dr.
Des Moines, IA 50321

MENTAL HEALTH DIVISION
Hoover State Office Bldg., 5th Fl.
1300 E. Walnut St.
Des Moines, IA 50319

MINING AND MINERALS, DEPARTMENT OF
Wallace State Office Bldg.
E. 9th & Grand Ave.
Des Moines, IA 50319

MOTOR VEHICLES, DEPARTMENT OF
5268 NW 2nd Ave.
Des Moines, IA 50313

NATURAL RESOURCES, DEPARTMENT OF
Wallace State Office Bldg.
E. 9th & Grand Ave.
Des Moines, IA 50319

NUCLEAR ENERGY, DEPARTMENT OF
Lucas State Office Bldg.
E. 12th & Walnut Sts.
Des Moines, IA 50319

OCCUPATIONAL SAFETY AND HEALTH
Lucas State Office Bldg., 2nd Fl.
E. 12th & Walnut Sts.
Des Moines, IA 50319

OIL AND GAS, DIVISION OF
Wallace State Office Bldg.
E. 9th & Grand Ave.
Des Moines, IA 50319

OMBUDSMAN
Capitol Complex
215 E. 7th St.
Des Moines, IA 50319

PARKS AND RECREATION, DEPARTMENT OF
Wallace State Office Bldg.
E. 9th & Grand Ave.
Des Moines, IA 50319

PERSONNEL, OFFICE OF
Grimes State Office Bldg.
E. 14th St. & Grand Ave.
Des Moines, IA 50319

PLANNING DEPARTMENT
State Capitol Bldg.
10th St. & Grand Ave.
Des Moines, IA 50319

POLICE DEPARTMENT
Wallace State Office Bldg.
E. 9th & Grand Ave.
Des Moines, IA 50319

PRINTING AND PUBLISHING DIVISION
Grimes State Office Bldg.
400 E. 14th St.
Des Moines, IA 50319

PROBATION AND PAROLE, STATE BOARD OF
Capitol Annex
523 E. 12th St.
Des Moines, IA 50319

UBLIC UTILITIES, DEPARTMENT OF
Lucas State Office Bldg., 5ht Fl.
E. 12th & Walnut Sts.
Des Moines, IA 50319

PUBLIC WORKS, DEPARTMENT OF
Hoover State Office Bldg., Level A
1300 E Walnut St.
Des Moines, IA 50319

PURCHASING DIVISION
Hoover State Office Bldg., Level A
1300 E Walnut St.
Des Moines, IA 50319

RAILROADS DIVISION
800 Lincoln Way
Ames, IA 50010

REAL ESTATE, COMMISSION ON
1918 SE Hulsizer Ave.
Ankeny, IA 50021

REFUGEE RESETTLEMENT, OFFICE OF
City View Plaza Bldg., Suite D
1200 University Ave.
Des Moines, IA 50314

RETIREMENT, DEPARTMENT OF
600 E Court Ave.
Des Moines, IA 50309

SECRETARY OF STATE
State House
Des Moines, IA 50319

SECRETARY OF THE SENATE
State House
Des Moines, IA 50319

SECURITIES REGISTRATION DIVISION
Lucas State Office Bldg.
E 12th & Walnut Sts.
Des Moines, IA 50319

SOCIAL SERVICES DIVISION
Hoover State Office Bldg., 5th Fl.
1300 E. Walnut St.
Des Moines, IA 50319

SOLID WASTE MANAGEMENT
Wallace State Office Bldg.
900 E. Grand Ave.
Des Moines, IA 50319

STATE-LOCAL RELATIONS
200 E. Grand Ave.
Des Moines, IA 50309

SURPLUS PROPERTY DIVISION
Hoover State Office Bldg., Level A
1300 E. Walnut St.
Des Moines, IA 50319

TAXATION AND REVENUE
Hoover State Office Bldg.
1300 E. Walnut St.
Des Moines, IA 50319

TOURISM, OFFICE OF
200 E. Grand Ave.
Des Moines, IA 50309

TRANSPORTATION, DEPARTMENT OF
800 Lincoln Way
Ames, IA 50010

TREASURER
State Capitol Bldg.
10th St. & Grand Ave.
Des Moines, IA 50319

UNCLAIMED PROPERTY DIVISION
Hoover State Office Bldg.
1300 E. Walnut St.
Des Moines, IA 50319

UNEMPLOYMENT
1000 E. Grand Ave.
Des Moines, IA 50319

VETERANS' AFFAIRS, DEPARTMENT OF
7700 NW Beaver Dr.
Johnston, IA 50131

VITAL RECORDS AND STATISTICS BUREAU
Lucas State Office Bldg.
321 E. 12th St.
Des Moines, IA 50319

WATER POLLUTION CONTROL
Wallace State Office Bldg.
E. 9th & Grand Ave.
Des Moines, IA 50319

WATER RESOURCES
Wallace State Office Bldg.
E 9th & Grand Ave.
Des Moines, IA 50319

WEIGHTS AND MEASURES DIVISION
Wallace Stte Office Bldg.
E 9th & Grand Ave.
Des Moines, IA 50319

WELFARE, DEPARTMENT OF
Hoover State Office Bldg., 5th Fl.
1300 E. Walnut St.
Des Moines, IA 50319

WOMEN
Lucas State Office Bldg., G Level
E 12th & Walnut Sts.
Des Moines, IA 50319

WORKERS' COMPENSATION
1000 E Grand Ave.
Des Moines, IA 50319

DICTIONARY OF PLACES

ACKLEY, City; Franklin & Hardin Counties; Pop. 1,696; Zip Code 50601; 75 miles N of Des Moines; Elev. 1092; Laid out in 1857 and named for J. W. Ackley.

ADAIR, City; Adair & Guthrie Counties; Pop. 894; Zip Code 50002; 90 miles SW of Des Moines; Lat. 41-30-31 N long. 094-38-48 W; Named for Gen. John Adair, Governor of Kentucky.

In 1873, Jesse James and his gang derailed a C.R.I. & P. train of five coaches. Estimates of the loot obtained from the dazed passengers ranged from a small amount to $3,000. Afterwards, the James boys said that the engineer's death made this the "only job we regret."

ADAIR COUNTY, S central Iowa, 569 sq. mi.; Pop. 8,409; Named for John Lynch Adair (1828-1896), one of the editors of the Indian Chiefton.

ADAMS COUNTY, SW Iowa, 426 sq. mi.; Pop. 4,866; Named for John Adams (1735-1826), second President of the United States.

ADEL, City; Dallas County Seat; Pop. 3,304; Zip Code 50003; 30 miles W of Des Moines; Lat. 41-37-02 N long. 094-01-49 W; An early spelling was Adell; named for the location on a dell of North Racoon River.

Adel was, in 1850, a station on the Dubuque Council Bluffs stagecoach route. When the town was settled in 1846, it was called Penoach, but the name was changed in 1849 when the place was made the county seat. The county was named for George M. Dallas (1792-1864), Vice President of the United States (1845- 49).

HISTORICAL PLACES...
Dallas County Courthouse.

AFTON, City; Union County; Pop. 953; Zip Code 50830; 50 miles SW of Des Moines; Lat. 41-01-35 N long. 094-11-48 W; Laid out in 1854, the city was named after the Afton River in Scotland by Mrs. Baker, wife of one of the proprietors.

Located on the banks of Twelve Mile Creek, it was selected as the seat of Union County in 1855. After the C.B. & Q.R.R. was built through the county in 1869, the seat was moved to Creston, where it has remained.

AGENCY, City; Wapello County; Pop. 616; Zip Code 52530; 55 miles W of Iowa City; Lat. 40-59-54 N long. 092-18-31 W; Named in 1838 for the Sac and Fox Indian Agency established here. After the Indians were removed to Kansas, the agency was abandoned, but the Fox Agency post office remained and the place became known as Agency.

Joseph M. Street selected the site on which was built an immense council house.

Street moved his family to Iowa from Prairie du Chien, Wisconsin, in 1838 and before his death in 1840 had gained respect of his charges. When Chief Wapello died, he was buried, as he had requested, beside his friend, Street. The chief's name was later adopted as the name of the county because he had furthered peaceful relations with the white men.

AINSWORTH, City; Washington County; Pop. 506; Zip Code 52201; 25 miles S of Iowa City; Lat. 41-17-38 N long. 091-33-30 W; Named for D. H. Ainsworth, a Civil Engineer.

AKRON, City; Plymouth County; Pop. 1,450; Zip Code 51001; 38 miles NW of Sioux City; Lat. 42-49-44 N long. 096-33-14 W; The name was first Portlandville, but was changed in the belief that it was going to grow to the size of Akron, Ohio. The name Akron means "summit" or "peak" in Greek.

ALBERT CITY, City; Buena Vista County; Pop. 779; Zip Code 50510; 75 miles ENE of Sioux City; 42-46-45 N long. 094-55-23 W.

ALBIA, City; Monroe County Seat; Pop. 3,870; Zip Code 52531; 60 miles SE of Des Moines; Elev. 959; Lat. 41-01-30 N long. 092-47-56 W. It was first known as Princeton.

Most of the early settlers came from Illinois, Indiana, and Ohio; those who were foreign-born were chiefly natives of Germany, Scandinavia, and Ireland.

Until 1861, the residents of the town used wood for fuel, unaware of the the rich deposit of coal beneath the surface in the vicinity. The first method of mining here was stripping. The principal vein, however, was from 200 to 300 feet underground, and shafts had to be sunk to reach it. This area was at one time among the chief coal fields of the State.

ALBION, City; Marshall County; Pop. 585; Zip Code 50005; 45 miles NE of Des Moines; Lat. 42-06-44 N long. 092-59-54 W; Probably titled after the ancient name for England.

ALDEN, City; Hardin County; Pop. 855; Zip Code 50006; 70 miles N of Des Moines; Lat. 42-31-31 N long. 093-23-28 W; Named for Henry Alden, who settled there in 1854.

ALGONA, City; Kossuth County Seat; Pop. 6,015; Zip Code 50511; 25 miles SE of Armstrong; Lat. 43-04-22 N long. 094-13-53 W; First known as Call's Grove for early residents. The name was changed to Algona, after Henry Schoolcraft's book "Algonquin", at the suggestion of Mrs. Call.

The only fortifications erected in the county were two built in the spring of 1857, immediately after the Spirit Lake Massacre, as protection against the Indians. One enclosed the Town Hall, and was called the Algona Stockade. After several baseless Indian scares, the building was torn down, and the material used for plank roads.

Born in this town were Gardner Cowles, publisher of the Des Moines *Register* and allied papers, and Harvey Ingham, editor of the same paper. L. J. Dickinson, born at Derby, Iowa, in 1873, and elected by Iowa to the Senate in 1930, lived here for many years.

POINTS OF INTEREST:

- Ambrose A. Call State Park. 1 1/2 miles SW on US 18, 1 1/2 mils Soon on paved road.
- Kossuth County Musum. Dodge & Nebraska Sts.

ALAMAKEE COUNTY, NE corner of Iowa, 636 sq. mi.; Pop. 13,855; Named for Allan Makee, Indian trader.

ALLISON, City; Butler County Seat; Pop. 1,000; Zip Code 50602; 110 miles NNW of Iowa City; Lat. 42-45-28 N long. 092-47- 46 W. Named after an early settler.

ALMA, City; Buena Vista County; Pop. 1,720; Zip Code 51002; Lat. 42-40-27 N long. 095-18-35 W.

ALTON, City; Sioux County; Pop. 1,063; Zip Code 51003; 40 miles NE of Sioux City; Lat. 42-58-49 N long. 096-01-09 W.

ALTOONA, City; Polk County; Pop. 7,191; Zip Code 50009; 15 miles N of Des Moines; Lat. 41-38-46 N long. 093-27-50 W; Named for its location at the highest elevation between the Des Moines and Mississippi rivers. The name Altoona is derived from the latin word altus, meaning "high".

AMES, City; Story County; Pop. 47,198; Zip Code 50010; 35 miles SW of Des Moines; Lat. 42-02-33 N long. 093-34-43 W; Named for Oakes Ames.

Ames lies on rolling prairie lands near the geographic center of Iowa. Squaw Creek bisects the town, the northeastern corner of which touches Skunk River. The site of Ames, slough and marshland, was not the kind early settlers usually chose for a town.

When Mrs. Cynthia Duff bought the farmland occupying the future town site in 1864, no one knew she was buying it for John I. Blair, who planned to build a depot for the Cedar Rapids and Missouri Railroad (later the North Western) on the land. Although Blair had been offered 20 acres of free land south of College Farm, located at this point in 1859, he built the station and laid out the town on the land acquired by Mrs. Duff.

Blair named the new town site for Oakes Ames, one of the proprietors of the railroad. Noah Webster (not the compiler of the dictionary) built the first home in this town in 1864. Until January 1866, Ames bore the post office name of College Farm because it was adjacent to the land purchased for the State Agricultural College and the Model Farm.

With the development of the railroad and the drainage of the land, more settlers began to come in. By the end of 1865, there were 300 people living here. Special laws were passed by the State legislature to safeguard the students of College Farm, including one prohibiting the sale of any kind of alcoholic beverages.

The town was incorporated in 1870; four years later, the Narrow Gauge line from Des Moines to Ames helped to complete what the college had already started--the making of a brisk small town from what had been little more than a flag station. Always an important railroad center, Ames for a time was also the terminal of the Cedar Rapids and Missouri, making it a place of "considerable railroad stir."

By 1886, the local timetables boasted that "there were 20 chances to leave Ames every 24 hours."

POINTS OF INTEREST:

- Iowa State University of Science and Technology (1858). N on US 30.
- Farm House. (1860). Near Dairy Industry Building, off Union Drive.

HISTORICAL PLACES...

Knapp-Wilson House (The Farm House).

ANAMOSA, City; Jones County Seat; Pop. 5,100; Zip Code 52205; 35 miles NE of Iowa City; Lat. 42-06-44 N long. 091-17-05 W; Laid out in 1845 and named Lexington, it was renamed Anamosa to avoid duplication with another place called Lexington. Anamosa is derived from an Indian word meaning *white fawn* for the daughter of a Winnebago chief. It is said that the girl fell in love with a young white engineer, and rather than marry the Indian her father had chosen, ended her life by jumping from a high bluff into the Maquoketa River.

ANITA, City; Cass County; Pop. 1,068; Zip Code 50020; 65 miles WSW of Des Moines; Lat. 41-26-45 N long. 094-47-04 W. The city is named for Anita Cowles, niece of the surveyor who laid out the town.

ANKENY, City; Polk County; Pop. 18,482; Zip Code 50021; 15 miles NW of Des Moines; Lat. 41-39-26 N long. 093-36-57 W. Named for founder, Col. J. F. Ankeny, as a station on a narrow-gauge railroad, now abandoned.

APLINGTON, City; Butler County; Pop. 1,034; Zip Code 50604; 45 miles SSE of Mason City; Lat. 42-35-04 N long. 092-53-01 W.
It was named for Zenas Aplington, the town's first storekeeper.

APPPANOOSE COUNTY, S central Iowa, 448 sq. mi.; Pop. 13,743; Named for Appanoose, an Indian Chief of the Sac and Fox Indian tribes.

ARCADIA, City; Carroll County; Pop. 485; Zip Code 51430; 85 miles WNW of Des Moines; Lat. 42-04-54 N long. 095-02-45 W. Given a pleasant name meaning "ideal countryside."

ARION, City; Crawford County; Pop. 148; Zip Code 51520; 55 miles SE of Sioux City; Lat. 41-56-59 N long. 095-27-35 W.

It was named by N. Richards, a hotel proprietor. It has been almost abandoned since fire destroyed the business section in 1909.

ARLINGTON, City; Fayette County; Pop. 465; Zip Code 50606; 38 miles ENE of Waterloo; Lat. 42-44-18 N long. 091-40-25 W. Named for the area in Virginia.

ARMSTRONG, City; Emmet County; Pop. 1,025; Zip Code 50514; 25 miles NW of Algona; Lat. 43-23-38 N long. 094-29-06 W. Named after an explorer and early settler, it sprang into existence during the construction of the ALbert Lea-Estherville branch of the C.R.I. & P.R.R. The town lies on the East Fork of the Des Moines River.

ARNOLDS PARK, City; Dickinson County; Pop. 953; Zip Code 51331; 80 miles NE of Sioux City; Lat. 43-21-17 N long. 095-07-47 W.

Arnolds Park, now chefly a summer resort, was settled in 1856. Isaac Harriott, W.H. Granger, Carl Granger, and Bertell Snyder, of Red WIng, Minn., and James Mattock of Delaware County, chose the town site between east and West Okoboji lakes. They planned this as one of a series of towns to be platted by the Red Wing Land Site Co. along a proposed mail route which was to connect St. Paul with some point on the Missouri River. Rowland Gardner, his wife, and their four children, including a married daughter and her husband and two infants, arrived from the East and settled a mile from the Mattock and Granger sites. The Gardners were the first victims of the Indian uprising in the spring of 1857.

HISTORICAL PLACES...

Spirit Lake Massacre Log Cabin (Gardner Log Cabin).

ASHTON, City; Osceola County; Pop. 462; Zip Code 51232; 55 miles NNE of Sioux City; Lat. 43-18-57 N long. 095-47-00 W.

ATALISSA, City; Muscatine County; Pop. 357; Zip Code 52720; 25 miles ESE of Iowa City; Lat. 41-34-11 N long. 091-09-51 W; Established in 1848, one source says the name is taken from Thomas Campbell's famous poem, "Gertrude of Wyoming," in which a fictional Oneida chief, Outalissi, is mentioned; another says is was named by William Lundy, who named the village in honor of an Indian woman.

ATKINS, City; Benton County; Pop. 637; Zip Code 52206; 5 miles S of Cedar Rapids; Lat. 41-59-54 N long. 091-51-12 W.

ATLANTIC, City; Cass County Seat; Pop. 7,432; Zip Code 50022; 80 miles SW of Des Moines; Elev. 1,215; Lat. 41-24-08 N long. 095-00-43 W. Named after the Atlantic Ocean. The location was thought to be halfway between the two oceans, and its name was to be either Atlantic or Pacific. A coin was flipped, and Pacific won; but when it was learned that a number of other Middle Western towns already had that name, the decision was reversed.

POINTS OF INTEREST:

• Danish Windmill. 5 miles N of I-80 exit 54 Elk Horn. Built in Denmark (1848).

AUBURN, City; Sac County; Pop. 283; Zip Code 51433; 75 miles NW of Des Moines; Elev. 1,220; Lat. 42-17-09 N long. 094- 52-44 W. Given the name of the village in Oliver Goldsmith's famous poem.

AUDUBON, City; Audubon County Seat; Pop. 2,524; Zip Code 50025; 85 miles W of Des Moines; Elev. 1,373; Lat. 41-43-28 N long. 094-55-47 W; Named for John James Audubon, a famous orinthologist.

AUDUBON COUNTY, W Iowa, 448 sq. mi.; Pop. 7,334; Named for John James Audubon (1785-1851), naturalist and ornithologist.

AURELIA, City; Cherokee County; Pop. 1,034; Zip Code 51005; 50 miles NE of Sioux City; Lat. 42-42-55 N long. 095-26-22 W. Named after Aurelia Blair, daughter of John Blair.

AURORA, City; Buchanan County; Pop. 196; Zip Code 50607; 38 miles ENE of Waterloo; Lat. 42-37-08 N long. 091-43-32 W; The name is latin for "morning" or "dawn."

AVOCA, City; Pottawattamie County; Pop. 1,497; Zip Code 51521; 85 miles W of Des Moines; Lat. 41-16-46 N long. 095-50-10 W. Named for the Avoca River in Ireland.

POINTS OF INTEREST:

● Prairie Rose State Park. 2 miles N via US 59, then 6 miles E on I-68, exit 46, then 3 miles N on paved road.

AYRSHIRE, City; Palo Alto County; Pop. 195; Zip Code 50515; 80 miles W of Mason City; Lat. 43-01-35 N long. 094-49-27 W; Named for the town in Scotland.

BADGER, City; Webster County; Pop. 569; Zip Code 50516; 8 miles N of Fort Dodge; Lat. 42-36-56 N long. 094-09-24 W.

BAGLEY, City; Guthrie County; Pop. 303; Zip Code 50026; 55 miles WNW of Des Moines; Elev. 1,106; Lat. 41-51-24 N long. 094- 26-00 W. The city is named for an early farmer.

BANCROFT, City; Kossuth County; Pop. 857; Zip Code 50517; 54 miles W of Mason City; Lat. 43-17-42 N long. 094-13-19 W. Named in honor of historian, George Bancroft.

BARNUM, City; Webster County; Pop. 174; Zip Code 50518; 15 miles W of Fort Dodge; Lat. 42-30-30 N long. 094-221-04 W. Named after the famous 19th century showman.

BATAVIA, City; Jefferson County; Pop. 520; Zip Code 52533; 12 miles SE of Ottumwa; Lat. 40-59-41 N long. 092-09-46 W. It was first called Greaseville, in honor of one of the town's pioneers; it was later named after the Dutch city.

BATTLE CREEK, City; Ida County; Pop. 818; Zip Code 51006; 45 miles E of Sioux City; Elev. 1,194; Lat. 42-19-05 N long. 095- 36-01 W; Named for a skirmish that took place here in 1849 between a government survey party and Sioux Indians.

BAXTER, City; Jasper County; Pop. 938; Zip Code 50028; 25 miles N of Des Moines; Lat. 41-49-52 N long. 093-09-40 W. Baxter was an early settler.

BAYARD, City; Guthrie County; Pop. 511; Zip Code 50029; 55miles WNW of Des Moines; Elev. 1,135; Lat. 41-51-26 N long. 094-33-40 W.

BEACON, City; Mahaska County; Pop. 509; Zip Code 52534; 45 miles SE of Des Moines; Lat. 41-16-14 N long. 092-40-33 W; Named in honor of Lord Beaconsfield.

BEACONSFIELD, City; Ringgold County; Pop. 27; Zip Code 50030; Lat. 40-48-31 N long. 094-03-22 W; Most likely named for Lord Beaconsfield.

BEAVER, City; Boone County; Pop. 46; Zip Code 50031; Lat. 42-02-09 N long. 094-08-25 W; The Fox Indians called this place Amaqua, meaning "beaver," for the animals in the area. The English translation of the name was kept.

BEDFORD, City; Taylor County Seat; Pop. 1,528; Zip Code 50833; 90 miles SW of Des Moines; Lat. 40-40-22 N long. 094-43-26 W. Named after the city in Massachusetts.

BELLE PLAINE, City; Benton County; Pop. 2,834; Zip Code 52208; 45 miles NNW of Iowa City; Lat. 41-53-52 N long. 092-16-21 W; The name was first known as Gwinsville until 1862, when the post office was established; it was later named after a French name meaning "beautiful plain."

BELLEVUE, City; Jackson County; Pop. 2,239; Zip Code 52031; 70 miles NNE of Iowa City; Lat. 42-15-40 N long. 090-25-50 W; It was first called Bell View, in honor of one of the first settlers, named Bell, who built his home on a bluff overlooking the town site. It is also thought to be named after a French word for "beautiful view."

Here was staged the dramatic episode in early Iowa history known as the Bellevue war. In the later 1830s, the town was the rendezvous of an outlaw gang engaged in horse stealing and other acts of lawlessness. After a number of futile attempts to crush the gang, a posse of 40 men formed a vigilante committee with the purpose of capturing the outlaws. There followed a fierce encounter, in which 4 men on each side were killed and 13 bandits were captured. A vote to decide whether to hang the men or to whip and exile them was taken by dropping beans into a box--white beans for hanging, colored beans for whipping. The majority was three colored beans, and the men were whipped and placed on boats on the Mississippi, with three days' rations, and told not to return to the village.

BELMOND, City; Wright County; Pop. 2,500; Zip Code 50421; 90 miles N of Des Moines; Lat. 42-50-58 N long. 093-36-58 W. The city was named by the young men and women of the settlement in honor of Belle, the attractive daughter of Mr. and Mrs. Dumond.

BENNETT, City; Cedar County; Pop. 395; Zip Code 52721; 48 miles E of Iowa City; Lat. 41-43-48 N long. 090-58-33 W; Named for Chet Bennett, a railroad man.

BENTON COUNTY, E central Iowa, 718 sq. mi.; Pop. 22,429; Named for Thomas Hart Benton (1782-1858), senator from Missouri.

BLACK HAWK COUNTY, NE central Iowa, 568 sq. mi.; Pop. 123,798; Named for Black Hawk, chief of the Sauk and Fox Indian tribes; warrior, and the leader of the Black Hawk War, who was captured at the battle of Bad Axe River in 1832.

BLANCHARD, City; Page County; Pop. 67; Zip Code 51630; 125 miles SW of Des Moines; Lat. 40-35-13 N long. 095-13-28 W; An old French place name. Settlers from France and Canada gave the name Blanchard to many towns in the U. S.

BLOCKTON, City; Taylor County; Pop. 213; Zip Code 50836; 85 miles SW of Des Moines; Lat. 40-37-13 N long. 094-28-50 W. Block was a pioneer.

BLOOMFIELD, City; Davis County Seat; Pop. 2,580; Zip Code 52537; 90 miles SSW of Des Moines; Lat. 40-45-07 N long. 092-25- 15 W. The city's name was chosen at random by the county commissioners.

HISTORICAL PLACES...
Davis County Courthouse.

BLUE GRASS, City; Scott County; Pop. 1,214; Zip Code 52726; 2 miles S of Davenport; Lat. 41-30-25 N long. 090-46-12 W; The city takes its name from a variety of grass that grows in Kentucky.

170

BONAPARTE, City; Van Buren County; Pop. 465; Zip Code 52620; 25 miles W of Fort Madison; Lat. 40-42-51 N long. 091-48- 18 W; Named in honor of Napoleon Bonaparte, first emperor of France, who sold the Louisiana Territory to the United States.

BONDURANT, City; Polk County; Pop. 1,584; Zip Code 50035; 8 miles N of Des Moines; Lat. 41-36-05 N long.. 093-28-41 W; The city was named for A. C. Bondurant.

BOONE, City; Boone County Seat; Pop. 12,392; Zip Code 50036; 50 miles N of Des Moines; Lat. 42-05-22 N long. 093-56-00 W; Named for Captain Nathan Boone of the U.S. Dragoons, who captured the Des Moine Valley above Coon Forks.

         POINTS OF INTEREST:
- Mamie Doud Eisenhower Birthplace. 709 Carroll St.
- Ledges State Park. 6 miles S on IA 164.
- Ski Valley. 3 1/2 miles W on US 30.

BOONE COUNTY, Central Iowa, 573 sq. mi.; Pop. 25,186; Named for Nathan Boone (1782-1863) Dragoon Captain.

BOYDEN, City; Sioux County; Pop. 651; Zip Code 51234; 55 miles NNE of Sioux City; Lat. 43-11-19 N long 096-00-55 W. Originally a C.M. St. P & P. station known as Sheridan in 1878, it was renamed in honor of a local railroad man.

BRANDON, City; Buchanan County; Pop. 320; Zip Code 52210; 25 miles NNW of Cedar Rapids; Lat. 42-18-50 N long. 092-00-03 W.

BRAYTON, City; Audubon County; Pop. 148; Zip Code 50042; 65 miles W of Des Moines; Lat. 41-33-14 N long. 094-55-34 W. The city is named for a civil engineer who surveyed for the railroad here.

BREDA, City; Carroll County; Pop. 467; Zip Code 51436; 65 miles ESE of Sioux City; Lat. 42-10-38 N long. 094-58-40 W.

BREMER COUNTY, NE Iowa, 439 sq. mi.; Pop. 22,813; Named for Frederika Bremer (1801-1865), Swedish traveler and author.

BRIDGEWATER, City; Adair County; Pop. 209; Zip Code 50837; 65 miles WSW of Des Moines; Lat. 41-14-30 N long. 094-40-26 W. Descriptively named.

BRIGHTON, City; Washington County; Pop. 684; Zip Code 52540; 50 miles SW of Iowa City; Lat. 41-10-30 N long. 091-49-13 W; Probably named for Brighton, England.

BRITT, City; Hancock County; Pop. 2,133; Zip Code 50423; 120 miles NW of Des Moines; Lat. 43-05-48 N long. 093-48-21 W. The town is named after a local newspaper editor.

Britt was the home of John Hammill (1875-1936), Lt. Governor of Iowa (1921-25) and Governor for three terms (1925-31).

BROOKLYN, City; Poweshiek County; Pop. 1,439; Zip Code 52211; 60 miles W of Iowa City; Lat. 41-44-14 N long. 092-26-53 W. Named for the city in New York.

BUCHANAN COUNTY, E Iowa, 568 sq. mi.; Pop. 20,844; Named for James Buchanan (1791-1868), fifteenth President of the United States; Senator from Pennsylvania; U.S. Secretary of State in cabinet of President Polk.

BUENA VISTA COUNTY, NW Iowa, 572 sq. mi.; Pop. 19,965; Named for Buena Vista, Mexico, site of General Zachary Taylor's victory.

BUFFALO, City; Scott County; Pop. 1,260; Zip Code 52728; 3 miles S of Davenport; Lat. 41-27-23 N long. 090-43-24. Named for the Bison once found here.

BUFFALO CENTER, City; Winnebago County; Pop. 1,081; Zip Code 50424; 140 miles N of Des Moines; Lat. 43-23-05 N long. 093- 56-14 W. Buffalo dwelled in the area when the settlers first arrived, and this led to the city's name.

BURLINGTON, City; Des Moines County Seat; Pop. 27,208; Zip Code 52601; 65 miles S of Iowa City; Lat. 40-48-58 N long. 091- 06-22 W; Named after the city of Burlington, Vermont.

The region is scattered over four hills along the Mississippi River. The site of Burlington, called Sho-ko-kon (Flint Hills), was valued by the Indians for the flint found there.

Lieutenant Zebulon Pike referred to it when he wrote the story of his expedition (1805) to explore the Mississippi River from St. Louis to its source, in hopes of finding strategic locations for forts and to make friends with the Indians.

Tai-mah (Tama) set up his Indian village (Shokokon) on the site of Burlington in 1820, but later moved his band to Tama Town Prairie, nine miles north. Simpson S. White, Morton McCarver, and Amasa Doolittle were the first permanent settlers. After the Black Hawk treaty was signed in September 1832, the territory on the west side of the river was thrown open to white settlers; effective June 1833, some 10 or 12 families, too impatient to wait longer on the east side of the river, crossed over. Complaints by the Indians, however, forced the soldiers at Fort Armstrong to send them back. They reoccupied their claims in 1833, and in August of that year, Dr. William R. Ross opened the first store.

John Gray, a native of Vermont, arrived in Flint Hills in March 1834; upon purchasing a lot, he was allowed to name the settlement Burlington, after his hometown. The Reverend Peter Cartwright, presiding elder of a large part of Illinois and all of the Iowa country, organized a Methodist class at Dr. Ross's cabin in April; about the same time 16 children attended the first school, taught by Zadock C. Inghram. By the close of the year, Burlington was the chief settlement in Demoine County.

The second Legislature of the Territory of Wisconsin convened at Burlington on the first Monday in November 1837 in the temporary capitol erected to serve until the capitol at Madison was completed. In 1837, the town was incorporated. When the Territory of Iowa was created in 1838, the first Legislative Assembly convened that fall at Burlington, the temporary capital, and appointed a commission to select the permanent capital.

Drums rattled, fifes whistled, and bugles blew in Burlington when the first Iowa militia assembled there to settle the Iowa- Missouri boundary dispute, soon after the first assembly met. Roistering groups of would-be soldiers surged through the streets. Dropping plow handles and axes in the field, they came wearing make-shift uniforms and carrying an odd assortment of weapons. They jostled shoulders in the taverns and hunted excitement along the riverfront. Boisterous hilarity and drunken brawls marked their brief sojourn. Many companies were still en route to Burlington when settlement of the question was delegated to the United States Supreme Court.

On July 3, 1839, the body of Black Hawk, Indian chief, disappeared from its grave on James Jordan's farm near Iowaville. Burlington was aroused from a mid-summer doze when Nasheakusk, Black Hawk's son, with about 50 other Indians, marched through the streets to inform Governor Robert Lucas of what had happened. A year later, the bones were recovered from a dentist in Quincy, Illinois, who had received them from St. Louis. Black Hawk's widow left the bones in the care of the "good old man," Governor Lucas. Later they were placed in the museum of the Burlington Geological and Historical Society, and were lost when the building was burned in 1855.

The murder of John Miller and the subsequent public hanging of William and Stephen Hodges, convicted murderers, was an event in 1845. Thousands jammed the streets to see the condemned men paraded from the jail to the execution hill near the edge of town. Four companies of riflemen, marching to the dirge of a brass band, preceded the conveyance in which the condemned men, shrouded and in chains, sat astraddle their coffins.

In 1855, Dick, the first fugitive slave caught near Burlington, was tried in Marion Hall before a crowd that was determined to see him freed. Iowa had just elected its first anti-slavery Senator, and therefore, joyous shouts were heard when Judge Rorer dismissed the case.

The continual stream of immigrants that entered Iowa at Burlington reached its peak in August 1856, when 20,000 people crossed the Mississippi on the ferry. At that time the bustling town had three pork packing plants important enough to give Burlington the name "Porkopolis of Iowa." Hundreds of steamers docked to discharge freight that the prairie schooners were to carry inland, or to load pork, lard, and farm produce.

Railroads eventually changed Burlington from a lively river town to a bustling railroad center. A jubilant excursion from Chicago to a point opposite Burlington celebrated completion of the second continuous railroad from Chicago to the Mississippi in 1855. The next year, the Burlington & Missouri River Railroad, organized in 1851, began operations in Iowa. Temporarily, Burlington streets were crowded with the rough and hardy railroad workers, but they moved westward as the railroad approached the Missouri.

Marion Hall was crowded with men registering for service at the time of the Civil War, adding other companies to the Rifles, the Blues, the Irish Volunteers, the Washington Guards, and an artillery company already in existence. Camp Warren was established at the fairgrounds. During the war, railroad freight had to be rafted across the river, but a bridge was built in August 1868. The next year, the Chicago, Burlington & Quincy absorbed the Burlington & Missouri River Railroad, which then extended to the Missouri. From that time, river traffic gradually slackened.

In the 1870s, when livestock had become an increasingly important shipment from Omaha to Chicago, extensive stockyards grew up on the east side of the Mississippi, opposite Burlington. Here the bawling, restless cattle were unloaded, bedded, watered, and fed.

The year 1871 marked the peak of prosperity for the lumber industry. Burlington, a lumber shipping point, exported as much as 57,000,000 feet of lumber in a year. Raftsmen bringing the logs down the river from Wisconsin to the mills added, for a time, a lusty note to the growing town. In 1873, a disastrous fire destroyed five solid blocks of the business section, and temporarily held back the town's development. In 1874, after the city had been rebuilt, horse-drawn cars were inaugurated. The horses pulled the cars up the many hills, and then rested on the rear platform of the cars while they traveled downgrade.

In 1875, the city's special charter was abandoned when the municipality was organized under council form. In the period from the end of the Civil War to 1885, Burlington experienced its largest industrial, commercial, and cultural growth.

By 1890, the old-fashioned horse-drawn cars were supplanted by electric cars. Pleasure boats began to increase on the river about 1900, and regattas for speedboats became popular celebrations. In 1909, the city adopted the commission form of government. The last raft of lumber from the north, towed by the steamer *Ottumwa Bell,* with Captain Walter Hunter in charge, passed the city in 1915.

In May 1922, a cloudburst brought the waters from the hills nearby down into the city's center, but the losses suffered were soon replaced. In the last decades of the nineteenth and the first of the twentieth centuries, Burlington developed its manufacturing and jobs--furniture, baskets, coffins, and monuments--until, in 1925, factory output reached a high peak, valued at over $12,000,000.

Robert Jones Burdette (1844-1914) brought attention to the city through his humorous sketches in the *Hawk-Eye,* when he first began to publish them in the 1880s. Two other men associated with the city who received international fame were Charles Wachsmuth and Frank Springer, whose common interest-- collecting fossils--drew them together. In 1897, the two scientists published the results of their study of crinoids in a monumental book.

POINTS OF INTEREST:

- Crapo and Dankwardt Parks. On Great River Road at SE corner of city.
- Mosquito Park. 3rd & Franklin Streets.
- The Apple Trees Historic Museum. 1616 Dill Street in Perkins Park.
- Phelps House. (ca. 1851). 521 Columbia Street.
- Geode State Park. 6 miles W on US 34, then 6 miles W on County J20.

BURT, City; Kossuth County; Pop. 575; Zip Code 50522; 55 miles W of Mason City; Lat. 43-12-05 N long. 094-13-22 W; Called Burt after the President of the Union Pacific Railroad.

BUTLER COUNTY, NE central Iowa, 582 sq. mi.; Pop. 15,731; Named for William Orlando Butler (1791-1880), who was wounded at the Battle of the Thames on Oct. 6, 1813 and imprisoned at Canada. He was aide to Gen. Jackson and a member of the House of Representatives; he received gallantry at Monterey, Mexico.

CALAMUS, City; Clinton County; Pop. 379; Zip Code 52729; 25 miles N of Davenport; Lat. 41-49-33 N long. 090-45-29 W. Named for the wild marsh plant found in the area.

CALHOUN COUNTY, NW central Iowa, 571 sq. mi.; Pop. 11,508; Named for John Caldwell Calhoun (1782-1850), Vice President of the United States under presidents J. Q. Adams and Jackson 1825- 32; Senator from South Carolina; U.S. Secretary of State in Cabinet of President Tyler.

CALMAR, City; Winneshiek County; Pop. 1,026; Zip Code 52132; 110 miles N of Iowa City; Lat. 43-11-34 N long. 091-52-49 W.

CALUMET, City; O'Brien County; Pop. 160; Zip Code 51009; 45 miles NE of Sioux City; Lat. 42-56-49 N long. 095-33-04 W; Calumet was a word used by the French for the Indian peace pipe. A possible reason for the name for the place might be that the Indians obtained pipestone in the area.

CAMANCHE, City; Clinton County; Pop. 4,436; Zip Code 52730; 8 miles S of Clinton; A derivative of Comanche, the name of a Shoshone Indian tribe.

CAMBRIDGE, City; Story County; Pop. 714; Zip Code 50046; 25 miles N of Des Moines; Elev. 2,651; Lat. 41-55-00 N long. 093-30- 23 W. Named for the English University city.

CARBON, City; Adams County; Pop. 60; Zip Code 50839; 80 miles WSW of Des Moines; Lat. 41-02-51 N long. 094-49-28 W; The name may have been given to the place to indicate the presence of coal deposits.

CARROLL, City; Carroll County Seat; Pop. 9,579; Zip Code 51401; 85 miles NNW of Des Moines; Lat. 42-01-19 N long. 094-50- 53 W; Named for Charles Carroll, of Carrollton, Maryland, signer of the Declaration of Independence in 1776.

POINTS OF INTEREST:

- Black Hawk Lake State Park. 23 miles NW on US 71 in Lake View.
- Swan Lake. 3 miles SE.

CARROLL COUNTY, W central Iowa, 574 sq. mi.; Pop. 21,423; Named for Charles Carroll (1737-1832), Continental Commissioner to Canada 1776; signer of Declaration of Independence 1776; Senator from Maryland.

CARSON, City; Pottawattamie County; Pop. 705; Zip Code 51525; 18 miles E of Council Bluffs; Lat. 41-14-06 N long. 095- 25-15 W. Possibly named for explorer, Kit Carson.

CARTER LAKE, City; Pottawattamie County; Pop. 3,200; 90 miles SSE of Sioux City; Lat. 41-17-26 N long. 095-55-04 W.

CASCADE, City; Dubuque & Jones Counties; Pop. 1,812; Zip Code 52033; 40 miles ENE of Cedar Rapids; Lat. 42-17-49 N long. 091-01-01 W. Named for the cascades in the river.

Early settlers of Cascade, predominantly of Irish ancestry (a few of their descendants here still speak Gaelic) migrated from the East and attempted to utilize the natural waterfall here as a source of power. Because the dam they built was small and railroad facilities were inadequate, the town did not become the industrial center its founders planned. The dam is almost beneath the bridge just before the highway enters the town from the east. Following 1849, the influx of Irish and German farmers, who developed the fertile valley into a rich agricultural region, shifted the interest of the community to agrarian rather than to industrial pursuits.

CASS COUNTY, SW Iowa, 559 sq. mi.; Pop. 15,128; Named for Lewis Cass (1782-1866), Brig. General in 1813; U.S. secretary of war in cabinet of President Jackson, 1831-36; Senator from Michigan; Secretary of State in cabinet of President Buchanan.

CEDAR COUNTY, E Iowa, 585 sq. mi.; Pop. 17,381; a descriptive word.

CEDAR FALLS, City; Black Hawk County; Pop. 34,298; Zip Code 50613; 3 miles N of Waterloo; Lat. 42-31-35 N long. 092-25-33 W; Named for its proximity to the Cedar River.

The first settlers here were William Sturgis and his family, who built a cabin on the west side of the Cedar River in the spring of 1845, choosing this site because of the water power available. In 1851, the town was laid out, and in the next 40 years developed into one of the State's important milling centers. When Black Hawk County was organized (1853), Cedar Falls, then the principal town, was made the county seat. Two years later, however, an election moved the seat to Waterloo, which was nearer the center of the county.

In 1861 a railroad (later the Illinois Central) was completed as far west as Cedar Falls but, owing to a lack of funds and the outbreak of the Civil War, it went no farther until 1869. Farmers from a wide area brought stock and grain here for shipment to eastern markets, and the streets were crowded and the business houses so busy that they kept open until late at night. When construction of the railroad was resumed, it was found necessary to shut off the millrace in order to build the piers, but the owners of the gristmills and sawmills that had been running day and night charged the railroad company $300 a day damages. This so enraged the railroad officials that they made Waterloo the division point, and later built shops there, even though land for that purpose had been given to them at Cedar Falls. Local milling began to decline toward the end of the 19th century and, in the early 1900s, was supplanted by the manufacture of rotary pumps, elevator equipment, seed-corn sorting machines, automobile trunks, brooms, and concrete mixers.

POINTS OF INTEREST:

- University of Northern Iowa (1876). College Street between 23rd Street & University Avenue.
- Ice House Museum. First & Franklin Streets.
- Cedar Falls Historical Society Museum. 303 Clay Street.
- George Wyth Memorial State Park. Between Cedar River & US 20.
- Black Hawk Park. 3 miles N on US 218, 1 mile W on Lone Tree Road.

CEDAR RAPIDS, City; Linn County Seat; Pop. 108,751; Zip Code 52400; 30 miles NW of Iowa City; Lat. 41-59-02 N long. 091- 40-02 W; The area is named for the swift rapids in the river at this point. The city is the principal industrial center of east- central Iowa, in the midst of a rich agricultural area. The Cedar River, flowing southeast, divides the city neatly into the east and west sides. Sac and Fox Indians originally called it Mosk-wah-wah-wah or "red cedar"; they hunted and trapped in this region before 1838, the year Osgood Shepherd built his shack on the east side of the river at what is now First Avenue and First Street.

The first survey of the city was made in 1841 by N. B. Brown, George Greene, and others who purchased squatter rights held by Shepherd. These men gave the name of Rapids City to the newly formed town.

Early in the 1840s, a dam was constructed across the Cedar River, which furnished power for the grist and sawmills, already becoming lively industries. Robert Ellis, who settled on the west side of the river, built three flatboats at about the same time and loaded them with 4,000 bushels of wheat for New Orleans, the first outlet for the community's farm products. The first newspaper was established in 1851, and the next year, David W. King laid out the town of Kingston on the west side of the river. At this time the old ferry across the river was replaced by a toll bridge.

In 1858, the citizens of Cedar Rapids launched *The Cedar Rapids,* a steamer built for them at Beaver, Pennsylvania. It made several trips between St. Louis and Cedar Rapids, but a collision on the Mississippi River resulted in the loss of their investment. In June 1858, the railroad reached the city, and river traffic was abandoned.

With the coming of the railroad, interest turned to manufacturing and marketing. In 1870, the town of Kingston was annexed to Cedar Rapids; during the next ten years, the Douglas and Stuart oatmeal mills were established, gas for illumination was installed, streetcars drawn by horses began operations, and a boulevard was opened between Cedar Rapids and Marion, then the county seat. Also in that decade, Henry Ward Beecher spoke to a capacity audience at the Methodist Church, and William H. Seward, Secretary of State under Abraham Lincoln, stopped in the city while on a trip around the world. The following description of the town was credited to him: "Of the towns which have sprung up on the plains, we notice Cedar Rapids. During ten minutes' stay there we saw suburban cottages, with pointed roofs of the Norwegian settlers, surrounded by dark-green meadows, covered with flocks of geese and eider-ducks. We heard airs from *Trovatore* in a Chickering piano, in a dwelling not yet painted or plastered. We saw a Mansard mansion of the speculator in the city lots ... There seem to be all sorts of churches for all sects of Christians--one surmounted with a Catholic cross, and one with a dome and minaret borrowed from a Mohammedan mosque."

On December 27, 1880, Greene's Opera House was dedicated with a performance by the Emma Abbott Opera Company, and in the same year, the Cedar Rapids Business College was established, with Austin Palmer, later noted for his Palmer Method of Penmanship, as one of the teachers.

In the 1890s, churches and schools were rebuilt and enlarged; a new post office was constructed; electric cars were introduced; and the Union Station was built. With the advent of the 20th century, Cedar Rapids had become a prosperous city. In the span of 50 years, it had gone from Indians to automobiles.

Perhaps the most colorful of the city's characters were the Cherry sisters--Effie, Addie, and Jessie--who went on the stage at the turn of the 19th century with an act that was so poor it was good. Because of their performance, the Oscar Hammerstein Theatre in New York was able to pay off its mortgage and the audiences were "laid under the seats." It is said their act was at times presented behind nets to protect the sisters from vegetables, fruit, and other missiles hurled at them. The Cherry sisters, with the exception of their one season in New York, spent their entire lives in Cedar Rapids.

POINTS OF INTEREST:

- Czech Village. On 16th Avenue SW near downtown.
- Five Seasons Center. 370 1st Avenue NE.
- Indian Creek Nature Center. E via Mt. Vernon Road.
- Masonic Library and Grand Lodge Office Building (1955). 813 1st Avenue SE.
- May's Island. In Cedar River, linked to both banks by three bridges.
- Palisades-Kepler State Park. 12 miles SE via County W6E, IA 13, US 30.
- Wapsipinicon State Park. 27 miles NE, off US 151 in Anamosa.

CENTER POINT, City; Linn County; Pop. 1,693; Zip Code 52213; 40 miles N of Iowa City; Lat. 42-11-38 N long. 091-47-03 W.; it was settled in 1839 by Bartimeas McGonigle, and was then known as McGonigle's Point. J.M. Bartleson, who came here from Virginia in 1855, was one of the stage drivers on the mail route established by the Government between Cedar Rapids and Waterloo. Center Point was the half-way station between these cities.

CENTERVILLE, City; Appanoose County Seat; Pop. 5,936; Zip Code 52544; 55 miles SE of Des Moines; Lat. 40-44-08 N long. 092- 52-11 W.

Incorporated in 1855, it is in a coal-producing section, where more than 600,000 tons are mined annually. A 500-foot gypsum bed is also in the vicinity.

In 1846, the village was platted as Chaldea by J. F. Stratton. The residents, however, called the town Sentersville in honor of Governor Senter of Tennessee. When the name was submitted to the General Assembly in January 1847, the legislators changed it to Centerville, believing the original was an error in spelling. Appanoose County, of which Centerville is the seat, was named in honor of Chief Appanoose (a chief when a child).

POINTS OF INTEREST:

- Rathbun Lake. 7 miles NW.
- Sharon Bluffs State Park. 4 miles E on IA2, then S.

HISTORICAL PLACES...

Stringtown House.

CENTRAL CITY, City; Linn County; Pop. 1,063; Zip Code 52214; 40 miles N of Iowa City; Lat. 42-12-37 N long. 091-31-20 W. Descriptively named.

CENTRALIA, City; Dubuque County; Pop. 123; Platted in 1850 and first called Dakotah, the name was later changed to Centralia.

CERRO GORDO COUNTY, N Iowa, 575 sq. mi.; Pop. 46,733; Named for Cerro Gordo, Mexico, site of the battle of April 18, 1847 in the Mexican War.

CHARITON, City; Lucas County Seat; Pop. 4,616; Zip Code 50049; 40 miles S of Des Moines; Lat. 41-01-10 N long. 093-18-18 W. It lies along the banks of the Chariton River. In the description of the Lewis and Clark expedition, the men recorded seeing here two rivers," named by the French "The Two Charatons," a corruption of the the word Thieraton. Lewis designated the river as Charliton on his map of 1806, and Clark as Charaton in 1814. Pioneers believed the name to be of Indian origin, signifying *a country rich with honey.* According to another story, a French Canadian trader in Missouri, Joseph Chartran, sometimes referred to as Charitone, was so closely associated with the river that it was named for him. The town was first called Polk, then Chariton Point, and finally Chariton.

POINTS OF INTEREST:

- Lucas County Historical Society Museum. 123 17th Street & Braden Avenue.
- Red Haw Lake State Park. 1 mile E on US 34.
- Stephens State Forest. 10 miles W on US 34 to Lucas, then 2 miles S on US 65, then W on county road.
- Wayne County Historical Museum. On IA 2, approx. 25 miles S via IA 14 in Corydon.

CHARLES CITY, City; Floyd County Seat; Pop. 7,878; Zip Code 50616; 110 miles NNE of Des Moines; Lat. 43-04-15 N long. 092-40- 44 W.

It was first known as The Ford; there was once a Winnebago Indian village nearby. The name was later changed to Charles City in 1869 in honor of Charles, the son of Joseph Kelly, the town's founder.

POINTS OF INTEREST:

- Floyd County Historical Society Museum. 500 Gilbert Street on US 218 & 18.
- Little Brown Church in the Vale. 12 miles SE on IA 346 in Nashua.

CHARLOTTE, City; Clinton County; Pop. 359; Zip Code 52731; 13 miles NW of Clinton; Lat. 41-57-37 N long. 090-27-54 W. Named for the city in Virginia.

CHARTER OAK, City; Crawford County; Pop. 497; Zip Code 51439; 38 miles SE of Sioux City; Lat. 42-03-50 N long. 095-34-56 W. The town is named after a prominent oak tree.

CHELSEA, City; Tama County; Pop. 336; Zip Code 52215; 25 miles SW of Cedar Rapids; Elev. 792; Lat. 41-54-28 N long. 092- 25-48 W. Named after the city in England.

CHEROKEE, City; Cherokee County Seat; Pop. 6,026; Zip Code 51012; 50 miles NE of Sioux City; Lat. 42-44-28 N long. 095-33-16 W; Named for the Cherokee Indian tribe, which had no historical connection to the region. The first town named Cherokee was in Massachusetts. The name most likely came west with the settlers.

POINTS OF INTEREST:

- Sanford Museum and Planetarium. 117 E Willow Street.
- Sunset Ski Area. 3/4 mile E via IA 3.

HISTORICAL PLACES...

Cherokee Sewer Site; Phipps Site.

CHEROKEE COUNTY, NW Iowa, 573 sq. mi.; Pop. 14,098; Named for the Cherokee Indian tribe, meaning "cave people" in the Chickasaw language.

CHICKASAW COUNTY, NE Iowa, 505 sq. mi.; Pop. 13,295; Named for the Chickasaw Indian tribe.

CHILLICOTHE, City; Wapello County; Pop. 119; Zip Code 52548; 13 miles WNW of Ottumwa; Lat. 41-05-50 N long. 092-32-12 W; Derived from Chi-la-ka-tha, the name of one of the four divisions of the Shawnee Indian tribe.

CHURDAN, City; Greene County; Pop. 423; Zip Code 50050; 64 miles NW of Des Moines; Elev. 1,110; Lat. 42-08-38 N long. 094- 28-37 W.

CINCINNATI, City; Appanoose County; Pop. 363; Zip Code 52549; 37 miles SW of Ottumwa; Lat. 40-37-43 N long. 092-55-24 W. Named after the city in Ohio.

CLARENCE, City; Cedar County; Pop. 936; Zip Code 52216; 30 miles NNW of Davenport; Lat. 41-52-40 N long. 091-02-57 W. Named for a prominent early settler.
It was first called Onion Grove, because of the formerly abundant growth of wild onions in the timber along the banks of nearby Mill Creek. One source claims it was later named for a prominent early settler; another says it was named for Clarence, New York.

CLARKE COUNTY, S Iowa, 429 sq. mi.; Pop. 8,287; Named for James Clarke (1811-1850), third territorial governor of Iowa.

CLARINDA, City; Page County Seat; Pop. 5,104; Zip Code 51632; 100 miles SSW of Des Moines; Lat. 40-47-08 N long. 095-01- 34 W; Named for Clarinda Buck, the niece of the city founder.
POINTS OF INTEREST:
• Lake of Three Fires State Park. 18 miles E on IA 2.
HISTORICAL PLACES...
Hepburn, Col. William Peters, House.

CLARION, City; Wright County Seat; Pop. 2,703; Zip Code 50525; 27 miles NE of Fort Dodge; Lat. 42-43-50 N long. 093-44-03 W; it contains the only county seat in Iowa that is in the exact center of the county. Incorporated in 1881, the town was named for Clarion, Pennsylvania. It is a French word meaning "clear."

CLARKSVILLE, City; Butler County; Pop. 1,382; Zip Code 50619; 100 miles NNW of Iowa City; Lat. 42-47-13 N long. 092-40- 43 W. Named for the city's founder.

CLAY COUNTY, NW Iowa, 570 sq. mi.; Pop. 17,585; Named for Henry Clay Jr. (1807-1847), graduated from the U.S. Military Academy in 1831.

CLAYTON, City; Clayton County; Pop. 41; 85 miles of Iowa City; Lat. 42-54-14 N long. 091-08-50 W; Named in honor of John M. Clayton, Senator from Delaware.

HISTORICAL PLACES...
Clayton School.

CLAYTON COUNTY, NE Iowa, 779 sq. mi.; Pop. 19,054; Named for John Middleton Clayton.

CLEAR LAKE CITY, City; Cerro Gordo County; Pop. 8,183; 120 miles N of Des Moines; Lat. 43-08-17 N long. 093-22-45 W. Descriptively named for its location near the lake. This area was formerly a hunting and fishing ground of the Winnebago and Sioux, and the settlers had many difficulties with them in the early days.

POINTS OF INTEREST:
• Clear Lake. 2 miles S on IA 107.

CLEGHORN, City; Cherokee County; Pop. 275; Zip Code 51014; 33 miles NE of Sioux City; Lat. 42-48-44 N long. 095-42-52 W. Named in honor of a Dr. Cleghorn, who donated land to the town in 1901.

CLINTON, Pop. 29,201 Alt. 593'; The region, an industrial and railroad center, stretches seven miles along the west bank of the Mississippi River at the foot of a ridge of bluffs to the north and of hills to the south.

Elijah Buell, first settler in what is now Clinton, came to the Narrows at Fulton in 1835. He established a ferry across the Mississippi River to accommodate the many people on their way into the new West. Joseph M. Bartlett laid out a town in 1838 where the city now stands, naming it New York. In 1855, the Iowa Land Company, a promotion concern made up of the officers of the Chicago, Iowa & Nebraska Railroad, acquired the site and replatted it, naming it for DeWitt Clinton, one-time governor of the state of New York.

A post office was established in 1856 and, in the same year, the Randall Hotel was built. A spacious brick building, with marble mantels and hot and cold water, it had a five-story brick outside toilet, accessible from all floors, a marvel of convenience in those early days. The hotel was dubbed Randall's Folly by the skeptical who did not have faith in the city's growth. But where once had been swampland and slough, a city came into being. On the banks of a slough, where the courthouse now stands, was a boat-building factory. The finished boats were floated through a canal, crossing the main thoroughfare to the river.

Clinton was incorporated as a city in 1859. In 1864, striking railroad workers dumped the running gear of the freight cars into the Mississippi River, where they are said to remain. In those early days, streetcars were drawn by mules. Many of the wooden sidewalks were built on stilts, and frequently floated down the river during high water.

In 1878, the town of Ringwood was annexed to Clinton. The city's rapid growth followed the establishment of the sawmills, reaching the peak of production in the early 1880s, when Clinton was recognized as the largest lumber-producing city in the world, with five mills from Lyons on the north to Chancy on the south. In summer, an average of 40 to 50 steamboats passed daily up and down the river, and hundreds of log rafts were floated down from the north in the spring. Workers in the mills were mainly Irish, who came here in the days of famine in Ireland.

One of the biggest problems of the mills was the disposal of sawdust. The entire north end of Lyons, for two and half blocks west from the river, is still underlaid with sawdust to a depth of 20 feet or more. Sloughs and streams were filled in with it, and large portions of the city were built on sawdust bottoms. If exposed to air, spontaneous combustion starts smoldering fires in the buried sawdust, which sometimes takes days to extinguish.

The city in these days grew so fast that new papers of incorporation were taken out in 1881. In the 1890s, both Chancy and Lyons were annexed to the growing city. The interests of the people within the lumber industry were transferred to railroading with the last log raft arriving from the north in 1906; from then on, the city turned its attention to manufacturing, trading, and retailing.

Most of the business structures were built in the first two decades of the twentieth century, and public improvements were developed along with them. However, the city's development was not without labor troubles. In 1919, a strike in a local factory resulted in the death of one of the strikers; and in 1922, strikes on the North Western Railroad led machinists and clerks to walk out for six weeks, until a satisfactory agreement was reached.

Lillian Russell, the girl who first made the beauty of American woman internationally famous, was born in Clinton in 1861. Her home, the newspaper office where her father worked, and the Davis Opera House where she first made a stage appearance, have all been torn down.

CLINTON COUNTY, E Iowa, 693 sq. mi.; Pop. 51,040; Named for DeWitt Clinton (1769-1828), New York Senator and Governor; Mayor of New York City.

COLFAX, City; Jasper County; Pop. 2,462; Zip Code 50054; 8 miles N of Des Moines; Lat. 41-40-49 N long. 093-15-30 W. Named in honor of U.S. Vice President, Schuyler Colfax.

COLLINS, City; Story County; Pop. 455; Zip Code 50055; 20 miles N of Des Moines; Lat. 41-55-06 N long. 093-17-54 W.

COLO, City; Story County; Pop. 771; Zip Code 50056; Lat. 42-01-25 N long. 093-18-54 W. Railroad official John Blair remembered his favorite dog by naming the town after it.

COLUMBUS JUNCTION, City; Louisa County; Pop. 1,616; Zip Code 52738; 28 miles SSE of Iowa City; Lat. 41-16-48 N long. 091- 21-38 W. Named for the discoverer of America.

HISTORICAL PLACES...
Community Building.

CONRAD, City; Grundy County; Pop. 964; Zip Code 50621; 60 miles NE of Des Moines; Lat. 42-13-04 N long. 092-52-23 W. Named for a pioneer.

COON RAPIDS, City; Carroll County; Pop. 1,266; Zip Code 50058; 80 miles NNW of Des Moines; Lat. 41-52-24 N long.

094-41- 00 W; Named for nearby Coon Branch. The word coon is a colloquial abbreviation of racoon.

CORALVILLE, City; Johnson County; Pop. 10,347; 2 miles NE of Iowa City; Lat. 41-40-35 N long. 091-34-49 W; Named for the coral formation underlying the town.

HISTORICAL PLACES...

Coralville Public School.

CORNING, City; Adams County Seat; Pop. 1,806; Zip Code 50841; 90 miles SSW of Des Moines; Lat. 40-59-15 N long. 094-44- 26 W; The city took its name from famous merchant, Erastus Corning.

CORRECTIONVILLE, City; Woodbury County; Pop. 897; Zip Code 51016; 35 miles E of Sioux City; Lat. 42-28-34 N long. 095-47-41 W; So named because it was situated on a surveying correction line.

CORWITH, City; Hancock County; Pop. 354; Zip Code 50430; 42 miles WSW of Mason City; Lat. 42-59-52 N long. 093-57-41 W.

CORYDON, City; Wayne County Seat; Pop. 1,675; Zip Code 50060; 55 miles S of Des Moines; Lat. 40-45-34 N long. 093-19-24 W. Originally called Springfield, later named after the English city.

COUNCIL BLUFFS, City; Pottawattamie County Seat; Pop. 54,315; Zip Code 51501; 130 miles WSW of Des Moines; Elev. 986; Lat. 41-09-10 N long. 095-35-59 W; Native Americans first met along the river bluffs in this region to sell their furs to French traders; the explorers, Lewis and Clark, camped near the 2site in 1804. Itinerant traders and trappers, moving through the territory, later designated the whole bluff territory along this part of the Missouri as Council Bluffs.

Council Bluffs was early known as Hart's Bluff, named for a white man of unknown origin who, legend says, traded at this point before 1824. Francis Guittar settled at this point permanently in 1827 when he was appointed agent of the Hart's Bluff Post of the American Fur Company.

In 1937, the Potawatami Indians were moved into the region, and Federal troops were established in a temporary camp to protect them from other tribes. Other than Davis Hardin, a farming instructor provided by the Government in 1836, the Indians had no teacher until Father Pierre Jean DeSmet arrived in 1838. For the three years the mission was conducted, Father DeSmet used the camp block house as a church.

On June 14, 1846, the first Mormons arrived, and changed the name of the settlement first to Miller's Hollow, and then to Kanesville for Thomas L. Kane, an Army officer who was friendly to them. Kanesville, an unorganized section of Indian country, was ruled by Orson Hyde, priest, writer, editor, lawyer, and chief of the church's quorum of 18 apostles. Everything was controlled by the church, which did not tolerate idleness and dissipation. Wishing to participate in the Congressional election of 1848, Hyde and a group of Mormons applied at Albia for a township government and an election precinct. The candidates for Representative, knowing that the Mormon vote would decide the election, showered Kanesville with gifts. Controversy over the Mormon vote, however, made a second election necessary.

During the California Gold Rush in 1849, Kanesville, directly in the line of travel, was a stopping place where travelers rested and prepared for the long trip to the West Coast. Gamblers, traders, thieves, and desperadoes flocked to the town to prey on the gold-crazy throng. Vigilance committees, organized by the citizens, decided more than one trial by lynching.

In 1850, the number of Mormons in the vicinity reached 7,828. But in 1852, Brigham Young called all the faithful to join him in Utah. Selling farms, stores, and cabins, often at great sacrifice, most of the Mormons departed for Salt Lake City. After Orson Hyde and his high council left Kanesville in the spring of 1852, the town was without government. Later, the 1,000 people remaining in the town reorganized and renamed the community Council Bluffs. In 1853, the State legislature provided a government for the newly-named town, and it was incorporated the same year.

In 1852, Grenville M. Dodge came to Council Bluffs and surveyed the Platte River Valley for a railroad that is now part of the Rock Island system. In 1859, while Dodge was at the old Pacific House in Council Bluffs, he talked with a young lawyer, Abraham Lincoln, about railroads, telling him under a barrage of questions a good deal more than he had intended. It is said that Lincoln's visit to Council Bluffs and his chat with Dodge, influenced him, as President of the United States, in selecting this city as the eastern terminus of the Union Pacific in 1863. General Dodge returned from the Civil War in 1866, and was appointed chief engineer of the Union Pacific Railroad. By 1870, five railroads made connections with the Union Pacific at Council Bluffs.

OTHER FACTS ABOUT COUNCIL BLUFFS

Population in 1990: 54,315
Black population in 1990: 0.8 percent
Hispanic population in 1990: 2.42 percent
Persons with college education: 8.7 percent
Per capita income: $9,943
January mean temperature: 20.2 degrees Fahrenheit
July mean temperature: 77.7 degrees Fahrenheit
Annual precipitation: 30.3 inches

POINTS OF INTEREST:

- Golden Spike. 21st & 9th Aves (1939).
- Historic General Dodge House (1869). 605 3rd Street.
- Historic Potawattomie County Jail (1885). 226 Pearl Street.
- Lake Manawa State Park. 1 mile S on IA 192.
- Lewis and Clark Monument. Rainbow Drive.
- Lincoln Monument. Lafayette & Oakland Aves.
- Ruth Ann Doge Memorial. N 2nd & Lafayette Aves.

HISTORICAL PLACES...

Dodge, Grenville M., House; Pottawattamie County Jail.

CRAWFORD COUNTY, W Iowa, 716 sq. mi.; Pop. 16,775; Named for William Harris Crawford (1772-1834), Senator from Georgia; president pro tempore of the Senate 1812; U.S. Secretary of War in Cabinet of President and Secretary of the Treasury; Georgia Circuit judge.

CRESCENT, City; Pottawattamie County; Pop. 113; Zip Code 51526; 12 miles N of Council Bluffs; Lat. 41-22-04 N long. 095- 51-25 W. Descriptively named for the bluffs rising above the town.

It was formerly known as Crescent City. First settled by Mormons, Crescent was laid out in 1856. A prosperous future was anticipated, especially if a bridge should be constructed across the Missouri River at that point. The panic of 1857 put an end to this plan.

CRESCO, City; Howard County Seat; Pop. 3,669; Zip Code 52136; 120 miles N of Iowa City; Lat. 43-22-23 N long. 092-07-30 W; The name was derived from latin and means "it grows."

POINTS OF INTEREST:

● Green Valley State Park. 2 1/2 miles N off IA 25.

CRESTON, City; Union County Seat; Pop. 7,911; Zip Code 50801; 70 miles SW of Des Moines; Lat. 41-03-24 N long. 094-22-01 W; So named because it was located on a crest, the highest point on the Chicago, Burlington and Quincy Railroad line.

HISTORICAL PLACES...

Creston Railroad Depot.

CRYSTAL LAKE, City; Hancock County; Pop. 266; Zip Code 50432; 28 miles WNW of Mason City; Lat. 43-13-25 N long. 093-47- 43 W. Named after the nearby lake.

CUMBERLAND, City; Cass County; Pop. 295; Zip Code 50843; 50 miles E of Council Bluffs; Lat. 41-16-11 N long. 094-53-05 W.

CUSHING, City; Woodbury County; Pop. 220; Zip Code 51018; 30 miles E of Sioux City; Elev. 1,327; Lat. 42-27-53 N long. 095- 41-34 W.

CYLINDER, City; Palo Alto County; Pop. 112; Zip Code 50528; 68 miles E of Mason City; Lat. 43-04-39 N long. 094-34-05 W. The city is named after nearby Cylinder Creek, which was so dubbed because, when pioneers were trying to ferry a heavy machine across the creek, a cylinder from it became detached and was lost in the water.

DAKOTA CITY, City; Humboldt County Seat; Pop. 1,024; Zip Code 50529; 12 miles N of Fort Dodge; Lat. 42-43-34 N long. 094- 12-12 W; Named in 1855 by Edward McKnight. The word "Dakota" came from the name of the alliance of the Plains Indians.

DALLAS, City; Marion County; Pop. 451; Zip Code 50062; Lat. 41-13-56 N long. 093-14-33 W; The city was named for George M. Dallas, Vice-President of the United States.

DALLAS CENTER, City; Dallas County; Pop. 1,454; Zip Code 50063; Elev. 1,072; 25 miles W of Des Moines; Lat. 41-41-21 N long. 093-58-00 W. It was so named because early residents hoped that the seat of Dallas County would be established here.

DALLAS COUNTY, S central Iowa, 597 sq. mi.; Pop. 29,755; Named for George Mifflin Dallas, who was a Senator from Pennsylvania and Vice President of the United States under Polk.

DANBURY, City; Woodbury County; Pop. 430; Zip Code 51019; 39 miles ESE of Sioux City; Lat. 42-14-01 N long. 095-44-14 W; Probably named for the town of Danbury in Essex, England.

DANVILLE, City; Des Moines County; Pop. 926; Zip Code 52623; 8 miles N of Burlington; Lat. 40-51-40 N long. 091-18-19 W. Named for a local settler.

DAVENPORT, City; Scott County Seat; Pop. 95,333; Zip Code 52800; 8 miles WNW of Rock Island; Lat. 41-34-20 N long. 090-35- 26 W; The area is the third largest city in Iowa and stretches along the Mississippi River for nearly five miles, where the river widens to form Lake Davenport. The site of Davenport, important in the development of the territory beyond the Mississippi River, was a trading center of the American Fur Company, and a battleground of the War of 1812. Fort Armstrong, established on Rock Island in 1816, brought to the vicinity two men who were to influence the growth of the future city--Colonel George Davenport, for whom the city was named, and Antoine LeClaire, one of its pioneer founders. Colonel Davenport, an Englishman who had served in the United States Army, came to Fort Armstrong with the first troops to oversee the Army store. Becoming interested in the rich fur trade, he established a post of his own, and from this time, the Davenport area was a trading center. Antoine LeClaire, part French and part Indian, reared around trading posts at Milwaukee and Peoria, and later educated, was highly valued because he spoke French, Spanish, and English, as well as several Indian dialects.

General Winfield Scott (for whom the county was named) and John Reynolds, with Chiefs Keokuk and Wapello of the Sac and Fox tribes, negotiated a treaty here in 1832. LeClaire acted as interpreter. At the request of the tribes, the United States Government gave to LeClaire the section of land opposite Rock Island, and one section of land at the head of the first rapids above Rock Island, the site where the treaty was made. LeClaire's first Iowa home, built near this spot, was in fulfillment of his promise to Keokuk. LeClaire later acquired the land adjoining his reserve on the west and sold it, with the exception of an eighth interest, to Colonel Davenport and six other men. On this tract, Davenport was founded in 1836.

During the 1837-38 term of the Wisconsin Territorial Legislature, when Scott County was organized, there was a brisk fight between Davenport and Rockingham, now a part of Davenport, for county seat honors; three elections were held before the matter was finally settled in favor of Davenport. The city received its first charter in 1839 and its second in 1843. From 1850 to 1860, the population rose from 1,848 to 11,267, owing in large measure to German and other European immigrants who came to the United States to escape political difficulties abroad. The Germans organized their *turnmvereins* and singing societies, one of the first in Davenport being a *maennerchor,* organized in 1851.

Davenport was the first city in Iowa to have railroad service, and it was at this point that the first train crossed the Mississippi in 1856. The Mississippi and Missouri Railroad Company began construction of the road from Davenport to Council Bluffs in 1853. On August 25, 1855, the first passenger train to leave the city was drawn by a locomotive that had been ferried across the Mississippi. This road, completed to Iowa City by January 1, 1856, was not extended farther for several years. Almost at once the city was aroused to the possibilities of a bridge that would link the railroads on either side (later consolidated as the Chicago & Rock Island Railway). The Mississippi River Bridge Company, organized in 1853 to build a bridge at Davenport, began work in 1854 but encountered opposition. Rivermen and steamboat owners considered the river "a navigable waterway consecrated by nature" for their use alone. The steamboat men carried their fight to court to prevent the bridge's construction, but it was rushed to completion in April of 1856.

Events leading to the Civil War touched Davenport through two well-known men--Dred Scott and John Brown. Dred Scott, a slave, based his famous fight for freedom upon his residence in Davenport with his master, Dr. John Emerson, for whom he occupied a preemption shack. John Brown, the famed abolitionist, celebrated the 4th of July, 1857, in Davenport, buying supplies for the trip to Kansas that preceded the Harper's Ferry episode, which culminated in his arrest. At another time, he concealed a band of runaway slaves in a railroad boxcar as he took them through Davenport enroute to Chicago, then Canada and freedom.

During the Civil War, there were several camps in the vicinity of Davenport. Among the more important was Camp McClellan, where Sioux Indians who took part in the massacre of 1862 in Minnesota were imprisoned. Another was Camp Roberts, later Camp Kinsman, converted after the war into the Iowa Soldiers' Orphans' Home. Governor Samuel J. Kirkwood and his military staff had their headquarters in the city, for telegraph facilities terminated in Davenport at the opening of the war, thus giving the town an important position in relaying the news.

The river traffic of the 1860s, 1870s and 1880s added romance and color to life in Davenport, and gave it activities missing in inland towns. The city was an important port for boats plying between St. Paul and New Orleans.

During the 1880s, excellent limestone quarries were developed, making possible the establishment of the cement business, now a leading industry. The principal plants, fabricating steel and iron, were also started about this time. In 1888, the city developed the second electric trolley in the United States. By the 1890s, the immigration of Germans, which had been continuous for almost 40 years, came to a close. During World War I, more than 18,000 individuals were employed in the Rock Island arsenal just opposite Davenport.

Manufacturing in the city has ranged from pearl buttons to ready-made houses. Chiefly a sawmill town and exporter of raw foodstuffs in its earlier days, Davenport now manufactures cement, cigars, beer, foundry products, pumps, steel wheels, washing machines, men's clothing, wooden sole shoes, meat products, and wool products.

Davenport's third charter, adopted in 1851 and since amended, is still in use. This charter makes it possible for the city to secure, indirectly, special legislation to fit the particular needs of the city. Several times, the charter privileges have facilitated such local civic actions as the levee improvement commission and park board. No State law concerning municipal government affects Davenport unless it specifically mentions charter cities.

OTHER FACTS ABOUT DAVENPORT

Population in 1990: 95,333
Black population in 1990: 7.89 percent
Hispanic population in 1990: 3.46 percent
Persons with college education: 18.2 percent
Per capita income: $11,702
January mean temperature: 20.6 degrees Fahrenheit
July mean temperature: 75.8 degrees Fahrenheit
Annual precipitation: 33.7 inches

POINTS OF INTEREST:
- Museum-Art Center.
- Fejervary Park Zoo. W 12th Street a& Wilkes Avenue.
- Vander Veer Park. Lombard & Main Streets.
- West Lake Park. 4 miles S via US 61.

HISTORICAL PLACES...
Frick's Tavern; LeClair, Antoine, House; Schick Apartments; Trinity Episcopal Church.

DAVIS COUNTY, SE Iowa, 509 sq. mi.; Pop. 8,312; Named for Garrett Davis (1801-1872), Senator from Kentucky.

DAWSON, City; Dallas County; Pop. 174; Zip Code 50066; 45 miles WNW of Des Moines; Elev. 948; Lat. 41-50-12 N long. 094-13- 05 W.

DAYTON, City; Webster County; Pop. 818; Zip Code 50530; 20 miles SSE of Fort Dodge; Lat. 42-15-48 N long. 094-05-24 W. Named after the city in Ohio.

DECATUR CITY, City; Decatur County; Pop. 177; Zip Code 50067; 60 miles S of Des Moines; Lat. 40-45-21 N long. 093-49-12 W; Named in honor of Commodore Stephen Decatur.

DECATUR COUNTY, S Iowa, 530 sq. mi.; Pop. 8,338; Named for Stephen Decatur (1779-1820), who commanded the Schooner *Enterprise* in the Tripolitan War and U.S. in War of 1812.

DECORAH, City; Winneshiek County Seat; Pop. 8,063; Zip Code 52101; 52 miles NNE of Waterloo; Lat. 43-18-57 N long. 091-48-15 W; The name came from a noted Winnebago Indian, born in 1729, who was the son of Hopoekaw (a Winnebago woman) and a French officer, Sabrevoir de Carrie; the last name was corrupted to Decorah. Another variation to its naming is it was named for Chief Waukon Decorah (Indian, Waa-kaun-see-kaa, *the rattlesnake*), who aided the white men during the Black Hawk War. Waukon was the council chief and orator of his tribe.

POINTS OF INTEREST:

- Antonin Dvorak Memorial. In Spillville.
- Bily Clocks. 9 miles S on US 52, then 4 miles W on IA 325 in Spillville.
- Decorah Campgrounds. On US 52, 1 mile N of jct IA 9, exit Will Baker Park.
- Fort Atkinson State Preserve. 16 miles SW via US 52, IA 24.
- Nor-Ski-Runs. On US 52, 1 1/2 miles North of jct IA 9.
- St. Anthony of Padua Chapel. 17 miles S on IA 150 to Festina, then 2 miles SW on gravel road.
- Upper Iowa River.
- Vesterheim, the Norwegian-American Museum. 520 W Water Street.

HISTORICAL PLACES...

Painter-Bernatz Mill.

DEDHAM, City; Carroll County; Pop. 264; Zip Code 51440; 60 miles NE of Council Bluffs; Lat. 41-54-30 N long. 094-49-33 W.

DEEP RIVER, City; Poweshiek County; Pop. 345; Zip Code 52222; 32 miles SW of Cedar Rapids; Lat. 41-35-41 N long. 092-22- 51 W; Named after a nearby creek.

DEFIANCE, City; Shelby County; Pop. 312; Zip Code 51527; 45 miles NNe of Councl Bluffs; Elev. 1,283; Lat. 41-49-32 N long. 095-20-50 W.

DELAWARE, City; Delaware County; Pop. 176; Zip Code 52036; 40 miles W of Dubuque; Lat. 42-28-43 N long. 091-21-05 W; Named for Lord de la Narr, Governor and first Captain-General of Virginia.

DELAWARE COUNTY, E Iowa, 572 sq. mi.; Pop. 18,035; Named in appreciation of the services of Senator John Middleton Clayton of Delaware.

DELHI, City; Delaware County; Pop. 485; Zip Code 52223; 40 miles W of Dubuque; Lat. 42-25-44 N long. 091-20-16 W; Probably named for the city in India.

DELTA, City; Keokuk County; Pop. 409; Zip Code 52550; 19 miles N of Ottumwa; Lat. 41-19-18 N long. 092-19-47 W. Descriptively named.

HISTORICAL PLACES...
Delta Covered Bridge.

DENISON, City; Crawford County Seat; Pop. 6,604; Zip Code 51442; 55 miles NNE of Council Bluffs; Lat. 42-00-51 N long. 095- 20-04 W. The town is named after Baptist minister, J.W. Denison.

POINTS OF INTEREST:
• Yellow Smoke Park. RRi, 1 mile NE on US 30.

DENVER, City; Bremer County; Pop. 1,600; Zip Code 50622; 13 miles NNE of Waterloo; Lat. 42-40-30 N long. 092-20-07 W. It was originally called Jefferson City. After establishment of the Star Mail Route, a service provided persons who carried mail between towns having no Federal service, the town was called Breckenridge. The name was then changed to Denver, the city in Colorado.

DES MOINES, City; Polk County Seat; Pop. 193,187; Zip Code 50053; 32 miles NNW of Ames; Lat. 41-36-25 N long. 093-43-15 W; The city is the capital of Iowa, and is an important commercial center lying in the midst of a leading agricultural area. The gently rolling land of central Iowa is broken here by the Des Moines River that flows south through the city, and the Raccoon that winds east to empty into the Des Moines.

The name Des Moines is probably traceable to the mound builders who long ago lived near the banks of the rivers. The Indians called the main stream *Moingona* (River of the Mounds). French voyageurs, who followed Marquette and Joliet into the Midwest, called it *La Riviere des Moines,* from the monks who once dwelt in huts beside the water. It was spelled phonetically *De Moin, De Moyen, Demoine,* and *Des Moines.* The term, *De Moyen,* translated at "middle," was understood to refer to the principal river between the Mississippi and the Missouri. Another variation in the meaning is "the less" or "the smaller," referring to a small tribe of Indians living on the river.

The Raccoon Ford of the Des Moines River received official mention in December of 1834, when John Dougherty, Indian agent at Fort Leavenworth, wrote the War Department recommending a chain of military posts to protect the Indians as "untutored children." The territory was explored in the summer of 1835, when Colonel Stephen W. Kearny, with 150 men and officers, among them Lieutenant Albert M. Lea, studied the advantages of the site as a possible garrison.

In July, 1841, John C. Fremont was ordered west by the War Department to survey the Des Moines River, from the Raccoon Forks to its mouth, in order to complete Jean Nicholas Vicollel's map of the territory. He determined the astronomical position of Raccoon Forks, estimated the fall of the river, studied the flora of the valley, and returned to Washington in October.

The proposed military garrison was established in May 1843, when Captain James Allen and his company of First Dragoons arrived by the steamer *Ione* from Fort Sanford with another company from Fort Crawford. Captain Allen proposed to name the site Fort Raccoon, but this was vetoed by the War Department as being "shocking--at least in very bad taste," and Captain Allen was directed to use the name Fort Des Moines until further notice.

Wilson Alexander Scott, familiarly known as "Aleck," had preceded Captain Allen and his men by some months. When the fort was established, he obtained a permit to settle nearby and raise corn and hay for the garrison. At midnight, October 11, 1845, after the Sac and Fox had relinquished their rights, the territory was thrown open to white settlers. When the cannon at the fort boomed out the zero hour, settlers rushed in to take the land, setting fire to the deserted Indian tipis and staking out their claims. Captain Allen and his men occupied the fort until March 10, 1846, and in the same month, "Aleck" Scott purchased 500 acres of land on the east side of the Des Moines River. During the next year, he operated the first ferry, and later built the first bridge across the river at this point.

Fort Des Moines, after some dissension among rival settlements, was chosen to be the seat of Polk County. The first newspaper, *The Star,* appeared in the summer of 1849 under the editorship of Barlow Granger. The fort, situated on one of the main immigrant trails to California, was the stopping place of hundreds of gold seekers. Their contagious enthusiasm led many of the settlers to forsake their newly-acquired prairie homesteads and seek fortunes on the coast; but *The Star,* on May 1, 1851, noted another side to the picture: "Most of those who come from the east this year, remain here, satisfied that they can find no better country by going farther west."

The word Fort was dropped with the adoption of a city charter in 1857. The city officially assumed its role as State capital in January of 1858, after ten yoke of oxen had hauled into town two bobsleds of archives from Iowa City. During the growth and development of the city through the 1850s, the Des Moines River was a consequential, if precarious, waterway. One day in April 1859, five steamboats dropped anchor and loaded or discharged cargoes at the landing but, after the railroads entered, river traffic declined.

News of the outbreak of the Civil War aroused varied emotions in Des Moines. Stilson Hutchins, editor of the *State Journal,* Des Moines, wrote an editorial attacking the policy of coercion adopted by President Lincoln. At that time, mails were slow and uncertain, for there were no railroads. The "pony express" carried newspapers (The Burlington *Hawkeye*) from Eddyville to Des Moines in eight hours; letters from Keokuk reached the capital in from three to five days. When letters arrived in the city bringing news from Charleston, local patriots talked seriously of violence against the editor. Marcellus M. Crocker (later commended by General Grant as a leader "fit to command an independent army") presided at a mass-meeting when he asked for volunteers to accompany him to the front. One hundred responded immediately. On May 4, 1861, the "Capital Guards" started for Keokuk to be mustered in. Other units were formed from time to time, and a recruiting station was maintained on Capital Square.

"Copperheads" (Southern sympathizers) contended fiercely for control of the Democratic Party in Iowa. Henry Clay Dean, a leader of this group, held secret meetings nightly at the Demoine House, plotting to put every possible obstacle in the way of both State and national governments. One winter day, a large crowd assembled at the Methodist Church where Dean was scheduled to speak. The stovepipe functioned improperly and, as suffocating smoke thickened the air, the audience departed in a near panic. Frank Palmer of the *Register* commented, "Carnal-minded people might not regard this as a judgment, but we do."

Des Moines soldiers saw action at Fort Donelson, Pea Ridge, Shiloh, and Corinth. Crocker was made a brigadier general for "the masterly handling" of his troops in the two latter battles. Early in June 1862, casualties from the battle of Pittsburg Landing began to arrive in Des Moines. Women of the city encouraged enlistments and patriotic activities. When in May 1864, Governor Stone called for 100-day recruits, 41 married women signed a petition asking to take the places of business and working men to enable them to go to the front. Then 46 unmarried women made a similar offer, adding that the pay of the men should be continued. Recruits were found, however, without the aid of such stimulation.

Toward the end of the war, local citizens labored to expedite the extension of the Des Moines Valley Railroad to Des Moines. The company asked for stock subscriptions amounting to $100,000, and $33,000 was promptly raised. The first cars of this line ran into Des Moines on August 29, 1866.

Railroad passes were issued in 1870 to all Iowa veterans of the Civil War, to enable them to attend the Grand Reunion in Des Moines on August 31 of that year. Thirty thousand former soldiers were present. General William T. Sherman and General W. W. Belknap, Secretary of War, were guests of honor. The two generals again visited the city on September 9, 1875, when President Grant appeared to address the Ninth Annual Reunion of the Army of the Tennessee. Grant's speech before this gathering was considered epoch-making. He urged the Free School and "all needful guarantees for the more perfect security of free thought, free speech, a free press, pure morals, unfettered religious sentiment and of equal rights and privileges to all men irrespective of nationality, color or religion."

Late in April and early May 1894, "Kelly's Army" of nearly 1,000 unemployed men who were marching from Omaha to Washington to plead their cause in Congress, descended upon the city. The citizens of the community, anxious not to anger this formidable and determined throng, received them hospitably, providing ample meals and lodging. Crowds turned out to watch the parade, when Charles T. Kelly, "King of the Commons," rode a dark bay horse through the streets at the head of his men. But rain spoiled the reception and, continuing, tempted the visitors to linger in their dry and comfortable quarters. They refused to move on unless transportation was provided. Des Moines authorities feared the army might remain indefinitely, and were wondering how to meet the situation, when their attention was attracted by the rapidly swelling river. "It would float an army!" remarked someone, "Or a navy!" said another.

"General" Kelly and his men, invited to sail down the Des Moines River toward Keokuk on the next lap of their journey, set to work under the direction of the local carpenters' union and built 150 flatboats. Townspeople willingly contributed money to buy lumber. The boats were finished on May 9, and the "industrial fleet" got under way and started downstream. Each man was provided with a small American flag that he waved in salute; Des Moines's last sight of the adventurers was through a flurry of red, white and blue as the boats slipped around the bend of the river. Among the "sailors" was the writer, Jack London, who some years later referred to his experiences in Des Moines.

During the war with Spain (1898-99), the Fair Grounds, deeded to the State on June 26, 1885, were pressed into service for mobilization of the National Guard. Four regiments, the 49th, 50th, 51st, and 52nd Infantries, gathered there at Camp McKinley. Many Des Moines men enlisted in the 51st Infantry, and altogether 5,859 Iowans were mustered in or trained at the camp.

The city again gained military significance November 13, 1903, when the cavalry post, Fort Des Moines, was dedicated. Urged by Congressman John A. T. Hull, the 56th Congress passed a bill appropriating $219,000 for the establishment of the post, after a group of citizens had subscribed $40,000 toward the purchase of a 400-acre site. Troops from six other forts--Omaha, Crooks, Riley, Russell, Meade and Crawford--joined Fort Des Moines soldiers in

"The Great Tournament" in June of 1909. Infantry, cavalry, artillery, and other branches of the service competed for medals and corps area honors. President William Howard Taft reviewed the various units as they paraded in the finale of the five-day event, and presented the awards.

OTHER FACTS ABOUT DES MOINES

Population in 1990: 193,187
Black population in 1990: 7.11 percent
Hispanic population in 1990: 2.4 percent
Persons with college education: 16.6 percent
Per capita income: $11,616
January mean temperature: 18.6 degrees Fahrenheit
July mean temperature: 76.3 degrees Fahrenheit
Annual precipitation: 30.8 inches

POINTS OF INTEREST:

- Adventureland Park. NE on US 65 at jct. I-80.
- Botanical Center. 909 E River Drive.
- Civic Center. 221 Walnut.
- Des Moines Art Center. 4800 Grand Avenue, in Greenwood Park.
- Des Moines Center of Science and Industry. 4500 Grand Avenue, in Greenwood Park.
- Des Moines Zoo. 7401 SW 9th Street.
- Drake University (1881). University Avenue & 25th Street.
- Heritage Village. State fairgrounds, 4 miles E off I-80.
- Hoyt Sherman Place. 1501 Woodland Avenue (1877).
- Living History Farms. W via I-35, I-80, exit 125, to Hickman Rd.
- Polk County Heritage Gallery. 1st & Walnut Street.
- Salisbury House. 4025 Tonawanda Drive.
- State Capitol (1871). E 9th Street & Grand Avenue.
- Terrace Hill. 2300 Grand Avenue.

HISTORICAL PLACES...

Flynn Farm, Mansion, and Barn; Fort Des Moines Provisional Army Officer Training School; Iowa State Historical Building; Jordan House; Naylor House; Terrace Hill (Hubbell Mansion); U.S. Post Office.

DES MOINES COUNTY, SE Iowa, 408 sq. mi.; Pop. 42,614; Named after a french word meaning "river of monks."

DEXTER, City; Dallas County; Pop. 628; Zip Code 50070; Elev. 115; Lat. 41-31-08 N long. 094-13-49 W. Founded in 1865 and named for a racehorse.

DICKENS, City; Clay County; Pop. 214; Zip Code 51333; 60 miles NW of Fort Dodge; Lat. 43-08-05 N long. 095-01-06 W. Named after the English novelist.

DICKINSON COUNTY, NW Iowa, 380 sq. mi.; Pop. 14,909; Named for Daniel Stevens Dickinson (1800-1866), Governor and Senator of New York; U.S. Attorney General, south district of New York.

DIKE, City; Grundy County; Pop. 875; Zip Code 50624; 11 miles W of Waterloo; Lat. 42-27-53 N long. 092-38-09 W.

DONNELLSON, City; Lee County; Pop. 940; Zip Code 52625; 10 miles W of Fort Madison; 8-20 N long. 091-34-16 W. Donnellson was a pioneer.

DOON, City; Lyon County; Pop. 476; Zip Code 51235; 52 miles N of Sioux City; Lat. 43-17-21 N long. 096-13-26 W; Named after the Doon River in Scotland.

DOUGHERTY, City; Cerro Gordo County; Pop. 107; Zip Code 50433; 16 miles S of Mason City; Lat. 42-55-31 N long. 093-01-03 W; The city was named after one of its prominent residents, Daniel Dougherty.

DOW CITY, City; Crawford County; Pop. 439; Zip Code 51528; 47 miles NNe of Council Bluffs; Elev. 1,131; Lat. 41-55-11 N long. 095-26-30 W. Named for S.E. Dow, an early settler.

HISTORICAL PLACES...

Dow House.

DRAKESVILLE, City; Davis County; Pop. 172; Zip Code 52552; 19 miles SSW of Ottumwa; Lat. 40-48-01 N long 092-29-11 W; Laid out by John A. Drake, and named in his honor.

DUBUQUE, City; Dubuque County Seat; Pop. 57,546; Zip Code 52001; 65 miles ENE of Cedar Rapids; Lat. 42-29-58 N long. 090- 42-02 W; Located on the Mississippi River opposite the junction of the Wisconsin and Illinois state boundary lines, is one of the Iowa's oldest cities.

Julien Dubuque, a French Canadian, for whom the city was named, arrived in Prairie du Chien (Wisconsin) about 1785; three years later, he obtained permission to mine the lead ore in the river bluffs at Catfish Creek, near Kettle Chief's Indian 3village. The first white man to settle permanently in the Iowa region, Dubuque made his home just south of the present city. Later he certified his claim to the land doubly by naming it "The Mines of Spain," and obtaining formal recognition from Baron de Carondelet, then governor of Louisiana under the Spanish government.

"Little Night," as Dubuque was known to the Fox Indians, seemed to possess great power over them. There are several legends regarding this power, the most popular being associated with the refusal of the Fox to grant a request of Dubuque's. Dubuque threatened to burn the entire Mississippi, but even this did not move the stubborn Indians. So, while one of his associates emptied a barrel of oil into the water above the bend of Catfish Creek, Dubuque called the Indians from their lodges for consultation around the big bonfire he had built on the bank. Seizing a firebrand, he threw it on the water, smooth with oil. The sheet of flame rising instantly so terrified the Indians that they conceded all Dubuque asked. Then, supposedly at the exercise of his will, the fire went out. When Dubuque died, the Indians buried him with honors befitting a chief, competing with one another for the privilege of carrying his body to the grave. A tomb of wood and stone was erected, and upon a cross was inscribed: "Julien Dubuque, Miner of the Mines of Spain; died March 24, 1810, age 45 years, six months."

For years after Dubuque's death, the Fox did not allow any others to mine the lead. White men tried to take possession of the district in June 1830, but since they had violated agreements with the Indians, the United States Government forced them to return to the east side of the river. On June 1, 1833, under terms of the treaty with Chief Black Hawk, the territory was thrown open to white settlers.

Before Dubuque was a year old, stores, saloons, and cabins bordered both sides of the muddy main street. The first school, started in 1833, was taught by George Cubbage who, it was said, was captured by the Indians during the Black Hawk War. Later he was sold to a trader for a plug of tobacco because he was baldheaded and could not be scalped.

At this time there was no government in the Territory, and lawlessness prevailed. Patrick O'Connor, a miner, killed his partner, George O'Keaf, and readily admitted his crime, assuming that he could not be prosecuted since there were no laws. The settlers, however, took matters into their own hands; they established a court, tried, sentenced, and hanged O'Connor in June of 1834.

Shortly after this, the Methodists erected a log church, the first church building in Iowa. In September 1834, when the Territory of Wisconsin created the two original counties in Iowa, Dubuque was made the seat of government of Dubuque County, which included all of the Black Hawk treaty land north of Rock Island.

Dubuque, lusty and ambitious, was superior to other cities on the river. A boisterous mining town, it sheltered intellectuals side by side with illiterates. So great was the income from lead mining here that the Territorial Legislative Assembly of Wisconsin chartered the Miners' Bank of Dubuque, the first bank in Iowa, in 1836. In this year, too, the town boasted the first newspaper in what is now Iowa, the Du Buque *Visitor,* printed on the first press in the territory north of Missouri and west of the Mississippi.

The people of Dubuque expected their city to be made the capital of the Territory of Wisconsin. As one of its newspapers predicted: "A proud city shall be reared where at present stands our flourishing village ... when the lofty spires of the State house and churches glitter in the rays of the sun and the glossy bosom of the fair Mississippi shall swell beneath the weight of commerce." However, when another city was chosen, Dubuque did not lose its belief in its importance as the Queen City of the Northwest.

The settlers in Dubuque voted for their first representatives to the Legislative Assembly of the Territory of Wisconsin in the fall of 1836, almost a year before a local government was established. The city was not formally organized until the next spring, when the citizens met in the Methodist church building to elect a board of five trustees. In 1841, the town adopted the charter granted it by the Territory of Iowa.

During the 1840s and 1850s, Dubuque lost its place as the largest city in Iowa to Burlington. Three colleges were opened during this period: the University of Dubuque in 1852; Wartburg Seminary in 1854; and Clarke College in 1859.

In 1855, the Illinois Central Railroad reached the shore opposite Dubuque. Cannons roared and bands blared as Dubuque people turned out in the sweltering heat to celebrate the event and to hear Senator Stephen A. Douglas toast the railroad as "the great work of the age." The Dubuque & Pacific Railroad Company, which built the fourth railroad to cross Iowa, was formed on April 22, 1857, the people of the city and the county voting bonds for $600,000. Eleven years passed before the Mississippi was bridged at this point. In 1867, the two railroads were consolidated.

With the influx of many immigrants to the fertile prairies of northeastern Iowa, by 1860, Dubuque had again become Iowa's largest city. Lumbering had replaced mining as the important industry, and the mills were increasing their production daily. Huge log rafts were floated down from the north and converted into lumber and ties for the railroads that were opening new paths into Iowa. Another asset was the Dubuque-East Dubuque wagon bridge across the Mississippi, which opened in 1887, and brought in an external trade territory to the east.

Dubuque suffered disasters from 1876 to 1919. Thirty lives were lost in the Catfish Creek flood of 1876; in 1894, almost the entire lumbering district was wiped out by fire; and in 1911, a second conflagration destroyed practically the entire industry.

POINTS OF INTEREST:

- Bellevue State Park. 26 miles S on US 52, 67,near Bellevue.
- Clarke College (1843). 1550 Clarke Drive at W Locust Street.
- Crystal Lake Cave. 5 miles S off US 52.
- Eagle Point Park. Off Shiras Avenue, NE corner of city.
- Fenelon Place Elevator. 512 Fenelon Place at Raymond.
- General Zebulon Pike Lock and Dam. Can be seen from Eagle Point Park.
- Julien Dubuque Monument (1897). 1/2 mile from end of Julien Dubuque Drive.

- Loras College (1839). Alta Vista Street.
- Mathias Ham Museum (1857). 2241 Lincoln Avenue, near Eagle Point Park.
- Old Shot Tower (1856). River & Tower Streets.
- Sundown Ski Resort. 9000 Ashbury Road.
- University of Dubuque (1852). 2000 University Avenue.
- Woodward Riverboat Museum. 2nd Street Harbor.

HISTORICAL PLACES...

Dubuque City Hall; Dubuque County Courthouse; Dubuque County Jail; Orpheum Theatre and Site (Majestic Theatre); Johnson House and Barn.

DUBUQUE COUNTY, E Iowa, 612 sq. mi.; Pop. 86,403; Named for Julien Dubuque (1764-1810), the first white settler in Iowa. He received an option from the Indians to work the lead mines, the product of which he sold at St. Louis, Missouri.

DUMONT, City; Butler County; Pop. 705; Zip Code 50625; 27 miles SSE of Mason City; Lat. 42-45-13 N long. 092-58-35 W; Probably named for an early French settler.

DUNCOMBE, City; Webster County; Pop. 488; Zip Code 50532; 7 miles ESE of Fort Dodge; Lat. 42-28-18 N long. 094-01-11 W; The city was named for Hon. J. F. Duncombe.

DUNDEE, City; Delaware County; Pop. 174; Zip Code 52018; 43 miles E of Waterloo; Elev. 998; Lat. 42-34-45 N long. 091-33-04 W. Named for the city in Scotland.

EAGLE GROVE, City; Wright County; Pop. 3,671; Zip Code 50533; 16 miles NE of Fort Dodge; Lat. 42-39-24 N long. 093-54-20 W; Named for the many eagles that built nests in a grove here.

EARLHAM, City; Madison County; Pop. 1,157; Zip Code 50072; 39 miles WSW of Des Moines; Lat. 41-29-41 N long. 094-07-07 W.

EARLVILLE, City; Delaware County; Pop. 822; Zip Code 52041; 32 miles W of Dubuque; Lat. 42-28-52 N long. 091-16-35 W; The city was first called Nottingham, and later named for its first settler, G. M. Earl.

EARLY, City; Sac County; Pop. 649; Zip Code 50535; 50 miles W of Fort Dodge; Lat. 42-27-43 N long. 095-09-04 W. Named for D.C. Early, a pioneer who settled here in the 1870s.

EDGEWOOD, City; Clayton & Delaware Counties; Pop. 776; Zip Code 52042; 42 miles WNW of Dubuque; Lat. 42-38-49 N long. 091- 24-17 W.

ELBERON, City; Tama County; Pop. 203; Zip Code 52225; 26 miles W of Cedar Rapids; Lat. 41-59-40 N long. 092-21-00 W.

ELDON, City; Wapello County; Pop. 1,070; Zip Code 52554; 9 miles SE of Ottumwa; Lat. 40-54-29 N long. 092-12-45 W. Eldon is named in honor of an early settler.

HISTORICAL PLACES...
American Gothic House (Dibble House).

ELDORA, City; Hardin County Seat; Pop. 3,038; Zip Code 50627; 32 miles WSW of Waterloo; Elev. 1,088; Lat. 42-221-11 N long. 093-05-13 W; Derived from the Spanish words "el dorado", meaning "the gilded one."

ELDRIDGE, City; Scott County; Pop. 3,378; Zip Code 52748; 10 miles NNE of Davenport; Lat. 41-39-29 N long. 090-35-04 W. Given the name of a prominent citizen.

ELGIN, City; Fayette County; Pop. 637; Zip Code 52141; 48 miles NE of Waterloo; Lat. 42-57-52 N long. 091-37-55 W. Named after Elgin, Illinois.

ELKADER, City; Clayton County Seat; Pop. 1,510; Zip Code 52043; 48 miles WNW of Dubuque; Lat. 42-51-14 N long. 091-24-19 W. Named in 1845 for Algerian nationalist, Abd-el-Kader.

ELK HORN, City; Shelby County; Pop. 672; Elev. 1363; 42 miles NE of Council Bluffs; Lat. 41-35-30 N long. 095-03-35 W. Named after an elk horn once found in the area.

ELK RUN HEIGHTS, City; Blkack Hawk County; Pop. 1,088; 8 miles E of Waterloo; Lat. 42-28-01 N long. 092-15-23 W. Descriptively named.

ELLIOTT, City; Montgomery County; Pop. 399; Zip Code 51532; 29 miles ESE of Council Bluffs; Lat. 41-08-57 N long. 095-09-50 W.

ELLSWORTH, City; Hamilton County; Pop. 451; Zip Code 50075; 16 miles NNE of Ames; Lat. 42-18-25 N long. 093-34-28 W; Named for a banker who lived in Iowa Falls.

ELMA, City; Howard County; Pop. 653; Zip Code 50628; 27 miles ENE of Mason City; Lat. 43-14-42 N long. 092-26-08 W.

EMERSON, City; Mills County; Pop. 476; Zip Code 51533; 22 miles SE of Council Bluffs; Lat. 41-01-21 N long 095-27-08 W. Named in honor of the American philosopher and poet, R.W. Emerson.

EMMETSBURG, City; Palo Alto County Seat; Pop. 3,940; Zip Code 50536; 48 miles NW of Fort Dodge; Lat. 43-06-18 N long. 094- 41-01 W; Named in honor of Robert W. Emmet, an Irish patriot.

POINTS OF INTEREST:
• Kearney Park. NW edge of town.

EMMET COUNTY, N Iowa, 394 sq. mi.; Pop. 11,569; Named for Robert Emmet (1778-1803), Irish patriot and fighter.

EPWORTH, City; Dubuque County; Pop. 1,297; Zip Code 52045; 16 miles W of Dubuque; Lat. 42-28-38 N long. 090-56-55 W; The city takes its name from the town in Lincolnshire, England; another source says it was named for Epworth, England, the birthplace of John Wesley.

ESSEX, City; Page County; Pop. 916; Zip Code 51638; 35 miles SE of Council Bluffs; Lat. 40-49-43 N long. 095-17-50 W. Named for the county in England.

ESTHERVILLE, City; Emmet County Seat; Pop. 6,720; Zip Code 51334; 68 miles NNW of Fort Dodge; Lat. 43-24-18 N long. 094-48- 17 W; Called Estherville after Esther A. Ridley, wife of one of the original proprietors.

POINTS OF INTEREST:
- Fort Defiance State Park. 1 mile W on IA 9, then 1 1/2 miles S on County road N 26.
- Holiday Mountain Ski Area. 1 mile S on IA 4.

EVANSDALE, City; Black Hawk County; Pop. 4,638; Zip Code 50707; 8 miles E of Waterloo; Lat. 42-28-09 N long. 092-16-51 W.

EXIRA, City; Audubon County; Pop. 955; Zip Code 50076; 49 miles ENE of Council Bluffs; Lat. 41-36-01 N long. 094-53-06 W. The city was founded by Judge D. M. Harris and dates back to 1857. It is the oldest town in the county. The town was named after Exira Eckman of Ohio, who, with her father, Judge John Eckman, was visiting relatives when the town was platted. One of the promoters had intended to call it Viola, for his own daughter; when Judge Eckman offered to buy a town lot if the place were named for his daughter, the change was made at once.

FAIRBANK, City; Buchanan & Fayette Counties; Pop. 1,018; Zip Code 50629; 22 miles ENE of Waterloo; Lat. 42-37-38 N long. 092-02-51 W.

FAIRFAX, City; Linn County; Pop. 780; Zip Code 52228; 7 miles S of Cedar Rapids; Lat. 41-55-18 N long. 091-46-31 W. Named for the county in Virginia.

FAIRFIELD, City; Jefferson County Seat; Pop. 9,768; Zip Code 52556; 19 miles E of Ottumwa; Elev. 778; Lat. 41-00-21 N long. 091-57-21 W. Descriptively named for the area's beauty.

POINTS OF INTEREST:
Jefferson County Park. 1/2 miles SW on County Hwy V64 (Libertyville Road).
Old Settlers Park. B Street, N edge of town.

HISTORICAL PLACES...
Bentonsport National Historic District.

FARLEY, City; Dubuque County; Pop. 1,354; Zip Code 52046; 20 miles W of Dubuque; Lat. 42-26-35 N long. 091-

00-49 W. The town's name remembers railroad man, J.P. Farley.

FARMINGTON, City; Van Buren County; Pop. 655; Zip Code 52626; 19 miles W of Fort Madison; Elev. 569; Lat. 40-38-26 N long. 091-44-53 W. Named after farming, the area's main economic activity.

FARRAGUT, City; Fremont County; Pop. 498; Zip Code 51639; 37 miles NE of Waterloo; Lat. 40-43-05 N long. 095-29-12 W; The city was named for Admiral Farragut.

FAYETTE, City; Fayette County; Pop. 1,317; Zip Code 52142; 40 miles NE of Waterloo; Lat. 42-50-10 N long. 091-48-06 W; Named in honor of the Marquis de Lafayette, who served as French General in the American Army during the American Revolution.

It is the location of Upper Iowa University, a non-sectarian Christian college. The 14-acre campus lies in the center of town, along the banks of the Volga River. The school was organized in January 1857 as Fayette Seminary, after Col. Robert Alexander and Samuel H. Robinson had donated the land and a sum of $50,000. It was formerly sponsored by the Methodist Episcopal Church.

FAYETTE COUNTY, NE Iowa, 728 sq. mi.; Pop. 21,843; Named for Marquis de Lefayette (1757-1834), Commander-in-chief of the National Guard in 1789.

FENTON, City; Kassuth County; Pop. 346; Zip Code 50539; 48 miles NNW of Fort Dodge; Lat. 43-13-20 N long. 094-24-24 W.

FERTILE, City; Worth County; Pop. 382; Zip Code 50434; 18 miles WNW of Mason City; Lat. 43-16-07 N long. 093-25-21 W. Descritively named for the area's rich land.

FLOYD, City; Floyd County; Pop. 359; Zip Code 50435; 18 miles E of Mason City; Lat. 43-07-54 N long. 092-44-18 W; Named for William Floyd of Long Island, N.Y., one of the signers of the Declaration of Independence.

FLOYD COUNTY, N Iowa, 503 sq. mi.; Pop. 17,058; Named for Charles Floyd, a sargeant in the Lewis and Clark expedition; he was the first white man buried in Iowa.

FONDA, City; Pocahontas County; Pop. 731; Zip Code 50540; 35 miles W of Fort Dodge; Lat. 42-34-58 N long. 094-50-44 W. The town was first named Marvin in honor of Marvin Hewitt, a railroad official, but the post office was called Cedarville because of nearby Cedar Creek. The resulting confusion prompted the citizens to abandon both names and substitute Fonda, a name chosen because it was found in the United States post office directory only once.

FONTANELLE, City; Adair County; Pop. 712; Zip Code 50846; 63 miles WSW of Des Moines; Lat. 41-17-52 N long. 094-33-36 W; The town was formerly called Summerset. It was later either named after Louis Fontanelle, a trapper who worked for the American Fur Company, or for his son, Omaha Indian Chief, Logan Fontanelle.

FORT ATKINSON, City; Winneshiek County; Pop. 367; Zip Code 52144; Lat. 43-09-41 N long. 091-57-22 W. Named after an early military post.

FORT DODGE, City; Webster County Seat; Pop. 25,894; Zip Code 50501; 65 miles SW of Mason City; Lat. 42-30-23 N long. 094- 11-16 W; The area is situated on both sides of the Des Moines River at the point where Fort Dodge once stood. The city lies chiefly on the plateau land above the river flats, in the center of a productive agricultural and mining district, with one of the largest deposits of gypsum in the nation at its southeastern edge.

Early settlers in the territory were harassed by Sidominadotah's *Two Fingers* band of 500 Sioux Indians, who had been exiled from the tribe. One of the settlers, Henry Lott, was accused by Two Fingers in 1846 of illegal possession of his land. Mrs. Lott died shortly after the trouble started, and her 12-year old son also died while trying to follow the Des Moines River to the nearest settlement for help. Lott blamed Two Fingers for their deaths and in retaliation, killed him and his family. This trouble is believed to have been partly responsible for the Spirit Lake Massacre.

In 1850, the Federal Government established a fort here; it was first called Fort Clarke as a courtesy to the commander of the Sixth Infantry, Brevet Major Newman S. Clarke. The name was changed on June 25, 1851, to Fort Dodge for Henry Dodge, U.S. Senator from Wisconsin, who fought in the Black Hawk and other Indian wars. Roving bands of Indians who continued to plunder the country east, west, and southeast of the fort caused the only trouble, and in 1853, the fort, no longer necessary, was abandoned. Major William Williams, sutler for the United States troops, purchased the barracks and fort site in 1854, and laid out the town of Fort Dodge.

John F. Duncombe, described in an old newspaper as "an engine in pants," arrived in Fort Dodge in 1855. Through his efforts, Fort Dodge, then a tiny settlement, wrested the county seat from Homer, a thriving town. County histories only hint at the final chapter in the story by saying: "In April 1856, after a very exciting canvass, the citizens of the county decided by a large majority to move the county seat from Homer to Fort Dodge." The old and yellowed newspapers tell the story of the "exciting canvass" that ended in a wrestling match which finally decided the question. An election was eventually held, and both factions stuffed the ballot boxes. When the tabulated votes gave the county seat to Fort Dodge, John D. Maxwell, who led the fight for Homer, exploded. A suggestion that Maxwell and Duncombe wrestle it out brought action. In Homer's public square, with the whole town watching, the two wrestled for an hour. Whether it was a scissor-hold or half- nelson that gave Duncombe the victory is conjecture; but Fort Dodge was county seat without further controversy.

In 1858, clay resources of the city were first used commercially by Henry A. Flatt, an early brick-maker. In the same year, the first attempts to improve the wagon trails over the prairies were made by a horse-drawn scraper that cut off turf between wagon wheel ruts. Many of these wagon trails, according to legend, were pointed out by Wahkonsa, a Sioux Indian who frequently mapped with sticks the most available route over the prairies for the settlers. Intelligent and friendly, he sometimes reported movements of hostile bands. Fort Dodge citizens, hoping to profit by river navigation, purchased the *Charels Rogers* which arrived in Fort Dodge on April 6, 1859, although lower Des Moines River pilots declared the boat would never make it. The entire population lined the river bank to welcome the boat, but soon learned the river was navigable for steamboats only at flood stage.

A visit to Fort Dodge by George Hull of Binghamton, New York and H. B. Martin of Marshalltown, Iowa, in July 1868 resulted in the nationally famous Cardiff Giant hoax. The "prehistoric man" whose "discovery" caused a widespread stir of excitement during the last quarter of the 19th century, was cut for Hull and Martin by Michael Foley from a ledge of gypsum.

Freighted from Fort Dodge to Chicago, the slab was carved into a giant by two German stonecutters who pricked it with a leaden mallet faced with needles to give it a human-looking skin, then bathed the finished work in sulfuric acid to give the appearance of great age. The stone man, 10 feet long, two and one-half feet wide, and weighing 3,000 pounds, was encased in a strong box and arrived in Union, New York on October 12, 1858. A few weeks later, it was buried near Cardiff, New York by a Mr. Newell, brother-in-law of George Hull. A little later, Newell "discovered" the giant while digging a well. Soon the Cardiff Giant was famous. Sculptors, geologists, and writers believed him to be a "prehistoric man." James Hall, New York State geologist, pronounced him "the most remarkable archeological discovery ever made in this country." Hiram Powers, sculptor of the Greek Slave, declared "No chisel could carve such a perfect man."

Among the skeptics who did not believe the Cardiff Giant was a "petrified man" was Oliver Wendell Holmes. He drilled through the giant's head to prove to his own satisfaction that the statue was an old image, probably several hundred years old. Interest was so widespread that magazines and papers everywhere carried stores about the giant, and up-to-date encyclopedias mentioned it. During the time the giant was part of P. T. Barnum's show, millions of people paid 50 cents to see him. Interest flamed to such a peak that the New York Central changed its train schedules to permit passengers to stop and see the wonder when it was shown at Syracuse. In 1901, the giant attracted more people than almost anything else at the Pan American Exhibit at Buffalo, and it was the talk of the day until Professor Othniel C. Marsh of Yale exposed it as a fake. Afterward people forgot the Cardiff Giant for nearly a quarter of a century. He was then shown at Emmetsburg, Iowa, in July 1935, and featured in the Centennial Parade on August 17, 1935, at Fort Dodge. Shortly afterward, he was an attraction at the Iowa State Fair. The giant was later a part of the private museum of Gardner Cowles, Jr., a Des Moines newspaper executive.

It was during the period of the Cardiff Giant episode that Fort Dodge developed its gypsum resources. In 1869, two quarries were opened, one in Gypsum Hollow and the other on Soldier Creek. The first mill for the manufacture of wall plaster, the old Iowa Mill, was built about 1872 and stood between the Illinois Central tracks and the Des Moines River. The soft white gypsum, exposed on all sides of the hills, made quarrying easy after the soil was stripped off. By 1890 there were four mills for producing about 21,000 tons a year.

When the Cardiff Mill, named for the Cardiff Giant, sank a shaft in the open prairie to mine gypsum, a new era in the industry began. Most of it was marketed in the form of hard wall plaster, although some went into wallboard, partition, roof tile, insulating material, and fertilizer.

POINTS OF INTEREST:

- Blanden Memorial Art Museum. 920 3rd Avwenue South.
- Fort Dodge Historical Museum, Stockade and Fort. E at jct. US 20, 169.
- John F. Kennedy Memorial Park. 5 miles N on County P56.
- Kalsow Prairie. 15 miles W on IA 7 to Manson, then 2 miles N on county road.
- Site of Old Fort Dodge. 1st Avenue N & N 4th Street.

HISTORICAL PLACES...

Vincent House.

FORT MADISON, City; Lee County Seat; Pop. 11,618; Zip Code 52627; 13 miles WSW of Burlington; Lat. 40-37-17 N long. 091-21- 41 W; The city took its name from James Madison, President of the United States.

It was established as a Government trading post in 1808 for the Indian trade, but the natives regarded its presence as a treaty violation, and constantly harassed the place. In August 1813, Chief Black Hawk and his allies finally attacked. Unable to beat off the besiegers, those at the post decided to leave. On the night of September 3, with the Indians waiting in the hills, they gathered what remained of provisions and ammunition, and crawled on their hands and knees through a trench to the boats waiting on the river. As the Indians watched, they saw flames shoot up from the block houses. The last man had set fire to the buildings, and the men were safely away before their foes realized what had happened.

The town grew up around the lone chimney left after the post was deserted. In the intervening years, Indians called the site Potowanek (*place of fire*) and traders used the chimney as a landmark. In 1833, John Knapp estab-

215

lished a trading post. Many trains of prairie schooners were later ferried across the river here, one point in the southern part of the territory free from inundation at all seasons.

The Legislature of the Territory of Wisconsin established the city as the seat of Lee County in 1838, but a courthouse was not erected until 1842.

POINTS OF INTEREST:

- Fort Madison Marker. 300 Block of Avenue H.
- Lee County Courthouse (1841). 701 Avenue F.
- Riverview Park. Between river and business section at E end of town.
- Santa Fe Railway Bridge. E edge of town.
- Shimek State Forest. 25 miles W on IA 2, E of Farmington.

HISTORICAL PLACES...

Old Fort Madison Site.

FRANKLIN, City; Lee County; Pop. 152; 16 miles WSW of Burlington; Lat. 40-40-05 N long. 091-30-40 W; Like many places throughout the country, this city was named for Benjamin Franklin.

FRANKLIN COUNTY, N central Iowa, 586 sq. mi.; Pop. 11,364; Named for Benjamin Franklin (1706-1790), printer; deputy postmaster; general of the British No. American colonies; member of the Continental Congress; signer of Declaration of Independence, 1776; Governor of Pennsylvania.

FREDERICKSBURG, City; Bremer County; Pop. 1,011; Zip Code 50630; 34 miles NNE of Waterloo; Lat. 42-58-11 N long. 092-13-07 W. Founded in 1856 and named after founder, Frederick Padden.

FREDERIKA, City; Bremer County; Pop. 188; Zip Code 50631; 27 miles NNE of Waterloo; Lat. 42-52-58 N long. 092-18-36 W. The town's name remembers 19th century Swedish novelist, Frederika Bremer (1801-65).

FREMONT, City; Mahaska County; Pop. 701; Zip Code 52561; 14 miles NNW of Ottumwa; Lat. 41-12-49 N long. 092-26-19 W; The city was named for Gen. John C. Fremont.

FREMONT COUNTY, SW corner Iowa, 524 sq. mi.; Pop. 8,226; Named for John Charles Fremont (1813-1890), third provisional governor of California, and fifth territorial governor of Arizona; Senator from California; appointed a major general, U.S. Army on the retired list.

FRUITLAND, City; Muscatine County; Pop. 511; Zip Code 52749; 25 miles WSW Davenport; Lat. 41-21-22 N long. 091-07-45 W. Descriptivley named for the local horticulture.

GALVA, City; Ida County; Pop. 398; Zip Code 51020; 42 miles E of Sioux City; Lat. 42-30-29 N long. 095-25-01 W.

GARDEN GROVE, City; Decatur County; Pop. 229; Zip Code 50103; 53 miles E of Des Moines; Lat. 40-50-35 N long. 093-35-16 W. Descriptively named.

GARNAVILLO, City; Clayton County; Pop. 727; Zip Code 52049; 41 miles NW of Dubuque; Lat. 42-53-17 N long. 091-11-50 W. First named Jacksonville in 1844, it was given its present name in 1846 by Judge Samuel Murdock, for a town in Ireland.

GARNER, City; Hancock County Seat; Pop. 2,916; Zip Code 50438; 25 miles WSW of Mason City; Lat. 43-06-01 N long. 093-36- 33 W. The city's name remembers a prominent settler.

POINTS OF INTEREST:

- Pilot Knob State Park. 3 miles W via US 18, then 10 miles N on US 69, then 6 miles E on IA 9, then 1 mile S on IA 332 near Forest City.
- Rice Lake State Park. 3 miles W via US 18, then 24 miles NE on US 69, then S on unnumbered road.

GARRISON, City; Benton County; Pop. 320; Zip Code 52229; 18 miles WNW of Cedar Rapids; Lat. 42-08-44 N long. 092-08-25 W. Named after abolitionist, William L. Garrison.

GARWIN, City; Tama County; Pop. 533; Zip Code 50632; 42 miles W of Cedar Rapids; Lat. 42-05-32 N long. 092-40-30 W.

GENEVA, City; Franklin County; Pop. 169; Zip Code 50633; 36 miles WNW of Waterloo; Lat. 42-40-26 N long. 093-07-32 W. Named for the Swiss city.

GEORGE, City; Lyon County; Pop. 1,066; Zip Code 51237; 57 miles NNE of Sioux City; Lat. 43-21-03 N long. 095-58-35 W. Named after the founder.

GILBERT, City; Story County; Pop. 796; Zip Code 50105; 4 miles N of Ames; Lat. 42-06-52 N long. 093-36-59 W. Gilbert was a pioneer.

GILBERTVILLE, City; Black Hawk County; Pop. 748; Zip Code 50634; 11 miles ESE of Waterloo; Lat. 42-25-05 N long. 092-12-55 W.

GOOSE LAKE, City; Clinton County; Pop. 221; Zip Code 52750; 9 miles NW of Clinton; Lat. 41-58-03 N long. 090-22-58 W. Named after the nearby lake.

GOWRIE, City; Webster County; Pop. 1,028; Zip Code 50543; 18 miles SSW of Fort Dodge; Elev. 113; Lat. 42-19-02 N long. 094- 18-06 W.

GRAETTINGER, City; Palo Alto County; Pop. 813; Zip Code 51342; 56 miles NNW of Fort Dodge; Lat. 43-14-12 N long. 094-44- 56 W.

u[GRAND JUNCTION, City; Greene County; Pop. 808; Zip Code 50107; 28 miles W of Ames; Lat. 42-00-59 N long. 094-14-18 W; Named for its location at the junction of the Keokuk and Des Moines and the Chicago and Northwestern Railroads.

GRAND MOUND, City; Clinton County; Pop. 619; Zip Code 52751; 19 miles W of Clinton; Lat. 41-49-27 N long. 0909-38-52 W. Named for a nearby eroded glacial terminal moraine known as Sand Mound.

GRANDVIEW, City; Louisa County; Pop. 514; Zip Code 52752; 29 miles SW of Davenport; Lat. 41-16-33 N long. 091-11-18 W. Descriptively named.

GRANGER, City; Dallas County; Pop. 624; Zip Code 50109; 25 miles WNW of Des Moines; Lat. 41-45-44 N long. 094-49-57 W. The city's name honors railroad official, Ben Granger.

GRANT, City; Montgomery County; Pop. 123; Zip Code 50847; 38 miles E of Council Bluffs; Lat. 41-08-37 N long. 094-59-41 W; It was first named Milford. Later, when it was found that another Milford existed in Iowa, the name was changed to honor Ulysses S. Grant.

GRANVILLE, City; Sioux County; Pop. 298; Zip Code 51022; 37 miles NNE of Sioux City; Lat. 42-58-53 N long. 095-53-30 W; Was named after a French word for "large town."

GRAVITY, City; Taylor County; Pop. 218; Zip Code 50848; 58 miles SE of Council Bluffs; Lat. 40-45-40 N long. 094-44-41 W; Settled in 1881 and named by early resident, Sara Cox. She named the settlement Gravity because it was the main attraction in the area.

GREELEY, City; Delaware County; Pop. 263; Zip Code 52050; 37 miles WNW of Dubuque; Lat. 42-35-07 N long. 091-20-54 W. First called Plum Spring, but renamed in 1863 for the famous newspaper publisher, Horace Greeley.

GREENE, City; Butler County; Pop. 1,142; Zip Code 50636; 22 miles SE of Mason City; Lat. 42-06-07 N long. 092-49-16 W; Named for Judge George Green of Linn County.

GREENE COUNTY, W central Iowa, 569 sq. mi.; Pop. 10,045; Named for Nathaniel Greene (1742-1786), wh was a Brigadier General of Rhode Island troops and of the Continental Army in 1775, He was also a major general and Q.M. general. Greene commanded army of the South in 1780m, and was president of the court of inquiry for Maj. Andre.

GREENFIELD, City; Adair County Seat; Pop. 2,074; Zip Code 50849; 56 miles WSW of Des Moines; Lat. 41-18-34 N long. 094-27- 36 W; Greenfield took its name from the town in Massachusetts.

HISTORICAL PLACES...

Catalpa.

GRIMES, City; Polk County; Pop. 2,653; Zip Code 50111; 20 miles WNW of Des Moines; Lat. 41-39-41 N long. 093-47-29 W; Named for Senator Grimes.

GRINNELL, City; Poweshiek County; Pop. 8,902; Zip Code 50112; 34 miles ENE of Des Moines; Lat. 41-44-41 N long. 092-38- 56 W. Named after Josiah Bushnell Grinnell, a Congregational minister in New York City. In 1853, he went to Horace Greeley for advice. Greeley made his much-quoted statement: "Go West, young man, go West and grow up with the country!" In March 1854, accompanied by Dr. Thomas Holyoke of Scarsport, Maine, and the Rev. Homer Hamlin of Hudson, Ohio, Grinnell came West and founded the settlement that became Grinnell, on the barren treeless prairie between the Iowa and Skunk rivers.

Two important laws were made here: Land was to be set aside for a college campus, and no liquor could be sold in the town. The original deeds to town lots carried the liquor clause, and provided that the lots be reverted to the Grinnell estate on any breach of the contract.

POINTS OF INTEREST:

- Grinnell College (1846). On US 6, NE of business district.
- Grinnell Historical Museum. 1125 Broad Street.
- Poweshiek County National bank (ca 1914).
- Rock Creek State Park. 7 miles W on US 6, then 3 miles N on IA 224.
- Site of the Long Home. 1019 Broad Street.

GRISWOLD, City; Cass County; Pop. 1,049; Zip Code 51535; 29 miles E of Council Bluffs; Lat. 41-13-58 N long. 095-07-58 W; Named for J. N. A. Griswold, a railroad official.

GRUNDY CENTER, City; Grundy County Seat; Pop. 2,491; Zip Code 50638; 18 miles WSW of Waterloo; Elev. 1,026; Lat. 42-21-23 N long. 092-46-38 W; Grundy Center took its name from Felix Grundy, Senator from Tennessee.

GRUNDY COUNTY, NE central Iowa, 501 sq. mi.; Pop. 12,029; Named for Felix Grundy (1777-1840), Kentucky House of Representatives; Kentucky Supreme Court and Supreme Court Chief Justice; Rep. and Senator from Tennessee; Attorney General of the U.S. in cabinet of President Van Buren.

GUTHRIE CENTER, City; Guthrie County Seat; Pop. 1,614; Zip Code 50115; 48 miles NW of Dubuque; Elev. 1,150; Lat. 41-41-04 N long. 094-30-12 W; Named for Captain Edwin B. Guthrie.

POINTS OF INTEREST:

• Springbrook State Park. 8 miles NE on IA 25, then E on IA 384.

GUTHRIE COUNTY, SW central Iowa, 596 sq. mi.; Pop. 10,935; Named for Edwin Guthrie, Captain of Iowa Vol. in Mexian War; he died of wounds received in action at La Hoya, Mexico.

GUTTENBERG, City; Clayton County; Pop. 2,257; Zip Code 52052; 33 miles NW of Dubuque; Elev. 625; Lat. 42-44-32 N long. 091-05-30 W; It was first known as Prairie La Porte. The name was later changed to Guttenburg, for the German inventor of the printing press, Johann Gutenberg. The change in spelling was due to an error in the first plat of the site filed in the county records.

Guttenberg, lying along the west bank of the Mississippi River, is connected with the opposite side of the river by a ferry. The original settlement was made in 1834. In 1845, the Western Settlement Society of Cincinnati colonized the town with German immigrants, many of whom were intellectuals who had fled from military service in Europe. For more than half a century, the German language prevailed in the community, and Old World customs and traditions were held.

HAMBURG, City; Fremont County; Pop. 1,248; Zip Code 51640; 42 miles S of Council Bluffs; Elev. 914; Lat. 40-36-16 N long. 095-39-27 W; Probably named for the city in Germany.

HAMILTON, City; Marion County; Pop. 115; Zip Code 51016; 29 miles WNW of Ottumwa; Lat. 41-10-09 N long. 092-54-11 W; Named in honor of William W. Hamilton, president of the Senate in 1857.

HAMILTON COUNTY, N central Iowa, 577 sq. mi.; Pop. 16,071; Named for William H. Hamilton, president of Iowa Senate.

HAMPTON, City; Franklin County Seat; Pop. 4,133; Zip Code 50441; 28 miles S of Mason City; Lat. 42-44-31 N long. 093-12-08 W. The city was founded by Job Garner and George Ryan in 1856. The village was first named Benjamin. It was later named for the eastern city.

POINTS OF INTEREST:

• Beeds Lake State Park. 3 miles NW near jct. US 65, IA 3.

HANCOCK, City; Pottawattamie County; Pop. 201; Zip Code 51536; 21 ENE of Council Bluffs; Lat. 41-23-24 N long. 095-21-44 W; Like many places throughout the United States, this city was named for John Hancock, signer of the Declaration of Independence.

HANCOCK COUNTY, N Iowa, 570 sq. mi.; Pop. 12,638; Named for John Hancock (1737-1793), First governor and president of Mass., Continental Congress; first signer of the Declaration of Independence.

HARDIN COUNTY, N central Iowa, 574 sq. mi.; Pop. 19,094; Named for John J. Hardin, who was killed in the Mexican War.

HARLAN, City; Shelby County Seat; Pop. 5,148; Zip Code 51537; 32 miles NNE of Council Bluffs; Elev. 1250; Lat. 41-39-11 N long. 095-19-31 W; Named in honor of Senator Harlan.

HARRISON COUNTY, W Iowa, 696 sq. mi.; Pop. 14,730; Named for William Henry Harrison (1773-1841), ninth President of the U.S. and First Territorial Governor of Indiana. He defeated the Indians at Tippecanoe in 1811 and at the Thames in 1813, for which he was awarded a Congressional medal. Harrison was also a Senator from Ohio and U.S. Minister to Colombia.

HAWARDEN, City; Sioux County; Pop. 2,439; Zip Code 51023; 33 miles NNW of Sioux City; Lat. 42-59-45 N long. 096-29-06 W.

HAWKEYE, City; Fayette County; Pop. 460; 39 miles NE of Waterloo; Lat. 42-56-19 N long. 091-57-00 W; Named either for Sauk Chief, Black Hawk, or from the character "Hawkeye" in James Fenimore Cooper's novel, *The Last of the Mohicans.*

HAZLETON, City; Buchanan County; Pop. 733; Zip Code 50641; 26 miles ENE of Waterloo; Lat. 42-37-15 N long. 091-54-00 W. First known as Superior, it was renamed in 1863.

HEDRICK, City; Keokuk County; Pop. 810; Zip Code 52563; 10 miles N of Ottumwa; Lat. 41-10-21 N long. 092-18-31 W; Named for General Hedrick.

HENRY COUNTY, SE Iowa, 440 sq. mi.; Pop. 19,226; Named for Henry Dodge (1782-1867), Governor and Senator of Wisconsin Territory, who served in the Black Hawk and other Indian Wars.

HEPBURN, City; Page County; Pop. 41; Lat. 40-50-57 N long. 095-01-01 W; The city was named for Congressman Hepburn.

HIAWATHA, City; Linn County; Pop. 4,986; Zip Code 52233; 11 miles E of Cedar Rapids; Lat. 42-02-09 N long. 091-40-55 W; Named for the Indian in Longfellow's poem, *Song of Hiawatha.*

HILLS, City; Johnson County; Pop. 662; Zip Code 52235; 7 miles SE of Iowa City; Lat. 41-33-15 N long. 091-32-05 W. Descriptively named.

HINTON, City; Plymouth County; Pop. 697; Zip Code 51024; 7 miles N of Sioux City; Lat. 42-37-40 N long. 096-17-29 W.

HOLLAND, City; Grundy County; Pop. 215; Zip Code 50642; 18 miles WSW of Waterloo; Lat. 42-23-56 N long. 092-48-01 W. Named after the European country.

HOLSTEIN, City; Ida County; Pop. 1,449; Zip Code 51025; 37 miles E of Sioux City; Elev. 1437; Lat. 42-29-21 N long. 095-32- 41 W.
 It was founded in 1882 when a branch of the C. & N. W. R.R. was constructed through northern Ida County. The town was named for the area in Pressia, where many of the town's first residents lived before migrating to America.

HOPKINTON, City; Delaware County; Pop. 695; Zip Code 52237; 32 miles WSW of Dubuque; Lat. 42-20-38 N long. 091-14-54 W.

HISTORICAL PLACES...
Old Lenox College.

HOSPERS, City; Sioux County; Pop. 643; Zip Code 51238; 39 miles NNE of Sioux City; Lat. 43-04-19 N long. 095-54-15 W.

HOWARD COUNTY, N Iowa, 471 sq. mi.; Pop. 9,809; Named for Telgham Ashurst Howard (1797-1844), Tennessee State Senate in 1824, and District Attorney and Representative from Indiana.

HUBBARD, City; Hardin County; Pop. 814; Zip Code 50122; 25 miles NE of Ames; Lat. 42-18-20 N long. 093-18-00 W.
It was the boyhood home of Herbert Hoover, President of the United States (1929-1933). He lived at the home of an uncle near Hubbard, and his grandfather is buried here.

HUDSON, City; Black Hawk County; Pop. 2,037; Zip Code 56643; 5 miles S of Waterloo; Lat. 42-24-24 N long. 092-27-19 W. Named after the Hudson River.

HULL, City; Sioux County; Pop. 1,724; Zip Code 51239: 45 miles N of Mason City; Lat. 43-11-19 N long. 096-08-00 W; It was first named Pattersonville, and was later named for John Hull in 1882.

HUMBOLDT, City; Humdoldt County; Pop. 4,438; Zip Code 50548; 16 miles NNW of Fort Dodge; Lat. 42-43-15 N long. 094-12-54 W; Originally known as Springvale, it was settled by the Rev. S. H. Taft, with a little colony of abolitionists, on the West Fork of the river. It was renamed to honor geographer, Baron Alexander von Humboldt.

POINTS OF INTEREST:
- Frank A. Gotch Park. 3 miles SE off US 169.
- Humboldt County Historical Museum. E edge of Dakota City.

HUMBOLDT COUNTY, NW central Iowa, 435 sq. mi.; Pop. 10,756; Named for Freidrich Heinrich Alexander Von Humboldt (1769-1859), German naturalist, explorer, and statesman.

HUMESTON, City; Wayne County; Pop. 553; Zip Code 50123; 50 miles S of Des Moines; Lat. 40-51-32 N long. 093-29-50 W.

It was named for Alva Humeston, a railroad official who was active in promoting the extension of the railroad through the town.

IDA COUNTY, W Iowa, 431 sq. mi.; Pop. 8,365; Named for Ida Mountain in Crete, at the suggestion of Eliphalet Price.

IDA GROVE, City; Ida County Seat; Pop. 2,357; Zip Code 51445; 42 miles ESE of Sioux City; Elev. 1236; Lat. 42-20-42 N long. 095-28-17 W; Called Ida Grove by settlers from Ida Mountain in Greece.

HISTORICAL PLACES...

Ida County Courthouse; Moorehead Stagecoach Inn.

INDEPENDENCE, City; Buchanan County Seat; Pop. 5,972; Zip Code 50644; 26 miles E of Waterloo; Lat. 42-28-07 N long. 091-53- 21 W.

It was founded by Rufus B. Clark, a trapper, who saw the possibilities of utilizing water power from the river. The name of the town was determined by the fact that its organization was completed about July 4, 1847 (Independence Day); the county was named in 1837 for James Buchanan, then a U.S. Senator, who in 1857 became President.

INDIANOLA, City; Warren County Seat; Pop. 11,340; Zip Code 50125; 18 miles SSW of Des Moines; Lat. 41-21-29 N long. 093-33- 26 W.

It is said that the surveyors of the town were discussing a suitable name for it while eating lunch. One man had his food wrapped in a newspaper--a rare article in the new country. As the men read the paper before discarding it, they noticed an item from a now extinct Texas town called Indianola. The name pleased them and they selected it for the town.

POINTS OF INTEREST:

• Lake Ahquabi State Park. 5 miles S off US 69.

- Simpson College (1860). N Buxton Street & W Clinton Avenue.
- US National Balloon Museum. 711 N E Street.

INWOOD, City; Lyon County; Pop. 824; Zip Code 51240; 53 miles N of Sioux City; Lat. 43-18-26 N long. 096-25-54 W.

Known as Warren when settled in 1883, it was later called Pennington. When Jacob Rogers and his wife platted the town in 1891, they called it Inwood.

IOWA CITY, City; Johnson County Seat; Pop. 59,738; Zip Code 52240; 27 miles SSE of Cedar Rapids; Lat. 41-39-40 N long. 091- 31-48 W; Derived from the name of the Ioway Indian tribe. The word means "drowsy ones." This was the State's first capital, and is the home of the State University of Iowa. The city, lying along both sides of the Iowa River, extends from the river's bank over hills and bluffs.

Iowa City was founded as the capital of the Territory of Iowa. The founding act, approved by the first Legislative Assembly in Burlington (January 21, 1839), provided that three appointed commissioners select the most suitable 640 acres in Johnson County, employ surveyors and laborers to lay out the town, and supervise the plans and erection of the capitol, stipulating that the commissioners meet not later than May 1.

On March 3, Congress agreed to donate the section of land to be selected. Settlers flocked to Napoleon, Johnson County seat, May 1, 1839, to wait for the three commissioners, one from each judicial district, who were to meet there and select the capital site. Excitement ran high when noon came and only Chauncey Swan had arrived, as two commissioners had to be present to make the action legal. Delay might lose the capital, since other counties coveted the honor. Commissioner Swan sent a volunteer, Philip Clark, to bring John Ronalds of Louisa County, the nearest absent commissioner, to Napoleon before midnight. Ronalds lived only 35 miles away, but the distance was great in those days of prairie trails and bridgeless streams, and few believed he could arrive in time--but at five minutes to 12, by Swan's watch, he was there.

The justice of the peace swore the two men into office immediately so that the papers could be dated May 1. Observant persons noted, however, that the hours from midnight until sunrise were remarkably short. Swan and Ronalds selected a wild valley sloping up to one of the hilltops overlooking the Iowa River as the site and named it Iowa City.

Surveyors laid out wide city streets around the 12-acre capitol square before the first sale of town lots was held in August at Lean Back Hall, a rudely constructed rooming house and saloon. Funds from the land sale were used to start work on the capitol. Both the county seat and the post office at Napoleon were transferred to the new backwoods capital. Immigrants, the majority of them young men without families, began to arrive. Because travelers often lost the trail, the settlers hired Lyman Dillon in 1839 to plow a furrow from Iowa City to Dubuque. A road, well beaten by the wheels of the white-topped wagons of the incoming settlers, soon stretched beside the furrow, nearly 100 miles long. Later, Old Military Road followed this trail.

Log cabins and a few frame houses clustered around the site chosen for the capitol when its cornerstone was dedicated on July 4, 1840. Governor Lucas issued a proclamation designating Iowa City as the Territorial capital on April 30, 1841, and although the capitol was not finished, the Fourth Territorial Legislative Assembly convened in the city on December 6, 1841, in a frame building donated for temporary use by Walter Butler.

State constitutional conventions were held in the capitol during October, 1844 and May, 1946. Both the constitutions adopted at these conventions provided that Iowa City "shall be the seat of State Government until removed by law." With settlement moving rapidly toward the Missouri River, the western boundary, Iowa City was no longer near the population center of the State, and in spite of Iowa City's vigorous protests, the Assembly selected Monroe City as a new capital site in 1847, pacifying Iowa City by making it the seat of the State University. Public opinion, however, did not approve of Monroe City, so the capital remained at Iowa City until 1857, when Des Moines was selected. Iowa City had no municipal government until the General Assembly incorporated the town under a charter in 1853.

The episode of Hummer's Bell added spice to pioneer life in the late 1840s. Iowa City Presbyterians owed back salary to their pastor, the Reverend Michael Hummer, when he was excommunicated for his spiritual activities. In payment, he claimed most of the movable church property. When he was ready to take the bell, a crowd gathered to watch him climb the belfry and lower the bell to the ground. Just as it was lowered, several men removed the ladder, marooning the sputtering minister. The bell was loaded into a wagon, hauled to the mouth of Rapid Creek, and sunk in deep water. Hummer never recovered it. Later it was removed from the creek, taken to Utah, and sold to Brigham Young.

The first railroad company to lay tracks along the interior of Iowa, the Mississippi and Missouri, set the goal for reaching Iowa City before January 1, 1856. Tracks were still 1,000 feet from the station at nine o'clock the night before. Prominent citizens toiled side by side in zero weather with the railroad hands to complete the task. Great bonfires gave heat and light as each section of track was laid. Slowly the engine moved forward. At 11 o'clock, 200 feet from the station, the engine would not run. Undaunted, some of the men pushed the engine forward with crowbars while the others feverishly put down the remaining yards of steel. With only seconds to spare, the engine was crowbarred into the station, and the cheers echoed back from the hills.

On January 3, the first train from Chicago entered the city. For several years, Iowa City was a railroad terminus, resulting in a large transient population from the East, the South, and Europe, most of them headed for the far West.

The Mormon handcart expedition of 1856 brought about 1,300 European converts to Iowa City in answer to the call of Brigham Young. When the converts arrived, they camped during the spring and summer just west of the city, and constructed their own handcarts from the material available. With the inadequate wooden-wheeled vehicles ready, the first party of 226 set out June 9 toward the goal that lay more than 1,000 miles away over river, plain, and mountain. There was one pushcart for each five persons, piled with the allotted 17 pounds apiece, and one oxen- drawn wagon to each 100 individuals. Four other groups left Iowa City during the summer, the last party leaving July 28.

The act establishing the State University of Iowa was approved February 25, 1847, but the school did not open until 1855 when 75 students assembled, in answer to an advertisement for a short term of study under three professors. In 1857, when the capitol building was turned over to the university, there were 124 students. Lack of funds permitted only a normal department until 1860, when the university was reorganized. In 1861, the old Johnson County fairgrounds, now part of the city airport, was used as

Camp Fremont, the Civil War assembly ground for the 10th Iowa Infantry.

In the 1870s, the town had one of the largest breweries in the State. The Iowa City grape sugar factory produced 12,000 cases yearly of grape sugar, glucose, and corn syrup products during the 1880s. In the last years of the 19th and the first of the 20th century, a flint glass company and the Iowa City packing plant were important in the city's enterprise.

POINTS OF INTEREST:

- Coralville Lake. 3 1/2 miles N.
- Herbert Hoover National Historic Site. 10 miles E on I-80, exit 254 to West Branch.
- Herbert Hoover Presidential Library-Museum (1962).
- Lake Macbride State Park. 11 miles N on IA 1, then 4 miles W on IA 382 in Solon.
- Plum Grove (1844). 1030 Carroll Street.
- University of Iowa (1847). In W section of city on both sides of Iowa River.

HISTORICAL PLACES...

Close House; College Block Building; Congregational Chuirch of Iowa City; First Presbyterian Church; Kirkwood House; Old Capitol; Plum Grove (Robert Lucas House); South Summit Street District; Trinity Episcopal Church; Wentz, Jacob, House.

IOWA COUNTY, E central Iowa, 584 sq. mi.; Pop. 14,630; Named for the Iowa Indian tribe whose name means "sleepy ones" or "drowsy ones."

IOWA FALLS, City; Hardin County; Pop. 5,424; Zip Code 50126; 38 miles NNE of Ames; Lat. 42-31-21 N long. 093-15-04 W; Named for the falls in the nearby Iowa River.

IRWIN, City; Shelby County; Pop. 394; Zip Code 51446; Elev. 1264; 45 miles NE of Council Bluffs; Lat. 41-47-30 N long. 095- 12-20 W.

JACKSON COUNTY, E Iowa, 644 sq. mi.; Pop. 19,950; Named for Andrew Jackson (1767-1845), Seventh President of the United States; first Territorial Governor of Florida; Senator and judge from Tennessee. Jackson fought in the Creek War and defeated the British at the Battle of New Orleans in 1815; he received a gold medal and thanks of Congress.

JAMAICA, City; Guthrie County; Pop. 232; Zip Code 50128; 34 miles WSW of Ames; Elev. 1048; Lat. 41-50-46 N long. 094-18-34 W; Originally called Van Ness, the name was changed to avoid confusion with another town. The present name, Jamaica, is said to have been chosen randomly by pointing to a map blindfolded and landing on the island of Jamaica in the West Indies.

JANESVILLE, City; Black Hawk & Bremer Counties; Pop. 822; Zip Code 56647; 10 miles N of Waterloo. It was called Janesville in honor of the wife of founder, John T. Barrick.

JASPER COUNTY, S central Iowa, 734 sq. mi.; Pop. 34,795; Named for William Jasper (1750-1779), a private and sergeant in Col. William Moultrie's Second S.C. Infantry in 1775.

JEFFERSON, City; Greene County Seat; Pop. 4,292; Zip Code 50129; 35 miles W of Ames; Elev. 1078; Lat. 42-00-55 N long. 094-22-38 W; Like many towns throughout the country, this city was named for Thomas Jefferson.

It was founded after a group of settlers came to Des Moines about 1854 and borrowed $200 to purchase the town site. It was first called New Jefferson.

POINTS OF INTEREST:
- Mahanay Memorial Carillon Tower. Town center.

JEFFERSON COUNTY, SE Iowa, 436 sq. mi.; Pop. 16,310; Named for Thomas Jefferson (1743-1826), third President of the United States; second governor of Virginia; U.S. Minister to France; Vice President of the U.S.

JESUP, City; Buchanan County; Pop. 2,121; Zip Code 50648; 18 miles E of Waterloo; Lat. 42-28-32 N long. 092-03-49 W; Named for Morris K. Jesup of New York.

JEWELL JUNCTION, City; Hamilton County; Pop. 1,106; Zip Code 50130; 17 miles N of Ames; Lat. 42-18-25 N long. 093-38-24 W. Named for founder, David T. Jewell.

JOHNSON COUNTY, E Iowa, 619 sq. mi.; Pop. 96,119; Named for Richard Mentor Johnson (1781-1850), the Senator from Kentucky who fought at the Battle of the

Thames and was presented a sword by Congress for his heroism; he was also Vice President of the U.S.

JONES COUNTY, E Iowa, 585 sq. mi.; Pop. 19,444; Named for George Wallace Jones (1804-1896), Clerk of U.S. courts in Missouri and a Senator from Iowa.

KALONA, City; Washington County; Pop. 1,942; Zip Code 52247; 9 miles SSW of Iowa City; Lat. 41-28-59 N long. 091-42-21 W.

KAMRAR, City; Hamilton County; Pop. 203; Zip Code 50132; 20 miles ESE of Fort Dodge; Lat. 42-23-32 N long. 093-43-45 W.

KANAWHA, City; Hancock County; Pop. 763; Zip Code 50447; 31 miles NNE of Fort Dodge; Lat. 42-56-16 N long. 093-47-35 W; Named after the Kanawha River in West Virginia.

KELLERTON, City; Ringgold County; Pop. 314; Zip Code 50133; 68 miles SSW of Des Moines; Lat. 40-42-39 N long. 094-02-59 W. Named for Judge Isaac Keller.

KELLEY, City; Story County; Pop. 246; Zip Code 50134; 5 miles S of Ames; Lat. 41-57-02 N long. 093-39-54 W.

KELLOGG, City; Jasper County; Pop. 626; Zip Code 50135; 26 miles ENE of Des Moines; Lat. 41-43-05 N long. 092-54-26 W; Named for an early settler.

KEOKUK, City; Lee County Seat; Pop. 12,451; Zip Code 52632; 27 miles SSW of Burlington; Lat. 40-23-50 N long. 091-23-05 W; The area is rich in historical associations, and is also noted for the great dam that stretches across the Mississippi River. In the early days, the Indians called this place Puck-e-she-tuck, meaning "where the water runs shallow" or "at the foot of the rapids." Voyageurs and fur traders called it "The Point."
    The first white man to make a permanent settlement within the present limits of the city was Dr. Samuel C. Muir (1785- 1832)--a former surgeon in the United States Army--who erected a log cabin here in 1820 for his Indian wife and family. Moses Stillwell and Mark Aldrich opened a trading post in 1829 for the American Fur Company and that same

year, at the July 4 celebration, it proposed and adopted that the settlement be named for Chief Keokuk of the Sac tribe.

Chief Keokuk was three-quarters Indian. His father was full-blooded; his mother was a half-breed Sac. Keokuk was born in 1780 at the village of Saukenuk, not far from the present site of Rock Island, Illinois. Known as an orator of extraordinary eloquence, Keokuk culled his figures of speech from nature and based his arguments on skillful logic. After Black Hawk's defeat in the War of 1832, the Federal Government recognized Keokuk as the principal chief of the Sac and Fox Indians in this vicinity.

In 1831, the American Fur Company constructed a row of five hewn-log buildings; later these cabins were known as Rat Row. The first fully recorded religious services in Iowa took place from October 6 to 9, 1832. During that period, Father Van Quickenborne conferred the Sacrament of Baptism and performed five marriages. The first schoolmaster in Keokuk was Jesse Creighton, a shoemaker who, in 1834, had a class of eight pupils.

In the spring of 1837, the city was platted by Isaac Galland (1790-1858), an agent of the New York Land Company. Around this time, itinerant preachers of various faiths began to hold religious services in the town's auditorium (one of the Rat Row buildings), a long log building running along the levee near what is now the foot of Main Street.

Beginning with the 1840s, Keokuk was the manufacturing and jobbing headquarters for the pioneer Middle West. In the early days before the railroads, when rivers constituted the main means of transportation, it was known as the Gate City, not only for Iowa, but for the North and West as well, because of its position at the foot of the Des Moines rapids on the Mississippi. Steamboats were unable to go beyond this point. All passengers and freight had to be unloaded here and lightered over the rapids or continue the journey on land. Up to this time, the Half Breed Tract was involved in many disputes between Indians, white men, and half breeds as to title to individual holdings.

Francis Scott Key, who wrote *The Star Spangled Banner*, which became the U. S. national anthem, had a part in settling the litigation involved here. An attorney for the New York Land Company in 1841, he drew up the decree of partition of the lands. The plat established then is the basis for all titles today. The city of Keokuk was incorporated under a special charter in 1847.

A medical college that became the first medical department of the University of Iowa was established here in 1850, and moved to Iowa City in the 1860s. From a scientific standpoint, the geological formation of the Keokuk area proved interesting, the surrounding sections becoming classic in the annals of geology. Keokuk was the starting point for the classification of the Lower Carboniferous limestones throughout the entire Mississippi basin, being defined and described according to modern geological methods in 1858. Nearly the entire county is underlaid with this limestone, every variety of which affords a good grade of stone, easily quarried and readily dressed.

During the Civil War, Keokuk served as the port of embarkation of practically every Iowa regiment (except cavalry) and for those of several neighboring states. During this period, more than 200 Keokuk citizens were commissioned officers, many serving in the higher commands. Six war hospitals were established here to care for the wounded, later resulting in the creation of a National Cemetery.

Mrs. Annie Wittenmyer (1827-1900), who organized the Army diet kitchens during the Civil War, made her home in this city. Two Secretaries of War were among other Keokuk people to call the city home--W. W. Belknap, appointed in 1869, and George W. McCrary, in 1877. John W. Noble of this city took office as Secretary of the Interior under President Benjamin Harrison in 1889. Mary Timberman (1863-1899), actress, was born here and received her early dramatic training under a talented mother. Miss Timberman acted with Robert Keene, and in supporting roles with Richard Mansfield, Robert Mantell, and others. Cornelia Meigs, who was awarded the Newberry Medal for 1933-34 for *Invincible Louisa,* her biography of Louisa May Alcott, received her education in the Keokuk schools, where Rupert Hughes, another writer of repute, was also educated.

POINTS OF INTEREST:

- First Schoolhouse. River Road 13 miles N off US 61 in Galland.
- Keokuk Dam. (1910-13). End of N Water Street at riverfront.
- Keokuk River Museum. In Victory Park, foot of Johnson Street.
- National Cemetery. S 18th & Ridge Streets.
- Rand Park. Orleans Avenue between N 14th & N 17th Streets.

HISTORICAL PLACES...

Brown, Dr. Frank, House; Miller, Justice Samuel Freeman, House; U.S. Post Office and Courthouse.

KEOKUK COUNTY, SE central Iowa, 579 sq. mi.; Pop. 11,624; Named for Keokuk, chief of the Sauk Indians.

KEOSAUQUA, City; Van Buren County Seat; Pop. 1,020; Zip Code 52565; 27 miles SE of Ottumwa; Lat. 40-43-49 N long. 091-57- 44 W; The name is an Indian word meaning "great bend" and refers to a bend in the Des Moines River.

HISTORICAL PLACES...

Betonsport; Hotel, Manning.

KEOTA, City; Keokuk County; Pop. 1,000; Zip Code 52248; 23 miles SW of Iowa City; Lat. 41-21-53 N long. 091-57-12 W; First called Keoton, a combination of the first three letters of Keokuk County and the last three of nearby Washington County. The name was later altered for easier pronunciation.

KESWICK, City; Keokuk County; Pop. 284; Zip Code 50136; 28 miles NNE of Ottumwa; Lat. 41-27-20 N long. 092-14-19 W. Keswick was a pioneer's personal name.

KEYSTONE, City; Benton County; Pop. 568; Zip Code 52249; 19 miles W of Cedar Rapids; Lat. 42-00-07 N long. 092-11-40 W.

KINGSLEY, City; Plymouth County; Pop. 1,129; Zip Code 51028; 17 miles ENE of Sioux City; Lat. 42-35-06 N long. 095-57- 57 W; Named for Hon. J. T. Kingsley, a railroad official.

KIRKVILLE, City; Wapello County; Pop. 177; Zip Code 52566; 10 miles NW of Ottumwa; Lat. 41-09-31 N long. 092-30-18 W.

KLEMME, City; Hancock County; Pop. 587; Zip Code 50449; 26 miles WSW of Mason City; Lat. 43-00-37 N long. 093-36-21 W.

KNOXVILLE, City; Marion County Seat; Pop. 8,232; Zip Code 50138; 23 miles SE of Des Moines; Lat. 41-19-08 N long. 093-06-08 W. Named for General Henry Knox, Secretary of War under Washington.

KOSSUTH COUNTY, N Iowa, 979 sq. mi.; Pop. 18,591; Named for Lajos Kossuth (1802-1894), Minister of Finance in the Hungarian government; he was appointed governor or dictator of Hungary.

LACONA, City; Warren County; Pop. 357; Zip Code 50139; 28 miles S of Des Moines; Lat. 41-11-11 N long. 093-22-47 W.

LAKE CITY, City; Calhoun County; Pop. 1,841; Zip Code 51449; 34 miles WSW of Fort Dodge; Lat. 42-16-18 N long. 094-44- 14 W. Named for its geography.

LAKE MILLS, City; Winnebago County; Pop. 2,143; Zip Code 50450; 27 miles NW of Mason City; Lat. 43-24-39 N long. 093-32-02 W.
It was first known as Slauchville, later as Saylorville; it received its present name when a mill was built nearby on the edge of a small lake--now dry.

LAKE PARK, City; Dickinson County; Pop. 996; Zip Code 51347; 79 miles NE of Sioux City; Lat. 43-27-19 N long. 095-19-16 W.

LAKESIDE, City; Buena Vista County; Pop. 522; 51 miles W of Fort Dodge; Lat. 42-37-17 N long. 095-10-23 W. Descriptively named.

LAKE VIEW, City; Sac County; Pop. 1,303; Zip Code 51450; 46 miles WSW of Fort Dodge; Elev. 1,245; Lat. 42-17-57 N long. 095- 04-07 W. Named for its view of the adjacent lake.

LAKOTA, City; Kossuth County; Pop. 281; Zip Code 50451; 49 miles WNW of Mason City; Lat. 43-22-20 N long. 094-06-42 W; Derived from Dakota, the name for the Sioux Indian nation. Originally called Germania for its many German residents, the town name was changed during World War I, due to anti-German sentiment.

LAMONI, City; Decatur County; Pop. 2,319; Zip Code 50140; 71 miles SSW of Des Moines; Lat. 40-37-34 N long. 093-55-32 W. A Mormon name meaning "righteous king."

LAMONT, City; Buchanan County; Pop. 471; Zip Code 50650; 39 miles ENE of Waterloo; Lat. 42-35-58 N long. 091-38-23 W; The name is probably of French origin and comes from "le mont," which means "the mountain."

LA MOTTE, City; Jackson County; Pop. 219; Elev. 915; 10 miles S of Dubuque; Lat. 42-17-45 N long. 090-37-15 W; Most likely named for Pierre Sieur de la Motte, a French captian.

LANSING, City; Allamakee County; Pop. 1,007; Zip Code 51451; 67 miles NNW of Dubuque; Lat. 43-22-14 N long. 091-13-12 W. The city was named after Lansing, Michigan. The first claim on the town site was staked in 1848 by H. H. Houghton who, with John Haney, Sr., laid out the town in 1851 at the base of Mount Hosmer, a sheer rugged bluff rising abruptly from the river to a height of 400 feet.

HISTORICAL PLACES...
Lansing Stone School.

LA PORTE CITY, City; Black Hawk County; Pop. 2,128; 15 miles SE of Waterloo; Lat. 42-18-54 N long. 092-11-31 W; The name may either be from the French word meaning "door" or "opening", or from the La Porte family. Another source says it was first called La Porte for the city of that name in Indiana.

LARCHWOOD, City; Lyon County; Pop. 739; Zip Code 51241; 63 miles N of Sioux City; Lat. 43-27-23 N long. 096-27-03 W. Named for the many larch trees planted in the area by J.W. Fell, who founded the community in 1870 and planted more than 100,000 fruit and forest trees on land adjoining the town plat.

LARRABEE, City; Cherokee County; Pop. 175; Zip Code 51029; 42 miles ENE of Sioux City; Lat. 42-51-42 N long. 095-33-10 W. Larrabee was named for William Larrabee, Governor of Iowa (1886- 1890).

LATIMER, City; Franklin County; Pop. 430; Zip Code 50452; 30 miles SSW of Mason City; Lat. 42-46-01 N log. 093-21-57 W.

LAURENS, City; Pocahontas County; Pop. 1,550; Zip Code 50554; 41 miles WNW of Fort Dodge; Lat. 42-50-48 N long. 094-50- 43 W. The city was named for a nineteenth century resident.

HISTORICAL PLACES...
Laurens Public Library.

LAWLER, City; Chickasaw County; Pop. 517; Zip Code 52154; 41 miles NNE of Waterloo; Lat. 43-04-16 N long. 092-10-36 W. Named for a prominent resident.

LAWTON, City; Woodbury County; Pop. 482; Zip Code 51030; 5 miles ESE of Sioux City; Elev. 1,179; Lat. 42-28-52 N long. 096- 10-49 W.

LE CLAIRE, City; Scott County; Pop. 2,734; Zip Code 52753; 17 miles ENE of Davenport; Lat. 41-35-52 N long. 0909-20-47 W; Named in honor of Antoine Le Clair, the founder of Davenport.
Le Claire was the boyhood home of William F. (Buffalo Bill) Cody. Isaac Cody, father of Buffalo Bill, was a pioneer settler of Scott County. William, one of five children, was born Feb. 26, 1846, on what was then known as the John S. Wilson farm.

LE GRAND, City; Marshall County; Pop. 854; Zip Code 50142; 39 miles NE of Des Moines; Lat. 42-00-20 N long. 092-46-26 W; The name is French for "the big one." It was named for LeGrand Byington, an Iowa City politician.

LEE COUNTY, SE corner Iowa, 528 sq. mi.; Pop. 38,687; Named for Lee of Marsh, Delevan and Lee in Albany, New York, and of the New York Land Company.

LEHIGH, City; Webster County; Pop. 536; Zip Code 50557; 11 miles SSE of Fort Dodge; Lat. 42-21-15 N long. 094-04-04 W; Named for the Lehigh River, a tributary of the Delaware in Pennsylvania. The name Lehigh is derived from a Delaware Indian word meaning "forked stream."

LEIGHTON, City; Winnebago County; Pop. 142; Zip Code 50143; 29 miles NW of Ottumwa; Lat. 41-20-20 N long. 092-47-02 W.

LE MARS, City; Plymouth County Seat; Pop. 8,454; 20 miles NNE of Sioux City; Elev. 1231; Lat. 42-47-39 N long. 096-09-55 W; The name is composed of the initials of the six young ladies who accompanied the city's founder on his first visit to the site.

In 1876, William B. Close of Trinity College, Cambridge, England, acquired a blister while rowing with his team in a regatta at the Philadelphia Centennial. Sitting in the side lines, he became acquainted with Daniel Paullin, a banker and landowner of Quincy, Ill. Paullin, in glowing terms, described the Iowa lands newly opened to settlement by the United States Government. His enthusiasm inspired Close to visit the area with eastern speculators.

Later Close married Paullin's daughter. Close persuaded his brothers in England to come to America and formed a colonization company. They centered operations in Plymouth County, purchasing 30,000 acres; elsewhere they bought tracts of 14,000 18,000, 19,000, and 25,000 acres. The Iowa Land Co. published enthusiastic accounts of the opportunities in the new country in England, offering 40 percent and 50 percent profits to investors. Prospective colonists were assured that it would be safe to come to Iowa, "for no one carried revolvers or other firearms, bowie knives and such playthings."

By the early 1800s, a large group of colonists was on its way from England, and steamship companies specialized in tickets for "New York and Le Mars, Iowa, U.S.A."

The Close brothers aided English farmers in bringing their flocks of sheep, their fat cattle, and their families to the rolling hills of the new country. British customs were observed. All colonists punctiliously dressed for dinner. Here, as in other English settlements, the sun never rose or set on an unshaven British chin. Fashionable dinners and dances were held at the Albion House.

The drought, grasshopper sieges, bitter winters, and high expenses of the later 1880s and early 1890s caused many of the colonists to lose their enthusiasm. Fuel was scarce, too. Captain Moreton made an attempt at coal mining--a venture causing such rumors and speculations that mineral rights in the vicinity were leased at prices soaring from $100 to $300 an acre, and companies were formed to exploit possible strikes.

The operations, however, proved so costly that when an extensive boring revealed only lignite, the owners abandoned the project. Captain Moreton, himself a heavy loser, endeavored to justify himself. The fact that so much money had been expended locally, and caused a temporary boom, went far to mitigate the bitterness and discontent that might otherwise have resulted.

Eventually the colony disintegrated. William B. Close returned to England, and many other followed. Some went up to Pipestone, Minn., others to Canada.

People of German and other nationalities bought nearby land, and the British atmosphere of the settlement changed. Choice houses and herds were sold, and polo and cricket fields became neglected.

POINTS OF INTEREST:

- Plymouth County Historical Museum. Corner of 1st Avenue SW & 4th Street SW.
- Westmar College (1890). 3rd Avenue SE.

LEON, City; Decatur County Seat; Pop. 2,047; Zip Code 50144; 61 miles SSW of Des Moines; Lat. 40-45-11 N long. 093-44- 08 W. When the area was first surveyed, it was to be called Independence. But as a settlement of that name had already been established in Iowa, the town was called South Independence until the winter of 1854-55; then the name was changed to Leon in response to a petition to the Legislature submitted by citizens of the community.

LESTER, City; Lyon County; Pop. 257; Zip Code 51242; 62 miles N of Sioux City; Lat. 43-26-32 N long. 096-20-06 W.

LETTS, City; Louisa County; Pop. 390; Zip Code 52754; 29 miles WSW of Davenport; Lat. 41-19-42 N long. 091-14-13 W.

LEWIS, City; Cass County; Pop. 433; Zip Code 51544; 33 miles E of Council Bluffs; Lat. 41-18-18 N long. 095-04-41 W. Named for U.S. Senator, Lewis Cass.

LIBERTYVILLE, City; Jefferson County; Pop. 264; Zip Code 52567; 14 miles ESE of Ottumwa; Lat. 40-57-26 N long. 092-02-37 W.

LIME SPRINGS, City; Howard County; Pop. 438; Zip Code 52155; 43 miles ENE of Mason City; Lat. 43-26-55 N long. 092-17- 05 W; So named for springs in the rocks at this place.

LINCOLN, City; Tama County; Pop. 173; Zip Code 50652; 19 miles SW of Waterloo; Lat. 42-15-51 N long. 092-41-15 W. Named in honor of Abraham Lincoln.

LINDEN, City; Dallas County; Pop. 201; Zip Code 50146; 43 miles W of Des Moines; Elev. 1,120; Lat. 41-38-34 N long. 094-16- 16 W. The city was named after the beloved linden tree.

LINEVILLE, City; Wayne County; Pop. 289; Zip Code 50147; 66 miles WSW of Ottumwa; Lat. 40-34-49 N long. 093-31-29 W; Situated on the Iowa-Missouri state line, the town was named in 1871 for its location. It was first known as Grand River.

LINN COUNTY, E Iowa, 717 sq. mi.; Pop. 168,767; Named for Lewis Fields Linn (1795-1843), Surgeon in Col. Henry Dodges mounted riflemen in War of 1812; graduated Ph.d in 1815; Senator from Missouri.

LINN GROVE, City; Buena Vista County; Pop. 194; Zip Code 51033; 56 miles ENE of Sioux City; Lat. 42-53-32 N long. 095-14- 37 W; Named for Hon. Lewis F. Linn, U. S. Senator from Missouri.

LISBON, City; Linn County; Pop. 1,452; Zip Code 52253; 22 miles ESE of Cedar Rapids; Lat. 41-55-22 N long. 091-22-59 W. Lisbon takes its name from the great city in Portugal. It was colonized in the spring of 1847 by 61 people from Pennsylvania-- Christian Hershey, with his sons and grandsons, and their families.

LITTLE ROCK, City; Lyon County; Pop. 493; 65 miles NNE of Sioux City; Lat. 43-26-39 N long. 095-52-59 W; Named after the Little Sioux River, which was originally called "Petite riviere des Sioux" by the French.

LITTLE SIOUX, City; Harrison County; Pop. 205; Elev. 103; 41 NNW of Council Bluffs; Lat. 41-48-34 N long. 096-01-15 W.

LIVERMORE, City; Humboldt County; Pop. 436; Zip Code 50558; 23 miles N of Fort Dodge; Lat. 42-52-12 N long. 094-11-16 W.

LOGAN, City; Harrison County Seat; Pop. 1,401; ;Zip Code 51546; 27 miles N of Council Bluffs Elev. 1,104; Lat. 41-38-41 N long. 095-47-44 W. It was formerly known as Boyer Falls because of its proximity to the falls on the river. The name was changed in 1864 to honor Civil War general, John A. Logan.

LOHRVILLE, City; Calhoun County; Pop. 453; Zip Code 51453; 26 miles SW of Fort Dodge; Lat. 42-16-27 N long. 094-33-15 W.

LONE ROCK, City; Kossuth County; Pop. 185; Zip Code 50559; 46 miles NNW of Fort Dodge; Lat. 43-13-23 N long. 094-18-59 W; Named for a single tree which stood on the prairie.

LONE TREE, City; Johnson County; Pop. 979; Zip Code 52755; 14 miles SE of Iowa City; Lat. 41-29-17 N long. 091-25-33 W.

LONG GROVE, City; Scott County; Pop. 605; Zip Code 52756; 13 miles NNE of Davenport; Lat. 41-41-51 N long. 090-34-57 W.

LORIMOR, City; Union County; Pop. 377; Zip Code 50149; 45 miles SW of Des Moines; Lat. 41-07-42 N long. 094-03-37 W. Founded by Josiah Lorimar, and named in his honor.

LOST NATION, City; Clinton County; Pop. 467; Zip Code 52254; 28 miles WNW of Clinton; Lat. 41-58-06 N long. 090-50-36 W. A reference to the Indians.

LOUISA COUNTY, SE Iowa, 403 sq. mi.; Pop. 11,592; Named for Louisa Massey, pioneer heroine who shot and wounded her brother's murderer.

LOVILIA, City; Monroe County; Pop. 551; Zip Code 50150; 28 miles WNW of Ottumwa; Lat. 41-08-09 N long. 092-54-17 W.

LUCAS COUNTY, S Iowa, 434 sq. mi.; Pop. 9,070; Named for Robert Lucas (1781-1853), First Territorial Governor of Iowa. Lucas was also the twelfth governor of Ohio; a Col. in the U.S. Army 1812; and a governor of Ohio.

LYON COUNTY, NW corner Iowa, 588 sq. mi.; Pop. 11,952; Named for Nathaniel Lyon (1818-1861), who fought in the Seminole War and Mexican War. He was a captain in 1851, and commanded the U.S. arsenal at St. Louis, Missouri. He was killed while leading the First Iowa Infantry at the Battle of Wilson Creek, Missouri.

MACEDONIA, City; Pottawattamie County; Pop. 262; Zip Code 51549; 15 miles ESE of Council Bluffs; Lat. 41-11-19 N long. 095- 25-51 W. The city was named for the area in ancient Greece.

MCGREGOR, City; Clayton County; Pop. 797; 48 miles NW of Dubuque Lat. 43-01-06 N long. 091-10-57 W; Named for Alexander McGregor, an early proprietor.

MADRID, City; Boone County; Pop. 2,395; Zip Code 50156; 13 miles SW of Ames; Lat. 41-52-27 N long. 093-48-51 W. First named Swede Point in 1852, in honor of many settlers of that nationality. Following a disagreement, when additional land from the estate of Mrs. Anna Dalander was made available to the community, the place was in 1855 renamed for the capital of Spain, eulogized by a Spanish workman locally employed.

MADISON COUNTY, S central Iowa, 564 sq. mi.; Pop. 12,483; Named for James Madison (1751-1836), Fourth President of the United States; First general Assembly of Virginia; Continental Congress 1780-83 and 1786-88; U.S. Secretary of State in cabinet of President Jefferson.

MAGNOLIA, City; Harrison County; Pop. 204; 32 Miles NNW of Council Bluffs; Lat. 41-41-45 N long. 095-52-35 W; Named for the magnolia trees at this place.

MAHASKA COUNTY, SE central Iowa, 572 sq. mi.; Pop. 21,522; Named for Mahaska (1784-1834), Chief of the Iowa Indian tribe, whose name means "white cloud".

MALCOM, City; Poweshiek County; Pop. 447; Zip Code 50157; 42 miles E of Des Moines; Lat. 41-42-45 N long. 092-33-40 W; Named for an early Scotch settler.

MALLARD, City; Palo Alto County; Pop. 360; Zip Code 50562; 38 miles NW of Fort Dodge; Lat. 42-55-06 N long. 094-41-23 W.

MALVERN, City; Mills County; Pop. 1,210; Zip Code 51551; 17 miles SSE of Council Bluffs; Lat. 41-00-04 N long. 095-32-28 W.

MANCHESTER, City; Delaware County Seat; Pop. 5,137; Zip Code 52057; 41 miles W of Dubuque; Lat. 42-31-03 N long. 091-24- 31 W; The town was first known as Burrington, but this name was discarded in 1856 because of its similarity to Burlington. According to one story, the town name was created by twisting Chesterman, the name of an early settler, but it is more probable that the town was named for Manchester, England, whence came many of the early residents of the community.

HISTORICAL PLACES...
Spring Branch Butter Factory Site.

MANILLA, City; Crawford County; Pop. 898; Zip Code 51454; 49 miles NNE of Council Bluffs; Elev. 1317; Lat. 41-53-13 N long. 0-95-14-11 W.

MANLY, City; Worth County; Pop. 1,349; Zip Code 50456; 9 miles NNW of Mason City; Elev. 1198; Lat. 43-17-21 N long. 093- 12-16 W.

MANNING, City; Carroll County; Pop. 1,484; Zip Code 51432; 55 miles NE of Council Bluffs; Elev. 1355; Lat. 41-54-28 N long. 095-08-21 W; Named for a merchant who lived here.

MANSON, City; Calhoun County; Pop. 1,844; Zip Code 50563; 19 miles W of Fort Dodge; Lat. 42-32-06 N long. 094-32-26 W; The name "Manson" came from one of the town's residents.

MAPLETON, City; Monona County; Pop. 1,294; Zip Code 51034; 32 miles SE of Sioux City; Elev. 1157; Lat. 42-10-25 N long. 095-47-43 W.

MAQUOKETA, City; Jackson County Seat; Pop. 6,111; Zip Code 52060; 25 miles S of Dubuque; Lat. 42-03-51 N long. 090-40-14 W; Probably named for the Maquoketa River, which got its name from the Indian words meaning "there are bears" or "abundance of bears."

POINTS OF INTEREST:

- Jackson County Historical Museum. E Quarry Street at Fairgrounds.
- Maquoketa Caves State Park. 7 mile NW on County road.
- Old Mill Gallery. 1 mile E on IA 64.
- Sagers Museum. At entrance to Maquoketa State Park.

MARATHON, City; Buena Vista County; Pop. 320; Zip Code 50565; 46 miles WNW of Fort Dodge; Lat. 42-51-32 N long. 094-57- 38 W. Probably named after the site in Greece.

MARBLE ROCK, City; Floyd County; Pop. 361; Zip Code 50653; 16 miles SE of Mason City; Lat. 42-58-05 N long. 092-52-08 W. Descriptively named for a local feature.

MARCUS, City; Cherokee County; Pop. 1,171; Zip Code 51035; 32 miles NE of Sioux City; Lat. 42-49-23 N long. 095-48-34 W.

MARENGO, City; Iowa County Seat; Pop. 2,270; Zip Code 52301; 18 miles SW of Cedar Rapids; Lat. 41-47-25 N long. 092-04- 07 W; Named for the battlefield in Italy.

MARION, City; Linn County; Pop. 20,403; Zip Code 52302; 9 E of Cedar Rapids; Lat. 42-01-25 N long. 091-36-01 W; Named in honor of Gen. Francis Marion.

MARION COUNTY, S central Iowa, 567 sq. mi.; Pop. 30,001; Named for Francis Marion (1732-1795), Brig. general and commander of Marion's brigade. Marion was known as "the Swamp Fox." He harrassed English troops in the American Revolution and won the Battle of Eutaw Springs. He also served in S. C. State Senate.

MARNE, City; Cass County; Pop. 149; Zip Code 51552; 32 ENE of Council Bluffs; Lat. 41-27-03 N long. 095-06-12 W. Named after the area in France.

MARQUETTE, City; Clayton County; Pop. 479; Zip Code 52158; 48 miles NW of Dubuque; Lat. 43-02-44 N long. 091-11-28 W; This city was named in honor of Jacques Marquette, the Jesuit priest who explored the Illinois and Mississippi valleys with Joliet.

POINTS OF INTEREST:

- Effigy Mounds National Monument. 3 miles North on IA 76.
- Pikes Peak State Park. 5 miles Se on IA 340.
- Spook Cave-Beulah Falls Park. 5 miles W on US 18, then 2 miles N on unnumbered road.

HISTORICAL PLACES...

Effigy Mounds National Monument.

MARSHALLTOWN, City; Marshall County Seat; Pop. 25,178; Zip Code 50158; 37 miles NE of Des Moines; Lat. 42-02-07 N long. 092- 53-40 W. The town is situated on the prairie, stenciled with railroad tracks and hard-surfaced highways and bordered on the north by the Iowa River. The city was named for Marshall, Michigan, by the first permanent settler, Henry Anson, who emigrated from the East by covered wagon in the spring of 1851. The suffix "town" was added later to distinguish it from another town in the State.

The first court of Marshall County (created in 1846) was held by Judge Williams in the fall of 1851 in John Ralls's cabin in a grove north of Anson's home. In the same year, Marietta was chosen as the county seat. Henry Anson was furious. He roused his neighbors to action, insisting that their town should be chosen. The Marietta residents jeered at "Anson's Potato Patch." A bitter seven-year wrangle followed, drawn out by personal and political disputes and legal sparring. The Supreme Court of Iowa finally decided in favor of Marshalltown in December 1859.

On June 11, 1859, a group of Marshalltown businessmen, headed by Greenleaf M. Woodbury, formed the Cedar Rapids & Missouri River Railroad Company, in order to build a line west from Cedar Rapids to the Missouri River. The Government issued the company a land grant March 24, 1860, stipulating that the first 40 miles of the new road should be finished by January 1, 1862. A subscription list was started; those who could not spare money volunteered to work, give free room and board to other workers, or lend teams of horses. As the time limit approached, crews worked day and night to finish the required section of the road. The last spike was driven at midnight, December 31, 1861. A year later, in January of 1863, the line was completed to Marshalltown.

Many men from Marshalltown and the surrounding country fought with the Union forces in the Civil War. A local unit, the Bowen Guard, was mustered into service in July of 1861 as Company D, 5th Iowa Infantry. W. P. Hepburn, Marshall County prosecuting attorney, organized a company of the Second Cavalry, serving as its captain. Marshalltown, incorporated in 1863, was one of several cities that held sanitary fairs that year. A large amount of money was raised and sent to the front to improve first aid and hospital work.

Industrially, the city's development began in the first years after the Civil War with the establishment of flannel, blanket, woolen goods, wagon, and carriage factories and an iron foundry. Repair shops and terminal property of the Central Railroad of Iowa (Minneapolis & St. Louis) were located in Marshalltown when the railroad was built through in 1869.

Twice during the 1870s, flames threatened to destroy commercial Marshalltown. The first fire, on May 2, 1872, spread rapidly, owing to a high wind, and swept over an area of 15 acres which caused damages in excess of $200,000. The town was little more than rebuilt when, on April 6, 1876, another blaze burned $30,000 worth of elevators, warehouses, and lumberyards.

When hospitalization of Civil War veterans became a matter for State consideration, Marshalltown offered to donate 28 acres of ground for a home. The city also raised $12,000, later increasing the amount to $30,000, and adding to the acreage. The General Assembly in 1887 accepted the offer, appropriating $100,000 for the erection and maintenance of an institution.

When Henry Anson died on November 30, 1905, at the age of 79, the city he founded and fostered was an important shopping and manufacturing center. Since that time, Marshalltown has quietly expanded its manufactures in keeping with changing times.

POINTS OF INTEREST:
- Fisher Community Center. 709 S Center Street.
- Riverview Park. North on 3rd Avenue & Woodland.
- Susie Sower Historical House. 2nd Avenue & State Street.

HISTORICAL PLACES...
Marshall County Courthouse.

MARSHALL COUNTY, Central Iowa, 574 sq. mi.; Pop. 38,276; Named for Chief Justice, John Marshall.

MARTENSDALE, City; Warren County; Pop. 491; Zip Code 50160; 22 miles SW of Des Moines; Lat. 41-22-19 N long. 093-44-24 W. Named for an early settler.

MASON CITY, City; Cerro Gordo County Seat; Pop. 29,040; Zip Code 50401; 56 miles NW of Waterloo; Lat. 43-09-11 N long. 093- 12-49 W. The city began as a railroad and manufacturing town in north central Iowa. Rising from rolling prairies, it is the center of a fertile agricultural region.

Most of the pioneers in the territory were of the Masonic order, and the first settlement was named Shibboleth. Mason City was originally known as Masonic Grove, but when the town was platted in 1854, the name was changed. The county (Cerro Gordo) was organized in 1851 and named for a battlefield of the Mexican War.

John B. Long and John L. McMillan, said to have been Mason City's first settlers, arrived in 1853 and made extensive claims along Lime Creek. An Indian uprising (Grindstone War at Clear Lake) on July 4, 1854, pushed most of the settlers to the older towns on the Cedar River, leaving the county practically depopulated. Gradually the settlers returned and secured claims at a land auction, which opened on September 4, 1854. Cabins were built, sod was turned, and seeds were planted. The first mill was erected in 1855 on Lime Creek by Elisha Randall; at the same time, he built a lime kiln. In 1872, he invented and patented what was known as Randall's Perpetual Lime Kiln, which proved so successful that it was adopted in many parts of the country.

Until 1855, Mason City was without local government, as Cerro Gordo County had been attached to Floyd County for administrative purposes. In August, the citizens voted again for the organization of Cerro Gordo as an independent county, and three commissioners were appointed to determine the county seat. Mason City and Clear Lake were the chief competitors. Mason City, as the point nearest the geographical center of the county, was chosen. However, the Sixth General Assembly, in December 1856, designated Clark Lake, under the name of Livonia, as the seat. But at a county election held in April 1858, Mason City was again selected.

As early as 1869, Mason City gave promise of becoming a railroad center, with the Milwaukee Railroad laying its track to the city in that year. In 1870, it was completed northward to Austin, Minnesota. In 1870, the Iowa Central Railroad finished its line into the city. Sixteen years later, the Great Western arrived, followed by the Chicago & North Western short line (later Rock Island), which came in 1909.

POINTS OF INTEREST:

- Charles H. MacNider Museum. 303 2nd Street SE.
- Kinney Pioneer Museum. 7 miles W on US 18.
- Margaret M. MacNider Park. 841 Birch Drive at Kentucky Avenue NE.
- Prairie School Homes. List available from the Chamber of Commerce.

HISTORICAL PLACES...

Mason City National Bank Building (Hub Clothing Store, Adams Building); Park Inn Hotel.

MASSENA, City; Cass County; Pop. 372; Zip Code 50853; 47 miles E of Council Bluffs; Lat. 41-14-52 N long. 094-47-20 W; Named for French Marshall, Andre Massena.

MAXWELL, City; Story County; Pop. 788; Zip Code 50161; 18 miles N of Des Moines; Lat. 41-54-27 N long. 093-23-06 W.

MAYNARD, City; Fayette County; Pop. 513; Zip Code 50655; 32 miles NE of of Waterloo; Lat. 42-45-32 N long. 091-53-03 W.

MECHANICSVILLE, City; Cedar County; Pop. 1,012; Zip Code 52306; 28 miles ESE of Cedar Rapids; Lat. 41-53-56 N long. 091- 13-57 W. The first settlers here were mechanics, and thus named the town.

MEDIAPOLIS, City; Des Moines County; Pop. 1,637; Zip Code 52637; 15 miles N of Burlington; Lat. 41-00-38 N long. 091-09-28 W; Named for its location halfway between Burlington and Washington.

MELBOURNE, City; Marshall County; Pop. 669; Zip Code 50162; 25 miles NNE of Des Moines; Lat. 41-56-20 N long. 093-06-27 W. Probably named after the Australian city.

MELCHER, City; Marion County; Pop. 1,302; Zip Code 50163; 26 miles SSE of Des Moines; Lat. 41-13-21 N long. 093-14-33 W.

MELROSE, City; Monroe County; Pop. 150; Zip Code 52569; 35 miles W of of Ottumwa; Lat. 40-58-37 N long. 093-03-13 W.

MENLO, City; Guthrie County; Pop. 356; Zip Code 50164; 50 miles W of of Des Moines; Elev. 1,265; Lat. 41-32-37 N long. 094- 24-09 W.

MERIDEN, City; Cherokee County; Pop. 193; Zip Code 51037; 37 miles ENE of Sioux City; Lat. 42-47-37 N long. 095-38-01 W. Originally called Hazzard, it was later renamed by the Post Office.

MERRILL, City; Plymouth County; Pop. 729; Zip Code 51038; 14 miles N of Sioux City; Lat. 42-43-14 N long. 096-14-51 W. Named for a railroad man.

MIDDLETOWN, City; Des Moines County; Pop. 386; Zip Code 52638; 3 miles NW of Burlington; Lat. 40-49-46 N long. 091-15-02 W. It was first called Lewis Point, for an early settler, and was in 1847 descriptively renamed by John Sharp of Pennsylvania.

MILES, City; Jackson County; Pop. 409; Zip Code 52064; 13 miles N Clinton; Lat. 42-03-05 N long. 090-19-01 W; Founded by a man called Miles, and named for him.

MILFORD, City; Dickinson County; Pop. 2,170; Zip Code 51351; 72 miles NW of Fort Dodge; Lat. 43-20-24 N long. 095-09-30 W. Named after an early mill site.

MILLS COUNTY, SW Iowa, 447 sq. mi.; Pop. 13,202; Named for Major Frederick D. Mills, who was involved in the attack on San Antonio in Garita, Mexico.

MILO, City; Warren County; Pop. 864; Zip Code 50166; 20 miles S of Des Moines; Lat. 41-17-18 N long. 093-26-31 W. Named for an early pioneer.

MILTON, City; Van Buren County; Pop. 506; Zip Code 52570; 26 miles SSE of Ottumwa; Lat. 40-40-18 N long. 092-10-14 W. Named after the great English poet.

MINBURN, City; Dallas County; Pop. 346; Zip Code 50167; 32 miles WNW of Des Moines; Elev. 1,042; Lat. 41-45-25 N long. 094- 02-18 W. It was platted in 1869 by J. B. Hill and D. F. Rogers.

MINGO, City; Jasper County; Pop. 252; Zip Code 50127; 11 miles NNE of Des Moines; Lat. 41-46-43 N long. 093-12-21 W; The name may either have come from the eastern states where "mingo" was a term for certain Iroquois-speaking Indians, or from James Fenimore Cooper's books, in which he called the enemies of the Delaware Indians "mingos."

MISSOURI VALLEY, City; Harrison County; Pop. 2,888; Zip Code 51555; 22 miles NNW of Council Bluffs; Elev. 1,019; Lat. 41- 33-29 N long. 095-54-38 W; The first settler in Missouri Valley was H. B. Henricks, who arrived in 1854. In 1856, the McIntosh brothers came, and the place was first named McIntosh Point, and later St. Johns. When the C. & N. W. R. R. was built through the area, the name was changed to Missouri Valley Junction; later the Junction was dropped. The name "Missouri" came from the Indian word Miss-sou-li-au, which referred to "canoe men" or the Indians living east of the Mississippi River.

POINTS OF INTEREST:
- DeSota National Wildlife Refuge. 6 miles W on US 30.
- Harrison County Historical Village. 3 miles Ne on US 30.

MITCHELL, City; Mitchell County; Pop. 170; 14 miles NE of of Mason City; Lat. 43-19-19 N long. 092-52-03 W; Named for Irish patriot, John Mitchell.

MITCHELL COUNTY, N Iowa, 467 sq. mi.; Pop. 10,928; Named for John Mitchell.

MITCHELLVILLE, City; Polk County; Pop. 1,670; Zip Code 50169; 4 miles NNE of of Des Moines; Lat. 41-39-55 N long. 093- 21-39 W; Named for Thomas Mitchell.

MODALE, City; Harrison County; Pop. 289; Zip Code 51556; 29 miles NNW of Council Bluffs; Elev. 1,013; Lat. 41-36-58 N long. 096-02-47 W; The name is a combination of "Mo," the abbreviation for Missouri, plus dale, and is descriptive of the city's location near the Missouri River.

MONDAMIN, City; Harrison County; Pop. 403; Zip Code 51557; 35 miles NNW of of Council Bluffs; Lat. 41-42-37 N long. 096-03- 33 W; "Mondamin" is an Ojibwa Indian word meaning "corn."

MONMOUTH, City; Jackson County; Pop. 169; Zip Code 52309; 33 miles WNW of Clinton; Lat. 42-04-31 N long. 090-52-37 W.

MONONA, City; Clayton County; Pop. 1,520; Zip Code 52159; 54 miles NW of Dubuque; Lat. 43-03-18 N long. 091-23-38 W; One possibility is that it was named for the character "Monona" in Lewis Deffenbach's play, *Oolaita,* or the Indian Heroine. Another is it was named for an Indian girl who, believing her white lover had been slain by her people, jumped from a high rock into the Mississippi River. Although the group of men who named the town discovered the girl's name was Winona, the original name was not changed.

MONONA COUNTY, W Iowa, 699 sq. mi.; Pop. 10,034; Named for an Indian maiden who jumped from a high cliff into the Mississippi River, committing suicide in the belief that her tribesmen killed her white lover.

MONROE, City; Jasper County; Pop. 1,739; Zip Code 50170; 14 miles ESE of of Des Moines; Lat. 41-31-36 N long. 093-06-24 W; It was first named Tool's Point by Adam Tool, who laid it out. A year later, like many American towns, this city was renamed for President James Monroe.

MONROE COUNTY, S Iowa, 435 sq. mi.; Pop. 8,114; Named for James Monroe (1758-1831), Fifth President of the United States; twelfth and sixteenth governor of Virginia; Senator from Virginia; U.S. Secretary of State under President James Madison.

MONTEZUMA, City; Poweshiek County Seat; Pop. 1,651; Zip Code 50171; 42 E of Des Moines; Lat. 41-33-36 N long. 092-31-58 W; Named for Montezuma II, the Aztec ruler who was captured by the Spanish, under Hernando Cortes, in 1520.

MONTGOMERY COUNTY, SW Iowa, 422 sq. mi.; Pop. 12,076; Named for Richard Montgomery (1738-1775), Provincial Congress; Brig. general, Continental Army. He was captured in Montreal, Canada, and killed leading an assault against Quebec.

MONTICELLO, City; Jones County; Pop. 3,522; Zip Code 52219; 30 miles WSW of Dubuque; Lat. 42-14-14 N long. 091-25-22 W; Probably named for the famous Virginia estate of Thomas Jefferson.

MONTOUR, City; Tama County; Pop. 312; Zip Code 50173; 41 miles NE of Des Moines; Lat. 41-58-27 N long. 092-42-45 W; Thought to be named for an early settler from Quebec, Canada.

MONTROSE, City; Lee County; Pop. 957; Zip Code 52639; 20 SSW of Burlington; Elev. 530; Lat. 40-31-28 N long. 091-25-07 W. Originally called Cut Nose, in honor of Indian Chief Cut Nose, who lived nearby. It was later called Mount of Roses, because of the many wild roses on the nearby hillsides. This was later shortened to Montrose.

MOORHEAD, City; Monona County; Pop. 259; Zip Code 51558; 44 miles SSE of of Sioux City; Elev. 1,200; Lat. 41-56-37 N long. 095-51-09 W.

MOORLAND, City; Webster County; Pop. 209; Zip Code 50566; 8 miles WSW of Fort Dodge; Lat. 42-26-24 N long. 094-17-13 W. Originally swampy land before being drained, the named recalls its former character.

MORAVIA, City; Appanoose County; Pop. 679; Zip Code 52571; 25 miles WSW of Ottumwa; Lat. 40-54-16 N long. 092-49-03 W. Named after the province in central Europe.

MORNING SUN, City; Louisa County; Pop. 841; Zip Code 52640; 19 miles N of Burlington; Lat. 41-05-43 N long. 091-14-41 W. Descriptively named.

MOULTON, City; Appanoose County; Pop. 613; Zip Code 52572; 27 miles SW of Ottumwa; Lat. 40-41-18 N long. 092-41-17 W; Named for an engineer of the Chicago, Burlington and Quincy Railroad.

MOUNT AUBURN, City; Benton County; Pop. 134; Zip Code 52313; 20 miles NW of Cedar Rapids; Lat. 42-15-35 N long. 092-05- 40 W.

MOUNT AYR, City; Ringgold County Seat; Pop. 1,796; Zip Code 50854; 72 miles SW of Des Moines; Lat. 40-43-01 N long. 094-14-16 W. Located on a high rolling prairie and descriptively named.

MOUNT PLEASANT, City; Henry County Seat; Pop. 8,027; Zip Code 52641; 20 miles NW of Burlington; Lat. 40-58-48 N long. 091- 33-00 W. Presley Saunders, the founder of the town, chose the town site because of the elevation and good water, and because it was close enough to Burlington to enjoy the advantages of river commerce.

POINTS OF INTEREST:

- Iowa Wesleyan College (1842). 601 N Main Street.
- Midwest Old Settlers and Threshers Heritage Museum. S of town.
- Oakland Mills Park. 4 miles S, off US 34.

HISTORICAL PLACES...

Harlan-Lincoln House; Old Main.

MOUNT VERNON, City; Linn County; Pop. 3,657; Zip Code 52314; 20 miles ESE of Cedar Rapids; Lat. 41-55-33 N long. 091- 25-12 W; It was named by Elder George Bowman, a Methodist circuit rider. It is said that in 1851 he stopped his horse on the crest of a long hill and, inspired by the beauty of the scene, knelt to consecrate the spot to Christian education. It has also been said that it was named for George Washington's estate at Mount Vernon.

MOVILLE, City; Woodbury County; Pop. 1,306; Zip Code 51039; 10 miles E of Sioux City; Lat. 42-30-40 N long. 096-02-24 W; It was named for Moville, Ireland, home town of the first postmaster here. The name is a combination of "Mo," the abbreviation for Missouri, and "ville" which is French for "town."

MUSCATINE, Pop. 22,881 The city is located about 30 miles farther west on the Mississippi River than its neighbor city of Davenport. The name Muscatine is of Indian origin, derived from the Mascoutins, a tribe whose camping grounds were in a grove of oak trees on the river, four miles from the present city. In their language they referred to the site as "Burning Island," because of the underbrush and prairie fires that blazed every fall, and they themselves became identified as "People of the Place of Fire."

Muscatine first came into existence as a trading post in the summer of 1833, when Colonel George Davenport of Rock Island, Illinois, operator of a string of such posts, sent a Mr. Farnham into the territory to set up a store. James W. Casey staked a claim near the present Broadway Street and the river in 1835, and began the cutting of timber for fueling the steamboats that stopped, thus giving the place its early title of Casey's "Woodpile" or Landing. Prospector and adventurer, John Vanatte, along with Captain Benjamin Clark, paid $200 for quit-claim deeds from Colonel Davenport for the land where Farnham had held his trading post, later disposing of the land to new settlers.

During May of 1836, the site of the town was surveyed and called Bloomington, probably for Bloomington, Indiana, John Vanatta's birthplace. But in 1849, the name was changed to Muscatine. On August 22, 1837, the boiler of the steamer *Dubuque* exploded and 22 lives were lost. The steamer *Adventure* towed the disabled vessel to Muscatine, where 17 of the dead were buried in one grave. A post office was established in 1837, and new settlers, including many Germans, arrived daily, encouraged by tales of the rich farm lands in the Iowa country.

Muscatine became an important river stopping place. In 1839, records report 399 steamboats docked at the wharf. Ferryboats for many years formed an integral link in the transportation system. The first of these was the *Polly*

Keith, a flat-boat put into service in 1839, followed by a steam ferryboat, the *Iowa*, in 1842. The first sawmill in Muscatine was erected in 1843 at the foot of what is now Sycamore Street. It was built by Cornelius Cadle, who came to the Iowa country from New York. In those days, logs were floated down the river in huge rafts, and the town assumed importance as a lumbering center, maintaining this activity for years. Pork packing, another important industry, was introduced by Isett and Blaydes in 1844.

In 1853, the Mississippi & Missouri Railway Company was incorporated in Iowa, the first company to operate a train (1855) to Muscatine. During the Civil War, Muscatine was a military post with Camp Strong, on the island, a concentration point.

From the early 1860s to the late 1890s, Muscatine maintained an important position as both a lumber and river town. The packet boat *Muscatine* made its appearance on April 1, 1864. This 600-ton boat was 201 feet long, with 34-foot breadth of beam. It accommodated 200 persons. In 1870, a single order of 400,000 feet of lumber, lath, shingles, and pickets was shipped to a firm in Omaha, Nebraska. A sash and door factory, still in existence, was opened in 1872. In 1891, when the High Bridge was finished, the last of the ferryboats, the *Ida May,* owned by Captain Eaton, was discontinued.

About 1891, the manufacturing of pearl buttons began to supplant other river industries. A swimmer's mishap is said to have turned the attention of J. F. Beopple, a German immigrant, to the fresh-water mussels abundant in the Mississippi and its tributaries. Beopple cut his foot on a sharp object that turned out to be a mussel. Investigating further, he discovered that mussel shells grew in beds along the bottoms of fresh-water streams in the vicinity of Muscatine. When he attempted to get money for manufacturing buttons, he was laughed at, but he persisted and in 1891, constructed a machine somewhat like a turning lathe and operated by foot power. Continuing his experiments, Beopple jealously guarded his secrets, purchasing watch dogs, and even sleeping in his shop so the process could not be stolen. Beopple opened the first button-making factory in the city; others soon followed and Muscatine became the center of this industry. About 1910, when the industry was at its height, the annual output was more than $17,000,000 gross.

Samuel Clemens (Mark Twain) made his home in Muscatine at one time, and found here some of the material he used in his writings. He once said of the city: "I remember Muscatine for its summer sunsets. I have never seen any on either side of the ocean which equaled them."

MUSCATINE COUNTY, E Iowa, 443 sq. mi.; Pop. 39,907; Named for the Mascoutin Indian tribe.

HISTORICAL PLACES...

Bowman Livery Stable; McKibben, S. M. House; Old Jail; Sinnett Octagon; Trinity Episcopal Church.

NASHUA, City; Chickasaw County; Pop. 1,476; Zip Code 50658; 30 miles ESE of Mason City; Lat. 42-57-04 N long. 092-31-58 W; It was originally called Bridgeport, and later Woodbridge. It was renamed after the city of Nashua in New York, former home of resident, E. P. Greeley.

NEMAHA, City; Sac County; Pop. 112; Zip Code 50567; 46 miles W of Fort Dodge; Lat. 42-31-01 N long. 095-07-45 W; Either named for the Little Nemaha or the Nemaha River. The Indian word has been interpreted to mean "water of cultivation" or "muddy water."

NEOLA, City; Pottawattamie County; Pop. 894; Zip Code 51559; 15 miles NNE of Council Bluffs; Lat. 41-28-09 N long. 095- 35-31 W.

NEVADA, City; Story County Seat; Pop. 6,009; Zip Code 50201; 10 miles E of Ames; Elev. 1,003; Lat. 42-01-02 N long. 093-27-51 W; Thrift, a settler, named the village for his daughter, Sierra Nevada, who had been named for the California mountain range. In Spanish, "Nevada" means "snow- covered," and was applied to snow-capped peaks.

NEW ALBIN, City; Allamakee County; Pop. 534; Zip Code 52160; 76 miles NNW of Dubuque; Lat. 43-29-59 N long. 091-17-14 W.

NEWELL, City; Buena Vista County; Pop. 1,089; 42 miles W of Fort Dodge; Lat. 42-36-20 N long. 095-00-09 W.

NEW HAMPTON, City; Chickasaw County Seat; Pop. 3,660; Zip Code 50659; 38 miles E of Mason City; Lat. 43-03-32 N long. 092- 19-43 W. First known as Chickasaw Center, it was later renamed by Osgood Gowen for his old home town in New Hampshire. A controversy arose over the vote in 1856 to decide whether the county seat should be removed to Forest City (now Williamstown) from New Hampton. A tie vote threw the case into court, where Judge Bailey ruled in favor of Forest City. Refusal of New Hampton to relinquish the records led to a series of arrests, among them that of the judge.

A group of 24 men, led by the constable, forced Bailey into a wagon drawn by a yoke of oxen, but before they had gone far, friends who had secured a writ of habeas corpus from the clerk (acting for the judge in his absence), demanded his release. A pitched battle brought about the judge's release, and those resisting were arrested. Eventually the records were transferred to Forest City. But in 1880, when New Hampton subscribed $5,000 for a new courthouse if built there, the offer was accepted, and New Hampton once more became the county seat.

NEW HARTFORD, City; Butler County; Pop. 683; Zip Code 50660; 9 miles NW of Waterloo; Lat. 42-34-09 N long. 092-37-27 W. The city was named after Hartford, Connecticut.

NEW LIBERTY, City; Scott County; Pop. 139; Zip Code 52765; 15 miles NW of Davenport; Lat. 41-43-04 N long. 090-52-44 W.

NEW LONDON, City; Henry County; Pop. 1,922; Zip Code 52645; 11 miles NW of Burlington; Lat. 40-56-30 N long. 091-24-22 W. First named Dover in honor of Abraham C. Dover, owner of the site; it was renamed after New London, Connecticut.

NEW MARKET, City; Taylor County; Pop. 454; Zip Code 51646; 53 miles SE of Council Bluffs; Lat. 40-43-57 N long. 094-53-59 W.

NEW PROVIDENCE, City; Hardin County; Pop. 240; Zip Code 50206; 37 miles WSW of of Waterloo; Elev. 1,130; Lat. 41-16-05 N long. 093-10-00 W.

NEW SHARON, City; Mahaska County; Pop. 1,136; Zip Code 50207; 37 miles ESE of Des Moines; Lat. 41-28-11 N long. 092-38- 57 W. First called Sharon, it was later changed to New Sharon to avoid confusion with a town of that name in Warren County.

NEWTON, City; Jasper County Seat; Pop. 14,789; 14 miles ENE of Des Moines; Lat. 41-41-59 N long. 093-02-52 W.

The first known settlers in the territory now in Jasper County were Adam Tool, William Highland, John Frost, and John Vance, who came from Jefferson County in 1846. A commission named by the Legislature selected a site for the courthouse, placing a pole to mark the place. The city, incorporated in 1857, was named for a American Revolution soldier, Sergeant Newton, who served under General Marion with Sergeant Jasper, for whom the county was named.

The washing machine industry began here in 1898, when a local incubator firm undertook the manufacture of ratchet-slat washers, which were loaded on a one-horse spring wagon and sold in the countryside for $5.00 each. Fred H. Bergman, owner of the company, secured patent rights on the manufacture of a hand-power washer in 1904, and undertook its manufacture. Although discouraged by his associates, who believed it would be difficult to sell washers at $10 each, Bergman persisted and formed the One Minute Manufacturing Co.

F. L. Maytag, who became the "Washing Machine King," had a quarter interest in the Parsons Band Cutter and Self-Feeder Company; the manufacture of washing machines was a sideline. In 1907, Maytag introduced a hand-power designed by Howard Snyder, inventor and demonstrator for the self-feeder company. Snyder added the electric motor in 1911. The next Maytag improvement was the cabinet type of cylinder washer, employing the principle of the mill race, developed by Snyder in 1917. Snyder's most successful invention, "the gyrafoam washer," was placed on the market in 1922.

POINTS OF INTEREST:

- Fred Maytag Park. W 3rd Street South.
- Jasper County Historical Museum. 1700 S 15th Avenue West.
- Trainland, USA. 12 miles W via I-80, then 2 1/2 miles N on IA 117.

NEW VIENNA, City; Dubuque County; Pop. 376; Zip Code 52065; 25 miles WNW of Dubuque; Lat. 42-32-58 N long. 091-06-52 W.

NEW VIRGINIA, City; Warren County; Pop. 433; Zip Code 50210; 31 miles SSW of Des Moines; Lat. 41-11-01 N long. 093-43- 53 W.

NODAWAY, City; Adams County; Pop. 153; Zip Code 50857; 46 miles ESE of Council Bluffs; Lat. 40-56-03 N long. 094-53-51 W; Named after the Nodaway River, "Nodaway" is an Algonquin Indian word meaning "Shake," often applied to their enemies.

NORA SPRINGS, City; Floyd County; Pop. 1,505; Zip Code 50458; 4 miles E of Mason City; Lat. 43-08-49 N long. 093-00-38 W. It was formerly known as Woodstock, but acquired its present name because of the many springs feeding the river.

NORTHBORO, City; Page County; Pop. 78; Zip Code 51647; 46 miles SSE of Council Bluffs; Lat. 40-36-41 N long. 095-17-16 W.

NORTH LIBERTY, City; Johnson County; Pop. 2,926; 7 miles NNE of Iowa City; Lat. 41-44-57 N long. 091-35-52 W.

NORTHWOOD, City; Worth County Seat; Pop. 2,193; Zip Code 50459; 19 miles NNW of Mason City; Lat. 43-26-47 N long. 093-13- 09 W. It was largely settled by Norwegians; the first arrival was Gilbrand Nellum in 1853.

NORWALK, City; Warren County; Pop. 5,726; Zip Code 50211; 16 miles WSW of Des Moines; Lat. 41-30-27 N long. 093-36-47 W; Named from Norwalk, Connecticut.

NORWAY, City; Benton County; Pop. 583; Zip Code 52318; 7 miles SW of Cedar Rapids; Elev. 796; Lat. 41-54-18 N long. 091- 54-56 W. Settled by Norwegians who named the city for their former home.

OAKLAND, City; Pottawattomie County; Pop. 1,496; Zip Code 51560; Elev. 1,103; Lat. 41-17-46 N long. 095-20-54 W. It was first known as Big Grove, because of the oak trees that grow in abundance around the site.

OAKVILLE, City; Louisa County; Pop. 442; Zip Code 52646; Lat. 41-06-04 N long. 091-02-30 W.

O'BRIEN COUNTY, NW Iowa, 575 sq. mi.; Pop. 15,444; Named for William Smith O'Brien (1803-1864), a member of England's House of Commons, who was the leader of the Irish Independence movement. He was arrested, sentenced to life imprisonment, and fully pardoned in 1856.

OCHEYEDON, City; Osceola County; Pop. 539; Zip Code 51330; 70 miles NNE of Sioux City; Lat. 43-24-55 N long. 095-38-36 W; Named for the Ocheyedan River and Mound. The name is derived from a Dakota Indian word meaning "little hill" or "spot where they weep."

ODEBOLT, City; Sac County; Pop. 1,158; Zip Code 51458; 52 miles ESE of Sioux City; Elev. 1,377; Lat. 42-18-43 N long. 095- 14-46 W; Taken from Odebeau, the name of a French trapper who lived alone by the creek at this place.

In 1911, this community produced $400,000 worth of popcorn. This specialty brought the town much prosperity. Three nationally known popcorn companies did a large business here.

OELWEIN, City; Fayette County; Pop. 6,493; Zip Code 50662; 28 miles ENE of Waterloo; Lat. 42-39-17 N long. 091-55-04 W. The city was named after a German settler who donated land to the railroad. At one time it was known as "The Hub," because it is the central midwestern division point.

OKOBOJI, City; Dickinson County; Pop. 775; Zip Code 51355; 75 miles NW of Fort Dodge; Lat. 43-24-02 N long. 095-09-14 W; A Sioux name which has been interpreted as meaning "place of rest," "rushes," "a field of swamp grass" or "blue waters."

POINTS OF INTEREST:

- Gull Point. About 6 miles SW off US 71.
- Pikes Point. About 3 miles West.

OLIN, City; Jones County; Pop. 663; Zip Code 52320; 32 miles E of Cedar Rapids; Lat. 42-00-10 N long. 091-08-24 W.

ONAWA, City; Monona County Seat; Pop. 2,936; Zip Code 51040; 32 miles SSE of Sioux City; Elev. 1,052; Lat. 42-02-28 N long. 096-05-39 W; Platted in 1857 by the Monona

County Land Company, it was probably named for a song, "Onaway," in Longfellow's poem, *Hiawatha*.

ONEIDA, City; Delaware County; Pop. 49; Lat. 42-32-34 N long. 091-21-12 W; Named for the Oneida Indians who lived in the area around New York. The word "Oneida" means "standing stone."

ORANGE CITY, City; Sioux County Seat; Pop. 4,940; Zip Code 51041; 35 miles NNE of Sioux City; Lat. 42-59-56 N long. 096-04- 15 W. Founded by Henry Hospers in 1869, and named for Prince William of Orange.

ORIENT, City; Adair County; Pop. 376; Zip Code 50858; 57 miles WSW of Des Moines; Lat. 41-12-34 N long. 094-25-12 W.

OSAGE, City; Mitchell County Seat; Pop. 3,439; Zip Code 50454; 15 miles ENE of Mason City; Lat 43-22-53 N long. 092-43-33 W; First settled in 1853 by Hiram Hart, and named Coral in 1854 for the daughter of Dr. A. H. Moore, who first platted the town. This plat was never recorded, but on a later plat made by representatives of the banker, Orrin Sage, of Wareham, Mass., the town was called Osage (O. Sage) in his honor. He was known for his generous donation to the town library.

OSCEOLA, City; Clarke County Seat; Pop. 4,164; Zip Code 50213; 42 miles SSW of Des Moines; Lat. 41-01-56 N long. 093-45- 59 W; Named for Osceola, the famous Chief of the Florida Seminole Indians.

POINTS OF INTEREST:

- Nine Eagles State Park. 29 miles S on US 69 to Davis City, then 6 miles SE on County road.

OSCEOLA COUNTY, NW Iowa, 398 sq. mi.; Pop. 7,267; Named for the Indian Chief Osceola, who opposed cession of Seminole lands. He was seized in October 1837 under a flag of truce, and imprisoned at St. Augustine, Florida, later at Ft. Moultrie, S.C., where he died.

OSKALOOSA, City; Mahaska County Seat; Pop. 10,632; Zip Code 52577; 23 miles NW of Ottumwa; Lat. 41-17-21 N long. 092-38-16 W; Known for a short time as Mahaska, the name was changed to Oskaloosa in 1844. The city was named for Oskaloosa (*Last of the Beautiful*), a wife of Chief Osceola. Another possibility is it was named for Ouskaloosa, a fictional character in the book, *Osceola,* or *Fact and Fiction.*

The first coal mines in the State were developed (1870) in Mahaska County; for the most part, these were shallow workings of veins from three to six feet in thickness. By 1910, however, most of the large coal companies had removed to adjacent counties. After the closing of the Mahaska mines, the Welsh miners remained in the county to farm or carry on business in Oskaloosa and other towns.

The Welsh brought with them a love for music that had wide local influence, causing the establishment of various music- making groups. Among those born here were Frederic Knight Logan; Thurlow Lieurance, composer of *By the Waters of Minnetonka*; and Mason Slade, the organist. June Adele Skelton, known on the European concert stage as Mme. Salteni-Mochi, attended the public school here from 1898 to 1906. Homer Samuels, husband and accompanist of Mme. Galli-Curci, as well as Charles L. Griffith, the composer, came from the Welsh settlements near the city.

Samuel H. M. Byers, who wrote the words of the song, *Sherman Marched Down to the Sea,* while in a prison camp in South Carolina, was a native. With Byers in prison was a Lt. Tower who, after he was released, carried the lyrics to his home in Ottumwa, hidden in the hollow of his wooden leg.

POINTS OF INTEREST:

- Lake Keomah State Park. 5 miles E off IA 92.
- Nelson Pioneer Farm & Craft Museum. 2 miles NE of Penn College on Glendale Road.

HISTORICAL PLACES...

Nelson, Daniel, House and Barn.

OSSIAN, City; Winneshiek County; Pop. 810; Zip Code 52161; 55 miles NE of Waterloo; Lat. 43-09-51 N long. 091-46-17 W. Named after the Iowa poet, John Ossian Porter.

OTHO, City; Webster County; Pop. 529; Zip Code 50569; 5 miles S of Fort Dodge; Lat. 42-25-19 N long. 094-09-37 W.

OTTUMWA, City; Wapello County Seat; Pop. 24,488; Zip Code 50570; 64 miles SE of Des Moines; Lat. 42-54-00 N long. 094-22-54 W. The area is divided into two sections, North and South Ottumwa, by the Des Moines River, and spreads over bottomlands and rises on a series of terraces northward to the city limits.

The name Ottumwa is the white man's interpretation of the Indian word meaning "rippling waters." On May 1, 1843, the territory was opened to settlement by the whites. For days, men with their families camped on the outskirts waiting for the signal; at midnight of April 30, hundreds of pioneers in their covered wagons, buckboards, and other vehicles, dashed across the open country to stake out claims. Flaring torches lighted the night. For miles around, the sound of axes resounded. In the morning, it was found that many claims overlapped and some of the land had been forgotten. It is said that Wapello County received 2,000 men, women, and children in the few days of the land rush, and that the city of Ottumwa literally sprang up over night.

The Appanoose Rapids and Milling Company (organized in 1842) claimed much of the land in what is now Ottumwa. It promoted the town and donated lots to the county, providing that Ottumwa was made the seat of government. In 1844, the city was named Louisville, but the present name was adopted the following year. The first hotel was built in 1844, and by 1848, the place was a thriving village. Ottumwa was incorporated in 1851, and chartered as a city in 1857.

One of the first bridges to span the Des Moines River was constructed at Ottumwa in 1860. During the Lincoln-Douglas campaign, there was a mass meeting in Ottumwa. The meeting was held on the south side of the river, and since there were no bridges across the shallow stream, the farmers placed their wagons in two rows, end to end. End boards were removed so the people could pass easily from one wagon to the next. This unusual bridge, 800 feet in length, was built at the foot of Green Street. At the same spot 10 years later, a wooden tool bridge was constructed, but was later swept away in a flood.

From 1860 to 1880, the city grew slowly, little affected by the turbulent days of the Civil War, but gradually developed in the general expansion of the middlewest that followed the struggle. In 1888, with the establishment of the John Morrell and Company packing plant, the city began to turn its interest to industry, added impetus being given by the development of the deep beds of bituminous coal beneath the farms. In 1890, the city of Ottumwa built a "Coal Palace" to advertise the town. It was 230 feet long, and a central tower with high battlement walls rose to a height of 200 feet. The edifice had numerous turrets, and the tall narrow windows made it appear almost medieval, this effect being intensified by the glittering jet of the coal that veneered the walls. Underneath the palace was a reproduction of a coal mine. A Mardi Gras and fair were held, and visitors were attracted by the thousands. Among these visitors were President Benjamin Harrison in 1890, and William McKinley in 1891. The palace was torn down in 1892.

Honore Willsie Morrow (Honore McCue), the novelist, was born in Ottumwa, and Edna Ferber, author of *So Big, Show Boat,* and many other novels, lived here during her early childhood and began her education in the city's schools.

POINTS OF INTEREST:

- Lacey-Keosauqua. 18 miles S on US 63, then 24 miles E, off IA 2 near Keosauqua.
- Lake Waapello. 16 miles S on US 63, then 10 miles W on IA 273 near Drakesville.
- Ottumwa Park. At jct US 34.

HISTORICAL PLACES...

Mars Hill (Mars Hill Church and Cemetery).

OWASA, City; Hardin County; Pop. 37; Elev. 1085; Lat. 42-26-01 N long. 093-12-25 W; Possibly named for a character in Henry Schoolcraft's book of "Owaissa," the bluebird in Longfellow's *Hiawatha.*

OXFORD, City; Johnson County; Pop. 581; Zip Code 52322; 9 miles NW of Iowa City; Lat. 41-43-45 N long. 091-47-37 W. Named after the English city.

PACIFIC JUNCTION, City; Mills County; Pop. 548; Zip Code 51561; 14 miles SSW of Council Bluffs; Lat. 41-01-11 N long. 095- 45-00 W. Named as a favorite stopping place for emigrants bound for the west coast.

PAGE COUNTY, SW Iowa, 535 sq. mi.; Pop. 16,870; Named for John Page, Second Lieutenant, and Captain in 1831; he died of wounds received at the Battle of Palo Alto.

PALMER, City; Pocahontas County; Pop. 230; Zip Code 50571; 23 miles WNW of Fort Dodge; Lat. 42-37-50 N long. 094-35-57 W.

PALO, City; Linn County; Pop. 514; Zip Code 52324; 3 miles NNE of Cedar Rapids; Lat. 41-58-47 N long. 091-44-21 W; The name is a Spanish word which means "stick."

PALO COUNTY, N Iowa, 561 sq. mi.; Pop. 10,669; Named for the site of the battle of May 8, 1846 at Palo Alto, Texas.

PANAMA, City; Shelby County; Pop. 201; Zip Code 51562; 35 miles NNE of Council Bluffs; Elev. 1,325; Lat. 41-43-43 N long. 095-28-34 W; Probably named for "Pan-America." In Panama native languages, the word may mean either "place where many fish are taken", or refer to a river lacking fish which was thought to be "unlucky" or "panema."

PANORA, City; Guthrie County; Pop. 1,100; Zip Code 50216; 47 miles W of Des Moines; Elev. 1,071; Lat. 41-42-23 N long. 094- 21-54 W. The city's name is a contraction of "panorama."

HISTORICAL PLACES...
Panora-Linden High School.

PARKERSBURG, City; Butler County; Pop. 1,804; Zip Code 50665; 15 miles WNW of Waterloo; Lat. 42-34-52 N long. 092-47-32 W. The city was named after a prominent settler.

PARNELL, City; Iowa County; Pop. 209; Zip Code 52325; 18 miles W of Iowa City; Lat. 41-35-27 N long. 091-59-42 W. Named in honor of the famous Irish patriot.

PATON, City; Greene County; Pop. 255; Zip Code 50217; 30 miles WNW of Ames; Lat. 42-09-37 N long. 094-15-28 W.

PAULINA, City; O'Brien County; Pop. 1,134; Zip Code 51046; 42 miles NE of Sioux City; Lat. 42-58-55 N long. 095-41-14 W.

PELLA, City; Marion County; Pop. 9,270; Zip Code 50219; 27 miles ESE of Des Moines; Lat. 41-24-25 N long. 092-54-56 W; Settled by Dutch immigrants and named "Pella," a word that to them meant "In God is our hope and refuge."

POINTS OF INTEREST:

- Central University (1853). 812 University.
- Pella Historical Village & Wyatt Earp Boyhood Home. 507 Franklin Street.
- Red Rock Lake. 4 1/2 miles SW.

PEOSTA, City; Dubuque County; Pop. 128; Zip Code 52068; Lat. 42-27-37 N long. 090-50-44 W; Named for Peosta, an Indian warrior whose wife discovered lead in this area around 1780.

PERRY, City; Dallas County; Pop. 6,652; Zip Code 50220; 25 miles WSW of Ames; Elev. 998; Lat. 41-53-30 N long. 094-06-35 W. The city was named after a Colonel Perry, one of the owners of the Des Moines Valley Railroad.

POINTS OF INTEREST:

- Dallas County Forest Park & Museum. 16th Street, 1 mile S.

PERSIA, City; Harrison County; Pop. 312; Zip Code 51563; 23 miles NNE of of Council Bluffs; Elev. 1,273; Lat. 41-35-11 N long. 095-32-53 W. The city was named after the near eastern country.

PETERSON, City; Clay County; Pop. 390; Zip Code 51047; 53 miles ENE of Sioux City; Lat. 42-55-05 N long. 095-20-32 W.

PIERSON, City; Woodbury County; Pop. 341; Zip Code 51048; 18 miles E of Sioux City; Lat. 42-32-44 N long. 095-51-37 W.

PISGAH, City; Harrison County; Pop. 268; Zip Code 51564; 41 miles NNW of Council Bluffs; Elev. 1,060; Lat. 41-49-42 N long. 095-57-06 W.

PLAINFIELD, City; Bremer County; Pop. 455; Zip Code 50666; 25 miles NNW of Waterloo; Lat. 42-50-41 N long. 092-32-05 W. Named after the town in Illinois.

PLANO, City; Appanoose County; Pop. 75; Zip Code 52581; Lat. 40-45-26 N long. 093-02-34 W. Settled by Seventh Day Adventists from Plano, Illinois.

PLEASANT HILL, City; Polk County; Pop. 3,671; Zip Code 52767; 5 miles WSW of Des Moines; Lat. 41-35-02 N long. 093-31-11 W. Descriptively named.

PLEASANTVILLE, City; Marion County; Pop. 1,536; Zip Code 50225; 15 miles SSE of Des Moines; Lat. 41-23-14 N long. 093-16- 16 W.

PLYMOUTH COUNTY, NW Iowa, 863 sq. mi.; Pop. 23,388; Named for Plymouth, Mass., the landing place of the pilgrims.

POCAHONTAS COUNTY, NW central Iowa, 581 sq. mi.; Pop. 9,525; Named for Pocahontas (1595-1617), daughter of Powhatan, Indian chief, who married colonist John Rolfe. She interceded with her father to save the life of Capt. John Smith.

POLK COUNTY, S central Iowa, 594 sq. mi.; Pop. 327,140; Named for James Knox Polk (1795-1849), eleventh President of the United States; chief clerk of Tennessee Senate; Representative and Governor from Tennessee.

POMEROY, City; Calhoun County; Pop. 762; Zip Code 50575; 26 miles W of Fort Dodge; Lat. 42-33-17 N long. 094-41-09 W.
    Lying in Iowa's so-called "storm-belt," the city was struck by a terrific tornado on July 6, 1893; the storm destroyed every building on five nearby farms, then struck the town with full force, sweeping it of buildings. It was reported that "but 21 families were left with no dead or wounded of their own to take care of." The danger of storms has been lessened by the planting of large groves of trees that often serve to impede the progress of tornadoes.

PORTSMOUTH, City; Shelby County; Pop. 209; Zip Code 51565; 29 miles NNE of Council Bluffs; Elev. 1,237; Lat. 41-39-08 N long. 095-31-13 W. Named after the Connecticut town.

POSTVILLE, City; Allamakee & Clayton Counties; Pop. 1,472; Zip Code 52162; 57 miles NE of Waterloo; Lat. 43-06-10 N long. 091-34-32 W. The city was named after settler, Joel Post, who arrived here in 1841.

POTTAWATTAMIE COUNTY, SW Iowa, 963 sq. mi.; Pop. 82,628; Named for the Pottawattomi Indian tribe, from the Algonquin "Pottawatomink," meaning "people of the place of fire."

POWESHIEK COUNTY, SE central Iowa, 589 sq. mi.; Pop. 19,033; Named for Poweshiek, chief of the Sac Indians.

PRAIRIE CITY, City; Jasper County; Pop. 1,360; Zip Code 50228; 7 miles E of Des Moines; Lat. 41-37-30 N long. 093-14-46 W. It was platted in 1856 by James A. Elliott, and descriptively named for the surrounding prairie.

PRESCOTT, City; Adams County; Pop. 287; Zip Code 50859; 57 miles ESE of Council Bluffs; Lat. 41-01-18 N long. 094-36-49 W.

PRIMGHAR, City; O'Brien County Seat; Pop. 950; Zip Code 51245; 49 miles NE of Sioux City; Lat. 43-05-24 N long. 095-37-31 W; The name is a combination of the initials of the people present when the corner stone was laid.

PRINCETON, City; Scott County; Pop. 806; Zip Code 52768; 12 miles SSW of Clinton; Lat. 41-40-29 N long. 090-20-25 W. Named after the city in New Jersey.

PROMISE CITY, City; Wayne County; Pop. 132; Zip Code 52583; 43 miles WSW of Ottumwa; Lat. 40-44-28 N long. 093-08-52 W; Platted in 1855, it was named for the hope of early settlers that this would become an important center. It never did.

PULASKI, City; Davis County; Pop. 221; Zip Code 52584; 22 miles S of Ottumwa; Lat. 40-41-51 N long. 092-16-58 W. The city's name honors the Polish-American Revolutionary War hero.

QUASQUETON, City; Buchanan County; Pop. 579; Zip Code 52326; 32 miles E of Waterloo; Lat. 42-23-37 N long. 091-45-07 W; Settled in 1842, the name was taken from the Fox Indian language, and is thought to mean "swiftly running water."

QUIMBY, City; Cherokee County; Pop. 334; Zip Code 51049; 31 miles ENE of Sioux City; Lat. 42-37-48 N long. 095-38-30 W.

RADCLIFFE, City; Hardin County; Pop. 574; Zip Code 50230; 20 miles NNE of Ames; Lat. 42-18-51 N long. 093-27-27 W.

RALSTON, City; Carroll & Greene Counties; Pop. 119; Zip Code 51459; 47 miles W of Ames; Lat. 42-02-19 N long. 094-37-52 W. It was known for years as Slater Sliding. In 1891, when a station was built, the name was changed to honor an officer of the American Express Company.

RANDALL, City; Hamilton County; Pop. 161; Zip Code 50231; 13 miles NNE of Ames; Lat. 42-13-39 N long. 093-35-40 W.

RANDOLPH, City; Fremont County; Pop. 243; Zip Code 51649; 24 miles SSE of Council Bluffs; Elev. 977; Lat. 40-52-33 N long. 095-34-15 W.

RAYMOND, City; Black Hawk County; Pop. 619; Zip Code 50667; 9 miles E of Waterloo; Lat. 42-31-51 N long. 092-15-08 W. Named after an early settler.

READLYN, City; Bremer County; Pop. 773; Zip Code 50668; 17 miles NNE of Waterloo; Lat. 42-42-26 N long. 092-13-37 W.

REASNOR, City; Jasper County; Pop. 191; Zip Code 50232; 18 miles E of Des Moines; Lat. 41-34-56 N long. 093-01-31 W.

REDFIELD, City; Dallas County; Pop. 883; Zip Code 50233; 39 miles W of Des Moines; Lat. 41-35-27 N long. 094-12-12 W; It was first called New Ireland when the Cavanaugh brothers platted the town in 1850. The town was renamed in honor of Colonel James Redfield, a Civil War soldier.

RED OAK, City; Montgomery County Seat; Pop. 6,264; Zip Code 51566; 28 miles ESE of Council Bluffs; Lat. 40-57-27 N long. 095- 14-10 W; So named for a nearby grove of red oak trees.

POINTS OF INTEREST:

• Viking Lake State Park. 12 miles E on US 34.

HISTORICAL PLACES...

Chautauqua Park.

REINBECK, City; Grundy County; Pop. 1,605; Zip Code 50669; 12 miles SW of Waterloo; Lat. 42-19-02 N long. 092-36-05 W.

REMBRANDT, City; Buena Vista County; Pop. 229; Zip Code 50576; 54 WNW of Fort Dodge; Lat. 42-49-25 N long. 095-09-36 W. It was first named in honor of Barney Orsland, on whose farm the town was laid out in 1899. It was later renamed for the Dutch painter.

REMSEN, City; Plymouth County; Pop. 1,513; Zip Code 51050; 25 miles NE of Sioux City; Lat. 42-48-23 N long. 095-58-43 W. Named for landowner, Remsen Smith.

RENWICK, City; Humboldt County; Pop. 287; Zip Code 50577; 22 miles NNE of Fort Dodge; Lat. 42-49-53 N long. 093-58-39 W.

RICEVILLE, City; Howard & Mitchell Counties; Pop. 827; Zip Code 50466; 28 miles ENE of Mason City; Lat. 43-21-37 N long. 092-33-01 W; Named for the three Rice brothers.

RICHLAND, City; Keokuk County; Pop. 522; Zip Code 52585; 19 miles ENE of Ottumwa; Lat. 41-11-10 N long. 091-59-40 W. Descriptively named for the area's rich farm land.

RIDGEWAY, City; Winneshiek County; Pop. 295; Zip Code 52165; 54 miles E of Mason City; Lat. 43-18-23 N long. 092-00-44 W.

RINGGOLD COUNTY, S Iowa, 538 sq. mi.; Pop. 5,420; Named for Samuel Ringgold, Second Lieutenant, First Lieutenant, and Captain. He was brevetted a captain for ten years faithful service in one grade, and was brevetted a major for meritorious service against the Florida Indians. He died from wounds received at the Battle of Palo Alto, Mexico in 1846.

RINGSTED, City; Winneshiek County; Pop. 481; Zip Code 50578; 55 miles NNW of Fort Dodge; Lat. 43-17-54 N long. 094-30- 32 W.

RIPPEY, City; Greene County; Pop. 275; Zip Code 50235; 28 miles WSW of Ames; Elev. 1,077; Lat. 41-54-53 N long. 094-12-03 W; Named after Captain C. M. Rippey, an early settler.

RIVERSIDE, City; Washington County; Pop. 824; Zip Code 52327; 9 miles SSE of Iowa City; Lat. 41-28-55 N long. 091-34-53; This city was named for its location.

ROCKFORD, City; Floyd County; Pop. 863; Zip Code 50468; 9 miles SE of Mason City; Lat. 43-03-21 N long. 092-57-01 W.

ROCK RAPIDS, City; Lyon County Seat; Pop. 2,601; Zip Code 51246; 61 miles N of Sioux City; Lat. 43-26-00 N long. 096-09-38 W; The city takes its name from its location near the falls of the Rock River.

HISTORICAL PLACES...

Melan Bridge.

ROCK VALLEY, City; Sioux County; Pop. 2,540; Zip Code 51247; 46 miles N of Sioux City; Lat. 43-12-11 N long. 096-17-42 W; Named for the Rock River.

ROCKWELL, City; Cerro Gordo County; Pop. 1,008; Zip Code 50469; 13 miles SSW of Mason City; Lat. 42-59-16 N long. 093-10- 18 W. Named after original landowner, B.G. Rockwell.

ROCKWELL CITY, City; Calhoun County Seat; Pop. 1,981; Zip Code 50579; 25 miles WSW of Fort Dodge; Lat. 42-43-52 N long. 093-34-22 W. Named for settler, J.M. Rockwell. The town has been called "the golden buckle on the Corn Belt," because it is in the center of the Iowa corn region.

ROLAND, City; Story County; Pop. 1,035; Zip Code 50236; 8 miles NE of Ames; Lat. 42-09-54 N long. 093-28-54 W.

ROLFE, City; Pocohontas County; Pop. 721; Zip Code 50581; 27 miles NW of Fort Dodge; Lat. 42-48-41 N long.

094-32-01 W; Either named for the Englishman who married Pocahontas, or for the man who previously owned the townsite.

ROME, City; Henry County; Pop. 124; 26 miles WNW of Burlington; Lat. 40-58-53 N long. 091-40-56 W; Probably named for Rome, Italy.

ROSE HILL, City; Mahaska County; Pop. 171; Zip Code 52586; 20 miles NNW of Ottumwa; Lat. 41-19-15 N long. 092-27-32 W. Founded by James Ornabaum in 1875, it was a prosperous center of a purebred hog- and cattle-rearing area. Named after the many wild roses in the area.

ROWAN, City; Wright County; Pop. 189; Zip Code 50470; 30 miles ENE of Fort Dodge; Lat. 42-44-30 N long. 093-33-00 W.

ROYAL, City; Clay County; Pop. 466; Zip Code 51357; 60 miles NE of Sioux City; Lat. 43-03-50 N long. 095-17-00 W.

RUDD, City; Floyd County; Pop. 429; Zip Code 50471; 9 miles ESE of Mason City; Lat. 43-07-53 N long. 092-54-10 W.

RUSSELL, City; Lucas County; Pop. 531; Zip Code 50238; 42 miles W of Ottumwa; Lat. 40-59-29 N long. 093-12-18 W. Russell is named for an early settler.

RUTHVEN, City; Palo Alto County; Pop. 707; Zip Code 51358; 54 miles NW of Fort Dodge; Lat. 43-07-25 N long. 094-52-57 W. Named for the three Ruthven brothers, who were among the first settlers.

RYAN, City; Delaware County; Pop. 382; Zip Code 52330; 27 miles NE of Cedar Rapids; Lat. 42-21-14 N long. 091-28-59 W. Named for an Irish settler.

SABULA, City; Jackson County; Pop. 710; Zip Code 52070; 15 miles NNE of Clinton; Lat. 42-04-37 N long. 090-10-33 W. It was first named Carrolport, then Charlestown, and finally named Sabula in 1846, to honor Mrs. Sabula Wood.

SAC CITY, City; Sac County Seat; Pop. 2,492; Zip Code 50583; 42 miles W of Fort Dodge; Lat. 42-25-19 N long. 095-00-03 W; Named for the Sac, or Sauk Indian tribe.

SAC COUNTY, W Iowa, 578 sq. mi.; Pop. 12,324; Named after the Sac Indian tribe.

ST. ANSGAR, City; Mitchell County; Pop. 1,063; Zip Code 50472; Elev. 1,171; 15 miles NNE of Mason City; Lat. 43-22-40 N long. 092-55-07 W. Given a religious name by Czech settlers.

ST. CHARLES, City; Madison County; Pop. 537; Zip Code 50240; 31 miles SW of Des Moines; Lat. 41-18-03 N long. 093-12-28 W.

ST. MARYS, City; Warren County; Pop. 113; Zip Code 50241; Elev. 1,033; Lat. 41-18-29 N long. 093-43-53 W.

SCOTT COUNTY, E Iowa, 454 sq. mi.; Pop. 150,979; Named for Winfield Scott (1786-1866), who was brevetted a major general for services at Chippewa and Niagara Falls, Upper Canada, 1814; awarded gold medal by resolutions of Congress, 1814; commander- in-chief of U.S. Army; presented gold medals by Congress in 1848.

SEARSBORO, City; Poweshiek County; Pop. 164; Zip Code 50242; 31 miles E of Des Moines; Lat. 41-35-23 N long. 092-38-51 W.

SERGEANT BLUFF, City; Woodbury County; Pop. 2,772; Zip Code 51054; Elev. 1,092; Lat. 42-25-14 N long. 096-20-17 W; Established in 1854, it was first known as Floyd's Bluff. Later it was named Sergeant Bluff, both names honoring Sergeant Charles Floyd, the only man to die on the Lewis and Clark expedition. He was buried on a bluff on the Iowa side of the Missouri River.

SEYMOUR, City; Wayne County; Pop. 869; Zip Code 52590; 45 miles WSW of Ottumwa; Lat. 40-40-49 N long. 093-07-22 W.

SHARPSBURG, City; Taylor County; Pop. 116; Zip Code 50862; 61 miles ESE of Council Bluffs; Lat. 40-48-18 N long. 094-38-30 W.

SHEFFIELD, City; Franklin County; Pop. 1,174; Zip Code 50475; 17 miles SSW of Mason City; Lat. 42-54-22 N long. 093-12- 15 W; Named for James Sheffield, a railroad contractor.

SHELBY, City; Pottawamie & Shelby Counties; Pop. 637; Zip Code 51570; Like many places throughout the country, this city was named in honor of Gen. Isaac Shelby, Governor of Kentucky.

SHELBY COUNTY, W Iowa, 587 sq. mi.; Pop. 13,230; Named for Isaac Shelby (1750-1826), First and fifth governor of Kentucky who served in the American Revolution.

SHELDON, City; O'Brien & Sioux Counties; Pop. 4,937; Zip Code 51201; 49 miles NNE of Sioux City; Lat. 43-10-21 N long. 095-50-12 W; Named for Israel Sheldon, a stockholder in the first railroad to pass through town.

SHELL ROCK, City; Butler County; Pop. 1,385; Zip Code 50670; 16 miles NNW of Waterloo; Lat. 42-42-59 N long. 092-34-48 W.

SHELLSBURG, City; Benton County; Pop. 765; Zip Code 52332; 5 miles NNW of Cedar Rapids; Lat. 42-05-36 N long. 091-51-50 W.

SHENANDOAH, City; Fremont & Page Counties; Pop. 5,572; Zip Code 51602; 36 miles SSE of Council Bluffs; Lat. 40-45-35 N long. 095-22-53 W; Said to be named for the Shenandoah Valley in Virginia, which is similar to the Nishnabotna River Valley in which the town is located. The town was founded in 1870, when the railroad was completed through Page County. Many of the first settlers were Mormons, and most of them came from a small settlement called Manti, or Fisher's Grove.

SIBLEY, City; Osceola County Seat; Pop. 2,815; Zip Code 51249; 64 miles NNE of Sioux City; Lat. 43-24-10 N long. 095-44- 41 W. Named in 1872 to honor General G.H. Sibley.

SIDNEY, City; Fremont County Seat; Pop. 1,253; Zip Code 51652; 32 miles S of Council Bluffs; Lat. 40-44-44 N long. 095- 38-47 W. Named after Sidney, Ohio, where Milton Richard, who platted the town, once lived.

SIGOURNEY, City; Keokuk County Seat; Pop. 2,111; Zip Code 52591; 20 miles NNE of Ottumwa; Lat. 41-19-58 N long. 092-12-13 W; Called Sigourney after the poetess, Mrs. Lydia H. Sigourney.

Archilles Rogers, the only American Revolutionary War soldier buried in the county, is interred in the Pennington Cemetery; he died at the age of 102 during the cholera epidemic of 1864.

SIOUX CENTER, City; Sioux County; Pop. 5,074; Zip Code 51250; 38 miles N of Sioux City; Lat. 43-04-39 N long. 096-10-41 W; Named for the Sioux Indinas. "Sioux" is the last part of "Nadouessioux," the derogatory Ojibwa-French name for the Dakotas.

SIOUX CITY, City; Woodbury County Seat; Pop. 80,505; Zip Code 51100; Elev. 1,117; 88 miles NNW of Council Bluffs; Lat. 42- 30-05 N long. 096-23-43 W. The city lies along the Big Sioux and Floyd rivers at the point where they empty into the Missouri, and spreads over bluffs and the river valley at the western boundary line, where Iowa meets Nebraska and South Dakota.

The junction of the Missouri, the Big Sioux, and the Floyd rivers was important both to Indians and animals long before the invasion of the Europeans. Military Road, the main traffic artery northwest into South Dakota, was originally an old buffalo trail that traversed the entire length of what is now Sioux City and extended southward to Sergeant Bluff. Omaha, Oto, and Sioux Indians beat a trail along the buffalo's path, and French traders, penetrating into the region, followed. Explorers Lewis and Clark, on their expedition up the Missouri River, passed through this region in 1804. George Catlin, early painter of Indian life, described the site of Sioux City in enthusiastic terms on his return from a trip up the river in 1832. J. N. Nicollet, a geographer and scientist, also commented on the spot in 1839. The great naturalist, John James Audubon, who journeyed to Fort Union in 1843, remembered the region because he saw so many dead buffalo that had drowned while attempting to cross the thin ice above the mouth of the Big Sioux River.

In September, 1848, William Thompson came from Illinois and platted the town of Thompsonville, now within the southeastern limits of Sioux City. Theophile Bruguier, a French-Canadian trader, arrived in May of 1849 with his wives, their father, Chief War Eagle, and other Sioux Indians, and settled along the banks of the Big Sioux at a site he said he had seen in a dream. Later in the same year, Robert Perry established himself near the present Ninth Street on the creek that bears his name.

Bruguier's relationship to War Eagle and his tribe kept the Indians from seriously harassing the pioneer settlement. War Eagle indicated his attitude when he left the Santee Sioux tribe in the region of St. Paul, Minnesota, after it showed its hostility to white settlers. He joined the Yankton Sioux and was made their chief. War Eagle's friendship for the white settlers was so sincere that President Martin Van Buren called him to Washington in 1837 and presented him with a medal. Thus, to the founders of Sioux City, the Algonkian meaning of the word Sioux "the snakelike one," or "enemies," had little significance.

Joe Leonais, a trapper, in 1852, paid Bruguier $100 for his claim, 160 acres running from the Missouri River north to the present Seventh Street and lying between Perry Creek and the present Jones Street. Leonais' widowed sister, Mary Ann Lapore, the first white woman to settle in Sioux City, came from Canada to join him in 1854. Leonais had raised three crops of corn on his farm when, in 1855, he sold it to Dr. John K. Cook for $3,000. The latter platted it as Sioux City, East Addition.

Political favor seems to have played a large part in development of the town. Through the political connections of Dr. Cook, a land office and post office were opened in 1855, and for the next 20 years, the land office served the territory covered by 12 counties. Dr. S. P. Yeomans, the first registrar of the land office, described the location thusly: "The appearance at that time was very unpromising. There were but two cabins and the town site was pretty much covered by a large encampment of Indians. In the treetops at the mouth of Perry Creek were lashed a number of dead Indians, while upon scaffolds on the summits of the bluffs west of the town were more 'sleeping the long sleep.'"

Woodbury County was first called Wahkaw, but was changed to Woodbury in 1853, apparently for Judge Levi

Woodbury, a former United States Senator from New Hampshire. The Sioux City *Eagle,* in its first issue in 1857, stated there were more residents in Sioux City from New Hampshire than from any other state. In May of 1856, by popular vote, the county seat was established at Sioux City, which had 90 buildings and about 400 people. The town was incorporated in 1857.

Although the Missouri River was a canoe route for early fur traders, it was not until 1856 that the steamboat *Omaha* arrived with a $70,000 cargo of provisions and lumber from St. Louis, for which the consignee, James A. Jackson, son-in-law of Dr. Cook, paid a freight bill of $24,000. It included a sawmill, lumber, drygoods, hardware, and other commodities. Later Jackson had a frame store constructed in St. Louis and sent to Sioux City in sections.

This was the beginning of a regular freight service between St. Louis and Sioux City, and during the 1860s, there were usually four or five boats tied up at the levee discharging freight. When settlers first poured into the Northwest, the Missouri was one of the important arteries of travel, and both overland and river travelers made Sioux City their supply base for the long trip ahead of them.

The first African-Americans came to Sioux City in the 1860s as boat hands, and many remained. One of them, Henry Riding, a Civil War veteran, made a success of his hotel business and purchased other property. His subsequent actions provided table talk for the townspeople. When the railroad was put across his property without his consent, he seized a shotgun and drove the track-layers away. Later, the railroad company paid him $21,000 for the privilege of crossing his land. He later startled the residents by having his tombstone erected while he was still in prime health.

One of the more well-known African-Americans of the late 1860s was Aunty Wooden. Her opossum dinners were so famous that business and professional men often bid to get an invitation. Pearl Street, the city's first principal thoroughfare, was named for an African-American woman, a cook on one of the boats that docked at the foot of this street.

The Pacific Railroad was extended from Missouri Valley to Sioux City in 1868. The arrival of the Illinois Central in 1870, built directly across the State, made Sioux City an important shipping point. In these years, it was also the shipping center for the Army in its activity on the upper river.

In 1886, the floating population of traders, miners, adventurers, steamboat crews, and river travelers, had given the town of 20,000 a nationally unsavory reputation. When the Reverend George Channing Haddock came to Sioux City in October of 1885, he became the leader in the fight against licensed brothels, gambling houses, and saloons. Because no Sioux City lawyers would take the cases, Haddock hired an outside legal firm to work with him. While he was in the midst of his legal fight, he was murdered by his enemies. The public reaction after Haddock's assassination forced the proprietors of the saloons and kindred enterprises to leave the city.

An accident started the meat-packing industry that changed Sioux City from a village to an industrial city. When a boatload of wheat sank in the Missouri River opposite the city, James E. Booge recovered and purchased the grain. Finding that the water- soaked grain was good for nothing but feeding hogs, he started in that business. There was no market for live hogs, so Booge slaughtered them and sold the meat. He built a small plant and hired packing house butchers from St. Louis. Others soon began to traffic in livestock, furnishing feeders to a limited territory and giving farmers an opportunity to utilize their surplus corn and fodder by supplying stock to the packers. Out of this activity came the Live Stock Exchange, organized in 1887, and the Live Stock Exchange Building, erected in 1892.

In 1887, the citizens of Sioux City promoted a festival, the principal attraction being the world's first Corn Palace. It was designed by E. W. Loft, a local architect, and erected at Fifth and Jackson Streets. Over a skeleton of wood, volunteer workmen placed sheaves of grain and red, yellow, white, and vari-colored corn in diverse patterns. Circling the dome was an allegorical picture of Mondamin, the Indian god of corn, showering the products of the region from a horn of plenty, in company with the deities, Ceres and Demeter. An agricultural display and pictures designed in corn and other grain, notably a reproduction of Millet's *Angelus,* were inside. Four other Corn Palaces followed, all at Sixth and Pierce Streets. Color reproductions of the last one are curiously suggestive of the Church of St. Basil at Moscow. In the spring of 1889, a Corn Palace train toured the East, stopping at Washington for the inauguration of President Benjamin Harrison.

In 1889, a steam railroad line, one and a half miles of which was elevated to solve the problem of dangerous railroad tracks, and to avoid the often flooded lowlands, was opened between Third and Jones Streets and Morningside. Built at a cost of $586,000, it was electrified in 1893.

POINTS OF INTEREST:

- City Hall. Douglas Street.
- Floyd Monument. Glenn Avenue & US 75, on E bank of Missouri River.
- Grandview Park. 24th Street & Grandview Blvd.
- Morningside College (1894). 1501 Morningside Avenue.
- Sioux City Art Center. 513 Nebraska Street.
- Sioux City Public Museum. 2901 Jackson Street.
- Stone State Park. Off IA 12, in NW part of city.
- War Eagle Monument. Grave on N bank of Missouri River, near jct. Burton St., W 4th Street.

HISTORICAL PLACES...

Sergeant Floyd Monument; Sioux City Central High School; Woodbury County Courthouse.

SIOUX COUNTY, NW Iowa, 766 sq. mi.; Pop. 29,903; Named after the Sioux Indian tribe.

SIOUX RAPIDS, City; Buena Vista County; Pop. 761; Zip Code 50585; 54 miles WNW of Fort Dodge; Lat. 42-53-26 N long. 095-08- 33 W; it was platted in 1858 by Luther H. Barnes, who dreamed of seeing a great city grow here on the banks of the Little Sioux River. The community failed to thrive, and when Barnes left, heart-broken and impoverished, the other residents used his former town stakes for kindling wood. In 1869, When D. C. Thomas and David Evans replatted the town, they named it Sioux Rapids.

SLATER, City; Story County; Pop. 1,268; Zip Code 50244; 11 miles S of Ames; Lat. 41-54-10 N long. 093-39-06 W. Slater was an early settler.

SLOAN, City; Woodbury County; Pop. 938; Zip Code 51055; 17 miles S of Sioux City; Lat. 42-14-17 N long. 096-13-34 W.

SMITHLAND, City; Woodbury County; Pop. 235; Zip Code 51056; Elev. 1,090; 25 miles SE of Sioux City; Lat. 42-13-53 N long. 095-55-34 W.

SOLDIER, City; Monona County; Pop. 205; Zip Code 51572; 42 miles SE of Sioux City; Lat. 42-00-13 N long. 095-47-07 W; Named for the Soldier River, which runs through this region.

SOLON, City; Johnson County; Pop. 1,050; Zip Code 52333; 12 miles NNE of Iowa City; Lat. 41-48-51 N long. 091-30-38 W. A Greek word meaning "wise man."

SOUTH ENGLISH, City; Keokuk County; Pop. 224; Zip Code 52335; 25 miles WSW of Iowa City; Lat. 41-27-10 N long. 092-05-09 W.

SPENCER, City; Clay County Seat; Pop. 11,066; Zip Code 51301; Elev. 1,321; 64 miles NW of Fort Dodge; Lat. 43-08-32 N long. 095-08-28 W; This city was named in honor of George E. Spencer (1836-1893), U. S. Senator from Alabama.

POINTS OF INTEREST:
- East Leach Park Campground. 305 4th Street SE.
- Wanata State Park. 16 miles S on US 71, then 10 miles W on IA 10 in Peterson.

SPILLVILLE, City; Winneshiek County; Pop. 387; Zip Code 52168; 53 miles NNE of Waterloo; Lat. 43-13-04 N long. 091-58-30 W. It is the city where where Antonin Dvorak, the Bohemian composer, spent the summer of 1893. Along the banks of the quiet Turkey River at the southeast corner of town, Dvorak is said to have found inspiration for many beautiful melodies he used in his later works.

SPIRIT LAKE, City; Dickinson County Seat; Pop. 3,871; Zip Code 51360; 76 miles NW of Fort Dodge; Lat. 43-26-13 N long. 095- 05-57 W; Named for nearby Spirit Lake. The Indians called the lake Minnewauken because they believed its waters were haunted by spirits.

POINTS OF INTEREST:
- Gardner Cabin (1856). 5 miles SW on US 71 in Arnolds Park.

- Mini-Wakan state Park. Off IA 276 on N shore of Spirit Lake.
- Ocheyedan Mound. Approx. 25 miles W on IA 9, then N on IA 60.
- Spirit Lake. Access area at Marble Beach, 3 miles NW on IA 276.
- Spirit Lake Fish Hatchery. 1 mile N in Orleans.

SPRINGBROOK, City; Jackson County; Pop. 116; Zip Code 52075; 18 miles SSE of Dubuque; Lat. 42-10-03 N long. 090-28-44 W. Named for a local spring.

SPRINGVILLE, City; Linn County; Pop. 1,068; Zip Code 52336; 17 miles E of Cedar Rapids; Lat. 42-03-30 N long. 091-26-19 W. Named for a nearby group of springs.

STACYVILLE, City; Mitchell County; Pop. 481; Zip Code 50476; 24 miles NE of Mason City; Lat. 43-26-01 N long. 092-46-56 W.

STANHOPE, City; Hamilton County; Pop. 447; Zip Code 50246; 17 miles NNW of Ames; Lat. 42-16-48 N long. 093-47-00 W.

STANLEY, City; Buchanan County; Pop. 116; Zip Code 50671; 30 miles ENE of Waterloo; Lat. 42-38-33 N long. 091-48-38. Stanley was an early settler.

STANTON, City; Montgomnery County; Pop. 692; Zip Code 51573; 36 miles ESE of Council Bluffs; Lat. 40-59-22 N long. 095- 06-09 W. Named for Civil War cabinet officer, Edwin Stanton.

STANWOOD, City; Cedar County; Pop. 646; Zip Code 52337; 34 miles ESE of Cedar Rapids; Lat. 41-53-09 N long. 091-08-10 W. The city is named after a railroad official.

STATE CENTER, City; Marshall County; Pop. 1,248; Zip Code 50247; 23 miles E of Ames; Lat. 42-00-57 N long. 093-10-27 W; Descriptively named for its location at the center of the State.

STEAMBOAT ROCK, City; Hardin County; Pop. 335; Zip Code 50672; 30 miles W of Waterloo; Lat. 42-24-12 N long.

093-02-45 W; The city got its name from a large rock that resembles a steamboat found in a river nearby.

STOCKPORT, City; Van Buren County; Pop. 260; Zip Code 52651; 28 miles ESE of Ottumwa; Lat. 40-52-26 N long. 091-50-26 W.

STORM LAKE, City; Buena Vista County Seat; Pop. 8,769; Zip Code 50588; 52 miles W of Fort Dodge; Lat. 42-38-00 N long. 095- 10-54 W. Named after nearby Storm Lake.

POINTS OF INTEREST:
• Buena Vista County Historical Museum. 200 E 5th Street.

STORY CITY, City; Story County; Pop. 2,959; Zip Code 50248; 9 miles NNE of Ames; Lat. 42-11-15 N long. 093-33-34 W; The city was platted in 1855 and named Fairview. With the establishment of the post office the following year, the town name was changed to Story City, after Supreme Court Justice, Joseph Story.

STORY COUNTY, Central Iowa, 568 sq. mi.; Pop. 74,252; Named for Joseph Story (1779-1845).

STRATFORD, City; Hamilton & Webster Counties; Pop. 715; Zip Code 50249; 19 miles NW of Ames; Lat. 42-15-52 N long. 093-56-21 W. Named after Stratford, Connecticut.

STRAWBERRY POINT, City; Clayton County; Pop. 1,357; Zip Code 52076; 45 miles ENE of Waterloo; Lat. 42-41-22 N long. 091- 32-35 W; Named by soldiers who camped here, for the abundance of wild strawberries in the area. The name became well-known and was kept after the town was platted in 1853.

POINTS OF INTEREST:
• Wilder Memorial Museum. 123 W Mission Street.

STUART, City; Adair & Guthrie Counties; Pop. 1,522; Elev. 1210; 46 miles W of Des Moines; Lat. 41-30-31 N long. 094-25-16 W. Founded in 1869 by Charles Stuart.

SULLY, City; Jasper County; Pop. 841; Zip Code 50251; 25 miles E of Des Moines; Lat. 41-34-52 N long. 092-50-33 W.

SUMNER, City; Bremer County; Pop. 2,078; Zip Code 50674; 28 miles NNE of Waterloo; Lat. 42-51-04 N long. 092-06-30 W. The city's name honors abolitionist U.S. Senator, Charles Sumner.

SUPERIOR, City; Dickinson County; Pop. 128; Zip Code 51363; 71 miles NNW of Fort Dodge; Lat. 43-25-53 N long. 094-56-42 W. Named after Lake Superior.

SUTHERLAND, City; O'Brien County; Pop. 714; Zip Code 51058; 48 miles NE of Sioux City; Lat. 42-58-34 N long. 095-30-02 W. Sutherland was a prominent pioneer.

HISTORICAL PLACES...
Indian Village Site (Wittrock Area).

SWEA CITY, City; Kossuth County; Pop. 634; Zip Code 50590; 58 miles N of Fort Dodge; Lat. 43-22-52 N long. 094-18-22 W. It was first called Reynolds, it officially adopted its present name in 1893; it is derived from the Swedish word, "Svea,ø the affectionate nickname for Sweden.

SWISHER, City; Johnson County; Pop. 645; Zip Code 52338; 13 miles SSE of Cedar Rapids; Lat. 41-50-56 N long. 091-42-21 W.

TABOR, City; Fremont & Mills Counties; Pop. 957; Zip Code 51653; 22 miles S of Council Bluffs; Lat. 40-53-59 N long. 095- 39-02 W. The city has a Biblical name given by the first settlers.
It was the scene of some of John Brown's anti-slavery activities of 1858-59. In the southeast corner of City Park, a bronze marker indicates the campground of John brown and his followers.

TAMA, City; Tama County; Pop. 2,697; Zip Code 52339; 37 miles W of Cedar Rapids; Lat. 41-57-37 N long. 092-34-47 W; It was first named Iuca when it was platted in 1862; it was later renamed for Taimah, a famous chief of the Fox Indians.

TAMA COUNTY, E central Iowa, 720 sq. mi.; Pop. 17,419.

TAYLOR COUNTY, SW Iowa, 528 sq. mi.; Pop. 7,419; Named for Zachary Taylor (1784-1850), twelfth President of the United States.

TEMPLETON, City; Carroll County; Pop. 321; Zip Code 51463; 55 miles SW of Fort Dodge; Lat. 41-55-11 N long. 094-56-47 W.

TERRIL, City; Dickinson County; Pop. 383; Zip Code 51364; 66 miles NW of Fort Dodge; Lat. 43-18-20 N long. 094-58-16 W.

THOMPSON, City; Winnebago County; Pop. 498; Zip Code 50478; 34 miles WNW of Mason City; Lat. 43-21-55 N long. 093-46-21 W. Named after the original landowner.

THOR, City; Humboldt County; Pop. 205; Zip Code 50591; 11 miles NNE of Fort Dodge; Lat. 42-41-28 N long. 094-03-00 W. A settler's personal name.

THORNTON, City; Cerro Gordo County; Pop. 431; Zip Code 50479; 18 miles SE of Mason City; Lat. 42-56-45 N long. 093-22-42 W.

THURMAN, City; Fremont County; Pop. 239; Zip Code 51654; 27 miles S of Council Bluffs; Lat. 40-49-19 N long. 095-44-43 W.

TITONKA, City; Kossuth County; Pop. 612; Zip Code 50480; 45 miles W of Mason City; Lat. 43-12-44 N long. 094-09-19 W; Titonka is a variation of the Sioux Indian language, meaning "big house."

TOLEDO, City; Tama County Seat; Pop. 2,380; Zip Code 52342; 37 miles W of Cedar Rapids; Lat. 41-59-11 N long. 092-34-48 W. Named after Toledo, Ohio.

TORONTO, City; Clinton County; Pop. 132; Zip Code 52343; 29 miles W Clinton; Lat. 41-54-25 N long. 090-53-05 W; Named by George W. Thorn in 1844, for his former home of Toronto, Ontario.

TRAER, City; Tama County; Pop. 1,552; Zip Code 50675; 19 miles S of Waterloo; Lat. 42-11-22 N long. 092-27-12 W.

HISTORICAL PLACES...
Brooks and Moore Bank Building.

TREYNOR, City; Pottawattamie County; Pop. 897; Zip Code 51575; Lat. 41-13-52 N long. 095-36-50 W.

TRIPOLI, City; Bremer County; Pop. 1,188; Zip Code 50676; 23 miles NNE of Waterloo; Lat. 42-48-24 N long. 092-15-50 W. Named after the North African city.

TRUESDALE, City; Buena Vista County; Pop. 132; Zip Code 50592; 53 miles WNW of Fort Dodge; Lat. 42-43-43 N long. 095-10- 40 W. The city is named after railroad official, W.H. Truesdale.

TURIN, City; Monona County; Pop. 95; Zip Code 51059; 36 miles SSE of Sioux City; Lat. 42-03-53 N long. 095-57-40 W. The city is named for Turin, Italy.

UNDERWOOD, City; Pottawattamie County; Pop. 515; Zip Code 51519; Lat. 41-23-13 N long. 095-40-35 W.

UNION, City; Hardin County; Pop. 448; Zip Code 50258; 33 miles WSW of Waterloo; Lat. 42-13-45 N long. 093-02-38 W; Like many places in the United States, this city was named out of patriotic sentiment.

UNION COUNTY, S Iowa, 425 sq. mi.; Pop. 12,750; A descriptive word.

UNIVERSITY HEIGHTS, City; Johnson County; Pop. 1,042; 2 miles N of Iowa City; Lat. 41-39-18 N long. 091-33-24 W.

URBANA, City; Benton County; Pop. 595; Zip Code 52345; 14 miles N of Cedar Rapids; Lat. 42-13-35 N long. 091-52-23 W.

URBANDALE, City; Polk County; Pop. 23,500; 16 miles W of Des Moines; Lat. 41-37-36 N long. 093-42-43 W. Descriptively named.

UTE, City; Monona County; Pop. 395; Zip Code 51060; 41 miles SE of Sioux City; Lat. 42-03-53 N long. 095-42-42 W;

The city was most likely named by the Northwestern Railroad, for the Ute Indians.

VAIL, City; Crawford County; Pop. 388; Zip Code 51465; 60 miles WSW of Fort Dodge; Lat. 42-03-27 N long. 095-12-18 W. Named for a railroad official.

VAN BUREN COUNTY, SE Iowa, 487 sq. mi.; Pop. 7,676; Named for Martin Van Buren, eighth President of the U.S., eleventh Governor of New York; Senator of New York.

VAN HORNE, City; Benton County; Pop. 695; Zip Code 52346; 12 miles of Cedar Rapids; Lat. 42-00-36 N long. 092-05-06 W.

VAN METER, City; Dallas County; Pop. 751; Zip Code 50261; 28 miles WSW of Des Moines; Lat. 41-32-10 N long. 093-57-41 W.

VENTURA, City; Cerro Gordo County; Pop. 590; Zip Code 50482; 18 miles W of Mason City; Lat. 43-08-00 N long. 093-27-28 W.

VICTOR, City; Iowa & Poweshiek Counties; Pop. 966; Zip Code 52347; 28 miles SW of Cedar Rapids; Lat. 41-44-37 N long. 092-15- 27 W.

VILLISCA, City; Montgomery County; Pop. 1,332; Zip Code 50864; 42 miles ESE of Council Bluffs; Lat. 40-55-38 N long. 094- 59-13 W; Earlier spellings of the city name include Valiska and Vallisca. The name probably came from the Sauk and Fox Indian word, "Waliska" or "evil spirit."

VINCENT, City; Webster County; Pop. 185; Zip Code 50594; 6 miles NE of Fort Dodge; Lat. 42-35-24 N long. 094-02-25 W.

VINING, City; Tama County; Pop. 78; Zip Code 52348; 27 miles W of Cedar Rapids; Lat. 41-58-50 N long. 092-24-54 W; Named for Hon. Plynn Vinton.

VINTON, City; Benton County Seat; Pop. 5,103; Zip Code 52349; 15 miles NW of Cedar Rapids; Lat. 42-10-12 N long. 092-01- 09 W. Named after Congressman Plym Vinton.

VOLGA, City; Clayton County; Pop. 306; Zip Code 52350; 48 miles ENE of Waterloo; Lat. 42-05-30 N long. 091-23-09 W. Named for the great river in Russia.

WADENA, City; Fayette County; Pop. 236; Zip Code 52169; 44 miles NE of Waterloo; Lat. 42-50-16 N long. 091-39-28 W; Named for Ojibwa Indian Chief, Wadena, who was wounded in the last battle between the Ojibwa and the Sioux in 1858.

WAHPETON, City; Dickinson County; Pop. 484; 78 miles NW of Fort Dodge; Lat. 43-21-58 N long. 095-10-18 W; The name is taken from Wakhpetonwan, or "dwellers among the leaves," one of the seven divisions of the Sioux nation.

WALFORD, City; Benton & Linn Counties; Pop. 303; Zip Code 52351; 9 miles S of Cedar Rapids; Lat. 41-53-41 N long. 091-48-10 W.

WALKER, City; Linn County; Pop. 673; Zip Code 52352; 18 miles N of Cedar Rapids; Lat. 42-17-20 N long. 091-46-43 W. Probably named for an early settler.

WALLINGFORD, City; Emmet County; Pop. 196; Zip Code 51365; 62 miles NNW of Fort Dodge; Lat. 43-19-25 N long. 094-46-17 W.

WALNUT, City; Pottawattamie County; Pop. 857; Zip Code 51577; 29 miles ENE of Council Bluffs; Lat. 41-16-46 N long. 095- 50-10 W. Named after the walnut tree.

WAPELLO, City; Louisa County Seat; Pop. 2,013; Zip Code 52653; 27 miles N of Burlington; Lat. 41-10-56 N long. 091-11-11 W; Named for Wapello, Chief of the Fox Indians.

WAPELLO COUNTY, SE Iowa, 437 sq. mi.; Pop. 35,687; Named for Wapello, Chief of the Fox Indian tribe.

WARREN COUNTY, S central Iowa, 572 sq. mi.; Pop. 36,033; Named for Joseph Warren (1741-1775), physician; president of the Provincial Congress in 1775; and major general of the Continental Army in 1775.

WASHINGTON, City; Washington County Seat; Pop. 7,074; Zip Code 52353; 22 miles S of Iowa City; Lat. 41-17-51 N long. 091- 41-13 W; Named in honor of George Washington.

POINTS OF INTEREST:

- Lake Darling State Park. 12 miles SW on IA 1, then 3 miles W on IA 78, near Brighton.

HISTORICAL PLACES...

Blair House (City Hall); Conger, Jonathan Clark; Young, Alexander, Cabin.

WASHINGTON COUNTY, SE Iowa, 568 sq. mi.; Pop. 19,612; Named for George Washington (1732-1799), first President of the United States.

WASHTA, City; Cherokee County; Pop. 284; Zip Code 51061; 28 miles ENE of Sioux City; Lat. 42-34-31 N long. 095-42-56 W; The name is a variation of the Dakota word "waste," which means "good."

WATERLOO, City; Black Hawk County Seat; Pop. 66,467; Zip Code 50700; 43 miles NW of Cedar Rapids; Lat. 42-29-47 N long. 092-20-37 W. The Cedar River, wide and clear, flows through the city in a southeasterly direction.

In 1845, George W. Hanna established a home on the west bank of Cedar River, and by 1848, there were settlers on both sides of the stream. The place was first known as Prairie Rapids, the name given to it by the Hanna family. In 1851, the seven signers of the petition asking for a post office left the name blank when Charles Mullan took the document to Cedar Falls to obtain the signature of the postmaster there. While he was leafing through the post office directory, Mullan happened to see Waterloo listed. It had the "right ring to it," so it was inserted in the petition.

With eastern papers announcing the attractive possibilities in Iowa, Waterloo and the surrounding settlements were crowded with incoming settlers. In 1858, the Cedar River rose to one of the highest points recorded in local history. Two hundred feet of the Dubuque and Pacific Railway embankment were washed away. The flood waters poured in torrents through two ravines on the west side of the city, inundating the lowest portion. Settlers rowed boats through the streets, and post office officials had to build a raised platform from which the mail sacks were delivered by boat. The high waters made it possible for the *Black Hawk,* a small steamboat, to come up the river from Cedar Rapids, and, for a while, the people thought the Cedar to be a navigable stream, but the steamboat trips in this flood year were the only successful ones.

By 1860, Waterloo had 1,800 inhabitants. In the following decade, the Illinois Central arrived, wheat elevators were built, the first park areas were planned, a brick schoolhouse was erected, and a new dam across the river replaced the old log one. By 1870, the city had a population of 5,000. Beginning about 1875, and lasting until 1895, the city was known for its horse races, with some noted trotting and racing contenders being bred here in those years.

Free carrier mail delivery was started on July 1, 1887, and improved streets had their inception in 1891 when East Fourth Street was paved from the river to Franklin Street. In 1892, after John Froelich, of Alkader, Iowa, had successfully harvested a crop of grain with his newly invented gasoline engine, the Waterloo Gasoline Traction Engine Company was organized. From then on, the history of the city is closely paralleled by the history of the tractor industry.

POINTS OF INTEREST:

- Grout Museum of History and Science. W Park Avenue & South Street, on US 218.
- Renssalaer Russell House (1861). 520 W 3rd Street.
- Sunrise Children's Zoo. Cattle Congress Grounds, off Rainbow Drive.
- Waterloo Recreation and Art Center-Municipal Galleries. 225 Cedar Street on river.

HISTORICAL PLACES...

Russell, Rensselaer, House.

WAUCOMA, City; Fayette County; Pop. 277; Zip Code 52130; 42 miles NNE of Waterloo; Lat. 42-59-56 N long. 092-02-44 W; Probably named for Waucoma Creek (now known as Badfish Creek) in Wisconsin.

WAUKEE, City; Dallas County; Pop. 2,512; Zip Code 50263; 23 miles W of Des Moines; Lat. 41-36-32 N long. 093-52-48 W; The name was most likely derived from "Milwaukee," the from Ojibwa Indian word meaning "good land." The name "Waukee" alone, however, is meaningless.

WAUKON, City; Allamakee County Seat; Pop. 4,019; Zip Code 52172; 69 miles NE of Waterloo; Lat. 43-16-59 N long. 091-29-15 W; Named for the Winnebago Chief, Waukon Decorah.

WAVERLY, City; Bremer County Seat; Pop. 8,539; Zip Code 50677; 16 miles NNE of Waterloo; Lat. 42-43-53 N long. 092-28-39 W. The city is named after Walter Scott's "Waverly" novels.

POINTS OF INTEREST:

- Bremer County Historical Museum (1863). W Bremer Avenue, at jct US 218.
- Oak Highlands Ski Area. N on 1st Street NW over Stockwell Bridge, then W.
- Wartburg College (1852). 9th Street NW & Bremer Avenue.

WAYLAND, City; Henry County; Pop. 838; Zip Code 52654; 31 miles NW of Burlington; Lat. 41-09-20 N long. 091-41-00 W.

WAYNE COUNTY, S Iowa, 532 sq. mi.; Pop. 7,067; Named for Anthony Wayne (1745-1796).

WEBB, City; Clay County; Pop. 167; Zip Code 51366; 51 miles NW of Fort Dodge; Lat. 43-00-43 N long. 095-10-59 W.

WEBSTER, City; Keokuk County; Pop. 103; Zip Code 52355; 29 miles WSW of Iowa City; Lat. 41-26-16 N long. 092-10-09 W; Named for Daniel Webster, a famous statesman.

WEBSTER CITY, City; Hamilton County Seat; Pop. 7,894; Zip Code 50595; 15 miles E of Fort Dodge; Lat. 42-27-42 N long. 093- 48-35 W; Probably named in honor of Daniel Webster.

WEBSTER COUNTY, NW central Iowa, 718 sq. mi.; Pop. 40,342; Named for Daniel Webster (1782-1852), Senator from Mass.; U.S. Secretary of State in cabinet of President Tyler and President Fillmore.

WELLMAN, City; Washington County; Pop. 1,085; Zip Code 52356; 14 miles SW of Iowa City; Lat. 41-28-08 N long. 091-50-15 W.

WELLSBURG, City; Grundy County; Pop. 682; Zip Code 50680; 23 miles W of Waterloo; Lat. 42-26-00 N long. 092-55-34 W.

WELDON, City; Clinton County; Pop. 177; Zip Code 52774; 50 miles SSW of Des Moines; Lat. 41-54-29 N long. 090-35-430 W. Named for Welton Dale in Hull, England.

WESLEY, City; Kossuth County; Pop. 444; Zip Code 50483; 38 miles N of Fort Dodge; Lat. 43-05-30 N long. 094-01-10 W. Named for a local railroad man.

WEST BRANCH, City; Cedar County; Pop. 1,908; Zip Code 52358; 14 miles ENE of Iowa City; Lat. 41-37-27 N long. 091-09-53 W. Descriptively named for its location on a creek. It was the birthplace of Herbert Hoover.

> **HISTORICAL PLACES...**
> Herbert Hoover National Historic Site.

WEST BURLINGTON, City; Des Moines County; Pop. 3,083; Zip Code 52655; 3 miles NE of Burlington; Lat. 40-49-00 N long. 091- 09-34 W. In 1882, Joel West organized the community that had been known as Leffleer's Station by bringing workers from locomotive shops in the north part of town into a realty company, and enabling them to buy lots on the installment plan. Any religious denomination that wanted to build a church was given two lots.

WEST DES MOINES, City; Polk County; Pop. 31,702; 15 miles W of Des Moines; Lat. 41-34-38 N long. 093-42-40 W.

A former railroad center, it was first known as Valley Junction. The name was changed by popular vote to West Des Moines, effective January 1938. For years, the Chamber of Commerce has sponsored the slogan, "Next to the Largest City in Iowa."

WESTFIELD, City; Plymouth County; Pop. 160; Zip Code 51062; 22 miles NW of Sioux City; Lat. 42-45-32 N long. 096-36-24 W.

WESTGATE, City; Fayette County; Pop. 207; Zip Code 50681; 28 miles NE of Waterloo; Lat. 42-45-20 N long. 091-59-54 W.

WEST LIBERTY, City; Muscatine County; Pop. 2,935; 18 miles E of Iowa City; Lat. 41-34-12 N long. 091-15-49 W.

The trade center of a purebred-stock region, it lies near Wapsinonoc Creek, and was first called the Wapsinonoc Settlement. Joseph Smith, the Mormon leader, in 1836 considered this place for the site of the Mormon colony.

WEST POINT, City; Lee County; Pop. 1,079; 11 miles WSW of Burlington; Lat. 40-43-00 N long. 091-27-00 W.

WESTSIDE, City; Crawford County; Pop. 348; Zip Code 51467; 55 miles WSW of Fort Dodge; Lat. 42-04-32 N long. 095-06-39 W. Named by railroad officials for its western location to the roadbed.

WEST UNION, City; Fayette County Seat; Pop. 2,490; 44 miles NE of Waterloo; Lat. 42-57-46 N long. 091-48-29 W.

It was first called Knob Prairie, and became known by its present name in 1849.

POINTS OF INTEREST:

- Echo Valley State Park. 3 miles SE on IA 56.
- Montauk (1874). 9 miles NE on US 18, near Clermont.

WHAT CHEER, City; Keokuk County; Pop. 762; Zip Code 50268; 25 miles N of Ottumwa; Lat. 41-23-55 N long. 092-21-18 W.

It was a Scotch and German settlement, manufacturing pottery of national fame. The town dates back to 1865, when it was an Indian trading post and agricultural trade center. After the discovery of outcroppings of coal along the little stream, which the settlers named Coal Creek, mines were opened. Maj. Joseph Andrews, with the memory of early Rhode Island traditions, proposed the name of What Cheer. Neighbors were skeptical. Nobody had heard of a name like that, they argued. The Major told of how Roger Williams crossed the Seesonk River in a canoe, of how the Indians met him and exclaimed, "What cheer, Netop!"

What Cheer called itself the "Coal City of Iowa," but by 1889 several of the larger coal veins were worked out. The mines began to close, and many of the miners moved on westward. Then prospectors discovered another source of underground wealth- -white clay. A company to manufacture products of clay was formed, with a capital of half a million dollars. Tests later showed that the clay was suited to the manufacturing of table and kitchen ware.

HISTORICAL PLACES...

What Cheer Opera House.

WHEATLAND, City; Clinton County; Pop. 723; Zip Code 52777; 22 miles NNW Davenport; Lat. 41-49-54 N long. 090-50-17 W. It was named by John L. Bennett, who platted the town in 1858, for the home of President James Buchanan.

WHITING, City; Monona County; Pop. 683; Zip Code 51063; 26 miles SSE of Sioux City; Lat. 42-08-23 N long. 096-09-24 W; Named for Senator Whiting.

WHITTEMORE, City; Kossuth County; Pop. 535; Zip Code 50598; 39 miles NNW of Fort Dodge; Lat. 43-04-00 N long. 094-24-22 W. It was platted in 1878 by W. H. Ingham and L. H. Smith.

WILLIAMS, City; Hamilton County; Pop. 368; Zip Code 50271; 28 miles E of Fort Dodge; Lat. 42-29-10 N long. 093-32-35 W. Named in honor of U.S. Army Major, W. Williams of Fort Dodge, who commanded a detachment of soldiers sent to aid the settlers following the Spirit Lake Massacre. In the 1880s, the town was destroyed by a tornado.

WILLIAMSBURG, City; Iowa County; Pop. 2,174; Zip Code 52361; 18 miles W of Iowa City; Lat. 41-39-40 N long. 092-00-05 W; Named for an early settler.

WILLIAMSON, City; Lucas County; Pop. 166; Zip Code 50272; 35 miles S of Des Moines; Lat. 41-05-47 N long. 093-14-42 W.

WINFIELD, City; Henry County; Pop. 1,051; Zip Code 52659; 26 miles NNW of Burlington; Lat. 41-07-47 N long. 091-26-51 W. Named in honor of General Winfield Scott.

WINNEBAGO COUNTY, N Iowa, 401 sq. mi.; Pop. 12,122; Named after the Winnebago Indian tribe.

WINNESHIEK COUNTY, NE Iowa, 688 sq. mi.; Pop. 20,847; Named after Winneshiek, Chief of the Winnebago Indian tribe.

WINTERSET, City; Madison County Seat; Pop. 4,196; Zip Code 50273; 36 miles WSW of Des Moines; Lat. 41-20-43 N long. 094-00- 21 W.

POINTS OF INTEREST:

- John Wayne Birthplace Site. 224 S 2nd Street.
- Madison County Museum & Complex. 815 S 2nd Avenue 3.
- Pammel State Park. 5 miles SW on IA 162.

WINTHROP, City; Buchanan County; Pop. 742; Zip Code 50682; 33 miles E of Waterloo; Lat. 42-28-27 N long. 091-44-00 W.

WIOTA, City; Cass County; Pop. 160; Zip Code 50274; 43 miles ENE of Council Bluffs; Lat. 41-23-59 N long. 094-53-50 W; An Indian word with several possible explanations. In the Sioux language, it means "many moons;" in Winnebago, "much water." It has also been translated as "many snows."

WOODBINE, City; Harrison County; Pop. 1,500; Zip Code 51579; 32 miles N of Council Bluffs; Elev. 1,078; Lat. 41-44-18 N long. 095-41-51 W. Named for the popular flower.

WOODBURN, City; Clarke County; Pop. 240; Zip Code 50275; 41 miles SSW of Des Moines; Lat. 41-00-53 N long. 093-39-54 W.

WOODBURY COUNTY, W Iowa, 871 sq. mi.; Pop. 98,276; Named for Levi Woodbury (1789-1851), ninth governor of New Hampshire and Senator from New Hampshire.

WOODWARD, City; Dallas County; Pop. 1,197; Zip Code 50276; 18 miles SW of Ames; Lat. 41-51-16 N long. 093-55-38 W. Named by the railroad for an early pioneer.

WORTH COUNTY, N Iowa, 400 sq. mi.; Pop. 7,991; Named for William Jenkins Worth (1794-1849), who fought Seminole Indians in Florida. He was brevetted a brigadier general for heroism against the Florida Indians, and was brevetted a major general for heroism against the Mexicans; he was awarded a sword by Congress.

WORTHINGTON, City; Dubuque County; Pop. 439; Zip Code 52078; 25 miles W of Dubuque; Lat. 42-23-34 N long. 091-07-23 W.

WRIGHT COUNTY, N central Iowa, 577 sq. mi.; Pop. 14,269; Named for Joseph Albert Wright (1810-1867), Governor and Senator of Indiana; sixteenth governor of New York; Surrogate St. Lawrence County.

WYOMING, City; Jones County; Pop. 659; Zip Code 52230; 32 miles SW of Dubuque; Lat. 42-00-46 N long. 091-03-38 W; Named for the Wyoming Valley in Pennsylvania, the site of a famous massacre by British soldiers, Torries, and Iroquois Indians in 1778.

YALE, City; Guthrie County; Pop. 220; Zip Code 50277; 39 miles WSW of Ames; Lat. 41-47-17 N long. 094-21-36 W. Named for the famous university.

YORKTOWN, City; Page County; Pop. 100; Zip Code 51656; 44 miles SE of Council Bluffs; Lat. 40-44-10 N long. 095-09-23 W. The city is named after the final battle of the Revolutionary War.

ZEARING, City; Story County; Pop. 614; Zip Code 50278; 17 miles ENE of Ames; Lat. 42-09-33 N long. 093-17-25 W. Named for a Doctor Zearing, who promised the town a church if it was named after him.

ZWINGLE, City; Dubuque & Jackson Counties; Pop. 94; Zip Code 52079; 10 miles SSW of Dubuque; Lat. 42-17-44 N long. 090- 41-17 W; Named in honor of Ulrich Zwingle, a Swiss reformer.

GUIDE TO HISTORICAL PLACES

Designations of Historical Places

Frequently the designations NHL, HABS, HAER, and/or G follow the ownership and accessibility. These are explained as follows:

NHL — A National Historic Landmark is a building, structure, site, district, or object declared eligible for recognition as a property of national significance by the Secretary of the Interior under the provisions of the Historic Sites Act of 1935. These properties are not administered by the National Park Service.

HABS — A Historic American Buildings Survey designation indicates that documentation by photographs, measured drawings, and or data sheets has been made as evidence of a building's architectural or historical significance. The Historic American Buildings Survey is conducted by the National Park Service in cooperation with the American Institute of Architects and the Library of Congress where the records are deposited. A HABS designation is included in the description of historic districts when at least one property has been documented by the Historic American Buildings Survey.

HAER — A Historic American Engineering Record designation means that the property has been recognized and recorded as an important example of American engineering. The Historic American Engineering Record is conducted by the National Park Service in cooperation with the American Society of Civil Engineers. Records are kept at the Library of Congress.

G — A grant designation means that the properry has received a National Park Service grant-in-aid under the National Historic Preservation Act of 1966.

HISTORIC PLACES

Greenfield vicinity. **CATALPA, SE** of Greenfield, 19th C.. Frame, clapboarding covered with asbestos shingling; 1 1/2- and 2-story sections, L-shaped, gabled roof, 2 interior chimneys, shed porch; shingles added; barn. Home of Henry C. Wallace, owner and editor of the agricultural newspaper *Wallace's Farmer*, and U.S. Secretary of Agriculture; birthplace of his son Henry A. Wallace, U.S. Secretary of Agriculture, Vice President, and Secretary of Commerce. *Private.*

Lansing. **LANSING STONE SCHOOL, SW** corner Center and 5th Sts., 1864. Limestone, 2 stories, Latin cross shape, intersecting gabled roof sections with octagonal bell cupola over entrance facade. One of the oldest schoolhouses in continuous use in IA and the midwest. *Public.*

Marquette vicinity. **EFFIGY MOUNDS NATIONAL MONUMENT,** 3 mi. N of Marquette on IA 13 (also in clayton county), c.0600–1400. 29 mounds in the form of bird and bear effigies. Products of the Effigy Mounds people, a Middle and Late Woodland culture (c. 600–1400) thought to have developed from the earlier Hopewell people who constructed many conical and linear mounds during their occupation of the site (c.

297

1000B.C.–600 A.D.). Several other mounds date from the earlier Red Ochre Culture (c. 500 B.C.). *Non-Federal/federal/NPS.*

BLACK HAWK COUNTY

Waterloo. **RUSSELL, RENSSELAER, HOUSE,** 520 W. 3rd St., 1858–1861. Brick, 2 stories, rectangular with 1 1/2-story wing, flat roof with double bracketing, rectangular frame cupola with bracketing and round arched windows, small front and wrap-around porch on wing with similar Corinthian columns and decorative roof cresting. Italian Villa. One of first substantial brick houses in Waterloo; built for Rensselaer Russell, entrepreneur in real estate, dry goods, and banking. *Private.*

CEDAR COUNTY

West Branch. **HERBERT HOOVER NATIONAL HISTORIC SITE,** c. 1870. Site of Herbert Hoover's birth includes 3 areas: restoration of a portion of the late-19th C. midwestern village, the Presidential Library, and the graves of President and Mrs. Hoover. Village contains 2-room frame birthplace cabin (c. 1870, restored 1939) with some original furniture, a replica of Hoover's father's blacksmith shop, a restored Quaker meetinghouse, and homes. Birthplace (Aug. 10, 1874) of Herbert Hoover, engineer, administrator of disaster relief programs, U.S. Secretary of Commerce, 31st U.S. President, and lifelong public servant. *Federal/NPS/non-federal:* HABS.

CERRO GORDO COUNTY

Mason City. **MASON CITY NATIONAL BANK BUILDING (HUB CLOTHING STORE, ADAMS BUILDING)** , 4 S. Federal Ave., 1909,

Frank Lloyd Wright. Brick, 3 stories, rectangular, flat roof, overhanging eaves, 3 entrances, terra cotta trim; originally 2 stories with ground floor consisting of solid brick wall 16' high topped by row of small windows; 1930's alterations by E. F. Ramussen included addition of 1st-story storefront and division of large bank room into 2 stories. Prairie Style elements. Designed by Frank Lloyd Wright as part of double commission, which included adjacent Park Inn Hotel (see also Park Inn Hotel, IA). *Private.*

Mason City. **PARK INN HOTEL,** 15 W. State St., 1909, Frank Lloyd Wright, architect. Roman brick 1–3 stories, rectangular, flat roof sections, interior chimney, several entrances and storefronts, U-shaped plan for 2 upper floors, masonry trim emphasizes horizontality. Prairie School elements. Designed by Frank Lloyd Wright as a companion structure to the former City National Bank. *Private.*

CHEROKEE COUNTY

Cherokee vicinity. **CHEROKEE SEWER SITE,** Paleo-Indian–Archaic (8000–4000 B.C.). Stratified habitation site with 3 distinct cultural units: 2 Archaic (6000–4000 B.C.) and 1 Paleo-Indian (8000–6000 B.C.). Investigated, 1973. *Municipal.*

Cherokee vicinity. **PHIPPS SITE,** 3 mi. N of Cherokee, Mill Creek Culture (c. 1000–1600). Type site of the Mill Creek Culture, a Late Woodland-Mississippian people who utilized a dual agricultural-hunting subsistence pattern. Apparently a winter habitation site. Excavated, 1952 and 1955, by the Sanford Museums of Cherokee, IA. *Private; not accessible to the public:* NHL.

CLAYTON COUNTY

EFFIGY MOUNDS NATIONAL MONU-MENT, *Reference—see Allamakee County*

Clayton. **CLAYTON SCHOOL,** 1st St., 1860. Limestone, 2 1/2 stories, rectangular, gabled roof with intersecting center gables and front octagonal cupola, center entrance with transom, regular fenestration. Greek Revival elements. *Municipal.*

CRAWFORD COUNTY

Dow City. **DOW HOUSE,** Prince St. at S city limit, 1872–1874. Brick, 2 1/2 stories, modified rectangle, low hipped roof sections, interior chimneys, denticulated bracketed cornice, frieze with decorative molding, front center round arched section with oculus above cornice; front center entrance with 1-story porch with paired posts, scroll brackets, and balustraded deck; rear entrance, segmental arched hood molds; rear large frame wing with hipped porch added, early-20th C.; under restoration. Built for Simeon E. Dow, prominent local businessman and one of town's founders. *County:* G.

DALLAS COUNTY

Adel. **DALLAS COUNTY COURTHOUSE,** Town Sq., 1902, Proudfoot and Bird, architects. Stone, 3 1/2 stories; high-pitched irregular roof with ornately carved dormers, rounded conical corner towers, and 128' central clock tower with parabolic dome. Chateauesque. *County.*

DAVIS COUNTY

Bloomfield. **DAVIS COUNTY COURTHOUSE,**
Bloomfield Town Sq., 1877, T. J. Tolan and
Sons, architects. Brick, stone facing; 3 stories,
modified rectangle, mansard roof with cresting,
bell tower with round arched clock pediments
and a life-size statue of Justice, pedimented
dormers, pilastered entrance with bracketed
cornice, bracketed and pedimented windows,
quoins, bracketed and modillion cornice, roof
cresting. Second Empire. *County.*

Centerville vicinity. **STRINGTOWN HOUSE,** E
of Centerville on IA 2, 1832. Frame, clapboarding, shingled ends; 1 1/2 stories, rectangular, gabled roof with rear extension, 2 interior
chimneys, hipped front porch, lean-to rear
porch, double front and rear entrances.
Unusual area style. Built as double house; has
served as stagecoach stop and hotel. *Private.*

DELAWARE COUNTY

Hopkinton. **OLD LENOX COLLEGE,** College
St., Mid-19th–early-20th C.. Four-acre college
campus including 4 main brick buildings
around square with Civil War monument; ver-
nacular interpretations and elements of various
19th and 20th C. styles represented. Clark Hall,
1890, now county museum; other buildings in
use by local community school system. College
established as Bowen Collegiate Institute, 1859;
represents early example of IA higher education. *Public.*

Manchester vicinity. **SPRING BRANCH
BUTTER FACTORY SITE,** SE of Manchester
on National Fish Hatchery Rd., 1872. Foundation rubble of original creamery marks site of
first butter factory in state and possibly W of
the Mississippi River; in operation for 5 years

(1872–1877); produced butter which won award at the U.S. Centennial Exhibition at Philadelphia in 1876. *Private.*

DICKINSON COUNTY

Arnolds Park. **SPIRIT LAKE MASSACRE LOG CABIN (GARDNER LOG CABIN)**, Arnolds Park, W of Estherville on U.S. 71, 1856. Log construction, 1 1/2 stories over basement, rectangular, gabled roof, central chimney; protective 2nd roof with lattice ends and pole supports added after 1959; restored; adjacent museum and memorial. Built by early settler Rowland Gardner, who was killed along with 31 other settlers in raid by Sioux band under Inkpaduta, Mar. 1857; cabin operated as museum (1891–1921) by Gardner's daughter, Abigail, who was captured and later ransomed by the tribe. Museum. *State.*

DUBUQUE COUNTY

Dubuque. **DUBUQUE CITY HALL,** 50 W. 13th St., 1857, John Francis Rague, architect. Brick, 3 1/2 stories, rectangular, gabled roof with paired brackets, 2 interior chimneys, each segmental arched window set in its own recessed segmental arched panel, gable oculi. Italianate. Designed as market with 2nd-story offices and 3rd-story ballroom. *Municipal. 12 (9-14-72)*

Dubuque. **DUBUQUE COUNTY COURTHOUSE,** 720 Central Ave., 1891–1893, Fridolin Heer and Son, architects. Brick, stone, and terra cotta; 4 1/2 stories, rectangular, hipped roof, central tower with domed cupola, center and corner pavilions with corner pilasters, rock-faced stone ground floor, 2nd-floor Corinthian portico, 3rd–4th-floor round arched window bays with stone label molds, large round arched recess in center pedimented pavilion on main facade, bracketed cornice with metal frieze, statuary on pediment and pavilion roof; interior stained glass dome; altered. Beaux-Arts Classical. Monumental courthouse located on same block as Egyptian Revival jail (see also Dubuque County Jail, IA). *County.*

Dubuque. **DUBUQUE COUNTY JAIL,** 36 E. 8th St., 1857–1858, John Francis Rague, architect. Limestone, cast iron trim; 2 stories, L-shaped, flat roof, interior chimneys, gorge and roll cornice, N and W entrances; S section contains 3 tiers of cells; exercise yard; S wing added 1875. Rare area example of Egyptian Revival. *County.*

Dubuque. **ORPHEUM THEATRE AND SITE (MAJESTIC THEATRE)** , 405 Main St., 1910, Rapp and Rapp, architects. Brick, 3 1/2 stories on front facade, rectangular, flat roof sections with front convex mansard, arched dormers; front center theater entrances with marquee, flanked by storefront entrances; brickwork imitating quoins, Bedford stone trim on front facade; highly decorated interior. Early-20th C. eclectic theater design. Theater site since 1840; building was designed by Chicago architects C. W. and George L. Rapp, who designed several theaters. *Municipal.*

Dubuque vicinity. **JOHNSON HOUSE AND BARN,** S of Dubuque, 1850–1851, Hugh V. Gildea, architect. Limestone, 3 1/2 stories, rectangular, gabled roof, paired interior end chimneys, round arched entrance, fanlight in each gable end, modillion cornice; restored and adapted to residential use. Frame barn with SE overhang. Greek Revival. House is only remaining portion of 3-part seminary complex, Mount St. Bernard College and Seminary, one of state's oldest colleges, representing one phase in development of Catholic higher education in state. *Private; not accessible to the public.*

FAYETTE COUNTY

Clermont. **UNION SUNDAY SCHOOL,** McGregor and Larrabee Sts., 1858. Brick, 1 story, rectangular, gabled roof, front square wooden louvered belfry with narrow metal steeple, front pediment with floral frieze, brick pilasters separating bays; tin ceiling; Kimball pipe organ donated by state senator and governor E LARRABEE, WILLIAM WILLIAM LARRABEE. GREEK REVIVIAL ELEMENTS. CITY'S FIRST CHURCH. *Private.*

Clermont vicinity. **MONTAUK (GOV. WILLIAM LARRABEE HOUSE)** , 1 mi. NE of Clermont on U.S. 18, 1874. Brick, 2 1/2 stories, square, hipped roof with balustraded deck, interior end chimneys with corbeled caps, cornice with paired brackets and exaggerated modillions; slightly projecting front center gabled section with round arched entrance and 2nd-story window and 1-story entrance porch with brackets, pendants, and balustraded deck; round and segmental arched windows, each with hood mold; bay and attic windows, bays articulated by pilasters; original interior furnishings; outbuildings. High Victorian Italianate. Home of Gov. William Larrabee, state senator and governor who led crusade against rate abuses by the railroads in the 1880's and 1890's and was partially responsible for the formation of the Federal Interstate Commerce Commission. *Private.*

GUTHRIE COUNTY

Panora. **PANORA-LINDEN HIGH SCHOOL,** Bounded by Main, Vine, Market, and 2nd Sts., 1897, George E. Hallett, architect. Brick, 2 stories over basement, modified rectangle, hipped roof sections, 4 corner towers, triple arched entrance porch, round arched side entrances, rectangular and round and segmental arched windows, 1st-story rusticated effect; remodeled, 1950's and 1960's. Brick interpretation of Richardsonian Romanesque elements. *Municipal.*

HENRY COUNTY

Mount Pleasant. **HARLAN-LINCOLN HOUSE,** 101 W. Broad St., 19th C.. Frame, clapboarding; 2 stories, modified rectangle, hipped roof with paired brackets, central monitor, center double-door entrance with transom and 1-story porch, side bay windows, 2-story side wing with entrance, corner pilasters. Italianate. Home of James Harlan, U.S. senator and Secretary of the Interior under Presidents Abraham Lincoln and Andrew Johnson; summer home of Lincoln's son Robert Todd Lincoln after his marriage to Harlan's daughter. Museum. *Private.*

Mount Pleasant. **OLD MAIN,** Iowa Wesleyan College campus, 1854. Brick, 3 stories, rectangular, low hipped roof with paired brackets, central square wooden cupola with small dome; front center double-door entrance with fanlight, side lights, and pedimented porch with bracketed posts; round arched 1st-story windows set in recessed panels, segmental arched windows with granite moldings. Italianate. Built as library and classroom building for Mount Pleasant Collegiate Institute (rechartered as Iowa Wesleyan University, 1955) under president James Harlan. (See also Harlan-Lincoln House, IA). *Private.*

IDA COUNTY

Ida Grove. **IDA COUNTY COURTHOUSE,** 401 Moorehead St., 1883. Brick, 2 1/2 stories, Greek cross shape, intersecting hipped roof sections, center projecting gabled sections on 3 sides, projecting front center entrance tower with pyramidal roof with gabled dormers, limestone window sills and moldings; central hall plan. High Victorian Italianate elements. *County.*

Ida Grove. **MOOREHEAD STAGECOACH INN,** Off U.S. 59, 1856–1863. Frame, clapboarding; 1 1/2 stories, L-shaped, gabled roof, bargeboard in one gable end; interior alterations. Built as stagecoach stop by John H. Moorehead, first postmaster and county judge. As area's only building of significant size, became landmark for travelers and served as county courthouse (1860–1871), first area post office, hospital, church, and school. *County.*

IOWA COUNTY

Middle Amana vicinity. **AMANA VILLAGES,** NE Iowa County, 1855. Area composed of 7 villages founded by communal religious society. Towns feature numerous 2-story brick, stone, and frame structures, generally simple large edifices, which served communal purposes as kitchens, shops, mills, and factories, and were held in common by the society in the late-19th C. Organized by German pietist under leadership of Christian Metz; sect settled in NY in 1842, migrated to IA in 1854. One of the most successful Utopian settlements of 19th C. America, the Amana Society reorganized as a joint stock company in 1932 and continues to operate today. *Multiple private:* NHL; HABS.

JOHNSON COUNTY

Coralville. **CORALVILLE PUBLIC SCHOOL,**
402-404 5th St., 1876. Brick, 2 stories, rectangular, gabled roof, 1 interior chimney, windows
and 2 gabled-end entrances have brick
"eyebrow" arches and stone lintels. Unique triangular arrangement of star clamps on gabled
ends and 3 to each side. Primary educational
institution until mid-20th C. *Municipal.*

Downey vicinity. **SECREST-RYAN OCTAGON
BARN,** W of Downey, 1883, George Frank
Longerbeam, architect. Stone foundation,
frame, vertical flush siding; 3 working levels,
octagonal, bell-cast domed roof with central
cupola, connecting rectangular shed leading to
silo. One of state's largest and best preserved
octagonal barns. *Private.*

Iowa City. **CLOSE HOUSE,** 938 S. Gilbert St.,
1874. Brick, 2 1/2 stories, L-shaped, intersecting gabled roof sections, front porch and projecting 2-story bay, round and segmental
arched windows with dripstones, side bay,
elaborately bracketed cornice. City's best example of the Italianate style. *County.*

Iowa City. **COLLEGE BLOCK BUILDING,**
125 E. College St., 1883, Chauncey F.
Lovelace, architect. Brick, 2 stories, rectangular, flat roof, elaborate pressed tin segmental
arches over 2nd-story windows, flat roof; tin
cornice composed of alternating large and
small brackets and massive scroll brackets at
each corner, surmounted by ornamental center
crest, ground-floor storefront. High Victorian
Italianate. Represents late-19th C. appreciation
of massive ornamental detail. *Municipal.*

Iowa City. **CONGREGATIONAL CHURCH OF
IOWA CITY,** 30 N. Clinton St., 1868–1869,
Gurdon P. Randall, architect. Brick, 1 1/2 sto-

ries, rectangular, gabled roof; front corner tower with side entrance, louvered belfry, and octagonal broach spire; projecting front center gabled entrance vestibule with Tudor arched doorway and 3 pointed arched windows above, pointed arched windows, stone dripstones and string courses, rear tower; SW turret removed; extensive remodeling, 1934 and 1968–1969. Gothic Revival. *Private.*

Iowa City. **FIRST PRESBYTERIAN CHURCH OF IOWA CITY,** 26 E. Market St., 1856. Brick, 2 stories, L-shaped, low-pitched gabled roof with square battlemented belfry, front center piano nobile containing entrance and Palladian stained glass window, round arch form repeated in arcaded corbel table. Romanesque Revival with Gothic Revival elements. *Private.*

Iowa City. **KIRKWOOD HOUSE,** 1101 Kirkwood, 1864. Frame, clapboarding; 2 stories, L-shaped, gabled roof sections, interior chimney, hipped front porch, cornice with paired brackets; altered. Italianate elements. Built for Samuel J. Kirkwood, 3-time governor of IA, U.S. senator, and Secretary of the Interior. *Private.*

Iowa City. **OLD CAPITOL,** University of Iowa campus, Mid-19th C., John Francis Rague, architect. Limestone, 2 stories over high basement, rectangular, gabled roof, 4 interior chimneys, central 3-stage cupola with dome set on colonnaded base, E and 2-story center pedimented tetrastyle entrance porticos, front and rear bays articulated by pilasters; W balustraded terrace; W portico added, 1920's; major remodeling and rehabilitation including installation of steel structure and fireproofing, 1921–1924; under restoration. Greek Revival.

Designed as 3rd territorial capitol; became first state capitol; first permanent building of the University of Iowa. *State:* HABS; G.

Iowa City. **PLUM GROVE (ROBERT LUCAS HOUSE)** , 1030 Carroll Ave., 1844. Brick, 2 1/2 stories, rectangular, gabled roof sections, 1 exterior and 3 interior chimneys, off-center gable end entrance with transom, round window in gables, flat arches over windows, rear 1-story kitchen wing with recessed porch; restored 1941. Greek Revival elements. Built for Robert Lucas, first Territorial governor of IA. Museum. *State.*

Iowa City. **SOUTH SUMMIT STREET DISTRICT**, 301-818 S. Summit St., 19th–20th C.. Area containing 40 buildings, 3/4 of which date from 1860 to 1910; exhibit variety of architectural styles. Typical of upper middle class Midwestern Americans of late-19th C. Town green served as mustering for 22nd Iowa Infantry who in 1863 led first great frontal assault on Confederate entrenchments at Vicksburg. *Multiple private.*

Iowa City. **TRINITY EPISCOPAL CHURCH,** 320 E. College St., 1871. Frame, board-and-batten siding; 1 story, rectangular, steeply gabled roof, triangular dormers, gabled bell cote, small brackets in gable, pointed arched motif at top of each board, vestibule with pointed arched door and label molded windows, lancet side windows; recent side addition; slightly altered interior. Gothic Revival. Possibly built from designs of Richard Upjohn. *Private.*

Iowa City. **WENTZ, JACOB, HOUSE,** 219 N. Gilbert St., 1847. Sandstone (random ashlar), 2 1/2 stories, rectangular, gabled roof, 2 pairs of interior end chimneys, transom over entrance, full entablature with bracketed cornice, rear shed frame addition. Greek Revival. Built for

German immigrant shoemaker, Jacob Wentz. Only remaining 2-story native stone house from original town. *Private; not accessible to the public.*

KEOKUK COUNTY

Delta vicinity. **DELTA COVERED BRIDGE, S** of Delta off IA 108 across North Skunk River, 1869, Joseph Merrifield and James Harlan, builders. Frame with vertical siding, Burr arch truss of 80' single span, 12' wide, 40' and 50' approaches; 1 original stone end pier, the other rebuilt of concrete and steel. State's only bridge of Burr arch truss construction; last covered bridge in county. Now restricted to foot traffic. *County.*

What Cheer. **WHAT CHEER OPERA HOUSE,** 201 Barnes St., 1893. Brick, 3 stories, rectangular, modified hipped roof with deck, front center Masonic emblems, 2-story center entrance arch with 2 double-door entrances surmounted by a large rectangular window and fanlight, 3rd-story round arched windows, stone trim, corbeled table at cornice; horseshoe-shaped auditorium with balcony, restored; 3rd-floor Masonic temple; cast iron columns supporting balcony and temple. Eclectic. Important town entertainment center; converted to movie theater. *Private.*

LEE COUNTY

Fort Madison. **OLD FORT MADISON SITE,** 315–335 Ave. H, 1808. Partially excavated foundations, cobble walks, and numerous artifacts mark site of first official American occupation of IA; garrison's wheat field initiated large-scale agriculture in state; important link in frontier defense during War of 1812; abandoned under seige, 1813. *State/private.*

Keokuk. **BROWN, DR. FRANK, HOUSE,** 318 N. 5th St.,

Keokuk. **MILLER, JUSTICE SAMUEL FREEMAN, HOUSE,** 318 N. 5th St., 1859. Brick; 2 stories in front, 3 stories in rear; rectangular, hipped roof, 2 interior chimneys with blind arches; full-width entrance porch with flat deck, bracketing, and octagonal posts; center entrance with fanlight. Italianate. Built for Samuel Freeman Miller, who was appointed U.S. Supreme Court Justice in 1862. Museum. *County.*

Keokuk. **U.S. POST OFFICE AND COURTHOUSE,** 25 N. 7th St., 1887–1890. Brick with limestone trim, 2 1/2 stories, L-shaped, mansard roof with intersecting gabled and hipped sections, pedimented 1/2-story dormers, numerous interior paneled chimneys with corbeled caps, recessed round arched windows and doors, terra cotta ornamental panels and horizontal bands, 7-story corner tower, small corner towers on various projections; 1-story rear extension (1956). Excellent use of Queen Anne in public building. *Federal/USPS.*

LOUISA COUNTY

Columbus Junction. **COMMUNITY BUILD-ING,** 122 E. Maple St., 1882. Brick, 2 stories, L-shaped with square section inside L, hipped roof with broad cornice supported by diagonal brackets, brick and limestone voussoirs in arches over windows; interior subdivided in 1940's. High Victorian Italianate elements. Served as school until c. 1920; as community building since. *Municipal.*

Toolesboro vicinity. **TOOLESBORO MOUND GROUP,** N of Toolesboro, c. 1000B.C.–200 A.D.. Six conical burial mounds linked to Illinois Hopewell Culture; excavated, 1875 and 1886, by Davenport Academy of Science. Represents an extension of the "classic" Hopewellian mortuary practices of the Illinois River Valley center. *State; not accessible to the public:* NHL; G.

LYON COUNTY

Rock Rapids vicinity. **MELAN BRIDGE,** E of Rock Rapids in Emma Sater Park, 1893–1894, W. S. Hewett, builder. Reinforced concrete bridge, Melan arch of 30′ single span, 16′ wide; 2 stone posts at each end, iron handrail, sides faced in Jasper stone; moved. One of first reinforced concrete bridges of arched design built in U.S. Patented in U.S. by Frederick von Emberger, from design by Joseph Melan, Austrian pioneer in use of reinforced concrete. *Municipal.*

Sioux Falls vicinity. **BLOOD RUN SITE,** S of Sioux Falls at jct. of Blood Run Creek and Big Sioux River (also in Lincoln County, SD), Oneota (c. 1700–1750). Remains of an Oneota Indian village, once containing more than 158 visible conical burial mounds; and remains of an effigy earthwork believed to have been constructed after the mounds. *Private:* NHL.

MAHASKA COUNTY

Oskaloosa. **NELSON, DANIEL, HOUSE AND BARN,** SR 1, 19th C.. Site of farm complex originally containing 160 acres; now includes 2-story gabled brick farmhouse, large frame barn, and several frame outbuildings on less than an acre; restored. Well-preserved example of early homestead buildings. Museum. *Private.*

Historic Places

Marshalltown. **MARSHALL COUNTY COURTHOUSE,** Courthouse Sq., 1884–1886, John C. Cochrane, architect. Limestone, 3 1/2 stories over high basement, rectangular, gabled and hipped roof sections with cross gables, interior end chimneys, central clock tower with dome and cupola; front center projecting pavilion, entrance with 1-story portico with paired columns, figure sculpture on parapet above cornice; rock-faced stone foundation and 1st-story banding, 2nd- and 3rd-story bays articulated by pilasters. High Victorian eclectic. Designed by Chicago architect, John C. Cochrane, who also designed the Iowa State Capitol. *County.*

MILLS COUNTY

Glenwood vicinity. **PONY CREEK PARK,** Prehistoric. Two Central Plains Tradition villages consisting of earthlodge sites. Unexcavated. *Public/private.*

MONTGOMERY COUNTY

Red Oak. **CHAUTAUQUA PARK,** Oak St., 1908. Steel frame pavilion, polygonal wooden roof with large central octagonal clerestory; seating capacity, 3500–5000. State's only remaining permanent facility for Chautauqua assemblies, a church-related educational movement which began in NY in 1874 and became particularly popular in the Midwest. Opening addresses given by William Jennings Bryan, Jane Addams, and Gov. Robert M. La Follette; accommodated annual programs until 1929. *Municipal:* G.

MUSCATINE COUNTY

Muscatine. **BOWMAN LIVERY STABLE,** 219 E. Mississippi Dr., 1889. Brick, 3 stories, rectangular, flat roof, parapet with decorative center and end pediments and trefoil crenelations, bays articulated by pilasters, brick table corbeling under the cornice, ground-floor storefronts, 3 2nd-story arches, segmental arched 3rd-story openings; alterations include commercializing the original ground-floor livery area. Eclectic. *Private.*

Muscatine. **MCKIBBEN, S. M., HOUSE,** Walnut St. between Front and 2nd, 1866–1869. Brick double dwelling, 2 1/2 stories over basement, rectangular, gabled roof, 2 interior end chimneys, steps leading to paired entrances; numerous front 1st-story features removed. Federal elements. Built by Samuel McKibben, prosperous early businessman. *Municipal; not accessible to the public.*

Muscatine. **OLD JAIL,** 411 E. 4th St., 1856–1857, Hines and Milford, builders. Brick, 1–2 stories, T-shaped, gabled roof sections, tall rear chimney; front main block features center entrance with classical framing, regular fenestration, denticulated cornice with gabled end returns, and corner pilasters; rear cell block. Only remaining Greek Revival government structure in Muscatine; replaced 1838 jail. *County.*

Muscatine. **TRINITY EPISCOPAL CHURCH,** 411 E. 2nd St., 1852, Frank Will, architect. Irregular sandstone blocks set between raised mortar joints, 1 story, Latin cross shape, intersecting gabled roof sections, N gabled entrance section; slightly projecting gable end bell tower with lancet window, surmounted by recessed miter arched panel with trefoil with round arched bell opening above, set under gabled

314

roof; miter arched and lancet windows; oak interior furnishings and chancel and transepts added, 1855; High Victorian Gothic interior detailing added, 1894. Gothic Revival. Built for Trinity parish, reputedly the oldest Episcopal parish in IA. *Private.*

Muscatine vicinity. **SINNETT OCTAGON HOUSE,** N of Muscatine near IA 38, 1855. Brick, 2 1/2 stories, octagonal; low pitched roof with central octagonal cupola with pedimented sides, each with a window; shed dormers, bracketed eaves, SE entrance; S projecting bay, partially surrounded by 1-story porch; rear frame addition. Excellent example of the then popular Octagon Mode. *Private.*

O'BRIEN COUNTY

Sutherland vicinity. **INDIAN VILLAGE SITE (WITTROCK AREA),** 3 mi. E of Sutherland, Mill Creek Culture (1000–1500). Habitation site; contains 17 circular house depressions surrounded by a square fortification ditch. Investigated. *State:* NHL.

PAGE COUNTY

Clarinda. **HEPBURN, COL. WILLIAM PETERS, HOUSE,** 321 W. Lincoln St., 1867. Frame, clapboarding; 2 stories, modified T shape, gabled roof sections, interior chimney, NE tower with oculi in bell-cast hipped roof, wrap-around NE porch, screened W porch. Built for U.S.Representative William Peters Hepburn. *Private.*

POCAHONTAS COUNTY

Laurens. **LAURENS PUBLIC LIBRARY,** 263 N. 3rd St., 1910. Plaster cement on steel lath, brick, painted; modified T shape, gabled roof, interior chimney; front center gabled entrance section with half-timbered effect above doorway and flanking projecting window blocks, each with 3 windows with diamond-shaped panes; interior window seats; rear addition. Built from funds donated by Andrew Carnegie; early focal point of community activity. *Municipal.*

POLK COUNTY

Des Moines. **FLYNN FARM, MANSION, AND BARN,** 2600 111th St., 1867. Brick, 2 stories, square, hipped roof cut by two 2-story gabled projections, square central cupola, 1-story front and side porches; rear addition; board-and-batten gabled barn with cupola. High Victorian Italianate. Complex built by Martin Flynn, important farm and business leader from 1870 to 1906; maintained by honor prisoners of state from 1915 to 1965. *Private.*

Des Moines. **FORT DES MOINES PROVISIONAL ARMY OFFICER TRAINING SCHOOL,** 19th–20th C.. Portion of military installation that became first black officers' training camp in 1917; many buildings remain of 1917 era, including barracks that housed black officer trainees; post where Bernice Gaines Hughes, first black woman to become lieutenant colonel in the armed forces, trained. Third location of fort established as frontier post in 1833 to protect settlers against raiding Indians. *Multiple public:* NHL.

Des Moines. **NAYLOR HOUSE,** 944 W. 9th St., 1869, attributed to William Foster and W. W. Boyington, architects. Brick, 2 stories, T-shaped, gabled and hipped roof sections, off-center entrance with ornate moldings and small porch, side entrance with carved porch, segmental arched windows with fancy dripstones, side stone bay window with balustrade. High Victorian Italianate. *Private.*

Des Moines. **TERRACE HILL (HUBBELL MANSION)** , 2300 Grand Ave., 1867–1869, William W. Boyington, architect. Brick, stone trim; 2 1/2 stories, modified rectangle, mansard roof, decorative interior chimneys, round arched dormers, bracketed denticulated cornice, frieze panels; 4 1/2-story front center tower with round arched entrance with elaborate bracketed hood, arched front cornice section, 3rd-story oculi, 4th-story balcony surrounding tower; full-width 1-story E balustraded porch, rear entrance porch, side tower; round arched and rectangular windows, each with elaborate dripstones and some with ornate hoods; projecting sections, bay windows, precast cement quoining; 8 fireplaces; elaborate interior; under restoration. Second Empire. Built for B. F. Allen, state's first millioniare; later purchased by F. M. Hubbell, who became richest man in the history of the state and established a trust to maintain the house. *State:* HABS; G.

Des Moines. **U.S. POST OFFICE,** 2nd and Walnut Sts., 1908. Steel frame, limestone; 2 stories over full basement, rectangular, flat roof; colossal colonnade of 10 engaged Corinthian columns on main facade, Corinthian pilasters on other sides; nicely detailed interiors; 1935 rear addition in generally same style. Outstanding example of Neo-Classical Revival style in central IA. *Federal/USPS.*

West Des Moines. **JORDAN HOUSE,** 2251 Fuller Rd., Mid-19th C.. Frame, 2 stories, T-shaped, gabled roof with transverse gables, paired brackets, projecting center entrance pavilion, window cornices; W end addition,

1872. Second home of James Cunningham Jordan, one of city's earliest and most prominent settlers and twice state senator (1854, 1856). *Private.*

Council Bluffs. **DODGE, GRENVILLE M., HOUSE,** 605 S. 3rd St., 1869. Brick, 2 1/2 stories, modified rectangle, mansard roof, modillion cornice; wrap-around porch with Doric columns, square paneled posts, and classical arches in several bays; elaborate hoods over 1st- and 2nd-story windows, ornate dormers; fancy interiors; frame rear and side sections. Second Empire. Built for Grenville M. Dodge, Civil War general and chief engineer for Union Pacific RR. under whose supervision the first transcontinental railroad was completed (see also Golden Spike National Historic Site, UT). Museum. *Municipal:* NHL.

Council Bluffs. **POTTAWATTAMIE COUNTY JAIL,** 226 Pearl St., 1885. Brick, 3 stories, irregular shape, polygonal and gabled roof sections, central square cupola, front center projecting gabled section with 1-story projecting gabled entrance section, 2-story round arched panel containing windows in each projecting gabled section, stepped corbeled tables in some gables, bracketed cornice sections, projecting string courses; S wing added; 3 tiers of cells within circular enclosures divided into wedge-shaped cells and surrounded by stationary gridded cylinder, inner cylinder rotated by waterpower and hand cranking to provide access to single door on each level. Eclectic. One of few jails in U.S. designed with the rotary cell system. *County; not accessible to the public.*

SCOTT COUNTY

Davenport. **FRICK'S TAVERN,** 1402–1404 W. 3rd St., c. 1870's. Brick, 2 1/2 stories, rectangular, hipped roof with center attic cupola, heavy bracketed cornice, segmental arched windows; 1st floor altered, c. 1890 rear frame wing. Italianate. Served as social center for city's German residents for over a century. *Private.*

Davenport. **LECLAIRE, ANTOINE, HOUSE,** 630 E. 7th St., 1855. Brick, painted; 2 1/2 stories, irregular shape, hipped roof with monitor, interior chimneys, 3 porches; brackets and shutters removed; decorative ceiling rosettes and borders. Italian Villa. Home until 1861 of Antoine LeClaire, colorful pioneer who negotiated 22 Indian treaties; founded Davenport and its first church, ferry service, hotel, and foundry; and instigated the contruction of the first railroad bridge across the Mississippi River. *Public/private.*

Davenport. **SCHICK APARTMENTS,** 310–314 Gaines St., Mid-19th C.. Stone, 2 1/2 stories, rectangular; gabled roof with stepped gabled ends and divisions, each with paired chimneys; rectangular and segmental arched openings; built in 3 parts (1852, 1856, 1859), interior altered to meet need for more apartments. Italianate. One of the first multiple dwelling units built in Davenport. *Private.*

Davenport. **TRINITY EPISCOPAL CHURCH,** 121 W. 12th St., 1873, Edward Tuckerman Potter, architect. Limestone, 1 story, rectangular, gabled nave with shed side aisles, iron cresting, compound pointed arch entrance with rose window above, triple lancet windows, buttresses, dressed stone trim. Gothic Revival. *Private.*

McCausland vicinity. **CODY HOMESTEAD,** S of McCausland, 1854, 1880's. Frame, limestone, clapboarding; 2 stories, T-shaped, gabled roof, 3 interior end chimneys; rear lean-to (1930). Classical elements. Only known boyhood home (from 1847 to 1850) of Buffalo Bill Cody retained on original site. *County.*

STORY COUNTY

Ames. **KNAPP-WILSON HOUSE (THE FARM HOUSE)** , Iowa State University campus, 1860–1864. Brick, stuccoed; 2 1/2 stories, L-shaped, 4 interior chimneys, box cornice with end returns, balustraded front porch, center door with transom and side lights; later frame and brick additions. Greek Revival. Home of seaman Asahel Knapp, noted agriculturist and teacher, and later of James Wilson, Secretary of Agriculture. Now the residence for Dean of Agriculture of Iowa State University, the first formally authorized land-grant college. *State; not accessible to the public:* NHL; G.

TAMA COUNTY

Traer. **BROOKS AND MOORE BANK BUILD-ING,** 423 2nd St., 1873. Brick, 2 stories, modified rectangle, flat roof, entrance in angled corner wall, metal hood molds with keystones over flat-top arched windows and doors, bracketed entablature. Victorian Italianate elements. Building has served variety of commercial functions. *Private.*

UNION COUNTY

Creston. **CRESTON RAILROAD DEPOT,** 200 W. Adams St., 1899. Stone and brick, 2 1/2 stories, rectangular, hipped roof with 6 gabled dormers, high round arched openings on 1st floor. Largest, best constructed depot in IA on the Chicago, Burlington, and Quincy RR. when built; division point and depot for all southwestern IA business. *Municipal.*

VAN BUREN COUNTY

Keosauqua. **HOTEL MANNING,** River and Van Buren Sts., 1854. Brick, 2 1/2 stories, rectangular, mansard roof, gabled dormers, 3 front entrances; 2-story veranda, each level with blind frieze with brackets and posts with ornamental braces, 2nd-story balustrade; front corner polygonal bay; remodeled 1893, upper story added. Victorian eclectic. Built for Edwin Manning, who platted Keosauqua c. 1837; operated as general store and bank from 1854 until 1893 when it became a hotel. *Private:* HABS.

Keosauqua vicinity. **BENTONSPORT,** E of Keosauqua on the Des Moines River, 1839. Remains of prosperous rural village containing 1–2-story frame and brick domestic and commercial structures in various stages of repair. Founded 1839; site of state's first paper mill and dam with locks; stopover for steamboat captains and railroad men. Museums. *Multiple public/private:* G.

WAPELLO COUNTY

Eldon. **AMERICAN GOTHIC HOUSE (DIBBLE HOUSE)** , Burton and Gothic Sts., 1881–1882. Frame, board-and-batten siding and clapboarding; 1 1/2 stories, L-shaped, gabled roof sections, hipped wrap-around porch on slender turned columns, dominant pointed arched window with mullions in front gable; later rear ell, recent N porch. Picturesque

Gothic Revival elements. House that native IA painter Grant Wood depicted in his famous painting, *American Gothic*, 1931, which presently hangs in Chicago Institute of Art. *Private.*

Ottumwa vicinity. **MARS HILL (MARS HILL CHURCH AND CEMETERY)** , SE of Ottumwa, 1850's. Log construction, 1 story, rectangular, gabled roof, exterior end chimney; front center entrance, 2 windows on either side; many elements reconstructed; restored. Early log church still in use; believed to have been stop on Underground RR. *Private.*

WASHINGTON COUNTY

Washington. **BLAIR HOUSE (CITY HALL)** , E. Washington St. and S. 2nd Ave., 1880–1881, William Foster, architect. Brick, 2 1/2 stories, modified rectangle, mansard roof, pyramidal and gabled dormers, 3 1/2-story front tower, projecting front polygonal section, 1-story wrap-around porch with N entrance, round arched and rectangular windows with hood molds, bracketed modillion cornice; S addition contains gymnasium and club rooms. Second Empire. One of city's few remaining Victorian houses; built as private residence; later served community's social and civic needs. *Municipal.*

Washington. **CONGER, JONATHAN CLARK, HOUSE,** 903 E. Washington St., 1848, 1867, John Patterson Huskins, builder. Brick (cement facade), 2 1/2 stories, asymmetrical, gabled roof sections, interior chimneys, bracketed modillion cornice, segmental and round arched openings; front center gabled cement entrance and side porches replaced original wooden porches; original rear section expanded, 1867, by prominent businessman Jonathan Clark Conger. Italianate elements. *Public/private.*

Washington. **YOUNG, ALEXANDER, CABIN,** W. Madison St., between G and H Aves., 1840. Log construction, 2 stories, rectangular, gabled roof, rough stone exterior chimney; reconstructed; moved from original site, 1912. Built by pioneer Alexander Young; donated to DAR, 1912. *Private.*

WEBSTER COUNTY

Fort Dodge. **VINCENT HOUSE,** 824 3rd Ave. S., 1871. Brick, 2 1/2 stories, rectangular, mansard roof, central chimney, bracketed modillion cornice, front off-center double-door entrance with blind fanlight, 1-story wrap-around porch, paired round and segmental arched windows, side bay window; 3rd-story ballroom. Second Empire. Built for Webb Vincent, early promoter of gypsum, one of city's leading industries. *Private.*

WINNESHIEK COUNTY

Decorah. **PAINTER-BERNATZ MILL,** 200 N. Mill St., 1851–1853. Frame, stone; 2 1/2 stories, rectangular, gabled roof with gabled clerestory; lean-to (1914) on E; restored. Oldest building in Decorah; built by William Painter; later owned by Bernatz family. Conversion in 1875 from stone to roller milling machinery, flour shipped to many parts of the U.S.; operated until 1963. Museum. *Private.*

WOODBURY COUNTY

Sioux City. **SERGEANT FLOYD MONUMENT,** Glenn Ave. and Lewis Rd., 19th C.. 100' obelisk marks grave of Charles Floyd, who died nearby in 1804 on the Lewis and Clark Expedition. Frequently visited landmark during

first half of 19th C.; remains moved and rein-
terred, 1857; placed in monument, 1900–1901.
Municipal: NHL.

Sioux City. **SIOUX CITY CENTRAL HIGH
SCHOOL,** 1212 Nebraska St., 1892, F. S.
Allen, architect. Rough-hewn sandstone, 4 stories, modified rectangle, flat roof, central caste-
lated bell and entrance tower flanked by
stepped gabled projecting sections; originally 3
stories; 3-story addition, 1911–1912; raised to 4
stories, 1930. Richardsonian Romanesque elements. City's oldest community high school;
served as such until 1972. *Municipal.*

Sioux City. **WOODBURY COUNTY
COURTHOUSE,** 7th and Douglas Sts., 1918,
George Grant Elmslie, chief designer; Alfonso
Iannelli, sculptor; John W. Norton, muralist.
Brick and granite, 5-story lower block with 8-
story inner shaft, rectangular, flat roofs,
decorative leaded glass windows, polychro-
matic terra cotta molding and mosaic designs;
elaborate interior with tile floors and brick and
terra cotta walls; rooms distributed around central rotunda with glass dome. Art Deco. *County.*

PICTORIAL SCENES

State Capitol

Des Moines

General Dodge House

Pictorial Scenes

Greene County Courthouse

Clinton Riverfront

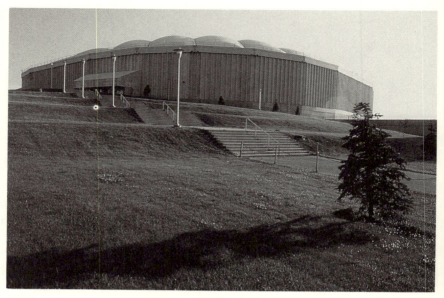

Unidome, University of Iowa

Lower Fox Creek School, Chase County

Pictorial Scenes

Iowa Great Lakes

Arnold's Park Amusement Park

College Hills Art Festival

Snake Alley

Pictorial Scenes

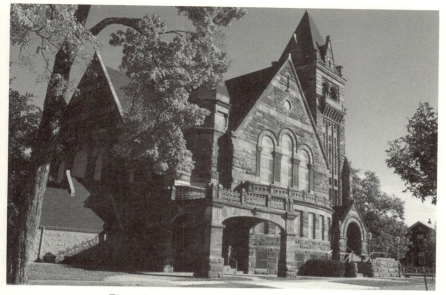

First Presbyterian Church of Davenport

Mississippi Belle Floating Casino

Pictorial Scenes

Maycrest College

Amana Colonies

Pictorial Scenes

Mississippi River Bluffs

RiverCenter, Davenport

George Wyth State Park

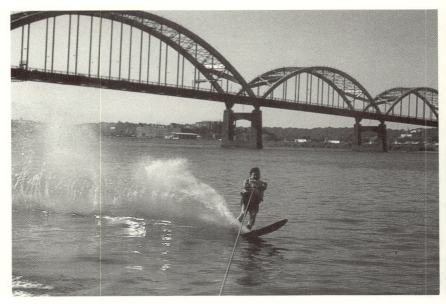

Mississippi River

Mummy at the Putnam Museum

Fort Dodge

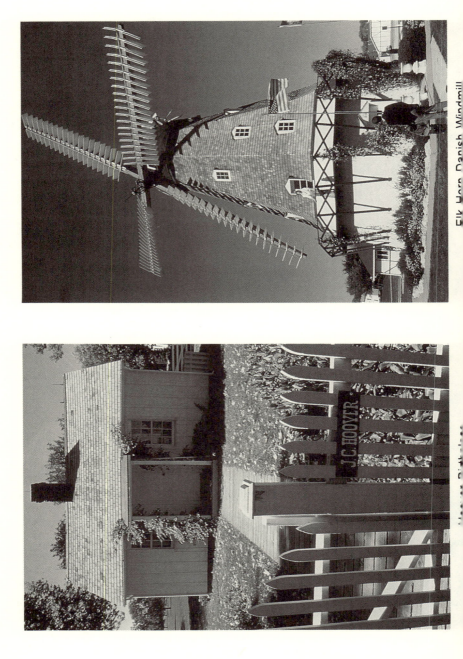

Elk Horn Danish Windmill

J.C. HOOVER

CONSTITUTION

Preamble. WE THE PEOPLE OF THE STATE OF IOWA, grateful to the Supreme Being for the blessings hitherto enjoyed, and feeling our dependence on Him for a continuation of those blessings, do ordain and establish a free and independent government, by the name of the State of Iowa, the boundaries whereof shall be as follows:

Boundaries. Beginning in the middle of the main channel of the Mississippi River, at a point due East of the middle of the mouth of the main channel of the Des Moines River, thence up the middle of the main channel of the said Des Moines River, to a point on said river where the Northern boundary line of the state of Missouri— as established by the constitution of that State—adopted June 12, 1820—crosses the said middle of the main channel of the said Des Moines River; thence Westwardly along the said Northern boundary line of the State of Missouri, as established at the time aforesaid, until an extension of said line intersects the middle of the main channel of the Missouri River; thence up the middle of the main channel of the said Missouri River to a point opposite the middle of the main channel of the Big Sioux River, according to Nicollett's Map; thence up the main channel of the said Big Sioux River, according to the said map, until it is intersected by the parallel of forty three degrees and thirty minutes North latitude; thence East along said parallel of forty three degrees and thirty minutes until said parallel intersects the middle of the main channel of the Mississippi River; thence down the middle of the main channel of said Mississippi River to the place of beginning.

See boundary compromise agreements at the end of Volume III of the Code

ARTICLE I. — Bill of Rights

Rights of persons. Section 1. All men are, by nature, free and equal, and have certain inalienable rights — among which are those of enjoying and defending life and liberty, acquiring, possessing and protecting property, and pursuing and obtaining safety and happiness.

Political power. Section 2. All political power is inherent in the people. Government is instituted for the protection, security, and benefit of the people, and they have the right, at all times, to alter or reform the same, whenever the public good may require it.

Religion. Section 3. The General Assembly shall make no law respecting an establishment of religion, or prohibiting the free exercise thereof; nor shall any person be compelled to attend any place of worship, pay tithes, taxes, or other rates for building or repairing places of worship, or the maintenance of any minister, or ministry.

Religious test—witnesses. Section 4. No religious test shall be required as a qualification for any office, or public trust, and no person shall be deprived of any of his rights, privileges, or capacities, or disqualified from the performance of any of his public or private duties, or rendered incompetent to give evidence in any court of law or equity, in consequence of his opinions on the subject of religion; and any party to any judicial proceeding shall have the right to use as a witness, or take the testimony of, any other person not qualified on account of interest, who may be cognizant of any fact material to the case; and parties to suits may be witnesses, as provided by law.

Dueling. Section 5. Any citizen of this State who may hereafter be engaged, either directly, or indirectly, in a duel, either as principal, or accessory before the fact, shall forever be disqualified from holding any office under the Constitution and laws of this State.

Laws uniform. Section 6. All laws of a general nature shall have a uniform operation; the General Assembly shall not grant to any citizen, or class of citizens, privileges or immunities, which, upon the same terms shall not equally belong to all citizens.

Liberty of speech and press. Section 7. Every person may speak, write, and publish his sentiments on all subjects, being responsible for the abuse of that right. No law shall be passed to restrain or abridge the liberty of speech, or of the press. In all prosecutions or indictments for libel, the truth may be given in evidence to the jury, and if it appear to the jury that the matter charged as libellous was true, and was published with good motives and for justifiable ends, the party shall be acquitted.

Personal security—searches and seizures. Section 8. The right of the people to be secure in their persons, houses, papers and effects, against unreasonable seizures and searches shall not be violated; and no warrant shall issue but on probable cause, supported by oath or affirmation, particularly describing the place to be searched, and the persons and things to be seized.

Right of trial by jury—due process of law. Section 9. The right of trial by jury shall remain inviolate; but the General Assembly may authorize trial by jury of a less number than twelve men in inferior courts; but no person shall be deprived of life, liberty, or property, without due process of law.

See also R.Cr.P. 16, 20(2), 48; R.C.P. 177, 178, 268

Rights of persons accused. Section 10. In all criminal prosecutions, and in cases involving the life, or liberty of an individual the accused shall have a right to a speedy and public trial by an impartial jury; to be informed of the accusation against him, to have a copy of the same when demanded; to be confronted with the witnesses against him; to have compulsory process for his witnesses; and, to have the assistance of counsel.

See §602.1601 of the Code

When indictment necessary. Section 11. All offences less than felony and in which the punishment does not exceed a fine of One hundred dollars, or imprisonment for thirty days, shall be tried summarily before a Justice of the Peace, or other officer authorized by law, on information under oath, without indictment, or the intervention of a grand jury, saving to the defendant the right of appeal; and no person shall be held to answer for any higher criminal offence, unless on presentment or indictment by a grand jury,* except in cases arising in the army, or navy, or in the militia, when in actual service, in time of war or public danger.

*As to indictment and the number of grand jurors, see Amendment [9], R.Cr.P. 3,4

For civil jurisdiction of Justice of Peace, see Art. XI, §1; but see 64GA, chapter 1124. Magistrate jurisdiction, §602.6405 of the Code

Twice tried—bail. Section 12. No person shall after acquittal, be tried for the same offence. All persons shall, before conviction, be bailable, by sufficient sureties, except for capital offences where the proof is evident, or the presumption great.

Habeas corpus. Section 13. The writ of habeas corpus shall not be suspended, or refused when application is made as required by law, unless in case of rebellion, or invasion the public safety may require it.

Military. Section 14. The military shall be subordinate to the civil power. No standing army shall be kept up by the State in time of peace; and in time of war, no appropriation for a standing army shall be for a longer time than two years.

Quartering soldiers. Section 15. No soldier shall, in time of peace, be quartered in any house without the consent of the owner, nor in time of war except in the manner prescribed by law.

Treason. Section 16. Treason against the State shall consist only in levying war against it, adhering to its enemies, or giving them aid and comfort. No person shall be convicted of treason, unless on the evidence of two witnesses to the same overt act, or confession in open Court.

Bail—punishments. Section 17. Excessive bail shall not be required; excessive fines shall not be imposed, and cruel and unusual punishment shall not be inflicted.

Eminent domain. Section 18. Private property shall not be taken for public use without just compensation first being made, or secured to be made to the owner thereof, as soon as the damages shall be assessed by a jury, who shall not take into consideration any advantages that may result to said owner on account of the improvement for which it is taken.*

*See Amendment [13]

Imprisonment for debt. Section 19. No person shall be imprisoned for debt in any civil action, on mesne or final process, unless in case of fraud; and no person shall be imprisoned for a militia fine in time of peace.

Right of assemblage—petition. Section 20. The people have the right freely to assemble together to counsel for the common good; to make known their opinions to their representatives and to petition for a redress of grievances.

Attainder—ex post facto law—obligation of contract. Section 21. No bill of attainder, ex post facto law, or law impairing the obligation of contracts, shall ever be passed.

Resident aliens. Section 22. Foreigners who are, or may hereafter become residents of this State, shall enjoy the same rights in respect to the possession, enjoyment and descent of property, as native born citizens.

Slavery—penal servitude. Section 23. There shall be no slavery in this State; nor shall there be involuntary servitude, unless for the punishment of crime.

Agricultural leases. Section 24. No lease or grant of agricultural lands, reserving any rent, or service of any kind, shall be valid for a longer period than twenty years.

Constitution

Rights reserved. Section 25. This enumeration of rights shall not be construed to impair or deny others, retained by the people.

An additional section (section 26) was added to article I by the amendment of 1882. The supreme court, however, in the case of Koehler v. Hill, 60 Iowa 543, on April 21, 1883, held that, owing to certain irregularities, the amendment did not become a part of the Constitution. [Prohibition of intoxicating liquors]

ARTICLE II. — Right of Suffrage

Electors. Section 1. [*Every (white)*]* *male citizen of the United States, of the age of twenty one years, who shall have been a resident of this State six months next preceding the election, and of the County in which he claims his vote sixty days, shall be entitled to vote at all elections which are now or hereafter may be authorised by law.***

*The above section was amended in 1868 by striking the word "white" from the first line thereof: See Amendment [1]

For qualifications of electors, see also Amendments 19 and 26, U.S. Constitution

A proposal to strike the word "male" was defeated in 1916

**In 1970, this section was repealed and a substitute adopted in lieu thereof: See Amendment [30]

Privileged from arrest. Section 2. Electors shall, in all cases except treason, felony, or breach of the peace, be privileged from arrest on the days of election, during their attendance at such election, going to and returning therefrom.

From military duty. Section 3. No elector shall be obliged to perform military duty on the day of election, except in time of war, or public danger.

Persons in military service. Section 4. No person in the military, naval, or marine service of the United States shall be considered a resident of this State by being stationed in any garrison, barrack, or military or naval place, or station within this State.

Disqualified persons. Section 5. No idiot, or insane person, or person convicted of any infamous crime, shall be entitled to the privilege of an elector.

Ballot. Section 6. All elections by the people shall be by ballot.

General election. Section 7. See Amendments [7], [11] and [14]

See §39.1 of the Code

ARTICLE III. — Of the Distribution of Powers

Departments of government. Section 1. The powers of the government of Iowa shall be divided into three separate departments—the Legislative, the Executive, and the Judicial: and no person charged with the exercise of powers properly belonging to one of these departments shall exercise any function appertaining to either of the others, except in cases hereinafter expressly directed or permitted.

Legislative Department.

General Assembly. Section 1. The Legislative authority of this State shall be vested in a General Assembly, which shall consist of a Senate and House of Representatives: and the style of every law shall be, "Be it enacted by the General Assembly of the State of Iowa."

Sessions. Section 2. [*The sessions of the General Assembly shall be biennial, and shall commence on the second Monday in January next ensuing the election of its members; unless the Governor of the State shall, in the meantime, convene the General Assembly by proclamation.*]*

*In 1968 this section was repealed and a substitute adopted in lieu thereof: See Amendments [24] and [36]

Special sessions, Art. IV, §11 and Amendment [36]

Representatives. Section 3. The members of the House of Representatives shall be chosen every second year, by the qualified electors of their respective districts, [*on the second Tuesday in October,* * except the years of the Presidential election, when the election shall be on the Tuesday next after the first Monday in November;*]* and their term of office shall commence on the first day of January next after their election, and continue two years, and until their successors are elected and qualified.

*For provisions relative to the time of holding the general election, see Amendment [14]: See also §39.1 of the Code

Qualifications. Section 4. No person shall be a member of the House of Representatives who shall not have attained the age of twenty-one years, be a [*free white*] [*male*]* citizen of the United States, and shall have been an inhabitant of this State one year next preceding his election, and at the time of his election shall have had an actual residence of sixty days in the County, or District he may have been chosen to represent.

*For amendments striking "free white" and "male", see Amendments [6] and [15]

Senators—qualifications. Section 5. Senators shall be chosen for the term of four years, at the same time and place as Representatives; they shall be twenty-five years of age, and possess the qualifications of Representatives as to residence and citizenship.

341

Number and classification. Section 6. [*The number of Senators shall not be less than one third, nor more than one half the representative body; and shall be so classified by lot, that one class, being as nearly one half as possible, shall be elected every two years. When the number of Senators is increased, they shall be annexed by lot to one or the other of the two classes, so as to keep them as nearly equal in numbers as practicable.*]*

*In 1968 this section was repealed and a substitute adopted in lieu thereof: See Amendment [26]

Officers—elections determined. Section 7. Each house shall choose its own officers, and judge of the qualification, election, and return of its own members. A contested election shall be determined in such manner as shall be directed by law.

Quorum. Section 8. A majority of each house shall constitute a quorum to transact business; but a smaller number may adjourn from day to day, and may compel the attendance of absent members in such manner and under such penalties as each house may provide.

Authority of the houses. Section 9. Each house shall sit upon its own adjournments, keep a journal of its proceedings, and publish the same; determine its rules of proceedings, punish members for disorderly behavior; and, with the consent of two thirds, expel a member, but not a second time for the same offense; and shall have all other powers necessary for a branch of the General Assembly of a free and independent State.

Protest—record of vote. Section 10. Every member of the General Assembly shall have the liberty to dissent from, or protest against any Act or resolution which he may think injurious to the public, or an individual, and have the reasons for his dissent entered on the journals; and the yeas and nays of the members of either house, on any question, shall, at the desire of any of any two members present, be entered on the journals.

Privileged from arrest. Section 11. Senators and Representatives, in all cases, except treason, felony, or breach of the peace, shall be privileged from arrest during the session of the General Assembly, and in going to and returning from the same.

Vacancies. Section 12. When vacancies occur in either house, the Governor or the person exercising the functions of Governor, shall issue writs of election to fill such vacancies.

Doors open. Section 13. The doors of each house shall be open, except on such occasions, as, in the opinion of the house, may require secrecy.

Adjournments. Section 14. Neither house shall, without the consent of the other, adjourn for more than three days, nor to any other place than that in which they may be sitting.

Bills. Section 15. Bills may originate in either house, and may be amended, altered, or rejected by the other; and every bill having passed both houses, shall be signed by the Speaker and President of their respective houses.

Executive approval—veto. Section 16. Every bill which shall have passed the General Assembly, shall, before it becomes a law, be presented to the Governor. If he approve, he shall sign it; but if not, he shall return it with his objections, to the house in which it originated, which shall enter the same upon their journal, and proceed to re-consider it; if, after such re-consideration, it again pass both houses, by yeas and nays, by a majority of two thirds of the members of each house, it shall become a law, notwithstanding the Governor's objections. If any bill shall not be returned within three days after it shall have been presented to him, Sunday excepted, the same shall be a law in like manner as if he had signed it, unless the General Assembly, by adjournment, prevent such return. Any bill submitted to the Governor for his approval during the last three days of a session of the General Assembly, shall be deposited by him in the office of the Secretary of State, within thirty days after the adjournment, with his approval, if approved by him, and with his objections, if he disapproves thereof.*

Statutory provisions, §3.4, 3.5 of the Code

*In 1968 an additional paragraph was added to this section: See Amendment [27]

Passage of bills. Section 17. No bill shall be passed unless by the assent of a majority of all the members elected to each branch of the General Assembly, and the question upon the final passage shall be taken immediately upon its last reading, and the yeas and nays be entered on the journal.

Receipts and expenditures. Section 18. An accurate statement of the receipts and expenditures of the public money shall be attached to and published with the laws, at every regular session of the General Assembly.

Statutory provisions, §14.10(5) of the Code

Impeachment. Section 19. The House of Representatives shall have the sole power of impeachment, and all impeachments shall be tried by the Senate. When sitting for that purpose, the senators shall be upon oath or affirmation; and no person shall

Constitution

be convicted without the concurrence of two thirds of the members present.

Officers subject to impeachment—judgment. Section 20. The Governor, Judges of the Supreme and District Courts, and other State officers, shall be liable to impeachment for any misdemeanor or malfeasance in office; but judgment in such cases shall extend only to removal from office, and disqualification to hold any office of honor, trust, or profit, under this State; but the party convicted or acquitted shall nevertheless be liable to indictment, trial, and punishment, according to law. All other civil officers shall be tried for misdemeanors and malfeasance in office, in such manner as the General Assembly may provide.

Members not appointed to office. Section 21. No senator or representative shall, during the time for which he shall have been elected, be appointed to any civil office of profit under this State, which shall have been created, or the emoluments of which shall have been increased during such term, except such offices as may be filled by elections by the people.

Disqualification. Section 22. No person holding any lucrative office under the United States, or this State, or any other power, shall be eligible to hold a seat in the General Assembly: but offices in the militia, to which there is attached no annual salary, or the office of justice of the peace, or postmaster whose compensation does not exceed one hundred dollars per annum, or notary public, shall not be deemed lucrative.

Failure to account. Section 23. No person who may hereafter be a collector or holder of public monies, shall have a seat in either House of the General Assembly, or be eligible to hold any office of trust or profit in this State, until he shall have accounted for and paid into the treasury all sums for which he may be liable.

Appropriations. Section 24. No money shall be drawn from the treasury but in consequence of appropriations made by law.

Compensation of members. Section 25. [*Each member of the first General Assembly under this Constitution, shall receive three dollars per diem while in session; and the further sum of three dollars for every twenty miles traveled, in going to and returning from the place where such session is held, by the nearest traveled route; after which they shall receive such compensation as shall be fixed by law; but no General Assembly shall have power to increase the compensation of its own members. And when convened in extra session they shall receive the same mileage and per diem compensation, as fixed by law for the regular session, and none other.*]*

Statutory provisions, §2.10 to 2.14 of the Code

*In 1968 this section was repealed and a substitute adopted in lieu thereof: See Amendment [28]

Time laws to take effect. Section 26. No law of the General Assembly, passed at a regular session, of a public nature, shall take effect until the *fourth** day of July next after the passage thereof. Laws passed at a special session, shall take effect ninety days after the adjournment of the General Assembly by which they were passed. If the General Assembly shall deem any law of immediate importance, they may provide that the same shall take effect by publication in the newspapers in the State.**

Supplementary provisions, §3.7 et seq. of the Code

*For provision changing effective date, see Amendment [23]

**In 1986 this section was repealed and a substitute adopted in lieu thereof: See Amendment [40]

Divorce. Section 27. No divorce shall be granted by the General Assembly.

Lotteries. Section 28. [*No lottery shall be authorized by this State; nor shall the sale of lottery tickets be allowed.*]*

*This section repealed by Amendment [34]

Acts—one subject—expressed in title. Section 29. Every act shall embrace but one subject, and matters properly connected therewith; which subject shall be expressed in the title. But if any subject shall be embraced in an act which shall not be expressed in the title, such act shall be void only as to so much thereof as shall not be expressed in the title.

Local or special laws—general and uniform—boundaries of counties. Section 30. The General Assembly shall not pass local or special laws in the following cases:

For the assessment and collection of taxes for State, County, or road purposes;
For laying out, opening, and working roads or highways;
For changing the names of persons;
For the incorporation of cities and towns;
For vacating roads, town plats, streets, alleys, or public squares;
For locating or changing county seats.

In all the cases above enumerated, and in all other cases where a general law can be made applicable, all laws shall be general, and of uniform operation throughout the State; and no law changing the boundary lines of any county shall have effect until upon being submitted to the people of the counties affected by the change, at a general election, it shall be approved by a majority of the votes in each county, cast for and against it.

Laws uniform, see Art. I, §6

Extra compensation—payment of claims—appropriations for local or private purposes. Section 31. No extra compensation shall be made to any officer, public agent, or contractor, after the service shall have been rendered, or the contract entered into; nor, shall any money be paid on any claim, the subject matter of which shall not have been provided for by pre-existing laws, and no public money or property shall be appropriated for local, or private purposes, unless such appropriation, compensation, or claim, be allowed by two-thirds of the members elected to each branch of the General Assembly.

See §3.14 of the Code

Oath of members. Section 32. Members of the General Assembly shall, before they enter upon the duties of their respective offices, take and subscribe the following oath or affirmation: "I do solemnly swear, or affirm, (as the case may be,) that I will support the Constitution of the United States, and the Constitution of the State of Iowa, and that I will faithfully discharge the duties of Senator, (or Representative, as the case may be,) according to the best of my ability." And members of the General Assembly are hereby empowered to administer to each other the said oath or affirmation.

Census. Section 33. [*The General Assembly shall, in the years One thousand eight hundred and fifty nine, One thousand eight hundred and sixty three, One thousand eight hundred and sixty five, One thousand eight hundred and sixty seven, One thousand eight hundred and sixty nine, and One thousand eight hundred and seventy five, and every ten years thereafter, cause an enumeration to be made of all the [white]* inhabitants of the State.]***

*The above section was amended in 1868 by striking the word "white" therefrom: See Amendment [2]

**This section repealed by Amendment [17]

Senators—number—method of apportionment. Section 34. [*The number of senators shall, at the next session following each period of making such enumeration, and the next session following each United States census, be fixed by law, and apportioned among the several counties, according to the number of [white]* inhabitants in each.]***

*The above section has been amended three times: in 1868 it was amended by striking the word "white" therefrom: See Amend [3]

**In 1904 this section was repealed and a substitute adopted in lieu thereof. See Amendment [12]: Also [16]: See also Amendment [26]

Senataors-representatives—number—apportionment—districts. Section 35. [*The Senate shall not consist of more than fifty members, nor the House of Representatives of more than one hundred; and they shall be apportioned among the several counties and representative districts of the State, according to the number of[white]* inhabitants in each, upon ratios to be fixed by law; but no representative district shall contain more than four organized counties, and each district shall be entitled to at least one representative. Every county and district which shall have a number of inhabitants equal to one-half of the ratio fixed by law, shall be entitled to one representative; and any one county containing in addition to the ratio fixed by law, one half of that number, or more, shall be entitled to one additional representative. No floating district shall hereafter be formed.]***

*The above section has been amended twice. In 1868 it was amended by striking the word "white" therefrom: See Amendment [4]

**In 1904 this section was repealed and a substitute adopted in lieu thereof: See Amendment [12]: See also Amendment [26]

Ratio of representation. Section 36. [*At its first session under this Constitution, and at every subsequent regular session, the General Assembly shall fix the ratio of representation, and also form into representative districts those counties which will not be entitled singly to a representative.]*

*In 1904 this section was repealed and a substitute adopted in lieu thereof: See Amendment [12]: See also Amendment [26]

Districts. Section 37. [*When a congressional, senatorial or representative district shall be composed of two or more counties, it shall not be entirely separated by any county belonging to another district; and no county shall be divided in forming a congressional, senatorial, or representative district.]*

See Amendment [12]

*In 1968 this section was repealed and a substitute adopted in lieu thereof: See Amendment [26]

Elections by general assembly. Section 38. In all elections by the General Assembly, the members thereof shall vote viva voce and the votes shall be entered on the journal.

Municipal home rule. Section 38A.

Amendment [25]

Legislative districts. Section 39.

Amendment [29]

Counties home rule. Section 39A.

Amendment [37]

Administrative rules. Section 40.

Amendment [38]

Constitution

ARTICLE IV. — Executive Department

Governor. Section 1. The Supreme Executive power of this State shall be vested in a Chief Magistrate, who shall be styled the Governor of the State of Iowa.

Election and term. Section 2. [*The Governor shall be elected by the qualified electors at the time and place of voting for members of the General Assembly, and shall hold his office two years from the time of his installation, and until his successor is elected and qualified.*]*

*In 1972 this section was repealed and a substitute adopted in lieu thereof: See Amendment [32]: See also Amendment [41]

Lieutenant governor—returns of elections. Section 3. [*There shall be a Lieutenant Governor, who shall hold his office two years, and be elected at the same time as the Governor. In voting for Governor and Lieutenant Governor, the electors shall designate for whom they vote as Governor, and for whom as Lieutenant Governor. The returns of every election for Governor, and Lieutenant Governor, shall be sealed up and transmitted to the seat of government of the State, directed to the Speaker of the House of Representatives, who shall open and publish them in the presence of both Houses of the General Assembly.*]*

For statutory provisions, see §50.35 of the Code

*In 1972 this section was repealed and a substitute adopted in lieu thereof: See Amendment [32]: See also Amendment [41]

Election by general assembly. Section 4. [*The persons respectively having the highest number of votes for Governor and Lieutenant Governor, shall be declared duly elected; but in case two or more persons shall have an equal and the highest number of votes for either office, the General Assembly shall, by joint vote, forthwith proceed to elect one of said persons Governor, or Lieutenant Governor, as the case may be.*]*

See Amendment [19] relating to death or failure to qualify

*In 1988 this section was repealed and a substitute adopted in lieu thereof: See Amendment [41]

Contested elections. Section 5. [*Contested elections for Governor, or Lieutenant Governor, shall be determined by the General Assembly in such manner as may be prescribed by law.*]*

*In 1988 this section was repealed and a substitute adopted in lieu thereof: See Amendment [41]

Eligibility. Section 6. No person shall be eligible to the office of Governor, or Lieutenant Governor, who shall not have been a citizen of the United States, and a resident of the State, two years next preceding the election, and attained the age of thirty years at the time of said election.

Commander in chief. Section 7. The Governor shall be commander in chief of the militia, the army, and navy of this State.

Duties of governor. Section 8. He shall transact all executive business with the officers of government, civil and military, and may require information in writing from the officers of the executive department upon any subject relating to the duties of their respective offices.

Duty as to state accounts, §79.8 of the Code

Execution of laws. Section 9. He shall take care that the laws are faithfully executed.

Vacancies. Section 10. When any office shall, from any cause, become vacant, and no mode is provided by the Constitution and laws for filling such vacancy, the Governor shall have power to fill such vacancy, by granting a commission, which shall expire at the end of the next session of the General Assembly, or at the next election by the people.

Convening general assembly. Section 11. He may, on extraordinary occasions, convene the General Assembly by proclamation, and shall state to both Houses, when assembled, the purpose for which they shall have been convened.

See Amendment of 1974 No. 2 [36]

Message. Section 12. He shall communicate, by message, to the General Assembly, at every regular session, the condition of the State, and recommend such matters as he shall deem expedient.

Adjournment. Section 13. In case of disagreement between the two Houses with respect to the time of adjournment, the Governor shall have power to adjourn the General Assembly to such time as he may think proper; but no such adjournment shall be beyond the time fixed for the regular meeting of the next General Assembly.

Disqualification. Section 14. No person shall, while holding any office under the authority of the United States, or this State, execute the office of Governor, or Lieutenant Governor, except as hereinafter expressly provided.

Terms—compensation of lieutenant governor. Section 15. [*The official term of the Governor, and Lieutenant Governor, shall commence on the second Monday of January next after their election, and continue for two years, and until their successors are elected and qualified. The Lieutenant Governor, while acting as Governor, shall receive* *the same pay as provided for Governor; and while presiding in the Senate, shall receive as compensation therefor, the same mileage and double the per diem pay provided for a Senator, and none other.]**

See §2.10 of the Code

*In 1972 this section was repealed and a substitute adopted in lieu thereof: See Amendment [32]: See also Amendment [42]

Pardons—reprieves—commutations. Section 16. The Governor shall have power to grant reprieves, commutations and pardons, after conviction, for all offences except treason and cases of impeachment, subject to such regulations as may be provided by law. Upon conviction for treason, he shall have power to suspend the execution of the sentence until the case shall be reported to the General Assembly at its next meeting, when the General Assembly shall either grant a pardon, commute the sentence, direct the execution of the sentence, or grant a further reprieve. He shall have power to remit fines and forfeitures, under such regulations as may be prescribed by law; and shall report to the General Assembly, at its next meeting, each case of reprieve, commutation, or pardon granted, and the reasons therefor; and also all persons in whose favor remission of fines and forfeitures shall have been made, and the several amounts remitted.

Lieutenant governor to act as governor. Section 17. In case of the death, impeachment, resignation, removal from office, or other disability of the Governor, the powers and duties of the office for the residue of the term, or until he shall be acquitted, or the disability removed, shall devolve upon the Lieutenant Governor.

President of senate. Section 18. [*The Lieutenant Governor shall be President of the Senate, but shall only vote when the Senate is equally divided, and in case of his absence, or impeachment, or when he shall exercise the office of Governor, the Senate shall choose a President pro tempore.]**

*In 1988 this section was repealed and a substitute adopted in lieu thereof: See Amendment [42]

Vacancies. Section 19. [*If the Lieutenant Governor, while acting as Governor, shall be impeached, displaced, resign, or die, or otherwise become incapable of performing the duties of the office, the President pro tempore of the Senate shall act as Governor until the vacancy is filled, or the disability removed; and if the President of the Senate, for any of the above causes, shall be rendered incapable of performing the duties pertaining to the office of Governor, the same shall devolve upon the Speaker of the House of Representatives.]**

*In 1952 this section was repealed and a substitute adopted in lieu thereof: See Amendment [20]: See also Amendment [42]

Seal of state. Section 20. There shall be a seal of this State, which shall be kept by the Governor, and used by him officially, and shall be called the Great Seal of the State of Iowa.

See chapter 1A of the Code for a description of the Great Seal of Iowa

Grants and commissions. Section 21. All grants and commissions shall be in the name and by the authority of the people of the State of Iowa, sealed with the Great Seal of the State, signed by the Governor, and countersigned by the Secretary of State.

Secretary—auditor—treasurer. Section 22. [*A Secretary of State, Auditor of State and Treasurer of State, shall be elected by the qualified electors, who shall continue in office two years, and until their successors are elected and qualified; and perform such duties as may be required by law.]**

*In 1972 this section was repealed and a substitute adopted in lieu thereof: See Amendment [32]

ARTICLE V. — Judicial Department

Courts. Section 1. The Judicial power shall be vested in a Supreme Court, District Courts, and such other Courts, inferior to the Supreme Court, as the General Assembly may, from time to time, establish.

Court of appeals, §602.5101 of the Code

Supreme court. Section 2. The Supreme Court shall consist of three Judges, two of whom shall constitute a quorum to hold Court.

But see sec. 10 following; see also §602.4101 of the Code

Election of judges—term. Section 3. [*The Judges of the Supreme Court shall be elected by the qualified electors of the State, and shall hold their Court at such time and place as the General Assembly may prescribe. The Judges of the Supreme Court so elected, shall be classified so that one Judge shall go out of office every two years; and the Judge holding the shortest term of office under such classification, shall be Chief Justice of the Court, during his term, and so on in rotation. After the expiration of their terms of office, under such classification, the term of each Judge of the Supreme Court shall be six years, and until his successor shall have been elected and qualified. The Judges of the Supreme Court shall be ineligible to any other office in the State,*

Constitution

during the term for which they shall have been elected.]*

*In 1962 this section was repealed: See Amendment [21]

Jurisdiction of supreme court. Section 4. The Supreme Court shall have appellate jurisdiction only in cases in chancery, and shall constitute a Court for the correction of errors at law, under such restrictions as the General Assembly may, by law, prescribe; and shall have power to issue all writs and process necessary to secure justice to parties, and exercise a supervisory control over all inferior judicial tribunals throughout the State.*

See §602.4102, 602.4201, 602.4202, 624.2 of the Code

*This section was amended in 1962: See Amendment [21]

District court and judge. Section 5. [*The District Court shall consist of a single Judge, who shall be elected by the qualified electors of the District in which he resides. The Judge of the District Court shall hold his office for the term of four years, and until his successor shall have been elected and qualified; and shall be ineligible to any other office, except that of Judge of the Supreme Court, during the term for which he was elected.]**

*In 1962 this section was repealed: See Amendment [21]; See also Amendment [21(1)]

Jurisdiction of district court. Section 6. The District Court shall be a court of law and equity, which shall be distinct and separate jurisdictions, and have jurisdiction in civil and criminal matters arising in their respective districts, in such manner as shall be prescribed by law.

Statutory provision, §602.6101 of the Code

Conservators of the peace. Section 7. The Judges of the Supreme and District Courts shall be conservators of the peace throughout the State.

Style of process. Section 8. The style of all process shall be, "The State of Iowa", and all prosecutions shall be conducted in the name and by the authority of the same.

Salaries. Section 9. [*The salary of each Judge of the Supreme Court shall be two thousand dollars per annum; and that of each District Judge, one thousand six hundred dollars per annum, until the year Eighteen hundred and Sixty; after which time, they shall severally receive such compensation as the General Assembly may, by law, prescribe; which compensation shall not be increased or diminished during the term for which they shall have been elected.]**

*In 1962 this section was repealed: See Amendment [21]

Judicial districts—supreme court. Section 10. *The state shall be divided into eleven judicial districts; and after the year eighteen hundred and sixty,* the general assembly may re-organize the judicial districts and increase or diminish the number of districts, or the number of judges of the said court, and may increase the number of judges of the supreme court; but such increase or diminution shall not be more than one district, or one judge of either court, at any one session; and no re-organization of the districts, or diminution of the number of judges, shall have the effect of removing a judge from office. Such re-organization of the districts, or any change in the boundaries thereof, or increase or diminution of the number of judges, shall take place every four years thereafter, if necessary, and at no other time.*

*Much of this section apparently superseded by Amendment [8]

Judges—when chosen. Section 11. [*The Judges of the Supreme and District Courts shall be chosen at the general election; and the term of office of each Judge shall commence on the first day of January next, after his election.]**

*In 1962 this section was repealed: See Amendment [21]

Attorney general. Section 12. [*The General Assembly shall provide, by law, for the election of an Attorney General by the people, whose term of office shall be two years, and until his successor shall have been elected and qualified.]**

*In 1972 this section was repealed and a substitute adopted in lieu thereof: See Amendment [32]

District attorney. Section 13. [*The qualified electors of each judicial district shall, at the time of the election of District Judge, elect a District Attorney, who shall be a resident of the district for which he is elected, and who shall hold his office for the term of four years, and until his successor shall have been elected and qualified.]**

*In 1884 this section was repealed and a substitute adopted in lieu thereof: See Amendment [10]. In 1970 this substitute was repealed: See Amendment [31]

System of court practice. Section 14. It shall be the duty of the General Assembly to provide for the carrying into effect of this article, and to provide for a general system of practice in all the Courts of this State.

For provisions relative to the grand jury, see Amendment [9]

Vacancies in courts. Section 15. Amendment [21].
State and district nominating commissions. Section 16. Amendment [21].
Terms—judicial elections. Section 17. Amendment [21].
Salaries—qualifications—retirements. Section 18. Amendment [21].
Retirement and discipline of judges. Section 19. Amendment [33].

347

ARTICLE VI. — Militia

Composition—training. Section 1. The militia of this State shall be composed of all able-bodied [*white*]* male citizens, between the ages of eighteen and forty five years, except such as are or may hereafter be exempted by the laws of the United States, or of this State, and shall be armed, equipped, and trained, as the General Assembly may provide by law.

*The above section was amended in 1868 by striking the word "white" therefrom: See Amendment [5]

Exemption. Section 2. No person or persons conscientiously scrupulous of bearing arms shall be compelled to do military duty in time of peace: Provided, that such person or persons shall pay an equivalent for such exemption in the same manner as other citizens.

Officers. Section 3. All commissioned officers of the militia, (staff officers excepted,) shall be elected by the persons liable to perform military duty, and shall be commissioned by the Governor.

ARTICLE VII. — State Debts

Credit not to be loaned. Section 1. The credit of the State shall not, in any manner, be given or loaned to, or in aid of, any individual, association, or corporation: and the State shall never assume, or become responsible for, the debts or liabilities of any individual, association, or corporation, unless incurred in time of war for the benefit of the State.

Limitation. Section 2. The State may contract debts to supply casual deficits or failures in revenues, or to meet expenses not otherwise provided for; but the aggregate amount of such debts, direct and contingent, whether contracted by virtue of one or more acts of the General Assembly, or at different periods of time, shall never exceed the sum of two hundred and fifty thousand dollars; and the money arising from the creation of such debts, shall be applied to the purpose for which it was obtained, or to repay the debts so contracted, and to no other purpose whatever.

Losses to school funds. Section 3. All losses to the permanent, School, or University fund of this State, which shall have been occasioned by the defalcation, mismanagement or fraud of the agents or officers controlling and managing the same, shall be audited by the proper authorities of the State. The amount so audited shall be a permanent funded debt against the State, in favor of the respective fund, sustaining the loss, upon which not less than six percent annual interest shall be paid. The amount of liability so created shall not be counted as a part of the indebtedness authorized by the second section of this article.

War debts. Section 4. In addition to the above limited power to contract debts, the State may contract debts to repel invasion, suppress insurrection, or defend the State in war; but the money arising from the debts so contracted shall be applied to the purpose for which it was raised, or to repay such debts, and to no other purpose whatever.

Contracting debt—submission to the people. Section 5. Except the debts herein before specified in this article, no debt shall be hereafter contracted by, or on behalf of this State, unless such debt shall be authorized by some law for some single work or object, to be distinctly specified therein; and such law shall impose and provide for the collection of a direct annual tax, sufficient to pay the interest on such debt, as it falls due, and also to pay and discharge the principal of such debt, within twenty years from the time of the contracting thereof; but no such law shall take effect until at a general election it shall have been submitted to the people, and have received a majority of all the votes cast for and against it at such election; and all money raised by authority of such law, shall be applied only to the specific object therein stated, or to the payment of the debt created thereby; and such law shall be published in at least one news paper in each County, if one is published therein, throughout the State, for three months preceding the election at which it is submitted to the people.

For statutory provisions, see §6.1 to 6.9 of the Code

Legislature may repeal. Section 6. The Legislature may, at any time, after the approval of such law by the people, if no debt shall have been contracted in pursuance thereof, repeal the same; and may, at any time, forbid the contracting of any further debt, or liability under such law; but the tax imposed by such law, in proportion to the debt or liability, which may have been contracted in pursuance thereof, shall remain in force and be irrepealable, and be annually collected, until the principal and interest are fully paid.

Tax imposed distinctly stated. Section 7. Every law which imposes, continues, or revives a tax, shall distinctly state the tax, and the object to which it is to be applied; and it shall not be sufficient to refer to any other law to fix such tax or object.

Motor vehicle fees and fuel taxes. Section 8.

Amendment [18]

ARTICLE VIII. — Corporations

How created. Section 1. No corporation shall be created by special laws; but the General Assembly shall provide, by general laws, for the organization of all corporations hereafter to be created, except as hereinafter provided.

Taxation of corporations. Section 2. The property of all corporations for pecuniary profit, shall be subject to taxation, the same as that of individuals.

State not to be a stockholder. Section 3. The State shall not become a stockholder in any corporation, nor shall it assume or pay the debt or liability of any corporation, unless incurred in time of war for the benefit of the State.

Municipal corporations. Section 4. No political or municipal corporation shall become a stockholder in any banking corporation, directly or indirectly.

Banking associations. Section 5. No Act of the General Assembly, authorizing or creating corporations or associations with banking powers, nor amendments thereto shall take effect, or in any manner be in force, until the same shall have been submitted separately, to the people, at a general or special election, as provided by law, to be held not less than three months after the passage of the Act, and shall have been approved by a majority of all the electors voting for and against it at such election.

State bank. Section 6. Subject to the provisions of the foregoing section, the General Assembly may also provide for the establishment of a State Bank with branches.*

*Sections 6 to 11, apply to banks of issue only. See 63 Iowa 11, also 220 Iowa 794 and 221 Iowa 102

Specie basis. Section 7. If a State Bank be established, it shall be founded on an actual specie basis, and the branches shall be mutually responsible for each others liabilities upon all notes, bills, and other issues intended for circulation as money.

General banking law. Section 8. If a general Banking law shall be enacted, it shall provide for the registry and countersigning, by an officer of State, of all bills, or paper credit designed to circulate as money, and require security to the full amount thereof, to be deposited with the State Treasurer, in United States stocks, or in interest paying stocks of States in good credit and standing, to be rated at ten per cent below their average value in the City of New York, for the thirty days next preceding their deposit; and in case of a depreciation of any portion of said stocks, to the amount of ten per cent on the dollar, the bank or banks owning such stock shall be required to make up said deficiency by depositing additional stocks; and said law shall also provide for the recording of the names of all stockholders in such corporations, the amount of stock held by each, the time of any transfer, and to whom.

Stockholders' responsibility. Section 9. Every stockholder in a banking corporation or institution shall be individually responsible and liable to its creditors, over and above the amount of stock by him or her held, to an amount equal to his or her respective shares so held for all of its liabilities, accruing while he or she remains such stockholder.

Bills—holders preferred. Section 10. In case of the insolvency of any banking institution, the bill-holders shall have a preference over its other creditors.

Specie payments—suspension. Section 11. The suspension of specie payments by banking institutions shall never be permitted or sanctioned.

Amendment or repeal of laws—exclusive privileges. Section 12. Subject to the provisions of this article, the General Assembly shall have power to amend or repeal all laws for the organization or creation of corporations, or granting of special or exclusive privileges or immunities, by a vote of two thirds of each branch of the General Assembly; and no exclusive privileges, except as in this article provided, shall ever be granted.

Analogous provision. §491.39 of the Code

ARTICLE IX. — Education and School Lands

1st Education*

See note at the end of this 1st division

Board of education. Section 1. *The educational interest of the State, including Common Schools and other educational institutions, shall be under the management of a Board of Education, which shall consist of the Lieutenant Governor, who shall be the presiding officer of the Board, and have the casting vote in case of a tie, and* one member to be elected from each judicial district in the State.

Eligibility. Section 2. *No person shall be eligible as a member of said Board who shall not have attained the age of twenty five years, and shall have been one year a citizen of the State.*

Election of members. Section 3. *One member of said Board shall be chosen by the qualified electors of each district, and shall hold the office for the term of four years, and until his successor is elected and qualified. After the first election under this Constitution, the Board shall be divided, as nearly as practicable, into two equal classes, and the seats of the first class shall be vacated after the expiration of two years; and one half of the Board shall be chosen every two years thereafter.*

First session. Section 4. *The first session of the Board of Education shall be held at the Seat of Government, on the first Monday of December, after their election; after which the General Assembly may fix the time and place of meeting.*

Limitation of sessions. Section 5. *The session of the Board shall be limited to twenty days, and but one session shall be held in any one year, except upon extraordinary occasions, when, upon the recommendation of two thirds of the Board, the Governor may order a special session.*

Secretary. Section 6. *The Board of Education shall appoint a Secretary, who shall be the executive officer of the Board, and perform such duties as may be imposed upon him by the Board, and the laws of the State. They shall keep a journal of their proceedings, which shall be published and distributed in the same manner as the journals of the General Assembly.*

Rules and regulations. Section 7. *All rules and regulations made by the Board shall be published and distributed to the several Counties, Townships, and School Districts, as may be provided for by the Board, and when so made, published and distributed, they shall have the force and effect of law.*

Power to legislate. Section 8. *The Board of Education shall have full power and authority to legislate and make all needful rules and regulations in relation to Common Schools, and other education institutions, but are instituted, to receive aid from the School or University fund of this State: but all acts, rules, and regulations of said Board may be altered, amended or repealed by the General Assembly; and when so altered, amended, or repealed they shall not be re-enacted by the Board of Education.*

Governor ex officio a member. Section 9. *The Governor of the State shall be, ex officio, a member of said Board.*

Expenses. Section 10. *The board shall have no power to levy taxes, or make appropriations of money. Their contingent expenses shall be provided for by the General Assembly.*

State university. Section 11. *The State University shall be established at one place without branches at any other place, and the University fund shall be applied to that Institution and no other.*

See Laws of the Board of Education. Act 10, December 25, 1858, which provides for the management of the state University by a Board of Trustees appointed by the Board of Education. See also sec. 2 of 2nd. division of this Article

Common schools. Section 12. *The Board of Education shall provide for the education of all the youths of the State, through a system of Common Schools and such school shall be organized and kept in each school district at least three months in each year. Any district failing, for two consecutive years, to organize and keep up a school as aforesaid may be deprived of their portion of the school fund.*

Compensation. Section 13. *The members of the Board of Education shall each receive the same per diem during the time of their session, and mileage going to and returning therefrom, as members of the General Assembly.*

Quorum—style of acts. Section 14. *A majority of the Board shall constitute a quorum for the transaction of business; but no rule, regulation, or law, for the government of Common Schools or other educational institutions, shall pass without the concurrence of a majority of all the members of the Board, which shall be expressed by the yeas and nays on the final passage. The style of all acts of the Board shall be, "Be it enacted by the Board of Education of the State of Iowa."*

Board may be abolished.* Section 15. *At any time after the year One thousand eight hundred and sixty three, the General Assembly shall have power to abolish or re-organize said Board of Education, and provide for the educational interest of the State in any other manner that to them shall seem best and proper.*

*The board of education was abolished in 1864 by 10GA, ch 52, §1. For statutory provisions, see chs 256 and 262 of the Code

2nd School Funds and School Lands

Control—management. Section 1. The educational and school funds and lands, shall be under the control and management of the General Assembly of this State.

Constitution

Permanent fund. Section 2. The University lands, and the proceeds thereof, and all monies belonging to said fund shall be a permanent fund for the sole use of the State University. The interest arising from the same shall be annually appropriated for the support and benefit of said University.

Perpetual support fund. Section 3. The General Assembly shall encourage, by all suitable means, the promotion of intellectual, scientific, moral, and agricultural improvement. The proceeds of all lands that have been, or hereafter may be, granted by the United States to this State, for the support of schools, which may have been or shall hereafter be sold, or disposed of, and the five hundred thousand acres of land granted to the new States, under an act of Congress, distributing the proceeds of the public lands among the several States of the Union, approved in the year of our Lord one thousand eight hundred and forty-one, and all estates of deceased persons who may have died without leaving a will or heir, and also such percent as has been or may hereafter be granted by Congress, on the sale of lands in this State, shall be, and remain a perpetual fund, the interest of which, together with all rents of the unsold lands, and such other means as the General Assembly may provide, shall be inviolably appropriated to the support of Common schools throughout the State.

Fines—how appropriated. Section 4. [*The money which may have been or shall be paid by persons as an equivalent for exemption from military duty, and the clear proceeds of all fines collected in the several Counties for any breach of the penal laws, shall be exclusively applied, in the several Counties in which such money is paid, or fine collected, among the several school districts of said Counties, in proportion to the number of youths subject to enumeration in such districts, to the support of Common Schools, or the establishment of libraries, as the Board of Education shall, from time to time provide.*]*

*This section repealed by Amendment [35]

Proceeds of lands. Section 5. The General Assembly shall take measures for the protection, improvement, or other disposition of such lands as have been, or may hereafter be reserved, or granted by the United States, or any person or persons, to this State, for the use of the University, and the funds accruing from the rents or sale of such lands, or from any other source for the purpose aforesaid, shall be, and remain, a permanent fund, the interest of which shall be applied to the support of said University, for the promotion of literature, the arts and sciences, as may be authorized by the terms of such grant. And it shall be the duty of the General Assembly as soon as may be, to provide effectual means for the improvement and permanent security of the funds of said University.

Agents of school funds. Section 6. The financial agents of the school funds shall be the same, that by law, receive and control the State and county revenue for other civil purposes, under such regulations as may be provided by law.

Distribution. Section 7. [*The money subject to the support and maintenance of common schools shall be distributed to the districts in proportion to the number of youths, between the ages of five and twenty-one years, in such manner as may be provided by the General Assembly.*]*

*In 1984 this section was repealed: See Amendment [39]

ARTICLE X. — Amendments to the Constitution

How proposed—submission. Section 1. Any amendment or amendments to this Constitution may be proposed in either House of the General Assembly; and if the same shall be agreed to by a majority of the members elected to each of the two Houses, such proposed amendment shall be entered on their journals, with the yeas and nays taken thereon, and referred to the Legislature to be chosen at the next general election, and shall be published, as provided by law, for three months previous to the time of making such choice; and if, in the General Assembly so next chosen as aforesaid, such proposed amendment or amendments shall be agreed to, by a majority of all the members elected to each House, then it shall be the duty of the General Assembly to submit such proposed amendment or amendments to the people, in such manner, and at such time as the General Assembly shall provide; and if the people shall approve and ratify such amendment or amendments, by a majority of the electors qualified to vote for members of the General Assembly, voting thereon, such amendment or amendments shall become a part of the Constitution of this State.

For statutory provisions, see §6.1 to 6.11, and 49.43 to 49.50 of the Code

More than one amendment. Section 2. If two or more amendments shall be submitted at the same time, they shall be submitted in such manner that the electors shall vote for or against each of such amendments separately.

Convention. Section 3. [*At the general election to be held in the year one thousand*

351

eight hundred and seventy, and in each tenth year thereafter, and also at such times as the General Assembly may, by law, provide, the question, "Shall there be a Convention to revise the Constitution, and amend the same?" shall be decided by the electors qualified to vote for members of the General Assembly; and in case a majority of the electors so qualified, voting at such election, for and against such proposition, shall decide in favor of a Convention for such purpose, the General Assembly, at its next session, shall provide by law for the election of delegates to such Convention.]*

*In 1964 this section was repealed and a substitute adopted in lieu thereof: See Amendment [22]

ARTICLE XI. — Miscellaneous

Justice of peace—jurisdiction. *Section 1. The jurisdiction of Justices of the Peace shall extend to all civil cases, (except cases in chancery, and cases where the question of title to real estate may arise,) where the amount in controversy does not exceed one hundred dollars, and by the consent of parties may be extended to any amount not exceeding three hundred dollars.*

Nonindictable misdemeanors, jurisdiction. Art. I. §11

[The office of Justice of Peace has been abolished by 64GA, chapter 1124.]

Counties. Section 2. No new County shall be hereafter created containing less than four hundred and thirty two square miles; nor shall the territory of any organized county be reduced below that area; except the County of Worth, and the counties west of it, along the Northern boundary of this State, may be organized without additional territory.

Indebtedness of political or municipal corporations. Section 3. No county, or other political or municipal corporation shall be allowed to become indebted in any manner, or for any purpose, to an amount, in the aggregate, exceeding five per centum on the value of the taxable property within such county or corporation — to be ascertained by the last State and county tax lists, previous to the incurring of such indebtedness.

Statutory limitation, §346.24 of the Code

See 64 GA. ch 1088

Boundaries of state. Section 4. The boundaries of the State may be enlarged, with the consent of Congress and the General Assembly.

See boundary compromise agreements at the end of Volume III of the Code

Oath of office. Section 5. Every person elected or appointed to any office, shall, before entering upon the duties thereof, take an oath or affirmation to support the Constitution of the United States, and of this State, and also an oath of office.

See §63.10 of the Code

How vacancies filled. Section 6. In all cases of election to fill vacancies in office occurring before the expiration of a full term, the person so elected shall hold for the residue of the unexpired term; and all persons appointed to fill vacancies in office, shall hold until the next general election, and until their successors are elected and qualified.

Land grants located. Section 7. The General Assembly shall not locate any of the public lands, which have been, or may be granted by Congress to this State, and the location of which may be given to the General Assembly, upon lands actually settled, without the consent of the occupant. The extent of the claim of such occupant, so exempted, shall not exceed three hundred and twenty acres.

Seat of government established—state university. Section 8. The seat of Government is hereby permanently established, as now fixed by law, at the City of Des Moines, in the County of Polk; and the State University, at Iowa City, in the County of Johnson.

See 5 GA. ch 72

ARTICLE XII. — Schedule

Supreme law—constitutionality of acts. Section 1. This Constitution shall be the supreme law of the State, and any law inconsistent therewith, shall be void. The General Assembly shall pass all laws necessary to carry this Constitution into effect.

Laws in force. Section 2. All laws now in force and not inconsistent with this Constitution, shall remain in force until they shall expire or be repealed.

Proceedings not affected. Section 3. All indictments, prosecutions, suits, pleas, plaints, process, and other proceedings pending in any of the courts, shall be prosecuted to final judgment and execution; and all appeals, writs of error, certiorari, and injunctions, shall be carried on in the several courts, in the same manner as now provided by law; and all offences, misdemeanors, and crimes that may have been committed before the taking effect of this Constitution, shall be subject to indictment, trial and punishment, in the same manner as they would have been, had not this

Constitution

Constitution been made.

Fines inure to the state. Section 4. [*All fines, penalties, or forfeitures due, or to become due, or accruing to the State, or to any County therein, or to the school fund, shall inure to the State, county, or school fund, in the manner prescribed by law.*]*

*This section repealed by Amendment [35]

Bonds in force. Section 5. All bonds executed to the State, or to any officer in his official capacity, shall remain in force and inure to the use of those concerned.

First election for governor and lieutenant governor. Section 6. The first election under this Constitution shall be held of the second Tuesday in October, in the year one thousand eight hundred and fifty seven, at which time the electors of the State shall elect the Governor and Lieutenant Governor. There shall also be elected at such election, the successors of such State Senators as were elected at the August election, in the year one thousand eight hundred and fifty-four, and members of the House of Representatives, who shall be elected in accordance with the act of apportionment, enacted at the session of the General Assembly which commenced on the first Monday of December One thousand eight hundred and fifty six.

First election of officers. Section 7. The first election for Secretary, Auditor, and Treasurer of State, Attorney General, District Judges, Members of the Board of Education, District Attorneys, members of Congress and such State officers as shall be elected at the April election, in the year One thousand eight hundred and fifty seven, (except the Superintendent of Public Instruction,) and such county officers as were elected at the August election, in the year One thousand eight hundred and fifty-six, except Prosecuting Attorneys, shall be held on the second Tuesday of October, One thousand eight hundred and fifty-eight: *Provided,* That the time for which any District Judge or other State or County officer elected at the April election in the year One thousand eight hundred and fifty eight, shall not extend beyond the time fixed for filling like offices at the October election in the year one thousand eight hundred and fifty eight.

For judges of supreme court. Section 8. The first election for Judges of the Supreme Court, and such County officers as shall be elected at the August election, in the year one thousand eight hundred and fifty-seven, shall be held on the second Tuesday of October in the year One thousand eight hundred and fifty-nine.

General assembly—first session. Section 9. The first regular session of the General Assembly shall be held in the year One thousand eight hundred and fifty-eight, commencing on the second Monday of January of said year.

Senators. Section 10. Senators elected at the August election, in the year one thousand eight hundred and fifty-six, shall continue in office until the second Tuesday of October, in the year one thousand eight hundred and fifty nine, at which time their successors shall be elected as may be prescribed by law.

Offices not vacated. Section 11. Every person elected by popular vote, by vote of the General Assembly, or who may hold office by executive appointment, which office is continued by this Constitution, and every person who shall be so elected or appointed, to any such office, before the taking effect of this constitution, (except as in this Constitution otherwise provided,) shall continue in office until the term for which such person has been or may be elected or appointed shall expire: but no such person shall continue in office after the taking effect of this Constitution, for a longer period than the term of such office, in this Constitution prescribed.

Judicial districts. Section 12. The General Assembly, at the first session under this Constitution, shall district the State into eleven Judicial Districts, for District Court purposes; and shall also provide for the apportionment of the members of the General Assembly, in accordance with the provisions of this Constitution.

Submission of constitution. Section 13. This Constitution shall be submitted to the electors of the State at the August election, in the year one thousand eight hundred and fifty-seven, in the several election districts in this State. The ballots at such election shall be written or printed as follows: Those in favor of the Constitution, "New Constitution - Yes." Those against the Constitution, "New Constitution - No." The election shall be conducted in the same manner as the general elections of the State, and the poll-books shall be returned and canvassed as provided in the twenty-fifth chapter of the code, and abstracts shall be forwarded to the Secretary of State, which abstracts shall be canvassed in the manner provided for in the canvass of State officers. And if it shall appear that a majority of all the votes cast at such election for and against this Constitution are in favor of the same, the Governor shall immediately issue his proclamation stating that fact, and such Constitution shall be the Constitution of the State of Iowa, and shall take effect from and after the publication of said proclamation.

Proposition to strike out the word "white". Section 14. At the same election that this Constitution is submitted to the people for its adoption or rejection, a proposition to amend the same by striking out the word "White" from the article on the Right of Suffrage, shall be separately submitted to the electors of this State for adoption or rejection in manner following — Namely:

A separate ballot may be given by every person having a right to vote at said election, to be deposited in a separate box: and those given for the adoption of such proposition shall have the words, "Shall the word 'White' be stricken out of the Article on the Right of Suffrage? Yes." And those given against the proposition shall have the words, "Shall the word 'White' be stricken out of the Article on the Right of Suffrage? No." And if at said election the number of ballots cast in favor of said proposition shall be equal to a majority of those cast for and against this Constitution, then said word "White" shall be stricken from said Article and be no part thereof.

This proposition failed to be adopted but see Amendment [1]

Mills county. Section 15. Until otherwise directed by law, the County of Mills shall be in and a part of the sixth Judicial District of this State.

Sec. 16. For provisions relative to biennial election, see Amendment [11]: See also Amendment [14]

Done in Convention at Iowa City, this fifth day of March in the year of our Lord One thousand eight hundred and fifty seven, and of the Independence of the United States of America, the eighty first.

In testimony whereof we have hereunto subscribed our names.

TIMOTHY DAY	JOHN EDWARDS
SHELDON G. WINCHESTER	J. C. TRAER
DAVID BUNKER	JAMES F. WILSON
D. P. PALMER	AMOS HARRIS
GEORGE W. ELLS	JOHN T. CLARK
J. C. HALL	SQUIRE AYERS
JOHN H. PETERS	HARVEY J. SKIFF
WILLIAM A. WARREN	J. A. PARVIN
HOSEA W. GRAY	W. PENN CLARKE
ROBERT GOWER	JEREMIAH HOLLINGSWORTH
H. D. GIBSON	WILLIAM PATTERSON
THOMAS SEELY	DANIEL W. PRICE
A. H. MARVIN	ALPHEUS SCOTT
J. H. EMERSON	GEORGE GILLASPY
RUFUS L. B. CLARKE	EDWARD JOHNSTONE
JAMES A. YOUNG	AYLETT R. COTTON
DANIEL H. SOLOMON	FRANCIS SPRINGER, *President*
M. W. ROBINSON	Attest:
LEWIS TODHUNTER	THOMAS J. SAUNDERS, *Secretary*
	ELLSWORTH N. BATES, *Asst. Secretary*

PROCLAMATION

Whereas an instrument known as the "New Constitution of the State of Iowa" adopted by the constitutional convention of said State on the fifth day of March A.D. 1857 was submitted to the qualified electors of said State at the annual election held on Monday the third day of August 1857 for their approval or rejection.

And whereas an offical canvass of the votes cast at said election shows that there were Forty thousand three hundred and eleven votes cast for the adoption of said Constitution and Thirty eight thousand six hundred and eighty-one votes were cast against its adoption. leaving a majority of sixteen hundred and thirty votes in favor of its adoption.

Now therefore I, JAMES W. GRIMES. Governor of said State, by virtue of the authority conferred upon me, hereby declare that said New Constitution to be adopted, and declare it to be the supreme law of the State of Iowa.

In the testimony whereof I have hereunto set my hand and affixed the Great Seal of the State of Iowa.

L.S.   Done at Iowa City this Third day of September A.D. 1857 of the Independence of the United States the eighty second and of the State of Iowa the eleventh.

JAMES W. GRIMES

By the Governor.
Elijah Sells,
Secretary of State.

AMENDMENTS TO
THE CONSTITUTION OF IOWA

Amendments of 1868

[1] 1st Strike the word "white," from Section 1 of Article II thereof; [Electors]
[2] 2d. Strike the word "white," from Section 33 of Article III thereof; [Census]
[3] 3d. Strike the word "white," from Section 34 of Article III thereof; [Senators]
[4] 4th Strike the word "white," from Section 35 of Article III thereof; [Apportionment]
[5] 5th Strike the word "white," from Section 1 of Article VI thereof; [Militia]
   The first of these amendments was submitted to the electorate with the Constitution in 1857 but was defeated.

Amendment of 1880

[6] Strike out the words "free white" from the third line of Section four (4) of Article three (III) of said Constitution, relating to the legislative department.

Amendments of 1884

[7] **General election.** [*Amendment 1. The general election for State, District County and Township officers shall be held on the Tuesday next after the first Monday in November.*]*
   *The above amendment, published as section 7 of Article II was repealed by Amendment [14]

[8] **Judicial districts.** Amendment 2. At any regular session of the General Assembly the State may be divided into the necessary Judicial Districts for District Court purposes, or the said Districts may be reorganized and the number of the Districts and the Judges of said Courts increased or diminished; but no reorganization of the Districts or diminution of the Judges shall have the effect of removing a Judge from office.
   See section 10 of Article V

[9] **Grand jury.** Amendment 3. The Grand Jury may consist of any number of members not less than five, nor more than fifteen, as the General Assembly may by law provide, or the General Assembly may provide for holding persons to answer for any criminal offense without the intervention of a Grand Jury.
   See section 11 of Article I

[10] Amendment 4. That Section 13 of Article V of the Constitution be stricken therefrom, and the following adopted as such Section.
   County attorney. SECTION 13. [*The qualified electors of each county shall, at the general election in the year 1886, and every two years thereafter elect a County Attorney, who shall be a resident of the county for which he is elected, and shall hold his office for two years, and until his successor shall have been elected and qualified.*]*
   *In 1970 this section was repealed: See Amendment [31]

Amendments of 1904

[11] Amendment 1. Add as Section 16, to Article XII of the Constitution, the following:
   General election. SECTION 16. [*The first general election after the adoption of this amendment shall be held on the Tuesday next after the first Monday in November in the year one thousand nine hundred and six, and general elections shall be held biennially thereafter. In the year one thousand nine hundred and six there shall be elected a governor, lieutenant-governor, secretary of state, auditor of state, treasurer of state, attorney general, two judges of the supreme court, the successors of the judges of the district court whose terms of office expire on December 31st, one thousand nine hundred and six, state senators who would otherwise be chosen in the year one thousand nine hundred and five, and members of the house of representatives. The terms of office of the judges of the supreme court which would otherwise expire on December 31st, in odd numbered years, and all other elective state, county and township officers whose terms of office would otherwise expire in January in the year one thousand nine hundred and six, and members of the general assembly whose successors would otherwise be chosen at the general election in the year one thousand nine hundred and five, are hereby extended one year and until their successors are elected and qualified. The terms of offices of senators whose successors would otherwise be chosen in the year one thousand nine hundred and seven are hereby extended one year and until their successors*]

are elected and qualified. The general assembly shall make such changes in the law governing the time of election and term of office of all other elective officers as shall be necessary to make the time of their election and terms of office conform to this amendment, and shall provide which of the judges of the supreme court shall serve as chief justice. The general assembly shall meet in regular session on the second Monday in January, in the year one thousand nine hundred and six, and also on the second Monday in January in the year one thousand nine hundred and seven, and biennially thereafter.]*

Practically the same amendment as the above was ratified in 1900, but the supreme court, in the case of State ex rel. Bailey v. Brookhart, 113 Iowa 250, held that said amendment was not proposed and adopted as required by the constitution, and did not become a part thereof

*The above amendment of 1904 has apparently been superseded by Amendment [14]

[12]   Amendment 2.* That Sections thirty-four (34) thirty-five (35) and thirty-six (36) of Article (III) of the Constitution of the State of Iowa, be repealed and the following be adopted in lieu thereof.

Senators—number—method of apportionment. SECTION 34. [*The Senate shall be composed of fifty members to be elected from the several senatorial districts, established by law and at the next session of the general assembly held following the taking of the state and national census, they shall be apportioned among the several counties or districts of the state, according to population as shown by the last preceding census.]***

*In 1968 this section was repealed and a substitute adopted in lieu thereof: See Amendment [26]

**See Amendment [16]; also Art. III. sec. 6

Representatives—number—apportionment. SECTION 35. [*The House of Representatives shall consist of not more than one hundred and eight members. The Ratio of representation shall be determined by dividing the whole number of the population of the state as shown by the last preceding state or national census, by the whole number of counties then existing or organized, but each county shall constitute one representative district and be entitled to one representative, but each county having a population in excess of the ratio number, as herein provided of three fifths or more of such ratio number shall be entitled to one additional representative, but said addition shall extend only to the nine counties having the greatest population.]**

*In 1968 this section was repealed and a substitute adopted in lieu thereof: See Amendment [26]

Ratio of representation. SECTION 36. [*The General Assembly shall, at the first regular session held following the adoption of this amendment, and at each succeeding regular session held next after the taking of such census, fix the ratio of representation, and apportion the additional representatives, as herein before required.]**

*In 1968 this section was repealed and a substitute adopted in lieu thereof: See Amendment [26]

Amendment of 1908

[13]   That there be added to Section eighteen (18) of Article one (I) of the Constitution of the State of Iowa, the following:

Drainage ditches and levees. The General Assembly, however, may pass laws permitting the owners of lands to construct drains, ditches, and levees for agricultural, sanitary or mining purposes across the lands of others, and provide for the organization of drainage districts, vest the proper authorities with power to construct and maintain levees, drains and ditches and to keep in repair all drains, ditches, and levees heretofore constructed under the laws of the state, by special assessments upon the property benefited thereby. The General Assembly may provide by law for the condemnation of such real estate as shall be necessary for the construction and maintenance of such drains, ditches and levees, and prescribe the method of making such condemnation.

Amendment of 1916

[14]   To repeal Section seven (7) of Article two (II) of the Constitution of Iowa and to adopt in lieu thereof the following, to-wit:

General election. SECTION 7. The general election for state, district county and township officers in the year 1916 shall be held in the same month and on the same day as that fixed by the laws of the United States for the election of presidential electors, or of president and vice-president of the United States; and thereafter such election shall be held at such time as the general assembly may by law provide.

The above amendment repealed Amendment [7], which was published as section 7 of Article II: See also Amendment [11]

For statutory provisions, see §39.1 of the Code

In 1916 a proposed amendment to extend the election franchise to women was defeated by the people

In 1917 a second proposed prohibition amendment was defeated by the people

In 1919 a second proposed amendment to enfranchise women was nullified by a procedural defect in failure to publish

Constitution

Amendment of 1926

[15]   Strike out the word "male" from Section four (4) of Article three (III) of said constitution, relating to the legislative department.

Amendment of 1928*

[16]   *[That the period (.) at the end of said section thirty-four (34) of Article three (III) of the Constitution of the state of Iowa be stricken and the following inserted: ", but no county shall be entitled to more than one (1) senator."]***

See Art. III, sec. 6

*The above amendment was repealed by Amendment [26]

**Applicable to Amendment [12]

Amendment of 1936

[17]   Amend Article three (III) by repealing Section thirty-three (33) relating to the state census.

Amendment of 1942

[18]   That Article Seven (VII) of the Constitution of the State of Iowa be amended by
adding thereto, as Section eight (8) thereof, the following:

Motor vehicle fees and fuel taxes. SECTION 8. All motor vehicle registration fees and licenses and excise taxes on motor vehicle fuel, except cost of administration, shall be used exclusively for the contruction, maintenance and supervision of the public highways exclusively within the state or for the payment of bonds issued or to be issued for the construction of such public highways and the payment of interest on such bonds.

Amendments of 1952

[19]   Amendment 1. Section four (4) of Article IV of the Constitution of Iowa is amended
by adding thereto the following:

Death of governor—elect or failure to qualify. *[If upon the completion of the canvass of votes for Governor and Lieutenant Governor by the General Assembly, it shall appear that the person who received the highest number of votes for Governor has since died, resigned, is unable to qualify, fails to qualify, or for any other reason is unable to assume the duties of the office of Governor for the ensuing term, the powers and duties of the office shall devolve upon the person who received the highest number of votes for Lieutenant Governor until the disability is removed and, upon inauguration, he shall assume the powers and duties of Governor.]**

*In 1988 this section was repealed and a substitute adopted in lieu thereof: See Amendment [41]

[20]   Amendment 2. Section nineteen (19) of Article IV of the Constitution of the State of Iowa is repealed and the following adopted in lieu thereof:

Gubenatorial succession. SECTION 19. *[If there be a vacancy in the office of Governor and the Lieutenant Governor shall by reason of death, impeachment, resignation, removal from office, or other disability become incapable of performing the duties pertaining to the office of Governor, the President pro tempore of the Senate shall act as Governor until the vacancy is filled or the disability removed; and if the President pro tempore of the Senate, for any of the above causes, shall be incapable of performing the duties pertaining to the office of Governor the same shall devolve upon the Speaker of the House of Representatives; and if the Speaker of the House of Representatives, for any of the above causes, shall be incapable of performing the duties of the office of Governor, the Justices of the Supreme Court shall convene the General Assembly by proclamation and the General Assembly shall organize by the election of a President pro tempore by the Senate and a Speaker by the House of Representatives. The General Assembly shall thereupon immediately proceed to the election of a Governor and Lieutenant Governor in joint convention.]**

Practically the same amendments were proposed in 1947 but nullified by a procedural defect in 1949 by failure to publish before the election

*In 1988 this section was repealed and a substitute adopted in lieu thereof: See Amendment [42]

Amendment of 1962

[21]   Article Five (V) is amended in the following manner:

1. Section four (4) is amended by striking from lines eight (8) and nine (9) of such section the words, " exercise of supervisory" and inserting in lieu thereof the words, "shall exercise a supervisory and administrative".

2. Sections three (3), five (5), nine (9) and eleven (11) are repealed.

3. The following sections are added thereto:

Vacancies in courts. SECTION 15. Vacancies in the Supreme Court and District Court shall be filled by appointment by the Governor from lists of nominees submitted by the appropriate judicial nominating commission. Three nominees shall be submitted for each Supreme Court vacancy, and two nominees shall be submitted for each District Court vacancy. If the Governor fails for thirty days to make the appointment, it shall be made from such nominees by the Chief Justice of the Supreme Court.

State and district nominating commissions. SECTION 16. There shall be a State Judicial Nominating Commission. Such commission shall make nominations to fill vacancies in the Supreme Court. Until July 4, 1973, and thereafter unless otherwise provided by law, the State Judicial Nominating Commission shall be composed and selected as follows: There shall be not less than three nor more than eight appointive members, as provided by law, and an equal number of elective members on such Commission, all of whom shall be electors of the state. The appointive members shall be appointed by the Governor subject to confirmation by the Senate. The elective members shall be elected by the resident members of the bar of the state. The judge of the Supreme Court who is senior in length of service on said Court, other than the Chief Justice, shall also be a member of such Commission and shall be its chairman.

There shall be a District Judicial Nominating Commission in each judicial district of the state. Such commissions shall make nominations to fill vacancies in the District Court within their respective districts. Until July 4, 1973, and thereafter unless otherwise provided by law, District Judicial Nominating Commissions shall be composed and selected as follows: There shall be not less than three nor more than six appointive members, as provided by law, and an equal number of elective members on each such commission, all of whom shall be electors of the district. The appointive members shall be appointed by the Governor. The elective members shall be elected by the resident members of the bar of the district. The district judge of such district who is senior in length of service shall also be a member of such commission and shall be its chairman.

Due consideration shall be given to area representation in the appointment and election of Judicial Nominating Commission members. Appointive and elective members of Judicial Nominating Commissions shall serve for six year terms, shall be ineligible for a second six year term on the same commission, shall hold no office of profit of the United States or of the state during their terms, shall be chosen without reference to political affiliation, and shall have such other qualifications as may be prescribed by law. As near as may be, the terms of one-third of such members shall expire every two years.

Terms—judicial elections. SECTION 17. Members of all courts shall have such tenure in office as may be fixed by law, but terms of Supreme Court Judges shall be not less than eight years and terms of District Court Judges shall be not less than six years. Judges shall serve for one year after appointment and until the first day of January following the next judicial election after the expiration of such year. They shall at such judicial election stand for retention in office on a separate ballot which shall submit the question of whether such judge shall be retained in office for the tenure prescribed for such office and when such tenure is a term of years, on their request, they shall, at the judicial election next before the end of each term, stand again for retention on such ballot. Present Supreme Court and District Court Judges, at the expiration of their respective terms, may be retained in office in like manner for the tenure prescribed for such office. The General Assembly shall prescribe the time for holding judicial elections.

Salaries—qualifications—retirement. SECTION 18. Judges of the Supreme Court and District Court shall receive salaries from the state, shall be members of the bar of the state and shall have such other qualifications as may be prescribed by law. Judges of the Supreme Court and District Court shall be ineligible to any other office of the state while serving on said court and for two years thereafter, except that District Judges shall be eligible to the office of Supreme Court Judge. Other judicial officers shall be selected in such manner and shall have such tenure, compensation and other qualification as may be fixed by law. The General Assembly shall prescribe mandatory retirement for Judges of the Supreme Court and District Court at a specified age and shall provide for adequate retirement compensation. Retired judges may be subject to special assignment to temporary judicial duties by the Supreme Court, as provided by law.

Constitution

Amendment of 1964

[22]   Section three (3) of Article ten (X) of the Constitution of the State of Iowa is repealed
and the following adopted in lieu thereof:

Constitutional convention. SECTION 3. At the general election to be held in the year one thousand nine hundred and seventy, and in each tenth year thereafter, and also at such times as the General Assembly may, by law, provide, the question, "Shall there be a Convention to revise the Constitution, and propose amendment or amendments to same?" shall be decided by the electors qualified to vote for members of the General Assembly; and in case a majority of the electors so qualified, voting at such election, for and against such proposition, shall decide in favor of a Convention for such purpose, the General Assembly, at its next session, shall provide by law for the election of delegates to such Convention, and for submitting the results of said Convention to the people, in such manner and at such time as the General Assembly shall provide; and if the people shall approve and ratify such amendment or amendments, by a majority of the electors qualified to vote for members of the General Assembly, voting thereon, such amendment or amendments shall become a part of the constitution of this state. If two or more amendments shall be submitted at the same time, they shall be submitted in such a manner that electors may vote for or against each such amendment separately.

Amendment of 1966

[23]   Section twenty-six (26) of Article III is amended by striking from line four (4) the word "Fourth" and inserting in lieu thereof the word "first".

Amendments of 1968

[24]   Amendment 1. Section two (2) of Article three (III) of the Constitution of the State of Iowa is hereby repealed and the following adopted in lieu thereof:

Annual sessions of General Assembly. SECTION 2. [*The General Assembly shall meet in session on the second Monday of January of each year. The Governor of the state may convene the General Assembly by proclamation in the interim.*]*

*In 1974 this section was repealed and a substitute adopted: See Amendment [36]

[25]   Amendment 2. Article three (III), legislative department. Constitution of the State of Iowa is hereby amended by adding the following new section:

Municipal home rule. SECTION 38A. Municipal corporations are granted home rule power and authority, not inconsistent with the laws of the General Assembly, to determine their local affairs and government, except that they shall not have power to levy any tax unless expressly authorized by the General Assembly.

The rule or proposition of law that a municipal corporation possesses and can exercise only those powers granted in express words is not a part of the law of this state.

[26]   Amendment 3. Section six (6) of Article three (III) section thirty-four (34) of Article three (III) and the 1904 and 1928 amendments thereto, sections thirty-five (35) and thirty-six (36) of Article three (III) and the 1904 amendment to each such section, and section thirty-seven (37) of Article three (III) are hereby repealed and the following adopted in lieu thereof:

Senators—number and classification. SECTION 6. The number of senators shall total not more than one-half the membership of the house of representatives. Senators shall be classified so that as nearly as possible one-half of the members of the senate shall be elected every two years.

Senate and House of Representatives—limitation. SECTION 34. The senate shall be composed of not more than fifty and the house of representatives of not more than one hundred members. Senators and representatives shall be elected from districts established by law. Each district so established shall be of compact and contiguous territory. The state shall be apportioned into senatorial and representative districts on the basis of population. The General Assembly may provide by law for factors in addition to population, not in conflict with the Constitution of the United States, which may be considered in the apportioning of senatorial districts. No law so adopted shall permit the establishment of senatorial districts whereby a majority of the members of the senate shall represent less than forty percent of the population of the state as shown by the most recent United States decennial census.

Senators and representatives—number and districts. SECTION 35. The General Assembly shall in 1971 and in each year immediately following the United States decennial census determine the number of senators and

359

representatives to be elected to the General Assembly and establish senatorial and representative districts. The General Assembly shall complete the apportionment prior to September 1 of the year so required. If the apportionment fails to become law prior to September 15 of such year, the Supreme Court shall cause the state to be apportioned into senatorial and representative districts to comply with the requirements of the Constitution prior to December 31 of such year. The reapportioning authority shall, where necessary in establishing senatorial districts, shorten the term of any senator prior to completion of the term. Any senator whose term is so terminated shall not be compensated for the uncompleted part of the term.

Review by Supreme Court. SECTION 36. Upon verified application by any qualified elector, the Supreme Court shall review an apportionment plan adopted by the General Assembly which has been enacted into law. Should the Supreme Court determine such plan does not comply with the requirements of the Constitution, the court shall within ninety days adopt or cause to be adopted an apportionment plan which shall so comply. The Supreme Court shall have original jurisdiction of all litigation questioning the apportionment of the General Assembly or any apportionment plan adopted by the General Assembly.

Congressional districts. SECTION 37. When a congressional district is composed of two or more counties it shall not be entirely separated by a county belonging to another district and no county shall be divided in forming a congressional district.

[27]   Amendment 4. Section sixteen (16) of article three (III) of the Constitution of the State of Iowa is hereby amended by adding the following new paragraph at the end thereof.

Item veto by Governor. The Governor may approve appropriation bills in whole or in part, and may disapprove any item of an appropriation bill; and the part approved shall become a law. Any item of an appropriation bill disapproved by the Governor shall be returned, with his objections, to the house in which it originated, or shall be deposited by him in the office of the Secretary of State in the case of an appropriation bill submitted to the Governor for his approval during the last three days of a session for the General Assembly, and the procedure in each case shall be the same as provided for other bills. Any such item of an appropriation bill may be enacted into law notwithstanding the Governor's objections, in the same manner as provided for other bills.

[28]   Amendment 5. Section twenty-five (25) of Article three (III) of the Constitution of the State of Iowa is hereby repealed and the following adopted in lieu thereof:

Compensation and expenses of General Assembly. SECTION 25. Each member of the General Assembly shall receive such compensation and allowances for expenses as shall be fixed by law but no General Assembly shall have the power to increase compensation and allowances effective prior to the convening of the next General Assembly following the session in which any increase is adopted.

Amendments of 1970

[29]   Amendment 1. Article three (III) of the Constitution of the State of Iowa is hereby
amended by adding thereto the following new section:

Legislative districts. SECTION 39. In establishing senatorial and representative
districts, the state shall be divided into as many senatorial districts as there are members of the senate and into as many representative districts as there are members of the house of representatives. One senator shall be elected from each senatorial district and one representative shall be elected from each representative district.

[30]   Amendment 2. Section one (1) of Article two (II) of the Constitution, as amended in 1868, is hereby repealed and the following is hereby adopted in lieu thereof:

Electors. SECTION 1. Every citizen of the United States of the age of twenty-one years, who shall have been a resident of this state for such period of time as shall be provided by law and of the county in which he claims his vote for such period of time as shall be provided by law, shall be entitled to vote at all elections which are now or hereafter may be authorized by law. The General Assembly may provide by law for different periods of residence in order to vote for various officers or in order to vote in various elections. The required periods of residence shall not exceed six months in this state and sixty days in the county.

See Amendments 19 and 26 to U.S. Constitution

Constitution

[31]   Amendment 3. Section thirteen (13) of Article five (V) of the Constitution of the State of Iowa as amended by Amendment 4 of the Amendments of 1884 is hereby repealed. [County Attorney].

Amendments of 1972

[32]   Amendment 1. Section two (2) of Article four (IV) of the Constitution of the State of Iowa is repealed and the following adopted in lieu thereof:
Election and term [governor]. SECTION 2. [*The Governor shall be elected by the qualified electors at the time and place of voting for members of the General Assembly, and shall hold his office for four years from the time of his installation, and until his successor is elected and qualifies.*]*

*In 1988 this section was repealed and a substitute adopted in lieu thereof: See Amendment [41]

Section three (3) of Article four (IV) of the Constitution of the State of Iowa is hereby repealed and the following adopted in lieu thereof:
Lieutenant governor—returns of elections. SECTION 3. [*There shall be a Lieutenant Governor who shall hold his office for the same term, and be elected at the same time as the Governor. In voting for Governor and Lieutenant Governor, the electors shall designate for whom they vote as Governor, and for whom as Lieutenant Governor. The returns of every election for Governor, and Lieutenant Governor, shall be sealed up and transmitted to the seat of government of the State, directed to the Speaker of the House of Representatives, who shall open and publish them in the presence of both Houses of the General Assembly.*]*

*In 1988 this section was repealed and a substitute adopted in lieu thereof: See Amendment [41]

Section fifteen (15) of Article four (IV) of the Constitution of the State of Iowa is hereby repealed and the following adopted in lieu thereof:
Terms—compensation of lieutenant governor. SECTION 15. [*The official term of the Governor, and Lieutenant Governor, shall commence on the second Monday of January next after their election, and continue until their successors are elected and qualify. The Lieutenant Governor, while acting as Governor, shall receive the same compensation as provided for Governor; and while presiding in the Senate, and between sessions such compensation and expenses as provided by law.*]*

*In 1988 this section was repealed and a substitute adopted in lieu thereof: See Amendment [42]

Section twenty-two (22) of Article four (IV) of the Constitution of the State of Iowa is repealed and the following adopted in lieu thereof:
Secretary—auditor—treasurer. SECTION 22. A Secretary of State, an Auditor of State and a Treasurer of State shall be elected by the qualified electors at the same time that the governor is elected and for a four-year term commencing on the first day of January next after their election, and they shall perform such duties as may be provided by law.

Section twelve (12) of Article five (V) of the Constitution of the State of Iowa is repealed and the following adopted in lieu thereof:
Attorney general. SECTION 12. The General Assembly shall provide, by law, for the election of an Attorney General by the people, whose term of office shall be four years, and until his successor is elected and qualifies.

[33]   Amendment 2. Article five (V), Constitution of the State of Iowa, is hereby amended by adding thereto the following new section:
Retirement and discipline of judges. SECTION 19. In addition to the legislative power of impeachment of judges as set forth in Article three (III), sections nineteen (19) and twenty (20) of the Constitution, the Supreme Court shall have power to retire judges for disability and to discipline or remove them for good cause, upon application by a commission on judicial qualifications. The General Assembly shall provide by law for the implementation of this section.

[34]   Amendment 3. Section twenty-eight (28) of Article three (III) of the Constitution of the State of Iowa is hereby repealed. [Lottery prohibition].

Amendments of 1974

[35]   Amendment 1. Section four (4), subdivision two (2), entitled "School Funds and
School Lands," of Article nine (IX) of the Constitution of the State of Iowa is hereby repealed.
Section four (4) of Article twelve (XII) of the Constitution of the State of Iowa is hereby repealed.

[36]   Amendment 2. Section two (2) of Article three (III) of the Constitution of the State of Iowa, as amended by amendment number one (1) of the Amendments of 1968 to the Constitution of the State of Iowa, is repealed and the following adopted in lieu thereof:
The General Assembly shall meet in session on the second Monday of January

of each year. Upon the written request to the presiding officer of each House of the General Assembly by two thirds of the members of each House, the General Assembly shall convene in special session. The Governor of the state may convene the General Assembly by proclamation in the interim.

Amendment of 1978

[37]   Article three (III), legislative department, Constitution of the State of Iowa is hereby amended by adding the following new section:

Counties Home Rule. SECTION 39A. Counties or joint county-municipal corporation governments are granted home rule power and authority, not inconsistent with the laws of the general assembly, to determine their local affairs and government, except that they shall not have power to levy any tax unless expressly authorized by the general assembly. The general assembly may provide for the creation and dissolution of joint county-municipal corporation governments. The general assembly may provide for the establishment of charters in county or joint county-municipal corporation governments.

If the power or authority of a county conflicts with the power and authority of a municipal corporation, the power and authority exercised by a municipal corporation shall prevail within its jurisdiction.

The proposition or rule of law that a county or joint county-municipal corporation government possesses and can exercise only those powers granted in express words is not a part of the law of this state.

Amendments of 1984

[38]   Amendment 1. Article three (III), legislative department, Constitution of the State of Iowa, is amended by adding the following new section:

Legislative veto of administrative rules. SECTION 40. The general assembly may nullify an adopted administrative rule of a state agency by the passage of a resolution by a majority of all of the members of each house of the general assembly.

[39]   Amendment 2. Section 7, subsection 2 entitled "School Funds and School Lands", of Article IX of the Constitution of the State of Iowa is repealed.

Amendments of 1986

[40]   Section 26 of Article III of the Constitution of Iowa, as amended by the Amendment of 1966, is repealed and the following adopted in lieu thereof:

An act of the General Assembly passed at a regular session of a General Assembly shall take effect on July 1 following its passage unless a different effective date is stated in an act of the General Assembly. An act passed at a special session of a General Assembly shall take effect ninety days after adjournment of the special session unless a different effective date is stated in an act of the General Assembly. The general assembly may establish by law a procedure for giving notice of the contents of acts of immediate importance which become law.

Amendments of 1988

[41]   Amendment 1. Section two (2) of Article four (IV) of the Constitution of the State of Iowa, as amended by amendment number one (1) of the Amendments of 1972, is repealed beginning with the general election in the year 1990 and the following adopted in lieu thereof:

SECTION 2. The governor and the lieutenant governor shall be elected by the qualified electors at the time and place of voting for members of the general assembly. Each of them shall hold office for four years from the time of installation in office and until a successor is elected and qualifies.

Section three (3) of Article four (IV) of the Constitution of the State of Iowa, as amended by amendment number one (1) of the Amendments of 1972, is repealed beginning with the general election in the year 1990 and the following adopted in lieu thereof:

SECTION 3. The electors shall designate their selections for governor and lieutenant governor as if these two offices were one and the same. The names of nominees for the governor and the lieutenant governor shall be grouped together in a set on the ballot according to which nominee for governor is seeking office with which nominee for lieutenant governor, as prescribed by law. An elector shall cast only one vote for both a nominee for governor and a nominee for lieutenant governor. The returns of every elections for governor and lieutenant governor shall be sealed and transmitted to the seat of government of the state, and directed to the speaker of the house of representatives who shall open and publish them in the presence of both houses of the general assembly.

Section four (4) of Article four (IV) of the Constitution of the State of Iowa, as amended by amendment number one (1) of the Amendments of 1952, is repealed

Constitution

beginning with the general election in the year 1990 and the following adopted in lieu thereof:

SECTION 4. The nominees for governor and lieutenant governor jointly having the highest number of votes cast for them shall be declared duly elected. If two or more sets of nominees for governor and lieutenant governor have an equal and the highest number of votes for the offices jointly, the general assembly shall by joint vote proceed, as soon as is possible, to elect one set of nominees for governor and lieutenant governor. If, upon the completion by the general assembly of the canvass of votes for governor and lieutenant governor, it appears that the nominee for governor in the set of nominees for governor and lieutenant governor receiving the highest number of votes has since died or resigned, is unable to qualify, fails to qualify, or is for any other reason unable to assume the duties of the office of governor for the ensuing term, the powers and duties shall devolve to the nominee for lieutenant governor of the same set of nominees for governor and lieutenant governor, who shall assume the powers and duties of governor upon inauguration and until the disability is removed. If both nominees for governor and lieutenant governor are unable to assume the duties of the office of governor, the person next in succession shall act as governor.

Section five (5) of Article four (IV) of the Constitution of the State of Iowa is repealed beginning with the general election in the year 1990 and the following adopted in lieu thereof:

SECTION 5. Contested elections for the offices of governor and lieutenant governor shall be determined by the general assembly as prescribed by law.

[42] Amendment 2. Section fifteen (15) of Article four (IV) of the Constitution of the State of Iowa, as amended by amendment number one (1) of the Amendments of 1972, is repealed beginning with the second Monday in January, 1991, and the following adopted in lieu thereof:

SECTION 15. The official terms of the governor and lieutenant governor shall commence on the Tuesday after the second Monday of January next after their election and shall continue until their successors are elected and qualify. The governor and lieutenant governor shall be paid compensation and expenses as provided by law. The lieutenant governor, while acting as governor, shall be paid the compensation and expenses prescribed for the governor.

Section eighteen (18) of Article four (IV) of the Constitution of the State of Iowa is repealed beginning with the second Monday in January, 1991, and the following adopted in lieu thereof:

SECTION 18. The lieutenant governor shall have the duties provided by law and those duties of the governor assigned to the lieutenant governor by the governor.

Section nineteen (19) of Article four (IV) of the Constitution of the State of Iowa, as amended by amendment number two (2) of the Amendments of 1952, is repealed beginning with the second Monday in January, 1991, and the following adopted in lieu thereof:

SECTION 19. If there be a vacancy in the office of the governor and the lieutenant governor shall by reason of death, impeachment, resignation, removal from office, or other disability become incapable of performing the duties pertaining to the office of governor, the president of the senate shall act as governor until the vacancy is filled or the disability removed; and if the president of the senate, for any of the above causes, shall be incapable of performing the duties pertaining to the office of governor the same shall devolve upon the speaker of the house of representatives; and if the speaker of the house of representatives, for any of the above causes, shall be incapable of performing the duties of the office of governor, the justices of the supreme court shall convene the general assembly by proclamation and the general assembly shall organize by the election of a president by the senate and a speaker by the house of representatives. The general assembly shall thereupon immediately proceed to the election of a governor and lieutenant governor in joint convention.

Amendment of 1992

[43] Section 5 of Article 1 of the Constitution of Iowa is repealed.

BOOKS ABOUT IOWA

Aurner, Clarence Ray. *History of Education in Iowa.* Iowa City, IA: State Historical Society, 1920.

-----*Iowa Stories.* Iowa City, IA: Clarence R. Aurner, 1917-21.

Barrows, Willard. *Notes on Iowa Territory.*, 1845.

Bennett, Henry Arnold. *The Mystery of the Iowa Buffalo.* IA: Iowa Journal of History and Politics, 1934.

Black Hawk. *Life of Black Hawk, Ma-ka-tai-me-she-kia-kiak.* Iowa City, IA: State Historical Society of Iowa, 1932.

Bogue, Allen G. *From Prairie to Cornbelt.* Chicago, IL: University of Chicago Press, 1963.

Briggs, John Ely. *The Grasshopper Plagues in Iowa.* IA: Journal of History and Politics, 1915.

-----*History of Social Legislation in Iowa.* Iowa City, IA: State Historical Society, 1915.

Brigham, Johnson. *Iowa, Its History and Its Foremost Citizens.* Chicago, IL: S. J. Clarke Publishing Co., 1915.

-----*The Sinclairs of Old Fort Des Moines.* Des Moines, IA: Hertzberg Bindery, 1927.

Briggs, John E. *The Removal of the Capital from Iowa City to Des Moines.* IA: Iowa Journal of History and Politics, 1916.

Bureau of Business and Economic Research. *Economic and Statistical Review of Iowa, 1950-1965.*, University of Iowa, 1967.

Capek, Thomas. *The Czechs in America.* Cambridge, MA: Riverside Press Co., 1920.

Carpenter, Allan. *Between Two Rivers: Iowa Year by Year, 1846-1939.*, 1940.

Christenson, Thomas P. *The State Parks of Iowa.* IA: Journal of History and Politics, 1928.

Clarke, S. J. *Prominent Iowans.* Chicago, IL: S. J. Clarke Publishing Co., 1915.

Cole, Cyrenus. *A History of the People of Iowa.* Cedar Rapids, IA: The Torch Press, 1921.

-----*I Am a Man--The Indian Black Hawk.* Iowa City, IA: State Historical Society of Iowa, 1938.

Dondore, Dorothy Ann. *The Prairie and the Making of Middle America: Four Centuries of Description.* Cedar Rapids: Torch Press, 1926.

Downey, E. H. *History of Labor Legislation in Iowa.* Iowa City, IA: State Historical Society of Iowa, 1910.

-----*History of Work Accident Indemnity in Iowa.* Iowa City, IA: State Historical Society of Iowa, 1912.

Dwelle, Jessie M. *Iowa, Beautiful Land.*, 1954.

Faust, Albert B. *The German Element in the United States.* Cambridge, MA: RIverside Press Co., 1909.

Federal Writers' Project. *Iowa: a Guide to the Hawkeye State.* New York, NY: Somerset, 1938.

Flom, George T. *The Growth of the Scandinavian Factor in the Population of Iowa.* IA: Iowa Journal of History and Politics, 1906.

Gallaher, Ruth A. *Legal and Political Status of Women in Iowa.* Iowa City, IA: State Historical Society of Iowa, 1918.

-----*The Tama Indians. Palimpsest,* (v. 7:44-53.), Feb., 1926.

Garland, Hamlin. *Main Travelled Roads.* Boston, MA: Arena Pub., Co., 1891.

Gillin, John L. *History of Poor Relief Legislation in Iowa.* Iowa City, IA: Stae Historical Society, 1914.

Glazer, Rabbi Simon. *The Jews in Iowa.* Des Moines, Koch Brothers Printing Co., 1904.

Grant, H. Roger, and L. Edward Purcell. *Years of Struggle: The Farm Diary of Elmer G. Powers, 1931-1936.*

Gue, Benjamin F. *History of Iowa.* New York, NY: Century History Co., 1903.

-----*Progressive Men of Iowa.* Des Moines, IA: Conaway & Shaw Pub., Co., 1899.

Bibliography

Hair, James T. *Iowa State Gazetteer.*, 1845.

Hamilton, Carl. *In No time at All.* Ames, IA: Iowa State University Press, 1974.

Harlan, Edgar R. *A Narrative History of the People of Iowa.* Chicago, IL: American Historical Society, 1931.

Hawley, Charles Arthur. *A Communistic Swedenborgian Colony in Iowa.* IA: Iowa Journal of History and Politics, 1906.

Haynes, Fred E. *History of Third Party Movements since the Civil War, with Special Reference to Iowa.* Iowa City, IA: State Historical Society of Iowa, 1916.

Hinkhouse, J. F. *One Hundred Years of the Iowa Presbyterian Church.* Des Moines, IA: Synod of Iowa, 1932.

Hoffman, M. M. *The Church Founders of the Northwest.* Milwaukee, WI: Bruce Publishing Co., 1937.

Hussey, Tacitus. *History of Steamboating on the Des Moines River, from 1837-1862.* IA: Annals of Iowa (Third Series), 1900.

Iowa Department of Agriculture. *Iowa Year Book of Agriculture.* Des Moines, IA: 1900.

Iowa Developmental Commission. *1985 Statistical Profile of Iowa.* Des Moines, IA 1985.

Kantor, MacKinlay. *God and My Country.*, 1954.

-----*Spirit Lake.*, 1961.

Kay, George F., and James H. Lees. *Sketch of the Geology of Iowa.* Des Moines, IA: Iowa Geological Survey, 1926.

Kempker, Father John F. *History of the Catholic Church in Iowa.* Iowa City, IA: Republican Press, 1887.

Keyes, Charles Reuben. *Prehistoric Man in Iowa.* Palimpsest, June, 1927 (v. 8:185-229)

Larrabee, William. *The Railroad Question.* Chicago, IL: Schulte Publishing Co., 1893.

Lea, Albert M. *Notes on the Wisconsin Territory, Particularly With Reference to the Iowa District.* Philadelphia, PA: H. S. Tanner, 1836.

MacMurtrie, Douglas C. *The Beginnings of Printing in Iowa.* IA: Annals of Iowa (Third Series), 1933.

Macbribe, Thomas H. *In Cabins and Sod-houses.* Iowa City, IA: State Historical Society of Iowa, 1928.

Mahan, Bruce E., and Ruth Augusta Gallaher. *Stories of Iowa for Boys and Girls.* New York, NY: The Macmillan Company, 1929.

Marple, Alice. *Iowa Authors and Their Work.* Des Moines, IA: Historical Department of Iowa, 1918.

Martin, Ethyl E. *The Expedition of Zebulon Montgomery Pike to the Sources of the Mississippi.* IA: Iowa Journal of History and Politics, 1911.

Morrison, Hugh. *Louis Sullivan.* New York, NY: W. W. Norton & Co., 1935.

Mott, Frank L. *The Lewis and Clark Expedition in its Relation to Iowa History and Geography.* IA: Annals of Iowa (Third Series-Oct., Jan.,), 1921-22.

-----*Literature of Pioneer Life in Iowa.*, 1923.

Newhall, J. B. *A Glimpse of Iowa in 1846.* Burlington: W. D. Skillman, 1846.

Osborn, Herbert. *A Partial Catalogue of the Animals of Iowa.* Ames, IA: State College of Agriculture and Mechanic Arts, 1892.

Owen, Mary A. *Folk-lore of the Musquakie Indians of North America.* London: David Nutt, 1904.

Peterson, William J. -----*Iowa History Reference Guide.* Iowa City, IA: State Historical Society of Iowa, 1952.

-----*Kearny in Iowa. Palimpsest, Aug.), 1931.*

-----*Lexington of the North. Palimpsest, 1932.*

-----*Steamboating on the Upper Mississippi.* Iowa City, IA: State Historical Society of Iowa, 1937.

-----*The Story of Iowa.* Iowa City, IA: State Historical Society of Iowa, 1952.

Plumbe, John. *Sketches of Iowa and Wisconsin.* St. Louis, MO: Chambers, Harris and Knapp, 1846.

Preston, Howard H. *History of Banking in Iowa.* Iowa City, IA: State Historical Society of Iowa, 1922.

Ross, Earl. *History of Agriculture in Iowa.*, 1950.

Bibliography

-----*Iowa Agriculture.* Iowa City, IA: State Historical Society, 1951.

Ross, Russell. *Government and Administration of Iowa.*, 1957.

Sabin, Henry, and Edwin L. *The Making of Iowa.* Chicago, IL: A Flanagan Company, 1916.

Sage, Leland. *A History of Iowa.* Ames, IA: Iowa State University Press, 1974.

-----*William Boyd Allison.*, State Historical Society of Iowa, 1956.

Schwieder, Dorothy. *Patterns and Perspectives in Iowa History.* Ames, IA: Iowa State University Press, 1973.

Shambaugh, Benjamin F. *The Constitutions of Iowa.* Iowa City, IA: State Historical Society of Iowa, 1934.

-----*Documentary Material Relating to the History of Iowa.* Iowa City, IA: State Historical Society of Iowa, 1897-1901.

Shetrone, Henry C. *The Mound-Builders.* New York, NY: Appleton, 1930.

Stephenson, George M. *The Religious Aspects of Swedish Immigration.* Minneapolis, MN: University of Minnesota Press, 1932.

Stewart, Ruth. *Capital City.* New York, NY: Sears Publishing Co., 1933.

Stong, Philip. *The Annals of Iowa 1863-74.*, 1903.

-----*State Fair.* New York, NY: Century, 1932.

-----*If School Keeps.*, 1940.

Suckow, Ruth. *Country People.*, 1952.

Swierenga, Robert P. *Pioneers and Profits.* Ames, IA: Iowa State University Press, 1968.

Swisher, Jacob A. *The Iowa Academy of Science.* IA: Iowa Journal of History and Politics, 1931.

Swisher, Jacob A., and Carl H. Erbe. *Iowa History as Told in Biography.* Cedar Falls, IA: Holst Printing Co., 1932.

Thompson, F. O. *Hunting in Northwestern Iowa.* IA: Iowa Journal of History and Politics, 1937.

Thornton, Harrison John. *History of the Quaker Oats Company, Chicago, IL: University of Chicago Press, 1933.*

Throne, Mildred. *Cyrus Clay Carpenter.*, 1974.

Van der Zee, Jacob. *The British in Iowa.* Iowa City, IA: State Historical Society of Iowa, 1922.

Wall, Joseph Frazier. *Iowa: A Bicentennial History.* New York, NY: Norton, 1978.

Ward, Duren J. H. *The Problem of the Mounds of Iowa.* Iowa Journal of History and Politics, (January, v. 3:20-40) 1905.

Wilkinson, Herbert E. *Sun Over Cerro Gordo.*, 1952.

Wilson, Margaret. *The Able McLaughlins.* New York, NY: Harper, 1923.

INDEX

Index

Aquifers, 18
Arcadia, 166
Archaeological
 Collections, 47
Archaeological
 Museums, 47
Archaeologists, 43, 44
Archives and Records
 Department of, 149
Arion, 166
Arlington, 166
Armstrong, 166
Army of the
 Tennessee, 200
Arnolds Park, 166, 331
Art Colony, 99
Arthur
 Chester Alan, 119
Artificial
 Lakes, 24, 30
Arts and Humanities
 Department of, 150
Ashton, 166
Astor
 John Jacob, 56
Atalissa, 167
Athletics Board, 150
Atkins, 167
Atlantic, 167
Atlantic Ocean, 167
Attorney General
 Office of, 150
Auburn, 167
Audit
 Department of, 150
Audubon, 267
Audubon County, 167
Audubon
 John James, 56,
 167, 275
Augsburg Seminary, 141

Auguel
 Antoine, 81
Augusta, 85
Aurelia, 167
Aurora, 168
Avenson
 Don, 106
Avoca, 168
Axes, 46
Ayers
 O. B., 120
Ayrshire, 168

Badfish Creek, 289
Badger, 168
Bagley, 168
Bailey
 Judge, 257
Bancroft, 168
Bancroft
 George, 168
Bank of Coon Rapids, 131
Bank of Denison, 129
Bank of Manilla, 129
Banking, 150
Banking Corporations, 92
Barbed Wire, 92
Barley, 24
Barnes
 Luther H., 279
Barnum, 168
Barnum
 P. T., 214
Barrick
 John T., 230
Bartleson
 J.M., 181
Bartlett
 Joseph M., 185
Baseball World Series, 96
Batavia, 168
Battle Creek, 168

Index

Index

Index

Constitution of 1857,
65, 74, 76, 78
Constitutional
Amendment, 99
Constitutional
Convention, 89, 92
Consumer Affairs
Office of, 151
Continental Army, 252
Continental
Congress, 216
Cook
John K., 276
Coon Branch, 188
Coon Forks, 171
Coon Rapids, 101,
131, 187
Cooper
James
Fenimore, 223, 250
Copperheads, 200
Coralville, 188
Coralville Lake, 229
Coralville Public
School, 188
Corn, 9, 22, 23, 24,
49, 94, 95, 100, 102
Corn Belt, 271
Corn Palace, 95, 278
Corn State, 101
Cornell College, 129
Cornell University, 74
Cornfields, 5, 49
Corning, 92, 188
Corning Academy, 135
Corning
Erastus, 188
Corrections
Department of, 151
Correctionville, 188
Cortes
Hernando, 252

Corwin
Thomas, 111
Corwith, 188
Corydon, 188
Council Bluffs, 84, 87,
90, 91, 94, 188
County Assessor
Law, 140
Court Administration
Office of, 151
Court Avenue
Speedway, 41
Cow War, 136
Cowles
Anita, 165
Gardner, 163, 214
Cox
Sara, 219
Crapo Park, 176
Crawford County, 190
Crawford
William Harris, 190
Crawshaw
Alice, 129
Credit
Island, 48, 55, 83
Creek War, 229
Creighton
Jesse, 232
Crescent, 190
Crescent City, 190
Cresco, 191
Creston, 191
Creston Railroad
Depot, 191
Cretaceous Period, 38
Cretaceous
System, 10, 38
Criminal Code, 104
Crittenden
John J., 110
Crops, 15, 23, 24, 46

Crystal Lake, 191
Crystal Lake Cave, 206
Cuba, 96
Cubbage
    George, 205
Culver
    John C., 105
Cumberland, 191
Cummins & Wright, 130
Cummins
    Albert Baird, 129, 133
    Hewitt & Wright, 130
    Thomas Layton, 129
Current Biography, 140
Curtis Airplanes, 136
Curtis
    Samuel R., 66
Cushing, 191
Cut Nose, 252
Cyclone, 96
Cylinder, 191
Cylinder Creek, 191
Cystic Fibrosis, 108
Czech Village, 181

Dakota City, 191
Dakota Formation, 38
Dalander
    Anna, 242
Dallas, 192
Dallas Center, 192
Dallas County, 192
Dallas County
    Courthouse, 161
Dallas County Forest
    Park & Museum, 266
Dallas
    George Mifflin,
    161, 192
Danbury, 192
Danish Windmill, 167
Dankwardt Park, 176

Danville, 192
Dartmouth
    College, 115, 122
Data Processing, 151
Daughters of the
    American Revolution, 3
Davenport, 16, 26, 90,
    91, 93, 94, 98, 192, 335
Davenport Museum, 47
Davenport
    George, 56,
    89, 192, 254, 333
Davis County, 195
Davis County
    Courthouse, 170
Davis County
    Republican, 132
Davis Opera House, 187
Davis
    Garrett, 195
    Jefferson, 57
Dawson, 195
Dayton, 195
De Carondelet
    Baron, 204
De Carrie
    Sabrevoir, 196
De Soto
    Hernando, 81
Dean
    Henry Clay, 200
Death Penalty, 144
DeBoer
    Jan, 107
    Roberta, 107
Decatur City, 195
Decatur County, 196
Decatur
    Stephen, 195
Declaration of
    Independence, 177, 211
Decorah, 196

Index

Decorah Campgrounds, 196
Dedham, 196
Deemer
  Horace E., 77
Deeny
  Cornell, 102
Deep River, 196
Deer, 19
Deffenbach
  Lewis, 251
Defiance, 196
Delaware, 197
Delaware County, 197
Delhi, 197
Delta, 197
Delta Covered
  Bridge, 197
Democratic
  Convention, 103
Democratic National
  Convention, 109
Democratic
  Party, 101, 102,
  103, 104, 105, 106
Demoine House, 200
Denison, 197
Denison
  J.W., 197
Denver, 197
Department
  of Environmental
  Quality, 146
Department of Public
  Safety, 139
Department of
  Transportation, 146
Des Moine Valley, 171
Des Moines, 1, 7, 26,
  41, 81, 91, 92, 94,
  95, 97, 98, 99, 101,
  102, 105, 197, 328

Des Moines
  Art Center, 202
Des Moines
  Center of Science
  and Industry, 202
Des Moines County, 203
Des Moines
  Lobe, 11, 13, 14
Des Moines
  Rapids, 83, 85, 232
Des Moines Register,
  105, 106, 163
Des Moines River
  Valley, 44, 47
Des Moines Series, 38
Des Moines Strata, 38
Des Moines Valley, 85
Des Moines Valley
  Railroad, 200, 266
Des Moines Zoo, 202
Des Noyelles, 81
Des Plaines, 23
DeSmet
  Pierre Jean, 189
DeSota National
  Wildlife Refuge, 250
Developmental
  Disabilities
  Division, 151
Devonian Age, 38
Dexter, 203
Dey
  Peter A., 67
Deyoe
  Albert, 73
Diamond
  Laboratories, 143
Dibble House, 208
Dickens, 203
Dickinson County, 203

383

Index

Index

Index

Grindstone War, 247
Grinnell, 116, 220
Grinnell College, 63,
  75, 90, 138, 220
Grinnell Historical
  Museum, 220
Grinnell
  Josiah Bushnell, 63,
  220
Griswold, 220
Griswold
  J. N. A., 220
Ground Moraine, 12
Groundwater, 18
Grout Museum of History
  and Science, 289
Grundy Center, 220
Grundy County, 220
Grundy
  Felix, 220
Guernsey County, 112
Guittar
  Francis, 188
Gulf Coast, 6
Gull Point, 260
Gutenberg
  Johann, 221
Guthrie Center, 221
Guthrie County, 221
Guthrie
  Edwin B., 221
Guttenberg, 221
Gypsum, 19, 38, 94, 97
Gypsum Hollow, 214

Hackberry Clay Banks, 41
Haddock
  George Channing, 278
Hail, 15, 23
Haines
  Perry V., 105

Hale
  John P., 121
Half-Breed Tract, 50,
  56, 84, 85, 232
Hall
  James, 214
Ham
  Mathias, Museum, 207
Hamburg, 221
Hamilton, 221
Hamilton County, 221
Hamilton University
  of Business, 141
Hamilton
  George E., 6
  William, 221
Hamlin
  Homer, 220
Hammerstein
  Oscar, Theatre, 181
Hammill
  George, 135
  John, 135, 172
Hampton, 222
Hampton Academy, 115
Hancock, 222
Hancock County, 222
Hancock
  John, 222
Handcart Expedition, 64
Handicapped
  Council on, 153
Haney
  John, Sr., 236
Hanna
  George W., 288
Hardin County, 222
Hardin
  Davis, 189
  John J., 222

Index

Index

Index

Iowa Wesleyan College
  Museum, 79
Iowa's Sixth
  District, 105
Iowa—
  Admission to
    Union, 1, 8, 9, 89
  Capital, 87
  Corn Song, 5
  Great Seal, 4
  Highest elevation, 1
  Highest point, 8
  Location of, 9
  Lowest elevation, 1
  Lowest point, 8
  Meaning of name, 1
  Nicknames, 2, 3
  Origin of name, 1, 2
  Proud Iowa, 5
  Settlement, 18
  State flag, 3, 4
  State flower, 5
  State historian, 1
  State song, 5
  State symbols, 1
  Surface area, 14
  Total area, 1, 8, 21
Iowa-Missouri
  Boundary Dispute, 173
Iowan Drift, 40
Irish Independence, 260
Irish Volunteers, 175
Irrigation, 17
Irwin, 229

Jackson County, 229
Jackson County
  Historical Museum, 244
Jackson
  Andrew, 109, 176, 229
  Frank D., 68, 126
  James A., 277

Jesse, 103
Jamaica, 230
James
  Jesse, 161
Janesville, 230
Japan
  Bombardment of, 100
Jasper County, 230
Jasper County
  Historical Museum, 258
Jasper
  Sergeant, 258
  William, 230
Jefferson, 230
Jefferson County, 230
Jefferson
  County Park, 210
Jefferson
  Thomas, 230, 242, 252
Jennings
  Berryman, 84
Jepsen
  Roger, 104, 105
Jesup, 230
Jesup
  Morris K., 230
Jewell Junction, 230
Jewell
  David T., 230
Jobless, 104
John Morrell
  Company, 142
John Wayne Birthplace
  Site, 294
Johnson County, 230
Johnson County Claim
  Association, 88
Johnson County
  Fairgrounds, 228
Johnson House
  and Barn, 207

401

Index

Index

Index

Index

Index

Index

Index

Index

Index

Index

Index

Wapello
  Chief, 48
Wapsinonoc Creek, 292
Wapsipinicon
  State Park, 181
War Department, 3
War Eagle Monument, 279
War of 1812, 48, 55,
  83, 110, 124, 192
War Production
  Board, 136
Warren County, 287
Warren
  Joseph, 287
Warship, 100
Wartburg College, 290
Wartburg Seminary, 206
Washing Machine
  Factory, 97
Washing Machine
  King, 258
Washing Machine
  Manufacturing, 95
Washington County, 288
Washington Guards, 175
Washington, 288
Washington
  George, 254, 288
Washta, 22, 288
Water, 17
Water Conservation, 26
Water Pollution
  Control, 159
Water Quality, 18
Water Resources, 159
Watercourses, 25
Waterfowl Refuge, 36
Waterloo, 288
Waterloo Gasoline
  Traction Engine
  Company, 289

Waterloo Recreation
  and Art Center
  Municipal Gallery, 289
Waterloo-Cedar Falls, 16
Waucoma, 289
Waucoma Creek, 289
Waukee, 289
Waukon, 47, 290
Waukon Decorah, 196
Waverly, 290
Wayland, 290
Wayne County, 290
Wayne County Historical
  Museum, 182
Wayne
  Anthony, 290
  John, Birthplace
  Site, 294
Waynesburg College, 130
Weaver
  James Baird,
  68, 95, 96
Webb, 290
Webster, 290
Webster City, 23, 290
Webster County, 290
Webster
  Daniel, 290
  Noah, 164
Weights and Measures
  Division, 159
Weldon, 291
Welfare
  Department of, 159
Wellman, 290
Wellsburg, 291
Wentz
  Jacob, House, 229
Wesley, 291
Wesley
  John, 209

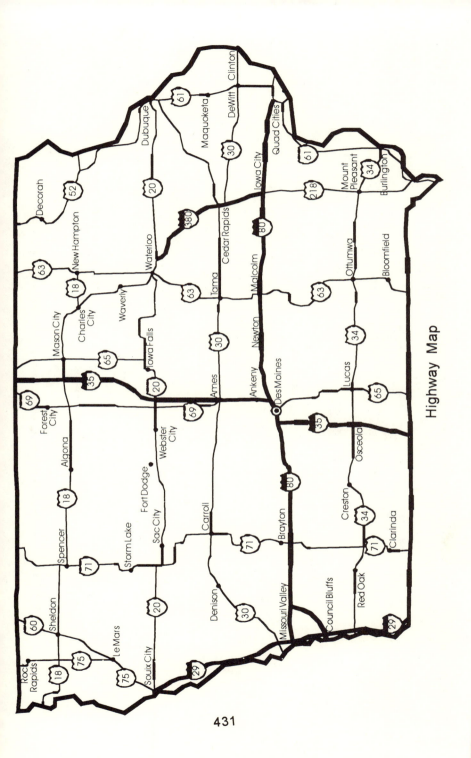

Highway Map

431

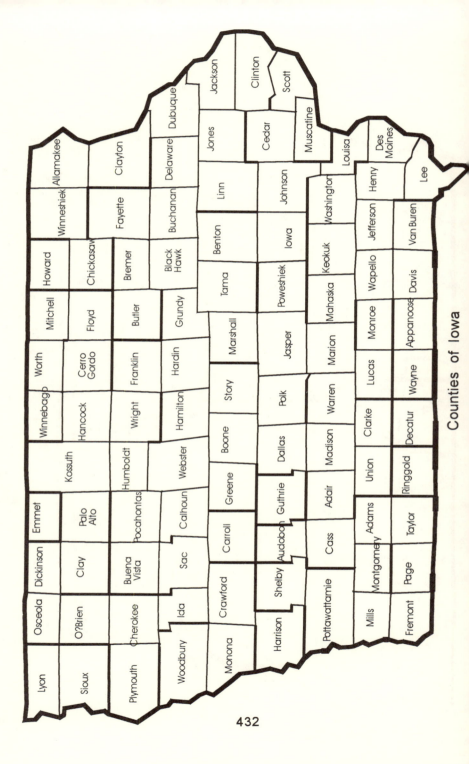

Counties of Iowa

432

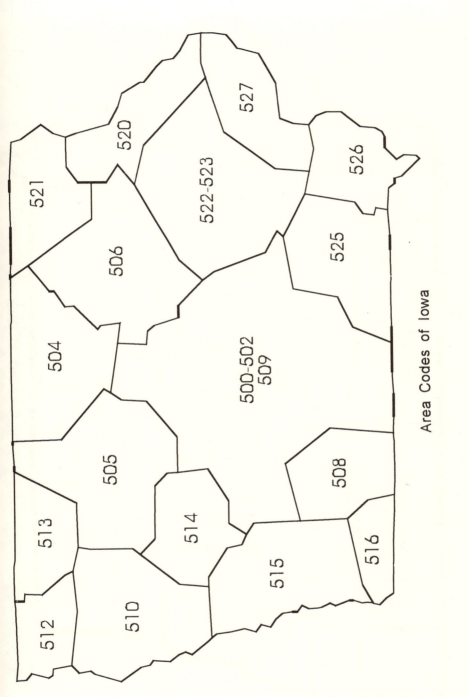

Area Codes of Iowa